Exeter Medieval English Texts and Studies
General Editor : M. J. Swanton

THE MEDIEVAL MYSTICAL TRADITION IN ENGLAND

Papers read at

Dartington Hall, July 1982

Edited by Marion Glasscoe

UNIVERSITY OF EXETER : 1982

Published with the aid of a grant
from The British Academy.

ISBN 0 85989 183 6

Printed and bound by CPI Group (UK) Ltd, Croydon, CR0 4YY

CONTENTS

Margery Kempe and the Eastern and Western Tradition of the 'perfect fool'.
R. Maisonneuve (Oyonnax)   1

The Choices of the Translator in the Late Middle English Period
R. Ellis (University College, Cardiff)   18

Henry Suso and the Medieval Mystical Tradition in England
R. Lovatt (University of Cambridge)   47

The Sources of *The Cloud of Unknowing*: A Reconsideration
A. Minnis (University of Bristol)   63

The Cloud of Unknowing and Vedanta
K. Watson (University College, Cardiff)   76

Augustine, Anselm and Walter Hilton
J. Clark (Longframlington Vicarage)   102

Christ the Teacher in Julian's *Showings*: the Biblical and Patristic Traditions
R. Bradley (St Ambrose College, Iowa)   127

Psychotechnological Approaches to the teaching of the *Cloud*-author and to the *Showings* of Julian of Norwich
D. Rogers (Loras College, Iowa)   143

The Mystical Experience of Julian of Norwich with reference to the Epistle to the Hebrews ch. ix: Semiotic and Psychoanalytic Analysis
B. Lorenzo (Orsay)   161

The Dynamics of the Signans in the Spiritual Quest (*Piers Plowman*, the Mystics and Religious Drama)
G. Bourquin (University of Nancy)   182

Mystic's Foot: Rolle and Affectivity
V. Gillespie (University of Oxford)   199

The Organization of the *Scale of Perfection*
M. Sargent (University of Salzburg)   231

MARGERY KEMPE AND THE EASTERN AND WESTERN TRADITION OF THE 'PERFECT FOOL'

ROLAND MAISONNEUVE

MARGERY KEMPE (c. 1373–1440) is a very controversial figure. In depth of spiritual perception or mystical doctrine, she is frequently judged as being inferior to the other fourteenth-century English mystics. Her critics are prone to view her as a mere eccentric or as an hysterical exhibitionist with strong neurotic tendencies. Her auto-biography has been appreciated more as a psychological document or for its historical value or background than for its religious meaning.

As a matter of fact, at first reading, her revelations sound verbose, diffuse, naïve and self-centred. They embarrass the reader with their outpouring of tears, shrill screams and wild gestures manifesting an overflow of sentimentality and superficial emotions, very difficult to harmonize with the peace and serenity which characterize true mysticism.

However a methodical and exhaustive study of Margery Kempe's text leads us to different conclusions. Too rigid criteria have been applied to her, which criteria do not cover the whole range of Christian mysticism. She appears actually as belonging to a category of mystics who have been often neglected or even overlooked in our western tradition and yet who are part of it. Mystics such as those have been glorified and studied in the eastern Christian tradition. They are known as the fools of God.[1]

I

Holy folly is a charism. The fool of God is called to live fully the absolute of God's requirements, to proclaim and live, through his word and daily life, the gospel of the beatitudes, to participate in Christ's *kenosis*, passion and divine folly of infinite love. Several texts by Paul delineate the spirit of this folly:

For it is written, I will destroy the wisdom of the wise, and will bring to

1

nothing the understanding of the prudent. Where is the wise? where is the scribe? where is the disputer of this world? hath not God made foolish the wisdom of this world? For after that in the wisdom of God the world by wisdom knew not God, it pleased God by the foolishness of preaching to save them that believe (1 Corinthans 1:19–21).

We are fools for Christ's sake, but ye are wise in Christ; we are weak, but ye are strong; ye are honourable, but we are despised. Even unto this present hour we both hunger, and thirst, and are naked, and are buffeted, and have no certain dwelling place. And labour, working with our own hands: being reviled, we bless; being persecuted, we suffer it: Being defamed, we intreat: we are made as the filth of the world, and are the offscouring of all things unto this day (1 Corinthians, 4:10–13).

The fool of God has to pass through what Christ has gone through:

And when his friends heard of it, they went out to lay hold on him: for they said, He is beside himself (Mark 3:21).

And many of them said, He hath a devil, and is mad; why hear ye him? (John 10:20).

Whether they belong to the eastern or western tradition, the fools of God have common traits.

1. All of them declare or hint that their call to become fools of God does not come from their own desire but from a vocation given by God, which is sometimes for them a weight they would willingly cast off. But they understand in their hearts that this folly is their divine lot and constitutes their own participation in Christ's redemption. Therefore they live it radically. One of the western fools of God, Francis of Assisi, will keep repeating it:

My brothers, my brothers, God has called me by the way of simplicity and humility. He told me that he wanted me to be a new fool.[2]

2. Their motto is: *Imitatio Christi*, the imitation of Christ's life. They do all they can to conform themselves to his total self-surrender. They want to live his mystery of self-emptying and nakedness. They even search for all possible humiliations. Their joy is to be subjected to mockery, incomprehension and be treated as insane people. Their inner eyes are fixed on the scene of the lord's crowning of thorns:

Then the soldiers of the governor took Jesus into the common hall, and gathered unto him the whole band of soldiers. And they stripped him, and put on him a scarlet robe. And when they had platted a crown of thorns, they put it upon his head, and a reed in his right hand: and they bowed the knee before him, and mocked him, saying, Hail, King of the Jews! And they spit upon him, and took the reed, and smote him on the head. And after that they had mocked him, they took the robe off from him, and put his own raiment on him, and led him away to crucify him (Matthew 27:27–31).

2

3. To be totally transformed into Christ's fools, they do not hesitate to perform very bizarre actions which puzzle or scandalize the deeply religious man who judges them to be contrary to modesty and decency or inspired by the devil. However such acts have most of the time a deep symbolical meaning.

In that respect, they follow the lines traced by the Prophets of the Old Testament. Isaiah walks naked and barefooted to announce in the name of the Lord that:

> the King of Assyria shall lead away the Egyptians prisoners, and the Ethiopians captives, young and old, naked and barefoot, even with their buttocks uncovered, to the shame of Egypt (Isaiah 20:4).

Ezekiel is ordered by God to eat human excrement as a sign that the children of Israel

> shall eat their defiled bread among the Gentiles, whither I will drive them (Ezekiel 4:10).

Palladius (c. 365–425), the historian of early monasticism, tells the story of one Serapion Sindonites, a vagabond ascetic, who wandered about, clothed with but a loincloth and living in the utmost poverty. From Egypt he went to Greece, then to Rome, and there met a female ascetic. To test her call, he enjoined her to undress, place her clothes on her shoulders and follow him, similarly naked, through the streets of the city. She objected that she would be a cause of scandal and would be accused of being insane and devil-ridden. 'What does that matter?', Serapion answered. And to prove that he was more dead to the world than she was, he walked away naked.[3] To proclaim God's self-abasement and humiliation, Francis of Assisi and brother Ruggini stripped themselves of their clothes and preached naked. The spectators first mocked at them and thought they 'had gone mad out of an excess of penance';[4] however, later on they understood, wept and repented.

In their folly, the 'perfect fools' transform themselves into sacred jesters, clowns or mimics. The monophysite historian, John of Ephesus (c. 507–586) gives an example of this in the lives of Theophilus and Maria, 'children of eminent men of Antioch, who despised the world and all that is in it and lived a holy life in poverty of spirit, wearing an assumed garb'.[5] Originally betrothed to one another, they were converted to celibacy and a life of simulated folly by one Procopius of Rome. From then, they dressed most strangely, Theophilus as a mime-actor, Maria as a prostitute. They went to the city of Amida, where

3

they used often to perform drolleries and buffooneries, being constantly in the courts of the church like strangers, making fun of the priests and the people, and having their ears boxed by everyone as mime-actors.[6]

The narrator followed them and surprised them one night over the pinnacle of the city wall:

I saw that both placed themselves standing with their faces towards the east, and stretched out their arms to heaven in prayer, and they stood up and again fell upon their faces in prayer . . . and they went through the same form for a long time.[7]

Their sanctity was unknown to the world. To everybody they were just a comedian and a whore.

Even through his strange gestures the perfect fool celebrates the most high: 'What are the servants of God but his minstrels?',[8] Francis of Assisi exclaims:

Drunken with the love and compassion of Christ, blessed Francis on a time did things such as these. For the most sweet melody of spirit boiling up within him, frequently broke out in French speech, and the veins of murmuring which he heard secretly with his ears broke forth into French-like rejoicing. And sometimes he picked up a branch from the earth, and laying it on his left arm, he drew in his right hand another stick like a bow over it, as if on a viol or other instrument, and, making fitting gestures, sang with it in French unto the Lord Jesus Christ[9]

4. Through his mad actions or gestures, the perfect fool wants to manifest the deep realities of the kingdom of God. He opposes the world of sin and the world of pure love, where you love and, in love, do what you like.[10] He is a prophet denouncing the evil, disparaging any form of hypocrisy, revealing the profound vices which hide under apparent virtues. In the orthodox east, St Basil the blessed (d. 1552) used to throw stones at the houses of respectable people and weep abundantly in front of the dwelling-places of sinners. In the west, to mock at human pride, or give lessons in humility or force himself to humility, St Philip Neri (1515–1595) played tricks, told jokes, performed rididulous dances before Cardinals, wore his clothes inside out, dressed in a cassock and large white boots, had his hair cut during the mass and shouted to the perplexed or scandalized faithful: 'See if my hair is not being well dressed'.

5. The perfect fool goes on a never-ending pilgrimage. He rambles along the roads or through the wilderness, or visits shrines. He is a nomad settling nowhere. Here again he reveals, through his peregrinations, that man's destiny is not limited to the earth but is boundless, always changing, always on the move. St Benedict-Joseph

4

Labre (1748–1783), the poor wanderer for Christ's sake—who lived in abject poverty, most of the time slept out of doors, ate what he found on rubbish heaps—travelled all over Europe, went to Loreto and Assisi in Italy, Einsiedeln in Switzerland, St James of Compostela in Spain. He is thought to have walked more than 30,000 kilometers: he kept moving restlessly from place to place, like a solitary man. Invited one day, he answered: 'Dinner? Dinner? I dine in the street'. Wherever he was, he irradiated just through his silence and presence.

6. The perfect fool is a soul of compassion. He feels akin to all the wretched and pariahs of the world. The beggars, the lepers or the prisoners are his brothers in Christ. He personally does not care for his reputation and feels drawn to all moral and mental outcasts. St Basil the blessed scandalized the righteous by making friends of loose women. Some Russian *yourodivyé* danced with prostitutes, hoping to make of a hellish dance a heavenly dance by frightening away Satan through the presence of Jesus whom they kept invoking while dancing.

7. As simple and pure children, the perfect fools live for God lives of spiritual infancy. They are intimate with their Creator, feel his presence everywhere, in nature, in man, in daily events. They seem to perceive acutely that everything comes from love, dwells in love, finds its end in love. The majorcan scholar-mystic Ramon Lull (c. 1233–1315), who called himself Ramon the Fool, kept travelling and working for the conversion of Jews and Moslems, and died in North Africa, stoned to death because of his preaching the Gospel in public; he used to repeat that God's love and God's intimacy are the inner fires of the fools of God:

> As one that was a fool went the Lover through a city, singing of his Beloved, and men asked him if he had lost his wits. 'My beloved', he answered, 'has taken my will and I myself have yielded up to Him my understanding; so that there is left in me naught but memory, wherewith I remember my Beloved.[11]
> 'Foolish Lover! Why dost thou weary thy body, cast away thy wealth, leave the joys of this world and go about as an outcast among the people?' – 'To do honour to the honours of my Beloved', he replied, 'for He is neglected and dishonoured by more men than honour and love him'.[12]

II

It is difficult to understand Margery Kempe unless one places her and studies her within the tradition of the perfect fool.

1. Her destiny seems to have been linked to madness. At the time of her conversion, and owing to inner anguishes and problems of conscience, she went out of her mind. Her biographer reports that she

was 'wondyrlye vexid & labowryd wyth spyritys hal ʒer wiij wekys & odde days.[13] More than once she felt attracted to mad people, visited them and succeeded in making them peaceful and serene.

After her conversion, her spiritual life and love of God were made manifest through three kinds of folly.

a. Her inner compassion provoked in her overabundant tears, sobs and screams, which occured everywhere and at any time,

sumtyme in þe cherch, sumtyme in þe strete, sumtyme in þe chawmbre, sumtyme in þe felde whan God wold sendyn hem, for sche knew neuyr tyme ne owyr whan þei xulde come.[14]

Margery fought against this overflow of emotion, which exasperated many people around her, but in vain, 'þe mor þat sche wolde labowryn to kepe it in er to put it a-wey, mech þe mor xulde sche cryen & þe mor lowder'.[15]

b. God ordered her to walk about, all dressed in white. She looked ridiculous, and as she was a married woman, she was thought to be insane and was constantly scoffed at:

'And, dowtyr, I say to þe I wyl þat þu were clothys of whyte & non oþer colowr, for þu xal ben arayd aftyr my wyl'.—A, der Lord, yf I go arayd on oþer maner þan oþer chast women don, I drede þat þe pepyl syl slawndyr me. Þei wyl sey I am an ypocryt & wondryn vp-on-me—ʒa, dowtyr, þe mor wondryng þat þow hast for my lofe, þe mor þu plesyst me. Than þis creatur durst non oþer-wyse do þan sche was comawndyd in hir sowle.[16]

More than once, in most diverse circumstances, she felt inwardly forced to talk to those she met of God, of God's love, of God's laws. She firmly reproved them for their faults and vices, and was judged to be both fanatic and insane.

Because of these three kinds of folly, she was often accused by priests or laymen of feigning her tears (ch. 3), being possessed (ch. 13) or sick (ch. 20), falsely deceiving people (ch. 57), drinking too much wine (ch. 84) or being a hypocrite (ch. 84). She was often forsaken by her friends. Her travelling companions 'wolde not knowyn hir'.[17] However God approved her ways:

Dowtyr, þe mor schame, despite, & reprefe þat þu sufferyst for my lofe, þe bettyr I lofe þe, for I far liche a man þat louyth wel hys wyfe, þe mor enuye þat men han to hir þe bettyr he wyl arayn hir in despite of hir enmys. & ryth so, dowtyr, xal I faryn wyth þe.[18]

2. Such was her participation in Christ's life. Jesus told her she would be totally bound to the cross with him:

Dowtyr, þu hast an hayr vp-on þi bakke. I wyl þu do it a-way, & I schal ʒiue þe an hayr in þin hert þat schal lyke me mych bettyr þan alle þe hayres in þe world.[19]

Þow xalt ben etyn & knawyn of þe pepul of þe world as any raton knawyth þe stokfysh.[20]

She suffered an inner martyrdom:

Sche ymagyned in hir-self what deth sche myght deyn for Crystys sake. Hyr þowt sche wold a be slayn for Goddys lofe, but dred for þe poynt of deth, & þerfor sche ymagyned hyr-self þe most soft deth, as hir thowt, for dred of inpacyens, þat was to be bowndyn hyr hed and hir fet to a stokke & hir hed to be smet of wyth a scharp ex for Goddys lofe. Þan seyr owyr Lord in hir mende, I thank þe, dowtyr, þat þow woldyst suffer deth for my lofe, for, as oftyn as þow thynkyst so, þow schalt haue þe same mede in Heuyn as þow þu suffredyst þe same deth.[21]

'Dowtyr, it is mor plesyng vn-to me þat þu suffyr despitys & scornys, schamys & repreuys, wrongys & disesys þan 3if þin hed wer smet of thre tymes on þe day euery day in sevyn 3er.[22]

Through her trials she learnt how to become one with Christ. Her autobiography shows that in Lynne, her native town, she suffered 'meche despite, meche reprefe, many a scorne, many a slawndyr, many a bannyng, & many a cursyng'.[23] And the same situations happened during her journeys and pilgrimages. She was insulted, ridiculed and threatened, both by lay and church people. 'Folke spitted at hir'.[24] She was accused of being 'a fals strumpet, a fals loller, & a fals deceyuer of þe pepyl',[25] threatened with being burnt alive,[26] taken several times to prison as a heretic, summoned to appear before bishops, archbishops and church courts.[27] Her inspired answers saved her.

When she was ill-treated or scoffed at, she answered meekly or remained silent, and prayed for those who persecuted her or accused her:

And on a tyme a rekless man, litil chargyng hys owyn schame wyth wil & wyth purpose kest a bolful of watyr on hir heuyd coming in þe strete. Sche, no-thyng meuyd perwyth, seyd, 'God make 3ow a good man', heyly thankyng God þerof, as sche dede of many mo oþer tymes.[28]

In her tribulations she followed the example of her Master with force and courage, remembering Christ's words to her: It wer vnpossibyl to þe to suffyr þe scornys & despytes þat þow schalt haue ne were only my grace supportyng þe.[29] She really lived the mystery of the crowning of thorns. In that respect, one episode in her life is deeply symbolical. Her companions, when she was going through the Holy Land,

dedyn hir mech shame & mech reprefe as þei wentyn in dyuers placys. They

cuttyd hir gown so schort þat it come but lytil be-nethyn hir kne & dedyn hir
don on a whyte canwas in maner of a sekkyn gelle, for sche xuld ben holdyn a
fool & þe pepyl xuld not makyn of hir ne han hir in reputacyon. Þei madyn
hir to syttyn at þe tabelys ende be-nethyn alle oþer þat ache durst full euyl
spekin a word.[30]

3. One must not wonder that Margery Kempe was so often
derided and thus made faithful to her call. Mad extravagant actions or
events abounded in her life and made of her a true fool of God. When
she was in Palestine and visited 'þe blysfule cite Ierusalem, þe cyte of
Heuyn',[31] she had the greatest difficulties in keeping on her donkey,
for 'sche myth not beryn þe swetnesse & grace þat God wrowt in hir
sowle'.[32] Two Dutch pilgrims had to help her and keep her from
falling, thinking she was sick! When she was walking up the Mount of
Calvary, she fell down because she could not stand or kneel,

walwyd & wrestyd with hir body, spredyng hir arms a-brode, & cryed wyth a
lowde voys as þow hir hert xulde a brostyn a-sundyr, for in þe cite of hir
sowle sche saw veryly & freschly how owyr Lord was crucifyed.[33]

Very often, while weeping, she 'wrestyd hir body turnyng fro þe o syde
in-to þe oþer & wex al blew & al blo as it had ben colowr of leed'.[34]
'sum scornyd hir and seyd þar sche howlyd as it had ben a dogge'.[35]

4. She has the prophetic insight and mission of the fools of God.
Not only does she know many 'secret thyngys boþe of qwyk & of ded as
owyr Lord schewyd to hir sowle'[36], but she has the courage of the
prophet. She 'spak boldly & mytily wher-so sche cam in London
a-geyn swerars, bannars, lyars & swech oþer viciows pepil, a-geyn þe
pompows aray boþin of men & of women'.[37] Through her words and
her ways of being, she obliges her interlocutors to reveal who they are
inside their hearts. When they reject her, they reject the truth they
more or less consciously apprehend. Some see their inner universes
crumble and begin to understand. Sometimes they feel remorseful and
begin to change. Thus, one day, reading into the soul of a wicked
monk, she strongly rebuked him and revealed to him what she knew of
his past: he amended. When she saw him again, later on, he was a new
man. He had been made

suppriowr of þe place, a wel gouernyd man & wel dysposyd, þankyd be
God, & made þis creatur gret cher & hyly blyssed God þat euyr he saw hir.[38]

Coming back from the Continent, she was summoned before the
Chapter House at York and examined as to her faith. She answered the
Archbishop's questions with force and wisdom:

8

Þan seyd þe Erchebischop to hir, 'Þow schalt sweryn þat þu ne xalt techyn ne chalengyn þe pepil in my diocyse'—'Nay, syr, I xal not sweryn,' sche seyde, 'for I xal spekyn of God & vndirnemyn hem þat sweryn gret othys wher-so-euyr I go vn-to þe tyme þat þe Pope & Holy Chirche hath ordeynde þat no man schal be so hardy to spekyn of God, for God al-mythy forbedith not, sor, þat we xal speke of hym. And also þe Gospel makyth mencyon þat, whan þe woman had herd owr Lord prechyd, sche cam be-forn hym wyth a lowde voys & seyd, 'Blyssed be þe wombe þat þe bar & þe tetys þat ȝaf þe sowkyn.' Þan owr Lord seynd a-ȝen to hir, 'Forsoþe so ar þei blissed þat heryn þe word of God and kepyn it.' And þerfor, sir, me thynkyth þat þe Gospel ȝeuyth me leue to spekyn of God.[39]

5. Like the fools of God, she is a nomad. She travelled a lot along the roads, went on pilgrimages in England and abroad, visited Rome, Jerusalem, Compostela, which journeys meant utter denial of herself. In her peregrinations she lived the life of the beatitudes. She knew all kinds of tribulations, thirst, hunger, fear, solitude. In Rome she found herself with 'no bed to lyn in ne no clothys to be cured wyth saf hir owyn mentil. & þan was sche ful of vermyn & suffyrd gret peyn þerwyth'.[40] She was frequently helped by poor people, but had also to suffer many trials and humiliations. Crossing Germany, on her way back to England, she had several unpleasant adventures:

Þe nyght fel up-on hyr, & sche was ryth heuy, for sche was a-lone. Sche wist not wyth whom sche myth reston þat nyght ne wyth whom sche xulde gon þe next day. Þer cam preistys to hir, þer sche was at oste, of þat cuntre. Þei clepyd hir Englische sterte & spokyn many lewyd wordys vn-to hir, schewyng vn-clenly cher & cuntenawns, proferyng to ledyn hir a-bowtyn yf sche wolde. Sche had mech drede for hir chastite & was in gret heuynes.[41]

. . . sche saw a cumpany of powr folke. Þan went sche to on of hem, speryng whidyr þei wer purposyd to gon. . . . He sayd, 'hast þu no man to gon wyth þe?' 'No', sche seyd, 'my man is gon fro me'. So sche was receyuyd in-to a cumpany of powr folke, &, whan þei comyn to any towne, sche bowte hir mete & hir felaschep went on beggyng. Whan þei wer wyth-owtyn þe townys, hir felaschep dedyn of her clothys, &, sittyng nakyd, pykyd hem. Nede compellyd hir to abydyn hem & prolongyn hir jurne & ben at meche mor cost þan sche xulde ellys a ben. Thys creatur was a-þauyd to putte of hir cloþis as hyr felawys dedyn, & þerfor sche thorw hir comownyng had part of her vermyn & was betyn & stongyn ful euyl boþe day & nyght tyl God sent hir oþe felaschep.[42]

6. As the true perfect fool, she is a soul of compassion. She visited the poor. She assisted the sick and the dying. She approached the lepers and comforted the mad. During her stay in Rome, for six weeks she served an old woman who was a poor creature. 'Sche seruyd hir as sche wolde a don owyr Lady'.[43]

9

Sche fet hom watyr & stykkys in hir nekke for þe poure woman and beggyd mete and wyn bothyn for hir. And, when þe pour womans wyn was sowr, þis creatur hir-self drank þat sowr wyn & ȝaf þe powr woman good wyn þat sche had bowt for hir owyn selfe.[44]

She was also ordered by God to give away all her money and make herself 'bar for hys lofe'.[45]

& a-non sche wyth a feruent desyr to plesyn God ȝaf a-wey swech good as sche had & sweche as sche had borwyd also of þe broke-bakkyd man þat went wyth hir.[46]

She kept praying for all her enemies, for all sinners, for the souls in purgatory, for the conversion of all Jews and Saracens and all heathen people so that, as God told her, 'þei xulde comyn to Cristen feith þat my name myth be magnyfijd in hem'.[47] All in tears and sobs, she frequently implored Jesus to keep all men from hell:

Þis creatur seyd, 'Lord, I aske mercy & preseruying fro euyrlestyng dampnacyon for me & for all þe world, chastyse us her how þow wylt & in Purgatory, & kepe us fro dampnacyon for þin hy mercy'.[48]
Þan sche preyed, Mercyful Lord Crist Ihesu, in þe is al mercy & grace & goodnes. Haue mercy, pyte, & compassyon of hem. Shew þi mercy & thy goodnes vp-on hem, help hem, send hem very contricyon, & late hem neuyr deyn in her synne'.[49]

Her autobiography reports that Christ said to her one day:

Dowtyr, I knowe alle þe thowtys of þin hert þat þu hast to alle maner men & women, to alle laȝerys, & to alle presonerys, & as mech good as þu woldist ȝeuyn hem be ȝer to serue me wyth I take it as yf it wer don in dede. &, dowtyr, I thanke þe for þe charite þat þu hast to alle lecherows men and women, for þu preyst for hem & wepist many a teer for hem, desyryng þat I xulde delyuyr hem owt of synne & ben as gracyows to hem as I was to Mary Mawdelyn & þat þei myth han as gret lofe to me as Mary Mawdelyn had . . .
Forþermore, dowtyr, I thanke þe for þe general charite þat þu hast to alle þe pepil þat is now in þis worlde leuyng & to alle þo þat arn for to come in-to þis worldys ende, þat þu woldist ben hakkyd as smal as flesche to þe potte for her lofe so þat I wolde be þi deth sauyn hem alle fro dampnacyon ȝyf it plesyd me.[50]

Isaac of Nineveh (7th century), who lived in the wilderness, among the hills, has written of the compassionate love of the perfect fool:

He who has such a heart cannot remember all creatures and see them without his eyes being filled with tears because of the immense compassion that invades his heart.[51]

Margery Kempe had that compassion.

7. Like all the fools of God, she loved God in a strange fashion,

but her love corresponded to her personal vocation as it was wanted by God, and such a love is more profound and contemplative than has been generally admitted. A searching study of the themes of love and union in her autobiography leads us to think that in, through and beyond her apparently oversentimental religious life, she reached high contemplation and experienced purgative, illuminative and unitive love. Her biographer tells of her:

> Be processe of tyme hir mende & hir thowt was so ioynyd to God þat sche neuyr forʒate hym but contynualy had mende of hym & behelde hym in alle creaturys. & euyr þe mor þat sche encresyd in lofe & in deuocyon, þe mor sche encresyd in sorwe & in contrycyon, in lownes, in mekeness, & in þe holy dread of owr Lord, & in knowlach of hir owyn frelte . . .[52].

Several episodes in her life reveal how she kept perceiving God through all the incidents of her existence:

> & Sumtyme, whan sche saw þe Crucyfyx, er yf sche sey a man had a wownde er a best wheþyr it wer, er ʒyf a man bett a childe be-for hir er smet an hors er an-oþer best wyth a whippe, ʒyf sche myth sen it er heryn it, hir thowt sche saw owyr Lord be betyn er wowndyd lyk as sche saw in þe man er in þe best, as wel in þe feld as in þe town, & be hir-selfe alone as wel as a-mong þe pepyl.[53]
>
> An-oþer tyme, ryth as sche cam be a powr womanys hows, þe powr woman clepyd hir in-to hir hows & dede hir sytten be hir lytyl fyer, ʒeuyng hir wyn to drynke in a cuppe of ston. & sche had a lytel manchylde sowkyng on hir brest, þe whech sowkyd o while on þe moderys brest; an-oþer while it ran to þis creatur, þe modyr syttyng ful of sorwe & sadnes. Þan þis creatur brast al in-to wepyng, as þei sche had seyn owr Lady & hir sone in tyme of hys Passyon, & had so many of holy thowtys þat sche myth neuyr tellyn þe haluendel, but euyr sat & wept plentyvowsly a long tyme þat þe powr woman, hauyng compassyon of hir wepyng, preyd hir to sesyn, not knowyng why sche wept. Þan owr Lord Ihesu Crist seyd to þe creatur, 'Thys place is holy'.[54]
>
> Also þer was a lady desyred to haue þe sayd creatur to mete. & þerfor, as honeste wolde, sche went to þe cherch þer þe lady herd hir seruyse, wher þis creatur sey a fayr ymage of owr Lady clepyd a pyte. And thorw þe beholdyng of þat pete hir mende was al holy ocupyed in þe Passyon of owr Lord Jhesu Crist & in þe compassyon of owr Lady, Seynt Mary, be whech sche was compellyd to cryyn ful lowde & wepyn ful sor, as þei sche xulde a deyd. Þan cam to hir þe ladys preste seying, 'Damsel, Ihesu is ded long sithyn.' 'Sir, hys deth is as fresch to me as he had deyd þis same day, & so me thynkyth it awt to be to ʒow & to alle Cristen pepil. We awt euyr to han mende of hys kendnes & euyr thynkyn of þe dolful deth þat he deyd for vs'.[55]

For her, God is not a mere matter of devotion. He is the one who is all-love.[56] It is of all-love that she wants to be the servant. All her tears spring from the overabundance of her love:

sumtyme duryng in wepyng ij owyres & oftyn lengar in þe mend of owyr
Lordys Passyon wyth-owtyn cesyng, sumtyme for hir owyn synne, sumtyme
for þe synne of þe pepyl, sumtyme for þe sowlys in Purgatory, sumtyme for
hem þat arn in pouerte er in any dysese, for sche desyred to comfort hem
alle. Sumtyme sche wept ful plentevowsly & ful boystowsly for desyr of þe
blys of Heuyn & for sche was so long dyfferryd þerfro.[57]
and þan oftyn-tymys xulde sche cryin and roryn as þow sche xulde a brostyn
for þe feyth & þe trost þat sche had in þe precyows Sacrament. Also þe sayd
creatur was desiryd of mech pepil to be wyth hem at her deying & to prey for
hem, for, þow þei louyd not hir wepyng ne hir crying in her lyfe-tyme, þei
desiryd þat sche xulde deyin, & so sche dede.[58]

Her visions and revelations, however material they may seem to
be sometimes, are meant to make her 'mythy & strong in þe lofe of owr
Lord & gretly stabelyd in hir heith & encresyd in mekenes & charite
wyth oþer good vertuys'[59]:

Sum-tyme owr Lady spak to hir & comfortys hir in hir sekenes. Sumtyme
Seynt Petyr, er Seynt Powle, sumtyme Seynt Mary Mawdelyn, Seynt
Kateryne, Seynt Margaret, er what seynt in Heuyn þat sche cowde thynke
on thorw þe wil & sufferawns of God, þei spokyn to þe vndirstondyng of hir
sowle, & enformyd hir how sche xulde louyn God & how sche xulde best
plesyn hym.[60]

She is asked by God to go from the visible to the invisible, from the
corporal to the spiritual: 'For sumtyme þat sche vndirstod bodily it was
to ben vndirstondyn gostly'.[61] Christ wants to lead her to mental
orison:

'And, dowtyr, I wyl þow þi byddyng of many bedys and thynk swych
thowtys as I wyl putt in þi mend. I schal ȝeuyn þe leue to byddyn tyl sex of þe
cloke to sey what þow wyld. Þan schalt þow ly stylle & speke to me be
thowt, & I schal ȝefe to þe hey medytacyon and very contemplacyon'.[62]

Though she finds it difficult to give up saying many prayers, her
autobiography shows she fundamentally makes use of contemplative
short prayers, and Jesus says he is pleased with her for her prayers tell
her love:

'þan þu ronne wyth al thy mynde to me, seying, "Lord, þer is no trost but in
þe alone." & þan þu crydist to wyth al þin hert, "Lord, for þi wowndys
smerte drawe alle my love in-o thyn hert". & dowtyr, so haue I do'.[63]

She is prone to repeat some jaculatory prayers such as 'Jesus, Mercy',
or sometimes, 'I die'. She thus enters the great spiritual current of
repetitive prayer, whose end is contemplation, and, through this
practice is akin to the Desert Fathers, the Hesychasts or the adepts of
the 'prayer of fire', who all aim at union with God. Whatever prayer

she says becomes part of her unceasing litanies of love: 'þu art my joye, Lord, my blysse, my comfort, & alle þe tresor þat I haue in þis world, for oþer werdlys joye coueyt I non but only þe'.[64]

She is not at all a sentimental bigot. Her inner life is focussed on Christ, and through Christ, on the alpha and omega of all-love, the blessed Trinity. She does have trinitarian graces, and God leads her in a symbolic way to meditate on the essence and intimate life of the Father, the Son and the Holy Ghost:

Sche teld hym how sum-tyme þe Fadyr of Hevyn dalyd to hir sowle as pleynly and as veryly as o frend spekyth to a-noþer be bodyly spech; sum-tyme þe Secunde Persone in Trinyte; sumtyme alle thre Personys in Trinyte & o substawns in Godhede dalyid to hir sowle & informyd hir in hir feyth & in hys lofe how sche xuld lofe hym, worshepyn hym, & dredyn hym. . . .[65]

'And ȝet I wot wel j-now, dowtyr, þat þu thynkyst þu maist not worschepyn þe Fadyr but þu worschep þe Sone, ne þu may not worschep þe Sone but þu worschep þe Holy Ghost. And also þu thynkyst sumtyme, dowtyr, þat þe Fadyr is al myghty & al witty & al grace & goodnes, & þu thynkyst þe same of þe Sone þat he is al myghty & al witty & al grace & goodnes. And þu thynkyst þat þe Holy Gost hath þe same propirteys euyn wyth þe Fadyr & þe Sone, procedyng of hem bothyn. Also þu thynkyst þat eche of þe iij personys in Trinite hath þat oþer hath in her Godhed, & so þu beleuyst verily, dowtyr in thy sowle þat þer be iij dyuers personys & oo God in substawnce, & þat eche knowyth þat oþer knowyth, & ech may þat oþer may, & eche will þat oþer wil. And, dowtyr, þis is a very feith & a ryght feyth, and þis feith hast þu only of my ȝyfte'.[66]

Even if this last passage sounds more like a theological lesson than like a living experience, it reveals how deeply Margery Kempe is centered by Christ on the living God. Both divinity and trinity are emphasized. However, Margery Kempe is at pains to understand the concept of Godhead, when, being in Rome, she hears from Jesus that she is going to be wedded to the Godhead. This announcement provokes in her a sort of crisis, as she is afraid of this unknown abyss and clings to the manhood of Christ. Such an episode witnesses to her deep religious life, but also unveils her simplicity of heart which tends to colour her deep experiences with the childish naive hues likely to lead the reader astray:

þe Fadyr seyd to þis creatur, 'Dowtyr, I wil han þe weddyd to my Godhede, for I schal schewyn þe my preuyteys & my cownselys, for þu xalt wonyn wyth me wyth-owtyn ende'. Þan þer creatur kept sylens in hir sowle & answeryd not þerto, for sche was ful sor afred of þe Godhed & sche cowde no skylls of þe dalyawns of þe Godhede, for al hir lofe & al hir affeccyon was set in þe

13

manhode of Criste & þerof cowde sche good skylle & sche wolde for no-thyng a partyd perfro. . . .

Than seyd þe Secunde Persone, Crist Ihesu, whoys manhode sche louyd so meche, to hir, 'What seyst þu, Margery, dowtyr, to my Fadyr of þes wordys þat he spekyth to þe? Art þu wel plesyd þat it be so?' And þan sche wold not answeryn þe Secunde Persone but wept wondir sor, desiryng to haue stille hym-selfe & in no wyse to be departyd fro him. Than þe Secunde Persone in Trinite answeryd to hys Fadyr for hir & seyde, 'Fadyr, haue hir excused, for sche is ȝet but ȝong & not fully lernyd how sche xulde answeryn'.

And þan þe Fadyr toke hir be þe hand in hir sowle be-fore þe Sone & þe Holy Gost & þe Modyr of Ihesu and alle þe xij apostelys & Seynt Kateryn & Seynt Margarete & many oþer seyntys & holy virgynes wyth gret multitude of awngelys, seying to hir sowle, 'I take þe, Margery, for my weddyd wyfe, for fayrar, for fowelar, for richar, for powerar, so þat þu be buxom & bonyr to do what I byd þe do. For, dowtyr, þer was neuyr childe so buxom to þe modyr as I xal be to þe boþe in wel & in wo, – to help þe and comfort þe. And perto I make þe suyrte'.[67]

The image of the child, applied to the Father, may seem incongruous, but in fact, it conveys deeply all the simplicity of love and the spirituality of childhood Margery Kempe is constantly led to. Her deepest relations with God are, in a similar way, suggested through other images: God tells her she is his sister, his mother, his wife.[68] And indeed the Autobiography shows how profoundly she lives each of these particular bonds with God. They both transmit and suggest her deep mystical life, which is also manifested by the outbursts of a mysterious fire of love in her soul, reminding us of similar experiences in the lives of other great mystics,[69] and by several important notations concerning her intimacy with God: her autobiography shows her as languishing in love (ch. 7), inebriated with love, wounded with love (ch. 41). The ring she wears on her finger, by order of Christ, contains an inscription which is, in fact, Margery's motto: 'Ihesus est amor meus'.[70] It is a union of will and love. Jesus celebrates it one day through a symbol:

'þu art so buxom to my wille & cleuyst as sore on-to me as þe skyn of stokfysche cleuyth to a manys handys whan it is sothyn, & wilt not forsake me for no schame þat any man can don to þe'.[71]

As so many of her brothers, she finally experiences her nothing-ness and perceives deeply God's ineffability:

Sche was so ful of holy thowtys & medytacyons & holy contemplacyons in þe Passyon of owyr Lord Ihesu Crist & holy dalayawns þat owyr Lord Jhesu Crist dalyed to hir sowle þat sche cowde neuyr expressyn hem aftyr, so hy & so holy þei weryn.[72]

Sche had many an holy thowt & many an holy desyr whech sche cowde neuyr tellyn ne rehersyn ne hir tunge myth neuyr expressyn þe habundawnce of grace þat sche felt. blissyd be our Lord of alle hys ʒyftys.[73]
It wer so holy & so hy þat sche was abaschyd to tellyn hem to any creatur, & also it weryn so hy abouyn hir bodily wittys þat sche myth neuyr expressyn hem wyth hir bodily tunge liche as sche felt hem.[74]

Examining Margery Kempe within the tradition of the perfect fool sheds a new light on her. However eccentric she may still appear, she participates, through her eccentricity of love, in a deeper experience that links her to the living current of mysticism. All the richness, strangeness and uniqueness of her call are summed in Christ's brief pronouncement on her in her Autobiography:

'Þu art to me a synguler lofe, dowtyr'.[75]

NOTES

1. On the tradition of the 'perfect fool', see 'Fous pour le Christ', *Dictionnaire de Spiritualité*, Paris, 1963, 1. En Orient, Thomas Spidlik, c. 752–761. 2. En Occident, (François Vandenbroucke), c. 761–770; John Saward, *Perfect Fools*, London, 1980; Mother Maria, *The Fool* and other writings, Greek Orthodox Monastery of the Assumption, Normanby, Whitby, North Yorkshire, 1980 (particularly 9, The Fool, p. 95–103); Gaston Zananin, 'Les Fous pour le Christ', *Sources*, Fribourg, 7 (1982), 58–73.
2. *Speculum Perfectionis*, ed. P. Sábatier, Manchester, 1928, ch. 67, p. 196.
3. Palladius, *Lausiac History*, ch. 37, trans. R. T. Meyer, Ancient Christian Writers, Westminster, Maryland, London, 34, 1965.
4. *The Little Flowers of St Francis*, ed. S. Hughes, New York, 1964, ch. xxx, pp. 107 f.
5. *Lives of the Eastern Saints*, ed. and tr. E. W. Brooks, Patrologia Orientalis, Paris, 1923, 19, 164.
6. Ibid., 166 f.
7. Ibid., 169 f.
8. *Speculum Perfectionis*, trans. R. Steele, London, 1903, ch. vi.
9. Ibid. 93. See also Thomas of Celano, *Vita Secunda*, 90.
10. According to St Augustine, 'caritas perfecta, perfecta justitia est', *De Natura et Gratia*, 70, II, 84.
11. Ramon Lull, *The Book of the Lover and the Beloved*, ed. E. A. Peers, London, 1945, p. 28.
12. Ibid., 12, p. 21.
13. All quotations from Margerie Kempe are from *The Book of Margery Kempe*, ed. Sanford B. Meech, and Hope Emily Allen, Early English Text Society O.S, 212, London, 1940. References are to chapter, page number and line number.See ch. 1, p. 7, 21–23.
14. Ch. 28, p. 69, 15–18.
15. Idem, p. 70, 2–3.
16. Ch. 15, p. 32, 16–24.
17. Ch. 30, p. 74, 22.
18. Ch. 32, p. 81, 28–33.

19. Ch. 5, p. 17, 6–9.
20. Idem, p. 17, 16–17.
21. Ch. 14, p. 29, 32; p. 30, 1–10.
22. Ch. 54, p. 131, 16–19.
23. Ch. 55, p. 137, 3–5.
24. Ch. 44, p. 105, 21.
25. Ch. 46, p. 112, 1–2.
26. One day she reproved the monks at Canterbury, who reacted violently. 'Sche went owt of þe monastery, þei folwyng & crying vp-on hir, þow xalt be brent, fals lollare. Her is a cartful of thornys redy for þe & a tonne to bren þe wyth'. And þe creatur stod wythowtyn þe ȝatys at Cawntyrbery, for it was in þe euenyng, mech pepyl wonderyng on hir. Þan seyd þe pepyl, 'Tak & bren hir' (ch. 13, p. 28, 28–34).
27. See ch. 45–48, 51–55.
28. Ch. 55, p. 137, 5–10.
29. Ch. 15, p. 29, 24–26.
30. Ch. 26, p. 62, 13–20.
31. Ch. 28, p. 67, 20–21.
32. Idem, p. 67, 25–26.
33. Idem, p. 68, 13–17.
34. Ch. 44, p. 105, 19–21.
35. Idem, p. 105, 22–23.
36. Ch. 15, p. 34, 1–2.
37. II Ch. 9, p. 245, 7–10.
38. Ch.12, p. 27, 14–17.
39. Ch. 52, p. 125, 37–38; p. 126, 1–13.
40. Ch. 34, p. 86, 1–3.
41. II Ch. 6, p. 236, 25–33.
42. Idem, p. 237, 11–27.
43. Ch. 34, p. 85, 37.
44. Idem, p. 86, 3–8.
45. Ch. 37, p. 92, 15.
46. Idem, p. 92, 15–18.
47. Ch. 84, p. 204, 19–20.
48. Ch. 8, p. 20, 14–18.
49. Ch. 20, p. 48, 12–16.
50. Ch. 84. p. 204, 3–12, 24–29.
51. *De perfectione religiosa*, Paris, 1909.
52. Ch. 72, p. 172, 11–17.
53. Ch. 28, p. 69, 1–8.
54. Ch. 39, p. 94, 8–21.
55. Ch. 61, p. 148, 2–17.
56. 'And also, dowtyr, þu seyst it is wel worthy þat I be callyd al lofe, & þu xalt fyndyn þat am al lofe to þe, for I knowe euery thowt of thyn hert' (Ch. 84, p. 203, 23–26).
57. Ch. 7, p. 19, 37–38; p. 20, 1–7.
58. Ch. 71, p. 172, 32–37; p. 173, 1–2.
59. Ch. 87, p. 215, 1–3.
60. Idem, p. 215, 10–17.
61. Idem, p. 220, 9–11.
62. Ch. 5, p. 17, 25–31.
63. Ch. 88, p. 217, 4–8.
64. Ch. 32, p. 81, 21–24.
65. Ch. 17, p. 39, 16–22.
66. Ch. 86, p. 211, 11–26.
67. Ch. 35, p. 86, 15–24; p. 87, 3–23.

16

68. See ch. 32, 35, 36.
69. See ch. 13, 28, 35, 41, 46, 59, 60, 85, 89. Mystics often pretend that they feel themselves being consumed by a fire which is both *real* and *immaterial*. The same experience is described in Margery's autobiography, see for example ch. 35: 'Also owr Lord ȝaf hir an oþer tokne, þe whech enduryd a-bowtyn xvj ȝer it encresyd euyr mor & mor, & þat was a flawme of fyer wondir hoot & delectabyl & ryth comfortabyl, nowt wasting but euyr incresyng, of lowe, for, thow þe wedyr wer neuyr so colde, sche felt þe hete brennyng in hir brest & at hir hert, as verily as a man schuld felyn þe material fyer ȝyf he put hys hand or hys fynger þerin. Whan sche felt fyrst þe fyer of loue brennyng in her brest, sche was a-ferd þerof, & þan owr Lord answeryd to hir mend & seyde, 'Dowtyr, be not a-ferd, for þis hete is þete of þe Holy Gost, þe whech schal bren a-wey alle þi synnes, for þe fyer of lofe qwenchith alle synnes. And þu xalt vndirstondyn be þis tokyn þe Holy Gost is in þe, and þu wost wel wher-þat-euyr þe Holy Gost is þer is þe Fadir, & wher þe Fadyr is þer is þe Sone, and so þu hast fully in þe sowle al þe Holy Trinite. (ch. 35, p. 88, 26–36; p. 89, 1–6). Such a fire is analyzed here in its trinitarian significance. In that respect, Margery Kempe's document is one of the richest and most important texts we have in the mystical tradition that refers to this sign in relation to the Trinity. It testifies to the seer's deep religious experience.
70. Ch. 31, p. 78, 14.
71. Ch. 37, p. 91, 14–17.
72. Ch. 29, p. 71, 34–35; p. 72, 1–3.
73. Ch. 78, p. 187, 6–20.
74. Ch. 84, p. 201, 34–37.
75. Ch. 22, p. 50, 32.

THE CHOICES OF THE TRANSLATOR IN THE LATE MIDDLE ENGLISH PERIOD[1]

R. ELLIS

I

NO ACCOUNT OF the Middle English mystics would be complete without reference to the vast body of translated material produced during the period. The originals of some were written by mystics; others were readily adaptable to mystical ends; the whole provides a necessary circumstance for, and accompaniment to, the production of mystical writings. This wide range of material is in no danger of being neglected, as will readily appear in the amount of familiar ground which this paper is proposing to cover. Yet familiar ground, and the possibility, in principle, of measuring accurately the relation of a translated work to its original, have not resulted, in practice, in anything like agreement about the qualities of a given translation, or of translation generally through the period. One view has it, for example, that Love's *Myrrour* is, for the most part, a faithful translation 'without any substantial alteration' (Salter, p. 301); another, that it is 'frequently no more than a paraphrase' (Ragusa, p. xxiv).[2] Such disagreements suggest that the study of translation in the Middle English period needs to be put on a more systematic footing than it has enjoyed until now: which is the main purpose of the present paper. A subsidiary purpose concerns the evaluation of those arguments advanced for the existence of a tradition of translation, with Love as one of its most illustrious members, and exemplified by such texts as *The Myroure of oure Ladye*, Þe *Seuen Poyntes of Loue*, Capgrave's *Life of St Gilbert*, the second version of the Wycliffe Bible, and even the Psalter of Rolle (Salter, ch. 6).

Like the author of an original work and the scribe who makes a copy of it, the translator realises his work only in relation to the competing demands of four elements whose collaboration vitally informs it: the demands of his original, his audience, himself, and the tradition within which he is working.[3] The first two elements regularly

18

receive comment from the translator: as Caxton put it, the translator needs not only 'to satysfye thauctour' but also to 'satysfye euery man' who reads his translation (Crotch, pp. 91, 108). The translator will seldom refer to the part his own needs have played in the creation of his work: normally they surface only when he is requesting reward, of whatever kind, for his undertaking.[4] He invokes the fourth element of our model, the tradition, only in order to explain departures from, or assert his faithfulness to, it.[5] Now, since a cause exists only as realised in particular choices—choices which, once made, have constantly to be renegotiated in the process of translation—the relations between the translator's particular choices provide the only sure foundation for this study. These choices can be deduced even from texts where the translator has left no word of his intentions.

Logically, the translator's first choice precedes the act of translation: that is, the choice of base text. If he has only one copy of the original work, he exercises this choice only notionally. He may emend obvious nonsenses in his copy, as MN tells us he did with his translation of Margaret Porete's work:

> the Frensche booke þat I schal write aftir is yuel writen, and in summe places for defaute of wordis and silables þe reson is aweie. Also . . . summe wordis neden to be chaunged or it wol fare vngoodly, not acordynge to þe sentence. (Doiron, p. 249)

Otherwise, he must take its reliability as given. Awareness of his inability to exercise this choice may lead him to publish his translation with a disclaimer for any errors in it (e.g. Caxton's prologue to *The Myrrour of the World*: 'and of such [faulte] so founden . . . repute not the blame on me but on my copie which I am charged to folowe as nyghe as God wil gyue me grace': Crotch, p. 54, cf. p. 58);[6] or with a request that it be corrected as necessary. When he has more than one copy of the original, he may compare versions in the hope of creating, in his translation, a new version closer to the original.[7] So the translator of the second version of the Wycliffe Bible tells us that he sought 'to gedere manie elde biblis, and other doctouris, and comune glosis, and to make oo Latyn bible sumdel trewe' (FM I.57) as the basis for his revision of the earlier version.[8] Likewise, Caxton compared three versions of *The Golden Legend*, one Latin, one French, one English, in order to make his own translation, and sought the agreement of French and Latin texts against the English in order to fill out the English text and improve its order (Crotch p. 72).[9] The translator explains these practices in the clear expectation that readers familiar

19

with an existing version of the work will need persuading of the defensibility, to say nothing of the superiority, of the new one. Thus the General Prologue of the Wycliffe Bible urges those disposed to find fault with its translation to examine rather their own Latin Bibles than the new translation, for 'the comune Latyn biblis han more nede to be correctid . . . than hath the English bible late translatid' (FM I.58). The practical implications of this choice are seldom very radical: the new text, typically, is the sum of the variants of the available copies or the suppression of one or more of them.[10] The author of the Wycliffite prologue may declare his intention to keep the Hebrew variants distinct from the preferred Latin readings by setting the former 'in the margyn, bi maner of a glose', (FM I.58), but a recent study of the Psalter of the Wycliffite Bible found only one manuscript that carried out this promise: in all other cases the variants were silently absorbed into the body of the text.[11] By contrast, Capgrave, though basing his life of St Katharine, for the most part, on an unfinished Middle English translation, occasionally suppressed its readings in favour of those of the Latin text which he was using to complete the translation.[12] The anonymous translation of the Brigittine Breviary of Syon, *The Myroure of oure Ladye*, provides the rare example of a translator actively drawing attention to textual variants:

> The letter of this antempne in youre bokes as I vnderstande ys thus, *Benedicta filia tua domino*. Therefore som thynke that they wolde amende yt sayng thus, *Benedicta filia tu a domino*, and so they make *tua* tow wordes. Other thynke that yt ys better to say after the use of Sarum thus, *Benedicta filio tuo domina*. . . . If the letter of this antempne be thus, *Benedicta filia tua domino* then yt is sayde to the father of heuen, Blyssed be thy dowghter that is oure lady to the lorde or by the lorde, that ys her sonne, for by hym she ys moste blyssed (Blunt, pp. 272–3).[13]

A translator's silence on this question of variant readings does not necessarily mean, of course, that he used only one copy of the original. The absence of such comment, though, makes more difficult to substantiate any claim that he was working from several texts, as Elizabeth Salter has sought to prove in the case of Love's translations from Suso and Ps.-Bonaventura.[14]

II

Once he has established his copy text, the translator's next choice governs the form of his translation. He can change the form of his original in a number of ways, usually because he judges his readers to

20

need something more or other than the original provides; occasionally because he reckons that the original itself is in need of improvement.[15] A good example of the first kind of change occurs in Simon Appleby's *The Fruyte of Redempcion*. There, the Virgin's account of the Passion of Christ in the *Liber Celestis* of St Bridget of Sweden (I, 10), is turned into a series of prayers of thanksgiving. Another example occurs in the anonymous Carthusian *Speculum Devotorum*, where a revelation delivered by St Bridget in first person (*Liber* VII, xv) is narrated by the author himself within the framework of a meditation:

> sche tellyth hyt in here owen persone . . . þe whyche I turne here into the forme of meditacyon, not goynge be the grace of God fro the menynge of here wordys. (Hogg, p. 267)

Formal changes of this kind, in themselves, carry little weight in any assessment of a translation.[16]

Other changes to the form are potentially more significant: they include major cuts, and major additions, to the original. Not every cut or addition to the original is major. Some, like the translation of a doublet by a single word, or the translation of a single word by a gloss of one or two words, clearly have no significance in relation to the larger structures of their original, and will be discussed later. The modifications I have in mind can be well illustrated by quotations from Love, Capgrave, and the anonymous translator of the *Orologium*:

> (Love): to edificacioun of suche men or wommen is this drawynge out of the forseide book . . . with more putte to in certeyn parties, and also with drawynge of dyuerse auctoritees and materes as it semeth . . . most spedeful and edifienge (Powell, p. 8); the forsaide Bonauenture in this book . . . maketh a longe processe, aleggynge many auctoritees . . . the whiche processe thou3 it so be that it is full good and fructuouse to men, as vnto many be gostly lyueres, neuertheles, so it semeth as inpertynent in grete partye to manye comoun persones and symple soules—that this booke in Englische is writen to . . . therfore, we passen it ouer schortly, takynge therof that semeth profitable and edificatyffe (Powell, p. 158);[17]
> (Capgrave: Seynt Gilbertis lif . . . I haue take on hand to translate out of Latyn rith as I fynde before me, saue sum addicionis wil I put þertoo whech men of þat ordre haue told me, and eke othir þingis þat schul falle to my mynde . . . whech be pertinent (Munro, p. 62);
> (þe *seuen poyntes*): for als miche as in þe forseyde boke þere beþ manye maters and long processe towchynge him þat wrote hit and oþere religiose persones of his degre, þe whiche, as hit semeþ to me, were lytel edificacione to write to 3owe . . . þerefore I leve seche materes and take onelye þat me þinkeþ edifiying to 3owe (Horstmann 1, p. 325).

Of course, as Elizabeth Salter claimed when she used this material

(Salter, pp. 226–8), these practices need not simply indicate a translator's readiness to bend his original to purposes of his own: they can issue just as well from his understanding of, and regard for, its spirit. As an instance of this, we note the regular indications Love gives his readers of the cuts he is making to his original, including reference even to the chapter numbers of the cut material in the original (e.g. Powell, p. 155). Likewise, he tells us, he will indicate any elaborations to the matter of his original by means of a marginal 'N', showing where his contribution begins, and a marginal 'B', for Bonaventura, where the original resumes (Powell, p. 6): a parallel practice occurs in Rolle's Psalter, though its prologue gives no indication of the visual means which will be used to distinguish Latin original, translation and commentary from one another.[18]) These practices make it possible, in principle, for a reader to have the translation without the commentary, and, where cuts have been made to the text of the *Meditationes*, to restore a full text by consulting the original afresh.

Capgrave does not mark his additions to the St Gilbert Life in this way, and since his actual source does not seem to have survived, it is more difficult to determine their extent and significance.[19] We can resolve this uncertainty only by considering whether, and to what extent, other features of the translation are consistent with Capgrave's declared intention of translating 'rith as I fynde before me'.

Useful evidence is offered, first, by Capgrave's translation of the original's grammatical relations. Concerning the spread of the Gilbertine order, for example, Capgrave's ultimate source, the canonization documents, tell us 'iam tempus advenit, ut egrederetur dilectus cum dilecta in agrum mundi' (Dugdale, p. viii*). Capgrave translated this very carefully: 'now is þe tyme come þat þe welbeloued masculyne with þe welbeloued feminine schuld go oute into þe feld of þis world' (Munro, p. 87). Then, we have the evidence of his care to translate a difficult word with due regard to its context. One of the translated miracles concerns the cure of a sick man by the application of a linen cloth worn by the saint. Capgrave had some trouble finding the right word for this cloth. The obvious version, 'shirt', would contradict what he had earlier written:

> I suppose veryly it was his awbe, for my auctor her setteth a word 'subucula' whech is both an awbe and a schert, and in þe ferst part of þis lyf þe same auctour seith þat þis holy man wered next his skyn non . . . lynand (Munro, p. 125).

More striking evidence comes with his claim to follow his original in the manner of its narration of the miracles:

lich þat inquysicion in sentens and in termes, whech inqwysicion þei sent þat tyme to Rome . . . lich þat forme wil we write here (Munro, p. 118);

a point which he echoes in bringing to a close his account of the miracles, some of which, he says,

wer eke wroute aftir tyme þat þis book was mad, wherfore þei be not ȝet browte onto þis forme. And because þat we be in no dowte þat þese wer do in þe same forme, þerfor haue we wrytin hem in swech language as we coude (Munro, p. 135).

Striking though it is, this latter evidence cannot be conclusive. Whether or not the words are his own, though, and whether or not he lived up to their promises, they provide valuable evidence of Capgrave's awareness that a translator ought not to tamper with the form of his original, and that additions ought, as far as possible, to harmonise with the formal structures of that original.[20]

The translator of the *Orologium* no more indicates his cuts to the original than Capgrave did his additions. Comparison with the original shows these to have been pretty substantial, often, as the translator alleged, because the original material was too narrowly autobiographical to be very useful to the reader. For all that, his cuts signify less than another feature of his work. He is well aware that the process of his original stands 'for þe moste parte in gostlye reuelaciones and deuowt ymaginaciones, in manere of spekynge byetwix þe maystre . . . and þe deuowt discyple! (Horstmann 1, p. 325). The original, that is, follows no very compelling narrative line. Rather, like Julian's *Revelations* and St Bridget's *Liber*, its structure exemplifies the processes of meditation.[21] The work is episodic, cumulative, repetitious; it derives its formal unity from the presence of the disciple figure, and its informing unity from the attempts of the disciple to connect the various meditation-events of his narrative with one another. That being so, a translator can make free with its order for purposes of his own: 'I folow not þe processe of þat boke in ordere, but I take þe materes insindrye, as þei acordene to mye purpos' (*Ibid.*). The practical consequences of this decision are extremely interesting. Building on the pattern laid down in *Orologium* II.2, where Christ promises to instruct the disciple on four points, the translator reduces his original's two books and twenty-four chapters to 'vii poyntes of . . . loue' (Horstmann 1, p. 328). His exposition of the first two, 'þe maner and properte' of love, seen first as heavenly wisdom and then as the crucified Christ, is followed by a third, 'gladde suffrynge of tribulaciones and aduersitees' for the love, and under the example, of

Christ. This third point, translating the single chapter I.13, serves as a kind of climax to the first part of the translation, since the earlier sections had explored this same theme in anticipatory counterpoint. The next two sections, translating II.2 and 3 in reverse order, presuppose a further development and propose to teach the art of living spiritually, and dying, for love.[22] Then, we have a section on Christ in the eucharist, translating II.4, and a section instructing the disciple to love all that is for Christ, and Christ above all that is, translating II.5–8, both of which, not surprisingly, develop strong links with materials used earlier in the work. Apart from that reversal of II.2 and 3, there is little in these later sections to suggest any very radical approach to the original. If we turn to the first two sections of the work, however, we shall find rather better what the translator meant by his declared intention to 'take þe materes insindrye'.

Chapter 2, for instance, translates material from several chapters (I.2–4, 14–16) and frequently disturbs their original order.[23] Sometimes a passage of dialogue loses one of its speakers.[24] Such a change need not count for much when, as is common with most medieval and all religious narrative, the actual speaker counts for less than the position he embodies.[25] A more important change concerns the bringing together of speeches from different places in the original, sometimes because verbal similarities between two passages have suggested their combination in translation.[26] So, for example, the translator brings together, so as to suggest a relation between them, two desires of the disciple widely separated in the original: the desire for tears of true compassion while the disciple is looking on the face of the crucified; and the desire for the wounds of Christ upon the person and within the soul (Horstmann 1, p. 339, 11.15–30). These practices are obviously weightier than the foregoing. Even so, their effect, typically, is not so much to contradict their original as to heighten it, and to focus more sharply its rather disparate elements. A certain amount of rewriting inevitably accompanies such changes to the original.[27] The translator assumes the status of author most clearly when he rearranges his original in this way, or, as happened in the *Speculum Devotorum*, translates only selected parts of it.

Of course, there was another choice open to him, not to tamper with the form of his original at all. Not surprisingly, he exercised this choice more often than not. One of the best examples of this is the translation of the Brigittine Breviary, *The Myroure of oure Ladye*. This work was intended for use in two different ways: as a source-book for public readings, additional to, and separate from, the recital of the office, and as a private supplement to the recital of the office (Blunt, pp. 70–71).[28] The reader who used it in this second way would need regular indications of the point which the service had reached. The translator therefore prefaced his translation of each period of the lessons, and each phrase of the hymns, antiphons, responses and versicles, with the first word(s) of the corresponding Latin unit.[29] As a further help to the reader, he proposed to have the Latin words, 'wryt . . . with reed, þat ye may knowe þerby wher it begynnethe' (Aberdeen University MS.134, f.55 ᵛ; the 1530 printing, Blunt, p. 70, was to use 'Romeyne letter' for these purposes). Like the scribes of Rolle's Psalter, he wished also to help his readers differentiate 'the bare englysshe of latyne' from material 'put þerto to expoune yt' (MS. 134, f.55 ᵛ), a distinction which would obtain ordinarily only in those parts of the office devoted to the hymns and other small elements. In such places, the 'bare englysshe' would appear 'wryte with blacke and stryke underneth withe reede'; the exposition, 'writte with blakk, safe in suche places where non exposicioun is': there, the reader would find 'the englissh of the latyne wryt all blake with [oute] eny rede stryk undyr yt' (*Ibid.*). The 1530 printing proposed to make this distinction by printing the 'bare englysshe' in 'smaller letter' (Blunt, p. 70), so that it would make use of three type-faces: small and larger black-letter, and Roman.[30]

This elaborate formal exercise, at several removes from anything we have so far seen, implies in the translator a very particular understanding of the status of his original: a point confirmed by his remarks on the original for the lessons of the office, the *Sermo Angelicus* of St Bridget:

> Lyke as holy scripture passeth all other scrypture, and as the gospell of saynt John passeth al other partes of holy scrypture, ryght so thys holy Legende passeth all other legendes that euer were wryten of oure lady (Blunt, pp. 102–3: for euer (*so* Aberdeen 134, f.80 ʳ) Blunt reads hath euer).

This comparison of the saint's writings with the Bible was a commonplace among the saint's more enthusiastic followers. Its occurrence here, in conjunction with the formal features already referred to, implies the creation of a translation as close to its original as authorised translations of the Bible were expected to be to theirs: a point given further weight by the translator's care to obtain episcopal permission to translate the Bible quotations in the office.[31] The specific lay-out of the work, then, shows us a translator who envisaged the closest possible relation of both the form and detail of his translation to those of his original.

This mention of detail brings us to the next major area of choice for the translator, the translation of the details of his original. He understands this area of his work most frequently as the translation of individual words, less often as the translation of grammatical relations. With the *Myroure* still fresh in our minds, we may begin with it.

III

The translator explains on two occasions that, while he wishes to keep strictly to the wording of his original, he will sometimes have to give himself greater scope:

> in many places where the nakyd letter is, thoughe yt be set in englyshe, ys not easy for some symple soulles to vnderstonde, I expounde yt and declare yt more openly, other before the letter, or after or else fourthewyth togyther (Blunt, p. 3).
>
> Yt is not lyght for euery man to drawe eny longe thynge from latyn into oure Englyshe tongue. For there ys many wordes in Latyn that we haue no propre englyssh accordynge therto. And then suche wordes muste be turnyd as the sentence may beste be vnderstondyd. And therfore though I laboure to kepe bothe the wordes and the sentence in this boke as farre as oure language wyll well assente: yet some tyme I folowe the sentence and not the wordes as the mater asketh. There is also many wordes that haue dyverse vnderstondynges, and some tyme they ar taken in one wyse, some tyme in an other, and som tyme they may be taken in dyuerse wyse in one reson or clause. Dyuerse wordes also in dyuerse scryptures ar set and vnderstonde some tyme other wyse then auctoures of gramer tell or speke of (Blunt, p. 7).

Except for the commonplace observation that he may need to follow 'the sentence and not the wordes', the translator has nothing to say about his translation of the grammatical relations of his original. Instead, he considers the translation of difficult individual words. These are of several kinds: technical words not readily understood by a layman; words with no simple English equivalent; words with more than one meaning; and words which, in context, yield a meaning not recorded in the dictionaries. In all such cases, a translator must deduce the meaning of the word from its context. If the English language has no simple equivalent for the word, he will 'turn' it in such a way that it 'may beste be vnderstondyd', typically by creating an explanatory gloss for his translation of it. Nor is that all. Since 'the commen maner of spekying in Englysshe of some contre can skante be vnderstonded in some other contre of the same londe' (Blunt, p. 8), the translator may

26

need to gloss words familiar to him but not to readers from other parts of the country.[32]

Practically every translator with anything to say about his work focusses on this use of the gloss for difficult and technical words, or words wanting a native equivalent:

> (þe *seuen poyntes*): I translate not þe wordes as þei bene wrytene, one for anoþere, þat is . . . þe englische worde for þe latyne worde, bycause þat þere beþ manye wordes in clergiale teremes, þe wheche wold seme vnsaverye so to be spokene in Englische (Horstmann 1, p. 325: the Caxton printing (so Salter, p. 227) reads 'chargeable' for 'clergiale');
> (Trevisa): in somme place I muste sette a reson for a worde, and telle what it meneth (Caxton printing, *sig.* 1.4 ᵛ).[33]
> (MN): At suche places þere me semeth moost nede, I wole write mo wordis þerto in maner of glose . . . And in þese fewe places þat I putte more yn þan I fynde writen I wole bigynne wiþ þe firste lettre of my name, 'M', and ende wiþ þis lettre 'N', þe firste of my surname (Doiron, p. 248);
> (Methley): in his Latin translation of *The Cloud*: vbi necesse fuerit explanare . . . in fine capitulorum quorumdam que quidem difficilia videntur ad intelligendum transferre [institi] (Hodgson 1, p. 177);
> (Caxton): prologue to a translation of Cicero's *De Senectute*: in latyn is specyfyced compendyously, whiche is in maner harde the texte. But this book reduced in Englyssh tongue is more ample expowned (Crotch, p. 42);
> (Gavin Douglas): Thoght venerabill Chauser . . . said
> That he couth follow word by word Virgill . . .
> Sum tyme the text mon have ane expositioun . . .
> And sum tyme of a word I mon mak thre
> (Coldwell, p. 10)[34]

Similarly, the author of the prologue to the Wycliffe Bible addresses himself to the question of 'words equiuok, that is, that hath many significacions under one lettre', and, like the author of the *Myroure*, urges context as the only safeguard of a word's meaning:

> a translatour hath greet nede to studie wel the sentence both bifore and aftir, and loke that suche equiuok wordis acorde with the sentence (FM I.60).

The gloss exists either as a simple doublet (commonest conjunctions 'and', 'or', occasionally 'of')[35] or as a more extensive addition to the text (commonly prefaced by 'that is', 'as if', and including what Fristedt, II.xxix, calls the 'elucidative attribute'). The gloss is so well-established and well-noted a feature in translations of the period—as an indication of that, we shall later note its regular use as an ornament of style—that a certain waywardness in the examples here offered may perhaps be pardoned.

1 When writing for women, translators occasionally gloss the

grammatical and pronominal relations of the original to show readers that they are included. Thus the translator of the *Orologium* renders 'amato' (Suso I.2, p. 45) by 'in a manne or womman þat is belovede' (Horstmann 1, p. 337); the translator of the *Speculum Devotorum*, also translating from the *Orologium*, renders 'felix qui . . . seriose intenderit' (Suso I.14, p. 271) by 'blyssyd ys he or sche that sadly takyth hede' (Hogg, p. 7), and translates Luke 2:14 'and pese in erthe to men and wymmen of a goode wyl' (Hogg, p. 80).[36] Similarly, the *Myroure* provides an interesting gloss for its unusual rendering of the Latin 'sponsam':

> O spousesse . . . this worde spouse ys taken often bothe for the man and for the woman in comoun englyshe; but for ther [so Bodley, Rawlinson, C 941, f.55 ᵛ; Blunt therfore] here is made mensyon of bothe togyther, therfore that the tone shulde be knowen from the tother, I calle hym the spouse and her the spousesse. And where the tone alone is spoken of, I calle her spouse (Blunt, pp. 238–9, and cf. Capgrave's translation of 'dilectus' and 'd¡lecta' earlier noted, p. 22);

Conversely, the translator might need to warn a reader not to take personally what he had intended generally. Thus, in the *Myroure*'s translation of the hymn *O Trinitatis gloria*, the translation of the words 'sibi gratos nos effice/quos sanguine redimerat' comes with an explanation:

> make vs kynde and acceptable to hym whome he boughte wyth hys bloude. Here ye may se, that ye pray not onely for youre selfe . . . for ye saye not *gratas* and *quas* that myghte be sayde onely of you, but ye say *gratos* and *quos*, that, whyle ye knytte *nos* therto, muste nedes be vnderstonde bothe of men and wymen (Blunt, p. 93).[37]

2 When translating Biblical allusions or quotations, writers often drew attention to their actual source (additions are underlined in the following examples):

(þe *seuen poyntes*): of whome sey<u>þe holye write</u> here delytes beþ for to dwelle with þe sones of menne (Horstmann 1, p. 333).
(Capgrave, *St Gilbert*): receyue him into euyrlastyng tabernacles <u>as þe gospel berith witnesse</u> (Munro, p. 67).

3 Lastly, we have in the *Speculum Devotorum* a nice instance of literal translation and close translation accompanied by gloss, all in the one passage:

> Non dabis sanctum tuum videre corrupcionem: thys ys in englyisch,
> thow schalt not ȝeue thy seyint to see corrupcyon;
> thys ys to seye in more opyn englyisch, thow schall not

28

suffre thy seyint, þat is the body of oure lorde Jhesu Cryste . . .
to see corrupcyon, þat is to seye to rote in the erthe . . . (Hogg, p. 297).

Not every writer, though, expressed himself in favour of the gloss as the instrument of elucidation. On the particular question of Bible translations, for example, the Dominican Thomas Palmer argued that the necessity for circumlocutions when translating Latin abstract nouns constituted an overwhelming argument against such translations (Deanesly, pp. 428–9).[38] We have also to reckon with the witness of Rolle's prologue to the Psalter. A work which all but sinks its translation in commentary, and of which its author says,

I seke na straunge ynglis, bot lyghtest and comonest. . . .
In the translacioun I folow the lettere as mykyll as I may,
and thare I fynd na propire ynglis I folow the wit of the
worde. . . . In expounynge, I fologh haly doctours (Bramley, pp. 4–5)

must, we might think, side with those who follow the 'wit' of their texts rather than with the literalists. But we correct this impression by noting two things. First, Rolle is drawing a clear distinction between the translation and its accompanying commentary: the latter is no part of the actual translation. Then, his professed avoidance of 'straunge', in favour of common and 'propre', English, and his willingness to follow the 'wit' when such English is unavailable, need to be related to his desire to find English 'that is mast lyke til the latyn, swa that thai that knawes noght latyn, by the ynglis may com til mony latyn wordis' (*Ibid.*). That is, Rolle's translation is not a substitute for the original, which, in any case, he copies out in full, but a means of familiarising the reader with the original Latin: almost an interlinear gloss. We can see the consequences of this choice if we compare the actual translation of a verse with the form it assumes in the commentary:

Ps. 4:3 vsquequo gravi corde: *translation* how lange of heuy hert, *commentary* how lange will ȝe be heuy of hert (Bramley, p. 15).

This extremely literal approach to the original—of a piece with the practices of the first version of the Wycliffe Bible as analysed by Fristedt (II. xx–xxxy)—inevitably leads one to ask what Rolle meant by his professed avoidance of 'straunge', and preference for common, English. I read it as meaning (i) that he does not intend to permit himself simply to transliterate a Latin word (e.g. *transgressio-transgression*);[39] (ii) that, where possible, he will provide native equivalents for both elements of compound Latin words, so that the whole translated word exactly duplicates its Latin original.[40] If this

29

view is correct, Rolle is here arguing for the translation of abstract and compound words in ways that will not be heard of again until the sixteenth century.[41]

Except for Rolle, translators are generally, and understandably, silent about the translation of individual words which they do not propose to gloss. The student of the Middle English mystics, however, regularly needs to know what scope a translator had in rendering a particular word, and whether any words were liable to erroneous or imperfect translation. The enormous task of providing this information has barely begun, and though we must be grateful to such as Riehle and Fristedt for the glossaries provided with their works, we must also press for all future editions of original and translated religious works to carry word lists, at least of the major spiritual terms in their original and translated forms.[42]

IV

Of course, translation involves not only the words, but also the grammatical relations, of its original. Most translators have nothing to say about this part of their work. It is probably significant that those who do, Trevisa and the author of the prologue to the Wycliffe Bible, were most actively engaged in translating the Bible, and aware of the need to defend themselves against the claim of the literalists that only those Bible translations could be permitted which exactly observed the grammatical forms of their original (so Palmer: see Deanesly, pp. 427–8). The prologue to the Wycliffe Bible allows for participial and absolute phrases to be resolved by cognate ('couenable') subordinate and co-ordinate clauses, and of relative clauses by cognate co-ordinate clauses:

> arescentibus hominibus prae timore/and men shulen wax drie for drede
> dicens/and seith, either that seith
> (qui currit)/which renneth, and he renneth (FM I.57).

More importantly, it recognises the need for the translation to reflect English word-order:

> where this reasoun *Dominum formidabunt adversarii ejus* shulde be Englisshid thus bi the lettre, *the Lord hise aduersaries shulen drede*, I Englishe it thus bi resolucion, *the aduersaries of the Lord shulen drede him* (*Ibid.*).

For the author of this Prologue, then, the basic consideration is the provision of native equivalents for the grammatical relations of his

30

original. Where the creation of these would result in unidiomatic English, the translator will abandon the strict wording of his original in favour of a reading which conveys as much of its meaning as possible while conforming to the requirements of English syntax. We shall call such resolutions, as the translators themselves did, 'open' rather than 'close' (these, or similar terms, are regularly used) only compared with a translation as literal as Rolle's: in themselves, they are perfectly consistent with close, or faithful, translation. Trevisa held a very similar view: since a literal translation 'word for worde . . . a-rowe right as it stondeth' might not always prove possible, the translator must sometimes 'chaunge the order of wordes'. He gives a specific example of such change: 'sette actyf for passyf, and ayenward' (Caxton printing, *sig.* 1.4 ᵛ). If by this he is thinking, say, of the need to resolve an impersonal passive (which English can express only periphrastically), by way of an active verb with impersonal subject, his example accords very well with the precepts of the Wycliffe Prologue. When, though, he suggests, as an equivalent, the translation of a Latin active by an English passive, we see that he is prepared to countenance more radical transformations of the original's grammatical relations than the author of the Wycliffe Prologue. A translation which regularly so treated its original would be more 'open'. Nevertheless, Trevisa is also right to claim that 'for al suche chaungyng, the menyng shal stande and not be chaunged' (*Ibid.*).

The foregoing evidence shows that a translator had at least three approaches open to him in his rendering of the original's grammatical relations: a literal one, of the sort favoured by Rolle; a slightly freer one, of the sort favoured by the second version of the Wycliffe Bible; and a still freer one, on the model of Trevisa's declared practice. *The Myroure of oure Ladye* offers an excellent example of the second approach. It regularly resolves ablative absolutes, participles used adverbially, and passive forms of the verb, according to the principles already enunciated.[43] Furthermore, it accommodates the word-order of its original to the requirements of English word-order.[44] A literal word-order is more likely to be kept in the translation of Bible passages (and we remember how the translator was content for the sisters to read the Psalms in Rolle's version: Blunt, p. 3). Even so, a comparison of the *Myroure*'s Bible translations with those of the two versions of the Wycliffe Bible will show the greater flexibility of its renderings:

Luc. I:48 beatam me dicent/E.V. schulen seie me blessid, E.V., L.V. shulen seie that Y am blessid; *Myroure* p. 159 shall call me blyssed;
Luc. I:74–5 ut sine timore de manu inimicorum nostrorum liberati serviamus

illi/E.V., L.V. that we withoute drede deliuerid fro the hond of oure enemyes serue to him; *Myroure* p. 132 that we so delyuered oute of the power of our enemys serue hym wythout drede.

The *Myroure* also provides for a number of other resolutions not so far touched on but no less clearly dictated by, or defensible by reference to, the requirements of English syntax, and found at least occasionally in the late version of the Wycliffe Bible. These include: abstract plural nouns resolved as singular; absolute adjectives, and participles used substantivally and adjectivally, resolved by a clause; adjectival dependence resolved by a cognate noun in the genitive; gerund resolved, according to case, as active infinitive or present participle; gerundive in adjectival relation resolved by a clause; and subjunctive resolved by periphrasis.[45]

Other translations not only use these resolutions, but also introduce others not favoured, or used only rarely, by the *Myroure*. Of these, very few are defensible by reference to the requirements of English syntax, though one such is the use of a clause to resolve accusative and infinitive constructions (and conversely, the use of an infinitive to resolve clauses of purpose).[46] More radical resolutions, while fairly preserving the sense of the original, involve transposition of parts of speech not required by the communication of the sense: thus, we have interchangeability of relations of genitive noun and adjectival dependence, and reversal of the original dependence; suppression of relations of co-ordination and apposition between nouns, or creation of new genitive dependence; resolution of noun, sometimes with auxiliary verb, by cognate verb, and consequent resolution of adjectives as adverbs; lastly, translation of paired elements by their opposites.[47] In all of these cases, a literal translation would not have resulted in any particularly unEnglish expression. Their absence in the *Myroure* points to the fundamentally conservative nature of the translation: their presence in any number, as in the Claudius B I translation of the *Liber* of St Bridget, points to a freer, not to say looser, translation.

But this range of practices does not exhaust a translator's options. Consider the following passage, for instance, from the other complete translation of St Bridget's *Liber*, that in British Library MS. Julius F II. Of wicked Christians St Bridget had written, using traditional imagery:

Ponunt eum in cruce quam sibi preparauerant quando de preceptis creatoris sui et domini non curant, et dehonestant eum quando ipse monet eos per seruos suos seruire sibi, et ipsi hoc contemnentes faciunt que sibi placent. (Liber I.37).

For this the translation offers us

> þei crucifie him whan thei rekke neuer of þer lord and makere and sett nowght be them þat has cure and charge of there sowlis vndir god neen will nat serue god f.33ᵛ.

We observe not only (i) obvious cuts to the Latin ('quam . . . preparauerant', 'preceptis', probably 'et dehonestant eum', 'faciunt . . . placent') but also (ii) a drastic rewriting of the periods 'quando . . . sibi' and 'et ipsi . . . placent'. In the first of these periods only the words 'serue god' clearly translate their equivalents 'seruire sibi'. 'Will nat serue', presumably, derives from the two words 'contemnnentes' and 'seruire'. From the period 'quando . . . curant' the words 'creatoris . . . et domini' have been translated ('of þer lord and makere') but their meaning lost by virtue of the writer's failure to render 'de preceptis'. We see further (iii) a watering-down of the meaning of 'contemnnentes' to make the new relationship with 'seruire' easier. (iv) 'Per seruos suos' receives a quite unwarranted gloss: 'them . . . vndir god'. (v) 'Sett nowght' duplicates 'rekke neuer', both translating the one form 'non curant'.

A translation of this sort takes us a very long way even from the 'sentence' of the original. Paradoxically, it differs from more faithful translations only in that degree to which each individual reading distorts the meaning, and insofar as the accumulation of such readings creates the impression of a text radically different from its original. We have, thus, the beginnings of an inventory of malpractice: (i) suppression of material necessary for the grammatical sense; (ii) rearrangement of grammatical relations resulting in error; (iii) substitution of stronger or weaker meanings for words or phrases in the original; (iv) creation of additional material, by way of forced or unnecessary glosses, to conceal gaps in the translation; (v) translation more than once of a single element of the original (contrast the simple doublet). To this list we could add, though the quotation does not reveal it, (vi) multiple transposition of parts of speech not required by the sense, and resulting in error.[48] Signs, if not formal causes, of these practices are: inattention to the grammatical relations of the original; and a, more or less, random quest for meaning among the more striking elements of the sentence.[49]

So far, then, as concerns the resolution of grammatical relations, I wish to argue for the existence of a model of practice along the lines of literal, close, free, and erroneous, resolutions. Given its very sketchy nature, I cannot claim for this model more than a notional existence in the mind of translator and critic alike. The categories cannot be rigidly distinguished from one another: in reality translation can no more be four categories than it was three for Dryden or two for the medievals. In any event, the categorising of material becomes increasingly difficult as we move from literal to free translation. Moreover, a translator is unlikely to achieve absolute consistency of practice. On the other hand, we can clearly distinguish between translator's solutions of the same problem (say, the resolution of an ablative absolute, whether by a participial or noun phrase, or by a co-ordinate or subordinate clause). Moreover, such practices have a cumulative and quantifiable effect. In any event, a translator is not likely to shoot too wide of the mark he has set himself. Thus Rolle, who favours very literal resolutions, also uses close translation regularly but never, I think, free or erroneous renderings; the *Myroure* favours close translation, while offering a sprinkling of literalisms and one or two free renderings; the Claudius translation moves consistently towards free, and fluent translation, with few instances of close, none of literal, and many of erroneous translation. Perhaps the Julius translation is the most interesting in this respect. The previous analysis could not demonstrate that, while Julius certainly includes many examples of erroneous translation, it also includes a great number of resolutions almost as literal as anything in Rolle.[50] A translator who sprays his target so unevenly may be presumed not to know his business very well.

V

The choices outlined in the previous section, though obviously important as the basis of any discussion about traditions of translation, are of little immediate interest to the student of mystical literature. The same is true of the remaining choices a translator has to make, governing the style and the medium of his work.

Style has received more attention, in my view, than it deserves.[51] I take it to be self-evident that the style of a translated work, if not actually parasitic on that of its original, can hardly be understood except in relation to it; emerges as the consequence of the choices outlined in the previous section of this work; and becomes interesting in itself only in proportion as the translation, for whatever reason, is becoming an original work. Furthermore, style exists only in relation to the conflicting demands, earlier outlined, of the original, the audience, the tradition, and the translator himself. That being so, it is hardly surprising that translators have little to say, and then only of the most general and conventional sort, about style. We find them talking about the fine or difficult style of their originals, the notable stylistic achievements of earlier translations, the low style to which their own poor abilities condemn them, explaining their style, that is, only by reference to their originals, to the expectations of their, usually courtly, audiences, and to their own limitations.[52] What is more, they understand style, typically, only as a question of vocabulary. When Capgrave tells us that the author of a particular translation seemed to be a west-country man 'be his maner of speche and be his style' (Horstmann 2, p. 15), he clearly implies style as no more than a writer's choice of individual words, in this case dialect words. The same is true even of Caxton's prologue to his translation of Guillaume le Roy's 'translation' of the *Aeneid*, where we find an attempt to treat the question of style more systematically. There, Caxton proposes a style midway between 'playn rude and curyous'; one to please both the 'gentylmen' who favour 'olde and homely termes' and the 'honest and grete clerkes' who prefer 'moste curyous termes'; one explicable by reference to its original ('in such termes as [are] . . . accordynge to my copye') and defensible by reference to 'Vyrgyll [and] . . . Ouyde' (Crotch, pp. 108–9). The proposals, though, have to do only with the choice of 'termes'; and the practical implications of such a choice are more curious than significant, as we can see from that model of high style set before us by the prologue to the *Aeneid*, the *Bibliotheca Historica* of Dyodorus Siculus, as translated by Skelton, 'in polysshed and ornate termes craftely' (*Ibid.*). The aureate style, as practised by Skelton in this work—of it the editors say, 'it is our most extreme example of "aureation and dilation" ' S.E II.xlvii) – consists of two principal features: literalisms of syntax and vocabulary; and extensive use of doublets and other devices of glossing.[53] The aureate style, that is, a bastard form (even as, for different reasons, the style of the Julius translation of St Bridget's *Liber* was), in which elements of embarrassing literalness combine with elements consistent with freer translation to produce an exotic hybrid, remote alike from the original and its audience, and answerable, finally, only to the taste of the translator.

The translator of a religious work was unlikely to give himself such airs. In his translations of the 'legendys of hooly wummen', for instance, Bokenham regularly apologises for his own limited abilities (Serjeantson, pp. 3, 6, 40, 111); struggles with the high style of St Jerome (p. 111), but finds it difficult, as any reader of the original can testify (he says) 'for most straungely/Amonge alle doctours and most vnkouthely/He endytyth' (p. 129); seeks to avoid prolixity and write 'compendiously' (pp. 112, 174, 200), in a humble imitation of his original which probably merely exposes his own little wit, like Chaucer's, and does not help the reader (p. 44); begs, lastly, to be protected in his rude simplicity from the 'capcyous/And subtyl' wits of Cambridge (p. 6). This conventional picture undergoes a subtle, though equally conventional, modification, in the prologue to one of the last-written works (if not *the* last-written: see p. 138), the life of St Mary Magdalen. If low style was a matter of necessity before, it has now become a deliberate choice. Like the captious wits of Cambridge, the 'curyals' to whom he refers in this prologue have great 'asperence/ In vttrynge of here subtyl conceyts':

> so craftyd vp, and wyth langwage so gay
> Uttryd, þat I trowe þe moneth of may
> Neuere fresshere embelshyd þe soyl wyth flours
> Than is her wrytyng wyth colours
> Of rethorycal speche both to and fro (Serjeantson, p. 143).

Bokenham will not attempt to match this deceitful eloquence. The source of inspiration is now not Apollo, that fount 'of gay speche . . . and of eloquencye', but Christ.[54] He will do better to write simply, and, as an old man at the end of his life, better still to leave off writing altogether (p. 39). The traditional ironies of the earlier passages are now turned to equally traditional good ends.

The fact that Bokenham wrote in verse brings us neatly to the last of the translator's choices, that of medium. He faces particular problems when his chosen medium is verse. He must turn his original into lines of verse of a more or less equal length, held together by rhyme and rhythm. Generally he pays most attention to the requirements of rhyme, leaving rhythm and even line length to fend for themselves. In order to translate his original into lines he breaks it into units of sense corresponding in some measure to the stanza form he has chosen, and then fills it out for the sake of the rhyme. The distinguishing feature of a verse translation is thus a, more or less continuous, gloss, dictated simply by the need for rhymes. The gloss occurs, typically, at the end of a line, as in the following example, from Caxton's epilogue to Lydgate's *Live of our Lady* (the gloss is underlined):

> Sancte et indiuiduae trinitati, Ihesu Cristi crucifixi humanitati, gloriose beate Marie virgini, sit sempiterna gloria ab omni creatura per infinita seculorum secula Amen.
> Vnto the holy and undeuyded trynyte

Thre persones in one veray godhede
To iesu crist crucefyed humanyte
And to our blessyd ladyes maydenhede,
Be geuyn laude and glorye in veray dede
Of euery creature whatsomeuer he be
World withouten ende amen say al we (Crotch, p. 85).

Apart from the gloss, whose use of the techniques of direct address of popular poetry merely reinforces the message of its original, we see very few changes to the original in this translation, and none that we have not already noted as compatible with close or free translation: (1) the cutting of 'sempiterna' as anticipating the final phrase of the original; (ii) the transformation of a relation of apposition ('Marie virgini') into one of genitive dependence by the creation of an abstract noun 'maydenhede' for the original's 'virgini'. This picture is, I suggest, not untypical.[55] And even when a translator chose verse to express his own literary pretensions—which he was more likely to do in the fourteenth and fifteenth centuries than before – the result was not likely to differ radically from the prose experiments with high style already noted. It follows, therefore, that the choice of medium was not, in itself, a matter of particular moment for the translator. No more substantial ground exists, that I know of, for preferring one medium to the other than is contained in Caxton's epilogue to Book II of the *Recuyell*: 'dyuerce men ben of dyuerce desyres, some to rede in ryme and metre, and some in prose' (Crotch, p. 7).[56]

Even then a translator's choices are not finished. Since the informing elements of a translation are not fixed qualities, but combine in a pattern of constantly shifting relationships, a translator may need from time to time to revise his text—as, to take parallel cases, the mystics constantly did with their texts, and Caxton was forced to do with his edition of *The Canterbury Tales* (see n.10 below). This is most likely to happen, I suppose, with a difficult original, like that of Margarete Porete. Of his translation of Margaret's *Mirror*, MN tells us

This boke . . . I . . . many ʒeeris goon wrote it out of French into Englisch. . . . Now I am stired to laboure it aʒen newe, for bicause I am enfourmed þat some wordis þerof haue be mystake. Þerfore . . . I shal declare þo wordis more openli . . . for . . . it is but schortli spoken, and may be taken oþirwise þan it is iment of hem þat reden it sodeynli and taken no ferþir hede. Þerfore suche wordis to be twies iopened, it wole be . . . more profite to þe auditoures (Doiron, p. 247).

The labour referred to results in the creation of new glosses for individual words (see above, p. 27, for quotation).[57]

VI

A few words by way of conclusion. The concept of a tradition of translation has little meaning if it is not founded on the systematic study of translation practices, the organising principle of which I have sought to locate in the concept of 'choice'. At the same time, we should not ignore the deeper truth lodged in this concept of tradition, one to which all the works here studied, in their different ways, bear manifest witness: the truth that 'yt is not lyght for euery man to drawe eny longe thyng . . . into oure Englysche tongue' (Blunt, p. 7); that 'I knaw quhat payn was to follow [myn auctor] fut hait' (Coldwell, p. 8); that the work of translation is accomplished 'not wythout labour' (Serjeant-son, p. 86). The translator well recognised his own limitations, and the consequent likelihood of failure in the work:

(Trevisa): no synfull man doth so well that it ne myght doo better, ne make so good a translacion that he ne might be better (Caxton printing, *sig.* 1.3 ˅);

(*Myroure*): for that I knowe myne owne feoblenes, as well in connyng as in verteu; therefore I will neyther seke defaulte in other ne maynteyne myne owne (Blunt, p. 8);

he also faced the possibility of censure and misreading from the ignorant:

(*Myroure*): the lesse good that he can, the more presumptuous will he be to fynde defaulte . . . ye often tymes tho thynges that he vnderstondyth not (Blunt, p. 8);

(Douglas): Beis not ourstudys to spy a moyt in myne e
That in your awyn a ferry boyt can nocht se (Coldwell, p. 14).

The translator saw clearly, too, the intimate, if not necessary, connection between the worth of a translation and a translator's moral state, and the moral status of the reader and his understanding of the work. Lastly, he was clear in his appreciation, and ready to make a virtue, of that very diversity of practice so strikingly demonstrated in the preceding pages:

(Caxton): dyuerce men haue made dyuerce bookes whiche in all poyntes acorde not (Crotch, p. 8);

(Wycliffite Prologue): it was Goddis wille that diuerse men translatiden . . . for where oon seide derkli, oon either mo seiden openli (FM I.59).

Of their translations we may say, as Caxton did of two by Earl Rivers (the *Dictes*, and the *Cordyale*)

translating in my iugement is a noble and a meritorious dede, wherfor [the translator] is worthy to be greetly commended and also singulerly remembred with our good prayers (Crotch, p. 39, cf. p. 18).

38

B.L.	C. Babington and J. R. Lumby, eds. *Polychronicon Ranulphi Higden*, Rolls Series 41, 1–9, London, 1865–86.
Blunt	J. H. Blunt, ed. *The Myroure of oure Ladye*, Early English Text Society, E.S, 19, London, 1873.
Bramley	H. R. Bramley, ed. *The Psalter . . . by Richard Rolle*, Oxford, 1884.
Coldwell	D. F. C. Coldwell, ed. *Selections from Gavin Douglas*, Oxford, 1964.
Crotch	W. J. B. Crotch, ed. *The Prologues and Epilogues of William Caxton*, Early English Text Society, O.S, 176, London, 1928.
Deanesly	M. Deanesly, *The Lollard Bible*, Cambridge, 1920, reissued 1966.
Doiron	M. Doiron, ed. *Margarete Porete. The Mirror of Simple Souls*, Archivio Italiano per la storia della pieta, 5, Rome, 1968, 241–381.
Dugdale	J. Caley, *et al*, eds. *Monasticon Anglicanum . . . originally published by . . . W. Dugdale*, VI:2, London, 1846.
E.V.	Early Version.
F.M.	J. Forshall and F. Madden, eds. *The Wycliffe Bible*, 5 vols., Oxford, 1850.
Fristedt	S. L. Fristedt, *The Wycliffe Bible*, Stockholm Studies in English 4, 21, Stockholm, 1953, 1969.
Glasscoe	M. Glasscoe, ed. *The Medieval Mystical Tradition in England*, Exeter, 1980.
Hodgson 1	P. Hodgson, ed. *The Cloud of Unknowing*, Early English Text Society, O.S, 218, London, 1944.
Hodgson 2	P. Hodgson, ed. *Deonise Hid Diuinite*, Early English Text Society, O.S, 231, London, 1955.
Hogg	J. Hogg, ed. *The Speculum Devotorum of an anonymous Carthusian of Sheen*, Analecta Cartusiana, 12–13, Salzburg, 1973–4.
Horstmann 1	C. Horstmann, ed. '*Orologium Sapientiae* or the Seven Poyntes of Trewe Wisdom', *Anglia*, 10 (1888), 323–89.
Horstmann 2	C. Horstmann, ed. *The Life of St Katharine of Alaxandria*, Early English Text Society, O.S, 100, London, 1893.

L.V.	Late Verson.
Munro	J. J. Munro, ed. *John Capgrave's Lives of St Augustine and St Gilbert*, Early English Text Society, O.S, 140, London, 1910.
Powell	L. F. Powell, ed. *The Mirrour of the Blessed Lyf of Jesu Christ*, London, 1908.
Ragusa	I. Ragusa, and R. B. Green, eds. and trans. *Meditations on the Life of Christ*, Princeton, 1961.
Salter	E. Salter, *Nicholas Love's 'Myrrour of the Blessed Lyf of Jesu Criste'*, Analecta Cartusiana, 10, Salzburg, 1974.
S.E.	F. M. Salter, and H. L. R. Edwards, eds. *The Bibliotheca Historica . . . translated by John Skelton*, Early English Text Society, O.S, 233, 239, London, 1956–7.
Serjeantson	M. S. Serjeantson, ed. *Osbern Bokenham, Legendys of Hooly Wummen*, Early English Text Society, O.S, 206, London, 1938.
Suso	(no edds.) *Colloquia Dominiciana . . . a beato Henrico Susone dictata*, Bibliotheca Mystica Sanctorum Ordinis Predicatorum, Monachii, 1923.
Workman	S. K. Workman, *Fifteenth Century Translation as an Influence on English Prose*, Princeton Studies in English, 18, Princeton, 1940.

NOTES

1. For an introduction to the extensive literature on the theory and practice of translation, consult the bibliographies in E. A. Neider, *Toward a Science of Translating*, Leiden, 1964, G. Steiner, *After Babel*, Oxford, London, 1975, and L. G. Kelly, *The True Interpreter*, Oxford, 1979. Of particular relevance to our enquiry are F. R. Amos, *Early Theories of Translation*, New York, 1920, pp. 15–18, Workman, and Salter ch. 6. The title and direction of this paper have, perhaps, a formal relation to that of J. Levy, 'Translation as a Decision Process', *To Honor Roman Jakobson*, The Hague, Paris, 1967, pp. 1171–82.

2. For this, and other abbreviations in the body of this article, see *Abbreviations*, above.

3. These categories correspond to those borrowed from Aristotle by Osbern Bokenham to explain his own translation of the Life of St Margaret (Serjeantson, p. 1), discussed by H. E. Allen, 'The *Manuel des Pechiez* and the Scholastic Prologue', *Romanic Review*, 8 (1917), 451–62.

4. An interesting variant of this request is provided by Osbern Bokenham at the end of his *Mappula Angliae* (quoted Serjeantson pp. xvi–xvii).

5. So, e.g., Caxton's defence of his new versions of the Troy Story and *The Golden*

Legend (Crotch, pp. 8, 72, the latter discussed in P. Butler, *Legenda Aurea, Légende Dorée, Golden Legend*, Baltimore, 1899; Bokenham's reference to the existence of a fuller version of the St Katherine story, by Capgrave, than the one he is undertaking (Serjeantson, pp. 173–4); the approving reference by the translator of the Brigittine Breviary (*The Myroure of oure Ladye*) to Rolle's translation of the Psalter (Blunt, p. 3) etc.

6. Compare the excuse when a translator cannot vouch for the truth of his original (Crotch, p. 8, Serjeantson, p. xvii) or needs to defend a fictional original against accusations of deceitfulness (Crotch, pp. 62, 93).

7. Parallel to this practice is the translation of a text with accompanying glosses: cf. the prologue to *Deonise Hid Diuinite*: 'I haue not onliche folowed þe nakid lettre of þe text, bot, for to declare þe hardnes of it, I haue moche folowed þe sentence of þe abbot of Seint Victore' (Hodgson 2, p. 2).

8. On the dangers of identifying this figure with Purvey, see A. Hudson, 'John Purvey: A Reconsideration of the Evidence for his Life and Writings', *Viator*, 12 (1981), 355–80.

9. On Caxton's treatment of the *Legenda Aurea*, see references above, n. 5.

10. The former noted, for instance, by S. S. Hussey 'Latin and English in *The Scale of Perfection*', *Medieval Studies*, 35 (1973), 467. For the latter, consider the parallel case, Caxton's printings of *The Canterbury Tales* (Crotch, pp. 90–91, discussed by W. W. Greg, 'The Early Printed Editions of *The Canterbury Tales*', *Proceedings of the Modern Language Association*, 39 (1924), 737–61. Comparison of the two printings with the Ellesmere MS. shows that in the second Caxton regularly made good the gaps in the first, and as regularly suppressed its spurious additions: the best example of the latter merits quoting, from *The Merchant's Tale*, after E 2353:

> A grete tente, a thrifty and a long
> She sayde it was the meriest fytte (*echoing* A 4230)
> That euer in her lif she was as yet
> My lordis tente seruith me nothing thus.
> He foldith twifolde be swete Jhesus.
> He may not swyue worth a leek,
> And yet he is ful gentil and ful meek.
> This is leuyr to me than an euynsong.

11. See H. Hargreaves, 'The Latin Text of Purvey's Psalter', *Medium Ævum* 24 (1955), 90.

12. For discussion of this work, see A. Kurvinen, 'The Source of Capgrave's Life of St Katharine', *Neuphilologische Mitteilungen*, 61 (1960), 268–324.

13. One MS. of the *Myroure* has survived, in two parts: Aberdeen University 134, and Bodley Rawlinson C 941. Blunt edited from the 1530 printing of Richard Fawkes, independent of the two MSS but related to them through a common original. Except where otherwise stated, quotation comes from Blunt, which, however, occasionally miscopies Fawkes and silently emends it on the authority of the appended printer's *errata*. Dr Roy Barkley of Michigan is currently preparing a critical edition. See also A. J. Collins, ed., *The Bridgettine Breviary of Syon Abbey*, Henry Bradshaw Society, 96, Worcester, 1969, pp. xxxv–xxxviii.

14. E. Zeeman, 'Continuity and change in the Middle English Versions of the *Meditationes Vitae Christi*', *Medium Ævum*, 26 (1957), 25–31; 'Two Middle English Versions of a Prayer to the Sacrament', *Archiv für das Studium der Neueren Sprachen*, 194 (1958), 113–21.

Thus the translation of *The Dictes . . . of the Philosophres*, which Earl Rivers supplied to Caxton for printing, contained 'diuerce lettres missiues' translated from the original which the Earl recommended Caxton to delete, as being too 'lityl appertinent vnto dictes . . . aforsayd' (Crotch, p. 20).

16. For discussion of these texts, see my 'Flores ad fabricandam coronam: an investigation into the uses of the *Revelations* of St Bridget of Sweden in fifteenth-century England', *Medium Ævum*, forthcoming. For modern editions of the Brigittine originals, see C. G. Undhagen, ed. *Sancta Birgitta Revelaciones: Book I*, Samlingar utgivna av Svenska Fornskriftsällskapet, Ser. 2, Bd. 7:1, Uppsala, 1978, bibliography *sub* Bergh, Eklund, Hollman. For other changes of this sort, see n. 25 below. In this context we need also to reckon with a work like Love's *Myrrour*, which preserves the overall narrative form of its original, but sets it in a liturgical context, as meditations appropriate to the different days of the week.

17. The original itself provided the precedent for this practice: thus *Ragusa*, p. 133, translated Powell, p. 100.

18. Commonly the translation is distinguished from the commentary by means of a red line under the former (a feature also observed in *The Myroure of oure Ladye*: see further below). Examples include British Library Mss, manuscripts Harley 1806, Arundel 158, Royal 18 C xxvi. The last named also underlines the Latin, and in other manuscripts the literal translation is sometimes additionally underlined when repeated in the commentary.

19. On the relation of Capgrave's life to its ultimate Latin original, see J. C. Fredeman, 'John Capgrave's *Life of St Gilbert of Sempringham*', *Bulletin of the John Rylands Library*, 55 (1972), 112–145.

20. Capgrave's other translations show a similar awareness of formal matters: e.g. 'this maner of wryting þat is cleped narratyf' (*St Augustine*, Munro, p. 33); 'ryght in this foorme and in this-maner-stile' (*St Katharine*, Horstmann, 2, p. 75, cf pp. 33, 127).

21. On Julian, see B. Windeatt, 'The Art of Mystical Loving: Julian of Norwich', *Glasscoe*, pp. 55–71, and my 'Revelation and the Life of Faith: the Vision of Julian of Norwich', *Christian*, 6 (1980), 61–71. On St Bridget, see my *A Revelation and its Editors: Book VI*, ch. 52, of the *Liber Celestis* . . . , Vision et Perceptions Fondamentales, Actes du Colloque I.R.I.S., ed. R. Maisonneuve, Oyonnax, 1981, pp. 77–96.

22. I say 'propose', because the translated material hardly sustains the claims of these chapter titles.

23. Horstmann, 1, p. 337, 1, 5–340, 1, 21 translates material from I, 2–4 in sequence, except at p. 341, 11, 25–31, where material from I, 4 is inserted into the translation of I, 3 (cf. 'Sed nunc tu doctrix discipline dei', Suso, p. 81); 340, 1, 21–346, 1, 28 translates material from I, 15–16, interrupted at pp. 341, 1, 10–343, 1, 22 by a long passage from I, 14 (cf. 'O peramabilis sapiencia', Suso, p. 271) and with material from I, 16 (cf. 'O eterna patris sapiencia', Suso, p. 307) inserted out of sequence at p. 346, 11, 4–12.

24. E.g. *Horstmann*, 1, p. 338, 11, 25–31 = *Orologium* I, 2, 'Discipulus: Vere et indubitanter . . . Sapiencia: Ad redivivam igitur . . .' (Suso, pp. 47–8).

25. Cf. my comments on this same point in 'A Revelation and its Editors' (see n. 21 above). Compare further the easy transformations of St Bernard's address to the Virgin, in his fourth homily on the *Missus Est* (Patrologiae Latina 183.83) into address to the reader (Ragusa, p. 13) and a speech by the angel Gabriel to the Virgin (K. S. Block, ed. *Ludus Coventriae*, Early English Text Society E.S, 120, 1922, p. lviii, 106; and see further R. Woolf, *The English Religious Lyric in the Middle Ages*, Oxford, 1968, pp. 141–2, and *The English Mystery Plays*, London, 1972, p. 166–8).

26. E.G. Horstmann, 1, p. 341, 11.3–17 = *Orologium* I, 15 'Discipulus: Scio domine quia non est . . .' (Suso, p. 289), conflated with I, 14 'Discipulus: O peramabilis sapiencia . . .' (Suso, p. 271).

27. Such changes could also arise when different passages in a volume of meditations supplied the material for a continuous narrative of the life of Christ: e.g. the life of Christ based on the *Liber celestis* of St Bridget in Bodley Rawlinson C41, discussed in my 'Flores ad fabricandam coronam' (see, n. 16 above).

28. For discussion of this point, in the larger context of contemporary attitudes to Bible translation, see Deanesly, pp. 339–40, and J. Bazire and E. Colledge, ed. *The Chastising of God's Children*, Oxford, 1957, pp. 76–7.

29. On the presence of Latin catch-phrases, cf Rolle's Psalter, which gives the full Latin text of each verse: a practice followed regularly by other writers when translating verses from the Bible (so Hilton, the cycle plays, and three of the *Cloud*-author's texts, *Privy Counselling, Preier* and *Discretion of Stirrings*). More importantly, compare translations of the *Distichs* of Cato by Caxton and Benedict Burgh, which provide the Latin text at the head of each unit of translation (i.e. each stanza of the Burgh verse translation: on Caxton's translation, see also Crotch, pp. 78–9).

30. In fact, the manuscripts only rarely distinguish the 'bare englysshe' and the 'exposicioun', e.g. MS. Rawlinson C941 f. 86 ᵣ 'blessed b[e] þi doughtir þat is our lady to the Lorde þat is hir sone' (underlinings in red). The Fawkes printing adheres more faithfully to the principles enunciated, a feature concealed in Blunt's edition by the use of only one type-face for 'bare englysshe' and 'exposicioun'.

31. The relevant quotation is as follows:

    for as moch as yt is forboden, vnder payne of cursynge, that no man shulde haue ne drawe eny texte of holy scrypture in to englysshe wythout lycense of the bysshop dyocesan, and in dyuerse places of youre seruyce ar suche textes of holy scrypture: therfore I asked and haue lysence of oure bysshop to drawe suche thinges in to englysshe (Blunt, p. 71).

32. E.g. Blunt, p. 109, on 'thorrocke': 'ye shall vnderstonde that there ys a place in the bottome of a shyppe . . . and yt ys called in some centre of thys londe a thorrocke. Other calle yt a hamron, and some . . . the bulcke of the shyppe'. Cf. Caxton's prologue to his translation of the *Aeneid* and epilogue to his edition of Trevisa's translation of the *Polychronicon* (Crotch, p. 68, 108).

33. For a modernised edition of Trevisa's writings on translation, see A. W. Pollard, *Fifteenth Century Prose and Verse*, London, 1903, pp. 203–10.

34. The last-quoted line, elucidated by Coldwell's note to 1.350, need not refer strictly to the creation of a gloss. Douglas's prologue contains other important observations about the general question of translating individual words.

35. Gloss with 'of' is uncommon enough to warrant a few examples from the British Library Claudius B I translation of St Bridget's *Liber* which I am currently editing: pluma/fedir of a plume f. 19 ᵣ; premeditacio/forthoght of premeditacion; premeditacion of forvisement f. 108 ᵛ.

36. Compare the translator's repeated comment that the Virgin is the mirror of perfection 'to alle wymmen' (Hogg, p. 53, 138).

37. For the Latin of this hymn, see C. M. Dreves, ed., *Analecta Hymnica MediiÆvi*, XLVIII, Leipzig, 1905, p. 411. On address to women, cf. the following, written by a woman to a woman in a compilation in Bodley Holkham Misc. 41, f. 91 ᵣ 'also I write in diuers places vs and we for ye schulde at swich places take youre euen cristen with you in youre preieres'.

38. Palmer's argument is based on the common view that English is impoverished by comparison with Latin. For a single expression of this view, see Coldwell, pp. 10–11. For the general content of Palmer's contribution (if indeed it is his) to the debate on Bible translation, see especially, A. Hudson, 'The Debate on Bible Translation, Oxford 1401', *English Historical Review*, 90 (1975), 1–18.

39. Clearest evidence of this can be seen when Rolle avoids the 'transliterated' form, even though it was already in existence in the language and so available to him, in favour of a native, or older, word: e.g. consilium (counsaile)/Psalm 20:11 redis; tribulacio (tribulacioun)/Psalm 19:1 anguys.

40. Thus, for example, Psalm 1:4 defluet/downren (*commentary*, rennes down); 3:1 multiplicati/manyfaldid (*commentary*, multiplide); 56:3 benefacit/wele did (*commentary trsp.*).

41. On the reopening of the debate in the sixteenth century, see F. R. Johnson, 'Latin

versus English: the sixteenth-century debate over scientific terminology', *Studies in Philology*, 41 (1944), 109–35.

42. For Riehle, see W. Riehle, *The Middle English Mystics*, trans. B. Standring, London, 1981. Valerie Lagorio, 'New Avenues of Research on the English Mystics', Glasscoe p. 238, has indicated the development of a computerised programme of devotional prose syntax.

43. Examples of (i) ablative absolute: creaturis omnibus . . . perfectis/and when . . . all creatures . . . were parfytly made (Blunt, p. 179); (ii) participles used adverbially percipiens/when she harde (p. 250); (iii) passive forms of verb e.g. periphrastic passive: gaudendum nobis est/it longeth to vs to ioye (p. 172), cf. Trevisa est credendum/me schal troure (B.L. I 70).

44. Compare, for example:

Deus, qui huic aquile comparatur, cuius conspectui omnia futura sicut et presencia clara sunt et aperta, dum vniuersa iusta et honesta coniugia, que a primi hominis creacione vsque in diem nouissimum fieri debebant, prospiceret, nullum simile Ioachim et Anne coniugio in omni diuina caritate et honestate preuidit (S. Eklund, ed. *Sermo Angelicus*, Samlingar utgivna av Svenska Fornskriftsällskupet, Ser. 2, Bd. 8:2, Uppsala, 1972, p. 103);

with the *Myroure*'s rendering:

God, to whome thys egle ys lykened, to whose syghte all thinges presente and to come are clere and open, whyle he behelde all the rightwys and honeste wedlockes that shulde be from the fyrste makeynge of man vnto the laste day, he se none lyke in godly charyte and honeste vnto the wedlocke of Ioachym and of Anne (Blunt, p. 207).

45. Examples of (i) abstract plural nouns resolved as singular: tenebre/derkenesse (Blunt, p. 171): (ii) absolute adjectives and participles used substantivally and adjectivally, resolved by a clause: reis/them that are gylty (p. 236), cf. Trevisa in nostro habitabili/in Londe þat men woneþ inne (B.L. I.66); increata/er thow were made (p. 105); credentibus/to them that beleued (p. 121), cf. Trevisa expertorum/ of hem þat assaiede (B.L. 1, 66); (iii) adjectival dependence resolved by cognate genitive noun: humanam carnem/mannes body (p. 192); cf *Fristedt* 2 48/28 paterno/ fadris; (iv) gerund resolved as infinitive or present participle: ad adiuuandum/to helpe (p. 81); corroborando/strengthynge (p. 112), cf. Trevisa ministrando/and servede (B.L., 4, 264); (v) gerundive in adjectival relation resolved by clause: omnia creanda/al creatures that were to be made (p. 106); (vi) subjunctive resolved by periphrasis: sanctificetur/be halowed (p. 74); vt . . . reficeretur/that . . . he shulde be fedde (p. 112).

46. Examples from the British Library MS. Claudius B I translation of St Bridget: (a) accusative and infinitive resolved by clause: iustum me esse negant/denies þat I ame rightwis, f.7 ᵛ; clause of purpose resolved by infinitive: paterer vt . . . penetrarent/ wald I suffir . . . to perishe, f.37 ʳ. Here, too, perhaps, we ought to record the translation of non-finite forms of the verb by abstract nouns (the alternatives, as noted nn. 43, 45 (iv–v), are not greatly more successful): in compatiendo/in compassion of, f.31 ᵛ; ipso opitulante/ by his helpe (Blunt, p. 106).

47. Examples from Claudius B 1: (a) interchangeability of genitive/adjectival dependence: desideriis mundi/werldli desires f.33 ʳ; feroure dilectionis/feruent lufe f.70 ʳ; os fetidum/þe stinke of his mouthe, f.71 ʳ; (b) relations of co-ordination, apposition resolved by new genitive dependence: molliciem et caritatem/softnes of charite f.31 ᵛ; sine splendore id est spiritu sancto/withoute brightnes of holigoste f.60 ʳ; (c) auxiliary + noun resolved as cognate, verb, and opposite: habet . . . fletum/sho wepis f.16 ᵛ; longa est mora domini/lorde taris lange f.62 ʳ; pedibus ut alacer sit/go gladli with his fete, f.111 ᵛ; (d) translation by 'negation': non bene/falsli f.17 ᵛ; que creatura non tenet/all oþir creatures kepes f.28 ʳ; recens enim natura mortem . . . amariorem facit/þe more febil þe kinde is, þe more esi is . . . dede f.27 ʳ.

48. An example, from the Claudius B translation: miserabiliter a bestiis . . . dis-

pergebantur/wreched bestis . . . disparpild þaime f.66 ʳ (just possibly the exemplar read 'miserabilibus'?)

49. For a nice example from another text, cf the following, in P. S. Jolliffe, 'Two Treatises on the Contemplative Life', *Medieval Studies*, 37 (1975), 118: 'ibi *cogitet de Passione domini* aliquantulum ut per *vulnus lateris* usque ad contactum divinitatis occultae latentis interius, per experimentum amoris, attingere mereatur'; 'and *thynke* than deply of *the wounde in his side* þat went vnto his herte. And streyne hym in al that he may for to haue compassion *of Cristis passion* ouer all thyngis'.

50. Examples: quibus stantibus/the wheche stondynge, f.58 ᵛ; cum approbata iustitia/ with rightwosnes approbate f.31 ʳ; erubescerent de nuditate/þei shamed þer nakednesse f.24 ᵛ; non decuit rex . . . iacere/it was not semynge þe kynge . . . to lygge f.29 ʳ. Note further the regular corrections by a later scribe to the translation, which replace the literalisms of the original translation with forms more in line with those of the Wycliffe Prologue and the *Myroure* e.g. letaremur/we . . . glad *corr.* we ar glad f.24 ᵛ; inaudita/dedys neuer before herd (neuer *corr.* þat neuer was) f.34 ʳ.

51. In this I see an indication of the exaggerated respect still accorded to R. W. Chambers, *On The Continuity of English Prose*, Early English Text Society, O.S, 191A, 1932, by writers as concerned to modify Chambers's conclusions as Salter, Workman, and N. F. Blake, 'Middle English Religious Prose and its Audience', *Archiv*, 90 (1972), 437–55. A saner approach to the question of style is revealed in the following: 'Malory and the devotional writers were chiefly concerned with their matter. They tried to reproduce, in English, material of absorbing importance or interest; the manner of its conveyance was left to look after itself, and it did' (S.E. 2, xxiii–xxiv).

52. On fine style in the original (variants 'high', 'strange', 'unkouth'), see Crotch, pp. 4, 104, 107, Serjeantson, p. xvi (and following paragraphs of this study); on success of previous translations, especially when undertaken by social superiors, Crotch, pp. 6, 20, 37, 76, 109; on the translator's 'simple and rude' style (variants 'brode and rude', 'rude and vnperfyght', 'rude and olde', 'old and homely' etc., and cf. Chaucer's Franklin), Crotch passim. (and cf. a translator's professed unwillingness to undertake his task, and his initial abandoning of the task after only a few pages: Crotch, p. 4, 108, Serjeantson, pp. 5, 139, and Horstmann 1, p. 326); on courtly audience, Crotch *passim*, especially pp. 43, 82, 109.

53. On literalisms, cf S.E. 2, xxx–xxxii; on glossing, S.E. 2 xl–xlvii.

54. On this opposition of Christ and Apollo, see further J. Seznec, *The Survival of the Pagan Gods*, New York, 1953, repr. 1961, pp. 48, 96 n. 56, and *Index s.v.* Apollo. As a consequence of his 'choice' of Christ, Bokenham makes Valentines for himself of Sts Faith, Cecilia and Barbara (Serjeantson, p. 225).

55. Another way of handling the gloss is that in the *Ludus Coventriae* play 'Mary in the Temple' (Early English Text Society, E.S, 120, pp. 74–7), where the author uses a quatrain for each opening verse of the Psalms of Degrees, the first pair to gloss the text, and the second to translate it: the whole is then *followed* by the Latin original. Equally interesting is the parallel case, when a prose text, the translation of the *Orologium*, discussed above, is versified in the Macro play *Wisdom* (on which, see Riehle, 'English Mysticism . . .', Glasscoe, pp. 202–15). By dextrous rearrangement of his original's word order the 'translator' managed to incorporate it almost whole into his work, but he still had to gloss the text for the sake of the rhymes (M. Eccles, ed. *The Macro Plays*, Early English Text Society, O.S, 262, 1969, p. 114, 11, 1–8, cf. Horstmann 1, p. 329, 11.19–23).

56. With this quotation cf. Horstmann 1, p. 326, though it is not referring directly to the medium of the translation: 'manne . . . haþ likynge in chaunge and diuerse þinges'. Note further that the existence of a translation in one medium might prompt the issuing of a new version in another. Thus Caxton offers a prose rendering of Book 3 of the *Recuyell* in the knowledge that Lydgate's verse translation is still to hand (Crotch, pp. 6–7), and of Cato's *Distichs* in the knowledge of his own earlier

45

printing of Benedict Burgh's verse translation (Crotch, p. 76–7). In both these cases, though, the defence for the new translation lies in its provision of new material not found in the earlier source (thus Caxton is translating the *Distichs* from a French text dependent on the glossed text of Philip of Bergamo, which Burgh seems not to have used.)

57. Other choices follow the act of translation, e.g. the choice of text(s) to accompany the translation (e.g. Crotch, pp. 44–7), and the choices the reader must make, to 'rente the leef out of the booke' (Crotch, p. 30) or complete it where it has left questions unanswered (Crotch, p. 76). Such choices, and others, can be neglected here.

HENRY SUSO AND THE MEDIEVAL
MYSTICAL TRADITION IN ENGLAND

ROGER LOVATT

I

SHORTLY BEFORE HIS retirement from the Privy Seal Office, probably in 1422, Thomas Hoccleve produced an English verse translation of the *ars moriendi* chapter from Book II of Suso's *Horologium Sapientiae*. The work has some literary value and has even been claimed as Hoccleve's finest poem. Certainly it accurately mirrors his remorseful later years and contains, in the form of additions to the Latin original, some of those passages of acute self-revelation which are one of the redeeming features of Hoccleve's *oeuvre*. Equally the poem has a place in literary history as an early, if not the first, treatment of the *ars moriendi* theme in English verse. However, from another point of view, Hoccleve's poem is of particular significance as exemplifying many of the central features of the circulation of Suso's work in late medieval England.

In terms of temperament it would be hard to envisage two figures more disparate than the embittered, garrulous, self-regarding Hoccleve and the austere, sensitive, unworldy Suso. In the same way the milieu of the Privy Seal clerk, immersed in clerical drudgery in his office at Westminster—interspersed with bouts of profligacy—and ambitious to establish himself as a successful court poet, was far removed from that of the contemplative Dominican friar teaching and preaching in the convents of southern Germany. Hence one might well regard Hoccleve's admiration for this chapter from the *Horologium*—'a bettar restreynte know I none fro vice', as he wrote—as a revealing indication of how widespread and enthusiastic was the reception of Suso's work in England.[1] Indeed, at first sight, there is much to be said in support of such a view.

It seems clear that the *Horologium* must have reached England by about 1375 (that is, some forty years after its original composition) although it may well, of course, have arrived considerably earlier and circulated without trace. As the date by which the book can be proved to have been available to English readers is of some consequence, it is worth briefly outlining the evidence on which this conclusion is based. The earliest explicit reference to Suso's work in England occurs in the will of a Bristol merchant, Henry Wyvelescombe, which is dated 18 April 1393 and which includes the bequest of an *Orologium Sapiencie* to a certain chaplain, Henry Inet.[2] However, there are persuasive grounds for believing that this book was a copy, not of the Latin *Horologium*, but of its English version more commonly—although not invariably—known as *The Treatise of the Seven Points of True Love and Everlasting Wisdom*. In general it is most unusual in late medieval England to find a Latin text of such length and complexity in the possession of a layman of Wyvelescombe's standing. More specifically, there is apparently no other unequivocal instance of an English layman owning a copy of the Latin *Horologium*, although *The Treatise* circulated quite widely among the laity. Certainly such a disparity between the readership of Latin and English versions of the same work is a noticeable feature of the circulation of many similar devotional texts. However, if Wyvelescombe's book was a copy of *The Treatise*, then the *Horologium* itself must have arrived in England well before 1393. In his preface to *The Treatise*, the anonymous translator remarked that he had been familiar with the Latin original for 'sumtyme' before starting work on the translation. At one stage he apparently abandoned the undertaking altogether and even after resuming the enterprise he worked on it sporadically, only 'whanne I have leysere and tyme' and 'in certeyne tymes, whanne myne affeccione falleth there-to'. Comments of this sort clearly imply that the translation was a lengthy process, and the nature of *The Treatise* itself points to the same conclusion. In effect *The Treatise* is a transformation, as much as a translation, of its source. The translator had the avowed aim of reducing the diversity and complexity of the *Horologium* to a single theme, 'to stirre devowte sowles to the trewe love of owre lorde Jhesu'.[3] In pursuit of this objective, large sections of the original were entirely omitted—so that the English version is only about half the length of the Latin—and passages which were far apart in the Latin text, but dealt with similar themes, were brought together to form complex patchworks of interconnected quotations. Such a drastic reconstruction of the original must in itself have prolonged the labour of translation. Equally, the translator's skill in re-ordering the Latin text so radically, while maintaining the coherence of his English version, indicates a mastery of the contents of the *Horologium* which can have been based only on long familiarity.

One might reasonably conclude that a decade or so elapsed between the time when the translator first became acquainted with the *Horologium* and the date when he eventually completed *The Treatise*. Hence, if Henry Wyvelescombe's book was indeed a copy of *The Treatise*, it follows that Suso's work had reached England by about 1380. Various other types of evidence point in the same direction. In the first place, the two earliest English manuscripts of the *Horologium* can both be attributed, on paleographical grounds at least, to the second half of the fourteenth century.[4] Furthermore, as both manuscripts were apparently written in England, they are both at least one stage removed from any imported, continental exemplar. Secondly, it is possible to show that texts of the *Horologium* were already quite widely diffused in England by about 1400. A pluralist clerk in the service of Archbishop Arundel could refer to the book in his will of 1405 in terms which clearly suggest that he had been familiar with the work for some years.[5] Quotations from the *Horologium* appear in *The Chastising of God's Children*, which has been persuasively dated by its editors as 'nearer in time to 1382 than 1408' and which was compiled by an anonymous spiritual advisor to a house of nuns in the south-east midlands or London area.[6] The Carthusian writer, Nicholas Love, almost certainly already a member of the Mountgrace Charterhouse in north Yorkshire, was familiar with at least part of the *Horologium* by 1410.[7] And, if the words of his preface are to be taken at their face value, the English translator of the *Horologium* – probably writing in the east midlands – was the chaplain to a noble lady.[8] However, if the work was available in such different milieux by about 1400, then the case is strengthened for believing that it must originally have reached England by 1375–80.

There is no need to emphasise the significance of such a date in the history of fourteenth-century English mysticism. Julian of Norwich received her 'showings' on 13 May 1373. For the next fifteen years and more she meditated on the meaning of her experiences and it was not until 1388 that she seems to have begun the composition of the longer text of her *Revelations*. This work appears to have occupied her until 1393 and, even after its completion, she continued to develop and elaborate on her earlier account.[9] Similarly, although the precise chronology of Walter Hilton's literary career remains unclear, there can be little doubt that all of his major writings were produced during the later years of his life, between *c*. 1380 and 1396.[10] For the moment, the present writer would share the views of those who have expressed scepticism concerning the possibility that Suso's book may have exercised a direct influence on Walter Hilton and Julian of Norwich. Nevertheless the fact that the work must have reached England by *c.* 1375–80 does mean, at the least, that the suggestion that Hilton and Julian were familiar with the *Horologium* in some form cannot simply be discounted on historical grounds alone – as can, for example, any argument for the direct influence of Eckhart or Tauler on the English Mystics. Equally it is of some importance in itself that the *Horologium*, in many ways the most remarkable and certainly the most popular product of the Rhineland school, can be shown to have been accessible in England at so creative a moment in the evolution of English spirituality.

II

During the course of the fifteenth century the *Horologium*—in whole or in part—became widely known in England. The enthusiasm shown for one particular chapter by Thomas Hoccleve has already been quoted as symptomatic of the way in which Suso's work penetrated into the most various, and even potentially improbable, areas of English religious life. However, it is important to define this process of absorption in more detail. In some respects the circulation of the work was almost predictable. It was only to be anticipated, for example, that the *Horologium* would prove to have a particular appeal for the English Carthusians. The book may very well have been imported in the first place through Carthusian channels, and the order's sympathetic interest in similar, modern devotional texts—often of European origin—has frequently been stressed. Nevertheless it is a revealing illustration of this interest, and of the capacity of the order to acquire and distribute such works, to discover that the *Horologium* was known in some form in the Charterhouses of Beauvale, Coventry, Hinton, London, Mountgrace and Witham, and probably also at Sheen.[11] There are also various other instances where the book can be shown to have been familiar in Carthusian circles, but where the particular communities cannot now be identified. In fact it is probably only our general lack of information about the libraries of the remaining two English Charterhouses, Axholme and Hull, that restricts the list to these seven. Similarly it is not unexpected to discover that there were three manuscripts of the *Horologium* in the Syon library before the end of the fifteenth century.[12] The Bridgettine house was by far the most distinguished monastery to be founded in late medieval England

and its library was especially well equipped with modern devotional literature. A comparably devout and learned environment existed at Eton College during the years immediately after its foundation, and it is again not surprising to find a copy of the *Horologium* in the hands of one Fellow in the 1450's and then being bequeathed to another in 1462.[13] The two universities also provided natural centres for the circulation of books, even apparently for those as explicitly anti-intellectual as the *Horologium*. Hence in 1425 a copy of Suso's work was to be found in the possession of a distinguished member of the house of Austin friars at Cambridge, a former vice-chancellor of the university; from him, it passed temporarily to an equally learned Fellow of Gonville Hall who was later to leave a library of some hundred volumes to his college and the university.[14] In rather the same way the corporate libraries of Oxford and Cambridge acted as obvious repositories for books of every type. Bishop Flemyng gave a copy of the *Horologium* to his new foundation of Lincoln College; another copy appears in the list of benefactions made to All Souls College by Archbishop Chichele, and a third text was bequeathed to the Cambridge University Library in 1440.[15]

The Carthusians, the Bridgettines, the Fellows of Eton and the senior members of the two universities were in many respects very different communities, but they did represent something of a spiritual and intellectual élite and therefore a natural environment—or series of environments—for the circulation of the *Horologium*. Even so, the appearance of the book in all of these milieux is in itself some indication of its widespread reception in England. However, what is more striking is the way in which the work also reached many more remote, provincial areas of the country and became familiar to a much less informed and sophisticated readership. For example, during the course of the fifteenth century it is possible to find several copies of the book in the possession of various members of the York clergy. Some were important functionaries, like the Sub-Treasurer of the Minster or the Examiner General in the Archbishop's Court. Others were merely members of the large clerical proletariat attached to the Minster, such as cathedral penitentiaries, chaplains or chantry priests.[16] Again, by 1499, there was a text of the *Horologium* in the library of the distant collegiate church of Bishop Auckland in County Durham.[17] With the notable exceptions of St John of Bridlington and Walter Hilton, the English Austin canons showed little obvious enthusiasm for the life of the spirit during the later middle ages. It is therefore all the more unexpected to discover that the canons of

Leicester owned two copies of the *Horologium* by the end of the fifteenth century, that in 1448 another text formed part of the small, and unremarkable, library attached to the Augustinian Hospital of Elsing Spital in the City of London, and that a fourth copy apparently belonged at one time to the canons of Kirkham Priory in the East Riding.[18] Similarly it is contrary to one's expectations to find a text of the *Horologium* amongst the collection of only seventeen books owned by one of the undistinguished group of religious houses that were dissolved by Cardinal Wolsey in the 1520s.[19] For the rest, it can be shown that Suso's work was familiar in one guise or another—and sometimes only in the form of extracts—to a highly heterogeneous readership in England, ranging from an aristocratic French prisoner-of-war captured at Agincourt and a fashionable London preacher, to a Dominican recluse and a poor hermit. Finally it was only to be expected that the English translation of the *Horologium* would reach an even wider audience than its Latin original, but here again it is possible to see that this expectation was more than realised. In the first place *The Treatise of the Seven Points of True Love* can be shown to have circulated amongst two groups who do not in general seem to have been familiar with the Latin text: that is women, both secular and religious, and laymen. The female readers of *The Treatise* included nuns, both Benedictine and Augustinian, as well as ladies as high born as the daughter of Edward IV, while its readership of laymen embraced a Bristol merchant, a Nottinghamshire knight and a royal judge.[20] Secondly, the process of dissemination was carried a stage further in about 1491 when William Caxton produced a printed version of *The Treatise*. The appearance of this edition was in itself some indication of the work's popularity. Not only was Caxton in general careful to publish only those books which already possessed a reasonably assured market, but the volume is specifically described as printed at the request of 'certeyn worshipfull persones'.[21] Equally the production of several hundred printed copies of *The Treatise* would obviously have further increased its availability to English readers.

In one form or another Suso's work might well be thought to have found a broad and varied audience in late medieval England, and in fact such an impression is further strengthened by various other indications. One revealing sign of the extent to which an imported text was accepted by its English readers is provided by the way in which they quoted from it in their own writings. From this point of view also the reception of the *Horologium* seems at first sight to have been unusually welcoming. A number of comparable modern devotional

52

texts, written in northern Europe, reached England during the later middle ages, and subsequently even achieved a measure of popularity, but seem never to have been exploited as a source by fifteenth-century English authors. One notable and instructive example is the *Imitatio Christi*, whose general popularity in late medieval Europe rivalled that of the *Horologium*. The two works have survived in roughly the same number of English manuscripts and, like the *Horologium*, the *Imitatio* was translated into English soon after its arrival. Indeed in many ways the *Imitatio* might be regarded as possessing the more universal appeal. Yet it was apparently never exploited as a source by fifteenth century English writers.[22] Quite the opposite was the case with the *Horologium*. Suso's work was extensively used by English authors, often in ways that were far removed from the purpose and circumstances of its origin. Part of *The Treatise of the Seven Points of True Love*, for example, was transformed into a substantial section of a morality play.[23] On another occasion a short passage from the *Horologium* was quoted by an English disciple of Richard Rolle in the course of a theological polemic defending the mystical teachings of his master.[24] In at least two instances extracts from the *Horologium* were rendered into English verse. Most unlikely of all, in about 1440 the *Horologium* was used as a source by the compiler of the earliest English-Latin dictionary.[25]

This type of exploitation of Suso's work suggests that its presence and availability were taken for granted, so to speak, by English writers but it is otherwise somewhat uncharacteristic. What is more revealing is the way in which the work was employed in England by the compilers of other devotional treatises. Reference has already been made to the early use of the *Horologium* by the author of *The Chastising of God's Children*, but rather similar quotations also appear in a number of other, comparable texts. One such work is the *Speculum Spiritualium*, a long and comprehensive guide to the spiritual life which was compiled early in the fifteenth century by an anonymous English Carthusian. The work is designedly eclectic. Indeed in his preface the author made a virtue of his methods, explaining that he had drawn upon many different sources in order to produce a compendium suitable for those who could not afford a large library of their own. He apparently possessed a quite detailed knowledge of the *Horologium*, quoting from it at several points and drawing on material from five different chapters. Otherwise his range of reference was remarkably broad. It embraced not only the standard patristic and early medieval authorities but also many of the fourteenth-century English writers.

He made use of the writings of Richard Rolle, of William Flete's *De Remediis contra Temptationes*, and of two of the works of Walter Hilton—one of his epistles and the Latin version of *The Scale of Perfection*.[26] The author of the *Speculum* was perhaps exceptionally well read but in a number of other devotional treatises, and also in various private spiritual commonplace books, the *Horologium* appears in a very similar context. The implication is that during the fifteenth century Suso's work came to be accepted in England as a standard text. He could appropriately be quoted alongside Richard Rolle and Walter Hilton as an equally authoritative guide to the life of the spirit, and his *Horologium* circulated in close proximity to the writings of the English Mystics. The manuscript which contains the unique shorter text of Julian's *Revelations* also includes an extract from the English version of the *Horologium*.[27] In a volume owned by a nun of Campsey Priory *The Scale of Perfection* appears alongside *The Treatise of the Seven Points of True Love*.[28] In 1467 a York priest bequeathed to one of his relations both a copy of the *Horologium* and also a work of Walter Hilton because, as his will explains, 'they are bound together'.[29] We might well feel that these words symbolise much more than a merely physical contiguity.

III

How valid is such a conclusion? Does the circulation of the *Horologium* really suggest that late medieval English spirituality was open and receptive towards stimulus from the mystics of the Rhineland? Is it possible to go beyond the mere mapping, so to speak, of inert copies and say something more positive about the actual response of English readers? In a word, how did they react to the *Horologium*? Such problems can best be approached by returning once again to Thomas Hoccleve and looking more closely at his attitudes. Fortunately we know something of the background to his verse translation of the *ars moriendi* chapter. In another poem, written a little earlier, Hoccleve had announced

> in latyn have I sene a small tretise,
> whiche 'lerne for to dye' I-callyd is . . .
> And that have I purposed to translate

and, at the end of the translation itself, he added the information that 'this booke of the tretice of deeth' was divided into four parts.[30] Such words prove that he cannot have been working from a complete version of the Latin *Horologium* but must have used some form of *ars moriendi* anthology which happened to include this particular chapter. In fact there is no evidence that Hoccleve knew anything of the complete work, still less of its author or the circumstances of its origin. Hoccleve's knowledge of the *Horologium* was both partial and vicarious, and in this respect—as in others—he exemplified the position of many English readers.

It is sometimes rather too easily, albeit conveniently, assumed that the reception in late medieval England of a devotional text can be defined simply in terms of its extant manuscripts and of its appearance in wills and library catalogues. Such an assumption ignores both the inveterate eclecticism of contemporary authors of religious literature and also the great popularity during this period of devotional commonplace books, or *florilegia*. The reception of the *Horologium* in England provides a good illustration of both phenomena, and hence a pertinent warning. There are, for example, more than twice as many extant English manuscripts containing extracts from the *Horologium* as there are English texts of the complete work. Similarly, more manuscripts have survived of the—heavily edited—vernacular translation, and of extracts from it, than there are English copies of the Latin original. Or, again, there are very nearly as many surviving manuscripts of *The Chastising of God's Children*, which contains quotations from the work, as there are English manuscripts of the *Horologium* itself. In other words much of the impact of the *Horologium* on English readers was made at second hand and in incomplete form. In all sorts of different guises parts of the *Horologium* became familiar to those who, like Hoccleve himself, were unlikely to be acquainted with the work in its full, original form. However, this process of penetration and absorption also entailed the dilution and impoverishment of Suso's distinctive message. As their audience widened, so Suso's teachings lost much of their characteristic flavour. At this stage it becomes quite misleading to speak of the reception of the *Horologium* in England as though this was a one-way process. Rather it was in the nature of a dialogue between Suso and his English readers, where Suso's words were tempered by a sense of what it was that his audience wished to hear. Hence English readers tended to find in the *Horologium* what they were already seeking, or what happened to coincide with existing devotional fashion. They imposed themselves on the work instead of allowing it to speak to them in its own language. As a result their reactions towards the *Horologium* reveal as much about their own religious attitudes as they do about any positive influence exercised by Suso's work. Instead of changing the pattern of English spirituality the *Horologium* was exploited in the interests of strengthening it.

Again, Hoccleve is entirely characteristic. His enthusiasm for the *ars moriendi* chapter sprang partly from his own melancholia, his broken health, his remorse over his mis-spent youth, his sense—as he wrote at the time—that

> . . . the hony fro the hyve
> Of my spirit withdrawith wondir blyve;
> Whan al is doon al this worldes swetnesse
> At ende torneth in-to bittirnesse.[31]

But as an aspiring court poet, always desperately seeking patronage, Hoccleve's translation must also be seen as his recognition of the general popularity of this literary genre. The concern with mortality, the 'vision of death', was of course one of the most fundamental features of late medieval piety.[32] In England its expression may not have been quite so dramatic as it was elsewhere in northern Europe but the cult was nevertheless widespread and influential. It was therefore entirely predictable that this particular chapter from the *Horologium* should prove to be by far the most popular section of the work amongst English readers. The chapter was rapidly separated from its source and distributed independently under many different guises. In several manuscripts it occurs as a self-contained treatise.[33] Elsewhere it appears alongside similar works as part of an *ars moriendi* anthology.[34] In the same way Hoccleve's version circulated in the company of Lydgate's *Danse Macabre* to form a brief English verse anthology on the same theme.[35] The chapter was also three times rendered into English prose. On two occasions it was translated as an independent text.[36] On the third it was included almost *in toto* in the generally much abbreviated English version of the complete *Horologium*. Then, in this form, the chapter was again removed from its source and circulated as a separate work.[37] Finally, the Latin text was reproduced *in extenso* in the *Speculum Spiritualium*, as well as in a number of private devotional *florilegia*. At first sight this might seem to provide a striking instance of the ready reception of the *Horologium*. But this is no more than a half-truth. The chapter was popular in England not because of the intrinsic, distinctive character of Suso's teachings but for almost the opposite reason, namely that it coincided with current devotional fashion and could therefore most easily be integrated into its new environment. What is more, in its generally sober and didactic tone

56

this particular section of the *Horologium* is in itself uncharacteristic of the more idiosyncratic, flamboyant flavour of the work as a whole.

Integration as dilution—absorption as emasculation—is equally noticeable in the full English translation, *The Treatise of the Seven Points of True Love*. *The Treatise* is only about half the length of the *Horologium* and is not so much a translation as a complete recasting of the original. The translator's treatment of his source was purposive and carefully premeditated. Explicitly in his preface, as well as implicitly in his editorial work itself, he made clear not only his own attitude towards the *Horologium* but also his views about how it might best be rendered more suitable for a wider, and potentially less sophisticated, readership. His approach to the work sprang from his perception that its central purpose, what he called the 'processe of the forseyde boke', was 'to stirre devowte sowles to the trewe love of owre lorde Jhesu'.[38] At first sight such an assessment might seem unexceptionable, at least as a brief generalisation; indeed the words echo one of Suso's own remarks in his preface. But to define the *Horologium* in these terms is to invest it with a unity and coherence of theme which it does not possess. By implication it disregards much of the material in the work, places a falsely exclusive emphasis on other elements, and generally over-simplifies its protean character. Furthermore, the translator's view of the *Horologium*, however acceptable in general terms, was applied in practice in a rigorous and scrupulous fashion. As a result, this translation of the *Horologium*, which was potentially a major instrument for disseminating Suso's teachings amongst an English audience, reduced his work to the level of a conventional, weakly affective, almost anodyne piety.

This is as apparent in what the translator omitted as in what he included. It was only to be expected that, with the needs of a largely lay audience in mind, he would reject the more philosophical and abstract passages. Equally, the chapters on the pains of hell and the joys of heaven might reasonably be seen as at least partly irrelevant to his chosen theme. But something central to Suso's message was lost with the omission of his lament over the decline of devotion in his own day, however unwelcome its criticisms of the worldliness of the clergy might be at a time when English churchmen were becoming sensitive towards Wycliffite anti-clericalism. Similarly, the *Horologium* contains many sharply personal reflections, redolent of Suso's individuality. There are bitter attacks on real, or imagined, persecutors and long, and at times overwrought, accounts of the author's own spiritual experiences. Throughout the work there is a general advocacy of ostentatious and extravagant devotional practices and, especially in Book I, what is—to a modern reader at least—an excessive concentration on the physical details of the Passion. In view of the enthusiasm for the *Horologium* expressed in his preface it is all the more paradoxical that the translator should have chosen to omit many such passages, fundamental as they are to the particular flavour of the work.[39] Some of these omissions may have been dictated by his wish to reduce the book to a more ordered scheme, but it is hard not to believe that the translator was also influenced by the reaction against exuberant, overcharged devotional attitudes which was widely articulated in the latter part of the four-teenth century, not least by Walter Hilton and the author of *The Cloud*.[40] This shift in emphasis towards the more sober, moralistic and didactic elements in the *Horologium* was further strengthened by the translator's decision to reproduce *in extenso* precisely those three chapters from Book II which are concerned most exclusively with matters of practical devotional observance—one providing a brief guide to the spiritual life, the other two dealing with the art of dying and with the reception of the sacrament of the eucharist. Hence the *Horologium* was remodelled to the pattern of contemporary English piety, its elevated passages often discarded in favour of the practical, the flamboyant in favour of the prosaic, the idiosyncratic in favour of the commonplace. In one sense the translation does indeed exemplify the receptivity of English spirituality towards stimulus from the Rhineland. It also shows no less clearly the way in which it absorbed such stimulus only on its own terms.

A similar response to the *Horologium* is apparent in other con-texts. There is, for example, persuasive evidence to suggest that at least some of the popularity of the work in England was due not so much to its own particular merits as to its coincidence with devotional tastes already established by Richard Rolle. There are important differences between the *Horologium* and Rolle's writings but they do also have much in common, and English readers seem to have seized on these similarities. The coincidence between the circulation of the *Horologium* and that of Rolle's works is especially striking. Nearly half of the numerous body of English manuscripts which contain extracts from the *Horologium* also include one or more treatises by Rolle. Again, those authors, like the compiler of the *Speculum Spiritualium*, who made use of the *Horologium* often also quoted from one or other of Rolle's works. It is tempting to assume that the—somewhat un-expected—popularity of the *Horologium* amongst the clergy of York can be attributed to the fact that the cult of Richard Rolle enjoyed an enthusiastic following in this milieu. At the least, several of the York clergy who owned copies of the *Horologium* also possessed works by Rolle.[41] Perhaps it was not simply ignorance that led the scribe of one English manuscript to attribute a passage from the *Horologium* to Rolle.[42] Certainly one English reader made the relationship explicit and claimed directly, in defence of Rolle's teachings, that his views found support in the words of Henry Suso.[43]

IV

Further examples of this phenomenon could readily be given but these are sufficient to suggest that the title of this paper is in a sense a misnomer. Suso's *Horologium* made little, if any, distinctive impact on the English mystical tradition. Yet the reasons for this are of great interest. The circulation of the *Horologium* in England was a process of dilution, almost a reduction to the lowest common denominator of English piety. English spirituality in this period was very different from that of the Rhineland; more sober, practical and moralistic. We should be wary of tracing analogies, and still less connections, between the English Mystics and Eckhart, Tauler or Suso. From this point of view it does not really matter whether the writings of Eckhart or Tauler were known in late medieval England. Had they been, they would certainly have lost much of their characteristic flavour and been smoothly integrated into a different world. English religious life was not isolated from the continent. As the reception of the *Horologium* demonstrates, such works could readily penetrate, in various forms, into diverse and unexpected milieux. The *Horologium* soon came to be quoted by English authors, alongside St Anselm, St Bernard or Walter Hilton, as an authoritative guide to the devotional life. A part of the work even came to the notice of a Thomas Hoccleve. The barriers were not physical but those of temperament and mentality. It was not a matter of isolation but of English conservatism; that is an insularity of spirit rather than of geography. The mystics of the Rhineland struck no answering chord in England not so much because their writings were unknown but because those which reached England went largely unrecognised. They were accepted not on their own terms but on those of their English readers. The scholastics recognised this process and formulated it in a wise axiom. *Quidquid recipitur, secundum modum accipientis recipitur.*

NOTES

This paper represents a brief, preliminary report on an extensive investigation into the reception of Suso's *Horologium Sapientiae* in England. Because of limitations of space many, often important, aspects of the subject have had to be omitted altogether and those issues which are discussed have often had to be treated in a partial or simplified manner. In particular it has not been possible even to mention many specific instances of the ownership of the work by English readers or to say anything in detail about the numerous devotional *florilegia* which contain extracts from the book. For the same reason it has not always seemed appropriate to provide completely comprehensive annotation, especially concerning the circulation and provenance of manuscripts of the *Horologium* where many conclusions rest upon lengthy and complex argument. Such information will be provided in full in a forthcoming study.

Pioneer accounts of the *Horologium* in England are contained in a series of articles by G. Schleich and W. Wichgraf in *Archiv für das Studium der Neueren Sprachen*, 152 (1927); 156 (1929); 157 (1930) and 169 (1936) and in *Anglia*, 53 (1929) and 54 (1930). All previous work on the *Horologium* has largely been rendered obsolete by the appearance of *Heinrich Seuses Horologium Sapientiae*, ed. P. Künzle, *Spicilegium Friburgense*, 23, Freiburg, 1977. At the same time it is only fair to say that Fr Künzle's study of the English sources has perhaps not been as comprehensive as his work on manuscripts elsewhere.

1. *Hoccleve's Works: The Minor Poems*, eds. F. J. Furnivall and I. Gollancz, revised by J. Mitchell and A. I. Doyle, Early English Text Society, E.S, 61 and 73, revised reprint in one volume, London 1970, pp. 117, 178–212. For the dating of the poem, see J. H. Kern, 'Die Datierung von Hoccleve's *Dialog*', *Anglia*, 40 (1916), 370–73. On the poem's relationship with its source, see B. P. Kurtz, 'The Relation of Occleve's *Lerne to Dye* to its Source', *Publications of the Modern Language Association*, 40 (1925), 252–75, and a corrective view by J. Mitchell, *Thomas Hoccleve*, London, 1968, pp. 40–43, 75–77.
2. T. P. Wadley, *Notes or Abstracts of the Wills Contained in the volume entitled The Great Orphan Book and Book of Wills*, Bristol and Gloucs. Archaeological Soc., 1886, pp. 35–6.
3. '*Orologium Sapientiae* or *The Seven Points of Trewe Wisdom* aus MS. Douce 114', ed. K. Horstmann, *Anglia*, 10 (1888), pp. 325–6. It should be added that the Douce MS. is not the best text. A proper edition of the work has more than once been projected but has so far not appeared.
4. St John's College, Cambridge, MS. 84 and Vatican, Bibl. Apostol., MS. Ottob. lat. 73.
5. *Testamenta Eboracensia*, III, pp. 28–31. Also, M. Aston, *Thomas Arundel*, Oxford, 1967, pp. 313–8.
6. *The Chastising of God's Children*, ed. J. Bazire and E. Colledge, Oxford, 1957, pp. 11, 37, 41–9.
7. For the details of this argument, see E. Zeeman, 'Two Middle English Versions of a Prayer to the Sacrament', *Archiv für das Studium der Neueren Sprachen*, 194 (1957), 113–21, esp. 118.
8. *Orologium Sapientiae*, ed. Horstmann, *op. cit.*, p. 325.
9. The complicated chronology of the composition of the *Revelations* has been elucidated in *A Book of Showings to the Anchoress Julian of Norwich*, ed. E. Colledge and J. Walsh, Toronto, 1978, pp. 18–25.
10. The best account of Hilton's career is still that of D. Knowles and J. Russell-Smith in the *Dictionnaire de Spiritualité, s.n.*
11. Bodleian Library MSS Douce 114 and Lat. th. d. 27; St John's College, Cambridge, MS. 125; *Testamenta Eboracensia*, II, pp. 78–9 and Lambeth Palace MS. 436. For

Mountgrace, see Zeeman, *art. cit.*; Aberystwyth, National Library of Wales, MS. Porkington 19 and Cambrai, Bibl. Communale. MS. 255.

12. *Catalogue of the Library of Syon Monastery*, ed. M. Bateson, Cambridge, 1898, see nos M. 22, M. 90 and 0.3.

13. Eton College, Register Book 1457–1536, p. 104.

14. Vatican, Bibl. Apostol., MS. Ottob. lat. 73, f. 189 ^{v}. Also, A. B. Emden, *A Biographical Register of the University of Cambridge to 1500*, Cambridge, 1963, pp. 168, 559, 683.

15. Lincoln College, Oxford, MS. 48. N. R. Ker, *Records of All Souls College Library, 1437_1600*, Oxford Bibliographical Soc. Publications, New Series, 16 (1971), p. 7. *Testamenta Eboracensia*, 2, pp. 78–9.

16. *Testamenta Eboracensia*, 2, pp. 78–9; 3, pp. 91, 126, 159–60.

17. *Wills and Inventories . . . of the Northern Counties of England*, I, Surtees Society, 2, 1835, pp. 101–3.

18. *Catalogue of the Library of Leicester Abbey*, ed. M. R. James in *Transactions of the Leicestershire Archaeological Society*, 19, (1936–7), pp. 122–3, 432, and 21, (1939–41), p. 9. J. P. Malcolm, *Londinium Redivivum*, London, 1802, 1 p. 29. Emmanuel College, Cambridge, MS. 65.

19. British Library, Harley Roll, Y. 24.

20. Gonville and Caius College, Cambridge, MS. 390; Corpus Christi College, Cambridge, MS. 268; British Library, Royal MS. 15. D. II, f. 211; T. P. Wadley, *loc. cit.*, and *Testamenta Eboracensia*, 2, pp. 227–8.

21. There is a copy of this edition in the Cambridge University Library; see f. c. iii ^{v}.

22. See R. Lovatt, 'The *Imitation of Christ* in Late Medieval England', *Transactions of the Royal Historical Society*, Fifth Series, 18 (1968), 97–121, esp. 113–4.

23. *The Macro Plays*, ed. M. Eccles, Early English Text Society, O.S, 262, 1969, pp. xxvii–xxxvi, 114–52. See also, W. K. Smart, *Some English and Latin Sources and Parallels for the Morality of Wisdom*, Menasha, 1912, and W. Riehle, 'English Mysticism and the Morality Play: Wisdom Who is Christ', in *The Medieval Mystical Tradition in England*, ed. M. Glasscoe, Exeter, 1980, pp. 202–15.

24. M. Sargent, 'Contemporary Criticism of Richard Rolle', in *Kartäusermystik und – Mystiker*, I, ed. J. Hogg, Analecta Cartusiana, 55, 1981, pp. 160–205, esp. p. 195.

25. *Promptorium Parvulorum*, ed. A. L. Mayhew, Early English Text Society, E.S, 102, 1908, p. 11.

26. The *Speculum Spiritualium* was printed in Paris in 1510, at the expense of a citizen of London, by Wolfgang Hopyl. The quotations from the *Horologium* occur in Books 3 and 5.

27. British Library, Add. MS. 37790, ff. 135 ^{v}–6 ^{v}.

28. Corpus Christi College, Cambridge, MS. 268.

29. *Testamenta Eboracensia*, 3, pp. 159–60.

30. *Hoccleve's Works: The Minor Poems, op. cit.*, pp. 117, 212.

31. *Ibid.*, p. 119.

32. The phrase is used by J. Huizinga in *The Waning of the Middle Ages*, London, 1924. It is now fashionable to argue that Huizinga exaggerated this morbidity. His picture is boldly drawn but no one familiar with the devotional literature of the period could deny its fundamental truth, and his book remains the best introduction to this subject. On a more detailed level, see M. C. O'Connor, *The Art of Dying Well: The development of the Ars Moriendi*, New York, 1942; R. Rudolf, *Ars Moriendi*, Cologne, 1957, and N. L. Beaty, *The Craft of Dying*, New Haven and London, 1970, esp. ch. 1.

33. For example, British Library, Lansdowne MS. 385, and several other similar volumes.

34. British Library, Sloane MS. 2515 and elsewhere. For the background to the Sloane anthology, see R. Lovatt, 'John Blacman: Biographer of Henry VI', in *The Writing of History in the Middle Ages: Essays Presented to Richard William Southern*, ed. R.

H. C. Davis and J. M. Wallace-Hadrill, Oxford, 1981, pp. 415–44, esp. pp. 426–8.
35. For example, Bodleian Library, Bodley MS. 221 and Laud Misc. MS. 735.
36. The earlier of these two translations occurs in Bodleian Library, Bodley MS. 789 and elsewhere; the later is in Lichfield Cathedral, MS. 6.
37. See, for example, British Library, Harley MS. 1706, as well as other comparable manuscripts.
38. *Orologium Sapientiae*, ed. Horstmann, *op. cit.*, p. 325.
39. *Ibid.*, p. 326, especially the translator's words concerning the 'love and likynge that I have hadde in the forseyde boke Orologium sapiencie'.
40. *The Chastising of God's Children*, ed. Bazire and Colledge, *op. cit.*, pp. 54–61; also Sargent, *art. cit.*, esp. pp. 176–87. It is only fair to add that Rolle's works are rather less uniform in tone than his enemies often seemed to imply. Some of his English writings possess a simplicity and straightforwardness which belie the extravagance to be found elsewhere.
41. *Testamenta Eboracensia*, 2, pp. 78–9; 3, pp. 91, 159–60. For the cult of Rolle in York, see H. E. Allen, *Writings Ascribed to Richard Rolle*, New York and London, 1927, pp. 414–5.
42. Cambridge University Library, MS. Kk. vi. 20, f. 7 ᵛ.
43. Thomas Basset, *Defensorium contra oblectratores eiusdem Ricardi*, edited by M. Sargent, *art. cit.*, pp. 188–205, esp. p. 195. More information can probably be added concerning the background of Thomas Basset.

THE SOURCES OF *THE CLOUD OF UNKNOWING*: A RECONSIDERATION

ALASTAIR J. MINNIS

IN THE PROLOGUE to his translation of the *De Mystica Theologia* of Pseudo-Dionysius, the *Cloud*-author states that he has 'moche folowed þe sentence of þe Abbot of Seinte Victore, a worþi expositour of þis same book' (2.10–12).[1] This 'worþi expositour' has been identified as Thomas Gallus, who was Abbot of St Andrew's at Vercelli from its foundation in 1219 until his death in 1246, a Canon Regular of the Congregation of St Victor.[2] Over a period of twenty years, 'Vercellensis' busied himself with the exposition of Dionysian theology.[3] That part of his work which concerns us here, his interpretation of *De Mystica Theologia*, took three forms: a brief commentary or gloss, hereafter referred to as the *Glossa* (written 1232), an explanatory paraphrase entitled the *Extractio* (1238), and a full commentary entitled the *Explanatio* (1241).[4] McCann and Hodgson have demonstrated beyond any reasonable doubt that, in translating Dionysius, the *Cloud*-author certainly used Gallus's *Extractio* and probably his *Glossa* and/or *Explanatio* on *De Mystica Theologia*. Both these scholars postulate the influence of Gallus on *The Cloud* as well, and it is this theory which I wish to support today. *Deonise Hid Diuinite* owes much of its characteristic flavour to the way in which Gallus had 'medievalized' *De Mystica Theologia*; *The Cloud of Unknowing* owes much of its characteristic flavour to Gallus's version of Victorine spirituality.

When the *Cloud*-author asserted the superiority of the will over the reason, and the power of love or affection over the power of the understanding, he tacitly was taking sides in a long-running debate on the nature of theology. Several schoolmen, notably Richard Fishacre, Robert Kilwardby and Giles of Rome, argued that theology is essentially affective, while others, including Albert the Great, Thomas Aquinas, and Henry of Ghent, sought to emphasize (in different ways and to different extents) the rational and intellectual nature of the science of theology.[5] Pseudo-Dionysius was cited often in this controversy; conversely, the terms of reference of the debate coloured medieval approaches to the Dionysian corpus. For example, in his commentary on *De Mystica Theologia* (1255) Albert the Great asserted the superiority of the intellect (*intellectus*), by means of which the soul is united with God.[6] Writing earlier, Thomas Gallus has assigned this supreme role to the affection or disposition (*affectus*), the loving power of the will.

If Gallus's expositions of *De Mystica Theologia* are read in the order in which they were written, one can see him building on Victorine ideas of contemplation – in particular, on the thought of Richard of St Victor (died 1173), who is acknowledged as a major source in the *Explanatio* – yet gradually moving towards a considerable modification of Richard's position in emphasizing the *principalis affectio* as the mental power through which the mystic union is effected.[7] By *principalis affectio* (or *apex affectus*) is meant the purest and most sublime activity of the affection; the will's capacity to love rising to its utmost limits with the aid of divine grace, leaving far behind all corporeal involvement and earthly emotion.[8] It is coterminous with the *synderisis scintilla*, the spark of conscience or discernment which leaps up to God like a spark shooting from a fire.[9] Gallus substituted *principalis affectio* for Richard's *intelligentia* (denoting the higher function of the intellect) as the medium of unitive experience – he did not identify the former with the latter, as Von Ivánka thought.[10] We should realise, however, that for Gallus the principal affection was a cognitive power; more precisely, it was the supreme cognitive power possessed by man, whereby the soul attained knowledge-in-love.[11] The precise ideological nature of the disagreement between Richard of St Victor and Gallus on the ultimate stage of contemplation remains a controversial issue in modern scholarship, but at least it is clear that in Gallus's rigidly hierarchical scheme of the human faculties, Richard's concern with cumulative process and gradual transition from one faculty to another has been excised. The result is a separation of natural and supernatural modes of knowledge.

Robert Grosseteste sided with Gallus in affording the *affectus* an elevated status in the mystical union; he believed that the highest knowledge possible in this life is acquired in and through love (*amor*).[12] The author of the most comprehensive study of Grosseteste's theology to appear in recent years can see no difference between the two schoolmen here, 'rather an identity of thought. . . . For the immense influence which this development had upon the history of western mysticism Gallus cannot be given the sole credit'.[13] This is a valuable corrective to Von Ivánka's unduly large claim for the importance of Gallus's theory of *principalis affectio*. But it should be recognised that Grosseteste's Dionysian scholarship was far too erudite for many medieval readers, while the more facile and succinct expositions of Thomas Gallus enjoyed a wide audience. It was Gallus who influenced those masterpieces of affective piety, Hugh of Balma's *De Mystica Theologia* or *Viae Sion Lugent* and St Bonaventure's *Itinerarium Mentis In Deum*.[14] He seems to have influenced *The Cloud of Unknowing* also, either directly, or indirectly through intermediate writings which reiterated his teaching. Two facts, the indubitable influence of Gallus on *Deonise Hid Diuinite* and the congruence of the thought in this work and *The Cloud*, strengthen the case for direct influence, especially in view of the prominent and distinctive position which Gallus occupies among medieval interpreters of Pseudo-Dionysius.

In *The Cloud of Unknowing*, the *Cloud*-author's emphasis on love or affection places him firmly beside Gallus. Their terminology is slightly different in some particulars: the *Cloud*-author speaks of 'loue' where Gallus spoke of *principalis affectio*; in the English treatise the words 'affeccion' and 'wille' designate the mental faculty which Gallus usually designated as *affectio* or *affectus*. These English terms represent small and natural developments of Gallus's theory of affection – one may point to the same process in *Viae Sion Lugent*, where Hugh of Balma substituted words like *affectio amoris*, *ardor amoris* and *amor ardentissimus* for Gallus's *principalis affectio* and *apex affectus*.[15] But there are no essential differences of doctrine: the *Cloud*-author shares Gallus's belief in the primacy of love in the soul's ascent to God.

'Þe Abbot of Seinte Victore' believed that the soul is united with God by the principal affection. Similarly, the *Cloud*-author states that the spiritual disciples of God may be 'onid vnto God in parfite charite' in so far as this is possible in this life (p.85,7–8). For the *Cloud*-author as for Gallus, love is the highest cognitive power, far superior to the powers of reason and intellect. God is incomprehensible to every created intellect (i.e. to the understanding of men and indeed of angels) but not to love (p.18,17–21). This echoes Gallus's doctrine of ascent 'by the principal affection to union with God, which is . . . incomprehensibly located beyond all knowledge both human and angelic'.[16]

According to the *Cloud*-author, there are two main mental powers, two types of 'principal worching miȝt', the knowing faculty and the loving faculty. God is incomprehensible to the 'knowable miȝt' but comprehensible to the 'louyng miȝt' (p.18,22–p.19,6). This contrast between the *intellectus* and the *affectus* is reiterated constantly throughout *The Cloud*. For the *Cloud*-author it is as rigid a distinction as it was for Thomas Gallus, and here both writers agree against Richard of St Victor, who postulated a progressive movement up the mental hierarchy, an ordered transition from one type of con- templation to another. The *Cloud*-author is not prepared to accom- modate human reason and intellection in the higher reaches of mystical experience: '[God] may wel be loued, bot not þouȝt. By loue may he be getyn & holden; bot bi þouȝt neiþer' (p.26,3–5). In a manner strongly reminiscent of the way in which Gallus expounded Dionysius's advice to his friend Timothy, the *Cloud*-author counsels his spiritual friend to reject all the normal processes of human thought, which depend on visible and substantial things. He who would be oned with God must suppress all knowledge and feeling about anything less than God (see especially p.81,21–p.83,5).

This emphasis on personal purification and preparation for grace squares with that ethical bias which is a distinctive feature of Gallus's medievalization of *De Mystica Theologia*. For example, Gallus inter- preted the Dionysian account of Moses's ascent of Mount Sinai in terms of the process whereby the contemplative separates himself from various material opinions and earthly affections in order to ascend to God.[17] One concomitant of this doctrine, in both the *Glossa* and the *Explanatio*, is discrimination between the gentile philosopher who believed that the intellect was supreme and the Christian mystic who recognises the superiority of the principal affection.[18] This may lie behind the *Cloud*-author's repeated attacks on learned men who suffer from intellectual pride: these latter-day philosophers refuse to recog- nise the superiority of love.

The point of the intelligence does not penetrate the divine incom- prehensibility, Gallus argues; the eye of intellectual cognition cannot reach so high,[19] whence mystical knowledge is said to be by ignorance. By the power of the principal affection the soul is united with God in that most excellent state which neither the reason reaches by inves- tigation nor the intellect contemplates by vision; by the full affection of the mind we long to be in the superlucent darkness of the 'cloud of ignorance' (*caligo ignorantiae*), i.e. in a state which is 'super- intellectual' since the intellect does not see or know it in any way. The parallels with the *Cloud*-author's depiction of the cloud of unknowing are striking. When the soul begins to ascend to God it finds a derknes, & as it were a cloude of vnknowyng, þou wost neuer what, sauyng þat þou felist in þi wille a nakid entent vnto God. Þis derknes & þis cloude is, how-so-euer þou dost, bitwix þee & þi God, & letteþ þee þat þou maist not see him cleerly by liȝt of vnderstonding in þi reson, ne fele him in swetnes of loue in þin affeccion (p.16,20–p.17,5).

But the eye of intellectual understanding is of limited avail. In this life knowledge cannot reach to God but love can (p.33,11), and so it is necessary to 'fele in þin affeccion goostly' a 'blynde steryng of loue vnto God for him-self' (p.34,5–14). One must beat away at the cloud of unknowing 'wiþ a scharpe darte of longing loue' (p.38,12–13), recognising that we can encounter him only in the darkness of this wonderful cloud:

þer was neuer ȝit pure creature in þis liif, ne neuer ȝit schal be, so hiȝe rauischid in contemplacion & loue of þe Godheed, þat þer ne is euermore a hiȝe & a wonderful cloude of vnknowyng bitwix him & his God (p.47,17–20).

While the 'cleer siȝt' of God is not possible to us in this life, by grace God can give men the 'felyng' of him (p.34,17–19). Hence, one should cease from intellectual activity and lift up one's love to that cloud, hoping that God will send out a beam of spiritual light to pierce it, thereby revealing some of his secrets. 'Þan schalt þou fele þine affeccion enflaumid wiþ þe fiire of his loue, fer more þen I kan telle þee . . .' (p.62,14–18).

Traces of Thomas Gallus's theory of affection may be found even in passages where the *Cloud*-author is following closely Richard of St Victor. Two examples must suffice. As Hodgson has pointed out, chapters 63–66 of *The Cloud* are indebted to the classification of mental faculties which Richard had provided in chapters 3–6 of his *Benjamin Minor*.[20] But there is one major difference – the *Cloud*-author has upgraded the will. Richard held that, in the normal course of events, reason is superior to affection, and when defining the soul's faculties he treated affection along with sensuality, and reason along with imagination: sensuality serves affection just as imagination serves reason.[21] In Richard's allegorical scheme of contemplative ascent, the children of Rachel (= reason) are born after those of Leah (= affection), and it is Rachel's lastborn son Benjamin who personifies contemplation in ecstasy. But Rachel dies at Benjamin's birth, signifying that when the mind of man is carried beyond itself all the limits of human reasoning are surpassed.[22] Attempting to describe how Benjamin is ravished in ecstasy, Richard reverts to the language of love; he returns, as it were, to Leah.[23] This is the central paradox of

Richard's mystical theology: a progressive system of affirmative knowledge, governed by reason and intellect, culminates in a dark night of unknowing in which the normal processes of reasoning and intellection are transcended. The *Cloud*-author will have none of this double standard. In chapter 64 he treats reason and will together, in chapter 65 he defines imagination, and in chapter 66 he defines sensuality. Thus, Richard's link between will and sensuality is broken. As the faculty by which we choose good after it has been approved by the reason, and the power by which we are united with God, will is placed unequivocally above reason:

> Wille is a myȝt þorou þe whiche we chese good, after þat it be determinid wiþ reson; & þorow þe whiche we loue God, we desire God, & resten us wiþ ful likyng & consent eendli in God (p.116,17–19).

This extension of the thought of Richard of St Victor bears the stamp of Thomas Gallus.

Our second example comprises chapters 71–73 of *The Cloud*, which are based on Richard's *Benjamin Major* iv.22–v.1.[24] From this portion of Richard's text the *Cloud*-author drew his account of Moses's ascent of Mount Sinai – and perhaps also the central image of his work, the cloud of unknowing itself, for here Richard described the darkness of unknowing as the *nubes ignorantiae*.[25] But there is one interesting change which may be attributed to the influence of Gallus's replacement of *intelligentia* with *principalis affectio*. The *Cloud*-author allegorizes the Ark of the Covenant as love: just as the Ark contained all the jewels and relics of the temple, 'riȝt so in þis lityl loue put ben contenid alle þe vertewes of mans soule' (p.126,21–4). There is nothing to parallel this in *Benjamin Major* iv.22–v.1, but in i.2 Richard had allegorized the Ark as intelligence:

> We know that every precious thing – gold and silver, and precious stones – is usually placed in an ark. Therefore, if we consider the treasures of wisdom and knowledge, we shall quickly discover what the storehouse of such treasures is. What ark will be suitable for this activity, except the human intelligence?[26]

For *intelligentia* the *Cloud*-author has substituted 'loue', in agreement with the thought of Gallus. In sum, it would seem that the English writer read the *Benjamin Minor* and *Benjamin Major* in the light of the opinions and emphases of Vercellensis.

A similar conclusion may be reached through comparison of the theories of imagination formulated by Richard of St Victor, Gallus and the *Cloud*-author. Richard placed considerable emphasis on the importance of imagination in the first three of his six stages of contemplation as described in the *Benjamin Major*.[27] In the first stage, the imagination plays a major role by bringing to one's attention the form or image of visible things, which leads to veneration of the power, wisdom and munificence of the creator who is their source. The second stage of contemplation is 'in imagination but according to reason' because it proceeds by means of reasoning concerning those things which are engaged in the imagination. The third stage is that which is 'formed in reason according to imagination', when by means of the similitude of visible things we are raised up to speculation concerning invisible things. Imagination is indispensable, it would seem, until the fourth stage of contemplation. Only in the sixth and final phase is the human reason transcended. The normal processes of human thought are, therefore, afforded considerable dignity by Richard of St Victor. As the imagination is left behind, the human intelligence is dilated more and more fully; the farther it moves away from lower things the more it grasps of higher things. Finally, the mind goes beyond the bounds of human capacity and, 'being transformed into a certain kind of supermundane affection, goes completely beyond itself'.[28] It was the suprahuman and suprarational nature of this highest type of contemplation which preoccupied Thomas Gallus as a commentator on *De Mystica Theologia*. In his interpretation of that work, a wedge is driven between philosophical wisdom and Christian wisdom, between the *intellectus* and the *affectus*. Consequently, the lower human faculties are denigrated, especially the imagination: their earth-bound operations must be left behind as the soul ascends to encounter the unknown God in darkness.

It is Gallus's emphasis which is present in *The Cloud*. While the soul dwells in 'þis deedly body' the sharpness of our understanding in beholding spiritual things, especially God, is unfortunately 'medelid wiþ sum maner of fantasie' which can lead us astray. Therefore, imaginative thinking, which always interferes when one is trying to engage in the 'blynd werk' of contemplation, must ruthlessly be suppressed: 'bot þou bere him doun, he wile bere þee doun' (p.33,11–20).[29] The *Cloud*-author was convinced that the 'bodely and fleschely conseytes of hem þat han corious & ymaginatyue wittys ben cause of moche errour' (p.94/22–4). By contrast, the 'deuoute steryng of loue' in a pure spirit is 'fer fro any fantasie, or any fals opynion þat may befal to man in þis liif' (p.91,14–18).

Richard of St Victor had praised the imagination as the willing handmaiden of reason: 'always and in all things, imagination is ready, and reason can employ her service everywhere'.[30] Indeed, without imagination the soul would not know corporeal things, and were she deprived of such knowledge she could not ascend to contemplation of heavenly things.[31] However, Richard felt obliged to enter the caveat that when the imagination is not controlled by the reason she will suggest phantasms and images to us which hinder greatly our spiritual progress. This warning is repeated with great relish in chapter 65 of *The Cloud*, where we are assured that, if the imagination is not restrained by the light of grace in the reason,

> it wil neuer sese, sleping or wakyng, for to portray dyuerse vnordeynd ymages of bodely creatures; or elles sum fantasye, þe whiche is nouȝt elles bot a bodely conseynte of a goostly þing, or elles a goostly conseynte of a bodely þing. & þis is euermore feynid & fals, & aneste vnto errour (p.117, 13–17).

This disobedience of the imagination is clearly revealed by the prayers of those who have recently turned aside from the world into a life of devotion. For until such times as their imagination is controlled (which will happen after constant meditation on spiritual things),

> þei mowe in no wise put awey þe wonderful & þe diuerse þouȝtes, fantasies & images, þe whiche ben mynystred & preentid in þeire mynde by þe liȝte & coriousitee of ymaginacyon. & alle þis inobedyence is þe pyne of þe original synne (p.118,3–6).

The positive aspect of Richard's theory of imagination, which makes considerable provision for 'ordered images' and recommends imaginative thinking to people who are at the lower stages of the contemplative ascent, has altogether been ignored. The influence of Gallus may account for this suppression of part of Richard's doctrine and the concomitant emphasis on that part which was most germane to Gallus's own thinking on the subject of imagination.

We are now in a position to question one of the opinions of a great medievalist to whom we are all highly indebted. In *The English Mystical Tradition* David Knowles voices his scepticism concerning the specific influence of Gallus on *The Cloud*:

> . . . it is not evident that the abbot of Vercelli inspired what are the peculiar characteristics of the *Cloud* and its companions: the insistence on the blind, 'naked' act of loving attention; the clear distinction between natural and supernatural knowledge, and the incommunicability and the imperceptibility to the natural powers of the light of contemplation. Likewise, there is no hint in Thomas Gallus of the abundant and shrewd practical advice of the *Cloud*. In other words, while the influence of Gallus is very real, it is not the specifying influence.[32]

In fact, the peculiar characteristics of *The Cloud* group here listed are substantially the same as distinctive doctrines of Thomas Gallus identified by recent scholarship. In particular, Gallus definitely emphasized the blindness of the affective ascent and firmly distinguished between natural and supernatural types of knowledge. The *Glossa* and the *Explanatio* make much of the Areopagite's exhortation of his beloved 'other self' Timothy to leave behind both sensible perceptions and intellectual operations, all sensible and intelligible things, and as far as is humanly possible to be raised up unknowingly to union with God, who is above every substance and all ordinary knowledge. Gallus relished the paradox that the divine light described by Dionysius is the secretly supershining darkness of spoken silence: this is incomprehensibility, he explains, said to be 'darkness' on account of the excess of light, to be 'spoken' because of the eternal word which speaks from eternity, to be 'secretly supershining' because of the most secret effusion of the divine light, and to be 'of silence' because the generation of such a word is not perceived by the intellectual hearing and therefore cannot be recounted by word of mouth.[33] In short, the light of contemplation is incommunicable and imperceptible to the natural powers of sense and reason. With regard to the absence of 'shrewd practical advice' in Gallus, it should be recognised that considerable differences of genre and audience are involved: Gallus was expounding the intention of his author through *explication de texte*, while the *Cloud*-author was offering advice to a budding contemplative. But it is perfectly possible to argue that the *Cloud*-author was amplifying and clarifying for his 'friend in God' the advice which Dionysius, viewed through the filter of Augustinian ethics, was supposed to have provided for his beloved friend Timothy.

It remains to consider briefly the possibility that the peculiar characteristics of *The Cloud of Unknowing* represent the influence of Gallus not directly but through an intermediate source. The intermediary can hardly have been Thomas Aquinas (as Knowles implies) since he believed that both the *intellectus* and the *affectus* were involved in the ultimate mystical experience. In a thesis which, it is hoped, will soon see the light in print in some form, Dr R. A. Lees offers Hugh of Balma as the most likely candidate.[34] Her argument turns on the belief that Hugh went beyond Gallus by disassociating knowledge-in-love from other types of knowledge; in this respect, she concludes, the *Cloud*-author followed Hugh rather than Gallus. The problem that we are faced with here is finding a principle on which Gallus and Hugh of Balma disagree to such an extent that precise identification of the *Cloud*-author's source is possible. If Von Ivánka's claim that Gallus identified the *principalis affectio* with the *intelligentia* is not true – and I for one am convinced that it is not – than one of the major grounds on which he distinguished between the two thinkers, namely that Hugh achieved the formal disassociation of natural and supernatural modes of knowledge, is seriously weakened.[35] It is, in my opinion, altogether destroyed when the following facts are brought to bear:

1. Natural and supernatural modes of knowledge are separated quite as much by Thomas Gallus as by Hugh of Balma. What we find in Hugh's discussions of the unitive way is a more precise and elaborate manner of speaking, together with more dramatically 'affective' idioms, but not a substantive difference in thought from Gallus.
2. For Hugh of Balma as for Gallus, the experience of loving union is a cognitive experience: some degree of super-knowledge, knowledge of the most sublime kind, is involved as the soul contemplates the beauty of God face to face.[36] Moreover, both thinkers suggest that, once such knowlege-in-love has been attained in the higher affection, an enlightenment of the higher function of the intellect (i.e. the *intelligentia*) can follow.

From our point of view, the similarities between Gallus and Hugh of Balma are more significant than the differences. Such differences as do exist in their accounts of the ultimate stage of contemplation are expressed in a technical Latin jargon far more discriminating than anything in the Middle English treatise.

All we can say with certainty is that Gallus's description of the respective roles of the *intellectus* and the *affectus* provides a quite sufficient precedent for all the major contrasts between 'understondyng' and 'loue' in *The Cloud of Unknowing*. Equally adequate are the precedents provided by Gallus's theory of the function of intellect in the lower stages of contemplation (cf. especially *The Book of Privy Counselling* p.158,17–25) and the function of superintellect in the highest possible stage (cf. especially *The Cloud* p.62,14–19 and *The Pistle of Preier* p.54,5–11). Significantly, the most distinctive single feature of Hugh's *Viae Sion Lugent*, its division of the contemplative way into the purgative, illuminative and unitive stages, is unparalleled in the English work, although it does seem to have influenced two fifteenth-century tracts on the contemplative life which contain borrowings from *The Cloud*.[37]

In the absence of clear evidence to the contrary, the claim for the direct influence of Gallus on *The Cloud of Unknowing* may be upheld. Sources must not be multiplied beyond necessity, especially when we know, on his own admission in *Deonise Hid Diuinite*, that the *Cloud*-author was familiar with Gallus's interpretation of *De Mystica Theologia*. Writing in the *Downside Review* in 1934, David Knowles toyed with the idea that 'there is a source of the *Cloud*, if only a great and inspiring teacher, whose name we shall never know'.[38] It is tempting to name that great teacher as Thomas Gallus, 'þe Abbot of Seinte Victore'. Of course, Vercellensis did not provide every doctrine and detail in *The Cloud*, but it is arguable that his teaching determined the tenor and tone of the work as a whole.

NOTES

1. *Deonise Hid Diuinite and Other Treatises on Contemplative Prayer*, ed. P. Hodgson, Early English Text Society, O.S, 231, rev. repr. London, 1958, p.2. All references to *The Cloud* and *The Book of Privy Counselling* are to the edition by P. Hodgson, Early English Text Society, O.S, 218, rev. repr. London, 1973.
2. See *The Cloud of Unknowing and Other Treatises*, ed. Justin McCann, London, 1924, pp.xiii–xxx, 249, 252, 276–283; cf. *Deonise Hid Diuinite*, ed. P. Hodgson, pp.xxxix–xl, xlii, 119–129.
3. On the life and works of Thomas Gallus see the series of articles by G. Théry in *Divus Thomas*, 40 (1934), 264–77, 365–85, 469–96; *Vie spirituelle*, supplements to vols 31 (1932), 147–67; 32 (1932), 22–43; 33 (1932), 129–54; *Archives d'histoire doctrinale et littéraire du moyen age*, 12 (1939), 141–208; also D. A. Callus, 'An Unknown Commentary on the Pseudo-Dionysian Letters', *Dominican Studies*, 1 (1949), 58–67. The most comprehensive study of Gallus's thought is by J. Walsh, '*Sapientia Christianorum': The Doctrine of Thomas Gallus, Abbot of Vercelli, on Contemplation*, D. Theol. diss., Pontifica Universitas Gregoriana, Rome, 1957; cf. the summary provided by Rosemary A. Lees, *The Negative Language of the Dionysian School of Mystical Theology: An Approach to the Cloud of Unknowing* PhD diss., University of York, 1981, 1, 203–212.
4. The *Glossa* is falsely attributed to John the Scot and printed among his works in Patrologiae Latina, 122, cols 267–284: see Théry, *Divus Thomas*, 37, 385. For a helpful discussion and comparison of the *Glossa* and the *Extractio* see W. Völker, *Kontemplation und Ekstase bei Pseudo-Dionysius Areopagita*, Wiesbaden, 1958, pp. 226–8.
5. For brief discussion and bibliography see A. J. Minnis, 'Literary Theory in Discussions of *Formae Tractandi* by Medieval Theologians', *New Literary History*, 11 (1979), 133–45. A fuller treatment is provided in Chapter 4 of my forthcoming book *Medieval Theory of Authorship: Scholastic Literary Attitudes in the Later Middle Ages*, London, 1982.
6. See Völker, *op. cit.*, pp. 241–5.
7. See E. Von Ivánka, 'Zur Überwindung des neuplatonischen Intellektualismus in der Deutung der Mystik. *Intelligentia* oder *Principalis Affectio*', in *Platonismus in der Philosophie des Mittelalters*, Wege der Forschung, 197 (Darmstadt, 1969), 147–60.

8. For a succinct explanation of these terms see James Walsh, 'The Cloud of Unknowing', The Month (1963), 325–336.

9. Völker, op. cit., p. 229 n.2; Von Ivánka, op. cit., pp. 149–50. See further, M. B. Crowe, 'The Term Synderesis and the Scholastics', Irish Theological Quarterly, 23 (1956), 151–164, 228–245.

10. Von Ivánka, op. cit., p. 150. In fact, in his interpretation of De Mystica Theologia Gallus does not distinguish clearly between intellectus and intelligentia, in respect of which his thinking resembles that of Richard of St Victor: see R. Javelet, 'Thomas Gallus et Richard de Saint-Victor mystiques', Recherches de théologie ancienne et medievale, 29 (1962), 206–33; 30 (1963), 88–121. Völker, op. cit., pp. 225–6, n.11; 231, n.3, points out that in the Extractio Gallus does not distinguish between the intellectus and the intelligentia and that in the Explanatio they are used as synonyms; moreover, at one point in the Explanatio the motus intelligentiae is placed in opposition to the motus affectionum.

11. See Walsh, 'Sapientia Christianorum', op. cit., pp. 99, 255–8; Lees, op. cit., pp. 205, 207–20. Von Ivánka, therefore, was right to stress the cognitive element in the affective union as described by Gallus; cf. Völker, op. cit., pp. 226–7. Indeed, Gallus seems to follow Richard of St Victor in believing that the affective and intellectual types of cognition tend to merge in the unitive experience: see Javelet, op. cit., 29, 232; 30, 88–121.

12. See Il Commento di Roberto Grossatesta al 'Di Mystica Theologie' del Pseudo-Dionigi Areopagita, ed. Elderico Gamba, Milan, 1942; cf. Grosseteste's sermon Ecclesia Sancta Celebrat, ed. James McEvoy, 'Robert Grosseteste's Theory of Human Nature, with the text of his conference, Ecclesia Sancta Celebrat', Recherches de Théologie Ancienne et Mediévale, 47 (1980), 131–87 (pp. 144–58).

13. McEvoy, 'Grosseteste's Theory of Human Nature', op. cit., p. 153. Professor McEvoy's monumental study of Robert Grosseteste is being published by the Oxford University Press. I am grateful to him for valuable discussion of Grosseteste's exposition of Pseudo-Dionysius, and for allowing me to read in typescript much of his forthcoming work.

14. See Völker, op. cit., pp. 231–7; Von Ivánka, op. cit., pp. 147–8, 150.

15. See for example the passages cited by Völker, pp. 232–35. I used the text of Hugh's Viae Sion Lugent printed among the works of St Bonaventure in S. Bonaventurae Opera Omnia, Venice, 1751–55, 11, 344–404.

16. Glossa, in Patrologiae Latina, 122, col. 272A.

17. Patrologiae Latina, 122, col. 274C.

18. Glossa, in Patrologiae Latina, 122, cols 269B, 272D–3A; Explanatio, in British Library, MS Royal 8,6,IV, fols 42ᵛ–3ʳ.

19. On Gallus's belief that the apex intellectus is inferior to the apex affectus see Walsh, 'Sapientia Christianorum', op. cit., p. 82; Lees, The Dionysian School, op. cit., p. 204.

20. The Cloud of Unknowing, ed. P. Hodgson, p. lxxv.

21. Patrologiae Latina, 196, col. 4C.

22. Benjamin Minor, cap. 73, in Patrologiae Latina, 196, col. 52D.

23. See especially Benjamin Minor, capi 75, 78, 80, in Patrologiae Latina, 196, cols 53–4, 55–7.

24. The Cloud of Unknowing, ed. Hodgson, pp.lxxiii–lxxxv; cf. Patrologiae Latina, 196, cols 164–9.

25. For discussion see The Cloud of Unknowing, ed. P. Hodgson, pp.lxii, lxx–lxxi.

26. Patrologiae Latina, 196, col. 65C; trans. G. A. Zinn, Richard of St Victor: The Twelve Patriarchs, The Mystical Ark, Book Three of the Trinity, the Classics of Western Sprituality, London, 1979, p.58.

27. Benjamin Major, I.6, in Patrologiae Latina, 196, cols 70B–71B; trans. Zinn, op. cit., pp. 161–2. Discussion of the commendable uses to which imagination can be put is included in my article 'Langland's Ymaginatif and Late-Medieval Theories of

Imagination', *Comparative Criticism*, 3 (1981), 71–103. I am preparing a monograph on late-medieval theory of imagination and imagery, with special reference to commentaries on the Dionysian corpus, especially *The Celestial Hierarchies*.

28. Patrologiae Latina, 196, 178D; trans. Zinn, *op. cit.*, p. 323.
29. Cf. *The Book of Privy Counselling*, p. 152, 3–18, 157, 27–158, 16.
30. *Benjamin Minor*, cap 5, in Patrologiae Latina, 196, col. 5B; trans. Zinn, *op. cit.*, p. 58.
31. Later schoolmen emphasized such positive and commendable functions of the imagination in discussing the imaginative or phantastic or cogitative power (these different terms and divisions having been used by different authorities). See N. H. Steneck, *The Problem of the Internal Senses in the Fourteenth Century*, PhD diss., University of Wisconsin, 1970, pp.15–16, 52–4, 63–4, 68–73, etc.
32. *The English Mystical Tradition*, London, 1961, p. 75.
33. Patrologiae Latina, 122, col. 271B; cf. the fuller account in the *Explanatio, op. cit.*, MS Royal 8, 6, IV, fols 43ᵛ–4ʳ.
34. For full reference see note 3 above.
35. For the scholarly controversy on these issues see the references in note 10 above. On Hugh's theory of affection see especially J. Krynen, 'La Pratique et la Théorie de l'Amour sans Connaissance dans la *Viae Syon Lugent* d'Hughes de Balma', *Revue d'Ascétique et de Mystique*, 40 (1964), 161–83.
36. See the references in note 11 above; also Lees, *op. cit.*, pp. 225–8.
37. See P. S. Jolliffe, 'Two Middle English Tracts on the Contemplative Life', *Mediaeval Studies*, 37 (1975), 85–121 (esp. pp.117–8).
38. 'The Excellence of the *Cloud*', *Downside Review*, 52 (1934), 71–92 (p. 81, n.1).

THE CLOUD OF UNKNOWING AND VEDANTA

KATHARINE WATSON

IN THIS PAPER the term 'Vedanta' will be used in its broadest sense, as the system of philosophy and teaching which is derived from the Vedas. It does not, therefore, refer to any particular branch or sect of Indian philosophy or religion. The word 'Vedanta' signifies the end, or goal, of the Veda. And what is that end? We might thus express it in a nutshell: that a soul may be 'onyd wiþ God'.

The word *Veda* itself literally means knowledge. It comes from the Sanskrit root *vid*, to know, from which are derived Greek *ouida*, Latin *videre*, Anglo-Saxon *witan*, and most appropriately, our modern word *wisdom*.

So what is this Veda, this knowledge? To most people, especially in the west, the Vedas means a collection of extremely obscure and ancient books, of which it is indeed very difficult to make head or tail. But tradition has it that Veda is in fact eternal – eternal wisdom, eternal knowledge. This knowledge – which is knowledge of all things – is implanted in man at the beginning of creation, and is natural to him, enshrined in his heart. The knowledge, which is said originally to have been instantaneously and naturally available, from within, to any human being whenever he needed it, extends to every detail of creation, and allows him wisely to care for every aspect of it.[1] At the other end of the scale, it gives him knowledge of himself, of his own true nature – which is divine – and also of God, and of man's relationship with God. In course of time, however, by a process very much analogous to the fall, this knowledge becomes obscured under an ever-thickening veil of ignorance, so that, although the knowledge is still there, stored, as it were, in the hearts of all men, it is no longer available to them, and they forget its very existence. When this happens, men become dependent upon knowledge imparted to them from without, which connects with and illumines the knowledge lying dormant within them. (Hence, say the teachers, it comes about that dawning knowledge so often feels like recognition.) Vedic tradition says that in course of time Sage Vyasa, realising that the Veda was beginning to be forgotten, first began to write down the knowledge, and that this is how the books now known as the Vedas came into being.[2] From time to time also wise men, prophets, teachers, law-givers arise among mankind to re-establish the ancient knowledge – always, of course, in a guise suited to that particular time and place. Thus what Moses taught is Veda, the teaching of Lao Tzu is Veda, the sayings of Buddha are Veda. When the Psalmist sings, 'Thy testimonies are wonderful, therefore doth my soul keep them'[3] he is praising the Veda. The scriptures, too, are divinely inspired, they exist and are preserved in order that men shall not entirely forget. Also, the tradition says, from time to time an incarnation of God – an *avatara* – is born into the world to lead men back to the truth. Thus lord Shrī Krishna says, 'Whenever spirituality decays and materialism is rampant, then, O Arjuna! I reincarnate Myself. To protect the righteous, to destroy the wicked, and to re-establish the kingdom of God, I am reborn from age to age'.[4] Christ himself says, 'Think not that I am come to destroy the law. . . . Verily I say unto you, Till heaven and earth pass, one jot or one tittle shall in no wise pass from the law, till all be fulfilled'.[5] That law is eternal; that law *is* the Veda. Clearly it follows that whatever the differences of style, traditions, practices and particular beliefs which have grown up around the different religions and philosophies, there can at this deeper, universal level, be no conflict between the Veda and Christianity.

For a number of reasons it is only now, in our time, gradually becoming possible for the thoughtful westerner to approach the oriental, and especially the Vedic, tradition with an open mind. The discovery of Sanskrit, and with it the vast corpus of sacred literature, came at what was, in some ways, an inauspicious time. The confident Victorian rulers of the British Raj blandly assumed the total superiority of their religion, culture and way of life over that of 'the native'. Monier Williams, earnestly attempting to promulgate under-standing by the British conquerors of the subject peoples of 'the Queen's Indian dominions',[6] even while advocating toleration speaks of 'looking down from our undoubted pre-eminence on the adherents of false systems'[7]—by which he means Buddhism, Islam and the Hindu religion. The theories of Darwin also encouraged the view that the ancient texts represented the work of primitive people, simple-minded and superstitious nature-worshippers—scarcely out of the trees. How great a misjudgement this was is only now becoming clear. The Vedas themselves, in particular, seem to have been very seriously misunderstood.

In 1958, during a visit to America, the great 'Jagadguru Shankarācharya' Shrī Bhāratī Krishna Tīrthajī Mahārāj drew his audience's attention to the absurdity of the situation where, throughout history, the followers of different religions 'deem it their duty to fight to the finish and bring forward before the world their own particular religion, not merely as the best of all, but as the only one leading to heaven; all the others being straight paths to hell'.[8] Even now, because of the way in which certain Biblical texts[9] are interpreted, many Christians feel themselves guilty of some sort of betrayal unless they uphold this view. Yet all exponents of Vedanta philosophy emphasise that there need be no conflict at all between Christianity and Vedanta.[10] Any differences are due to the different needs arising in the time and place of their origin.

During the latter part of this century Christians have at last begun to find the humility and the clear sightedness to recognise that there is no need for them to denigrate other religions, or try to prove the superiority of their own. There is, at least in some quarters – in the Julian Meetings for instance, in the writings of Henri Le Saux, (or 'Abhishiktananda' as he was known), and the work of Herbert Slade, and others of the Cowley Fathers a new spirit of willingness to learn and to share, and to put to use the remarkable insights of Vedanta. All this, of course, is not to deny that there are very real differences in doctrine and practice, but as Herbert Slade, writing on his community's use of the work of Patanjali says, 'We have used it as a way of by-passing many old theological differences by going behind the conditions of their origin to a wider and more general foundation in our human nature to which the work of Patanjali bears witness'.[11] He points out that to differ is healthful: 'It is not necessary to work for an artificial synthesis between differing theologies before using one of them for the contemplation of the Word. . . . This may seem an anti-ecumenical programme but . . . it can lead to a greatly enriched understanding and to a unity of life and a tension of thought much more alive than committee-framed and majority-accepted formula'.[12]

It was in this firm belief that the great truths of all religions point in the same direction that I first became interested in what seemed to me the many arresting correspondences between the teachings of Vedanta and *The Cloud of Unknowing*. It will only be possible in this paper to point to a few of them. I accept entirely William Johnstone's caveat that 'we must never overlook the great fact of tradition', and that we

78

may be wandering into serious error 'if we casually take similar words and phrases from [different cultures] and conclude that the underlying thought is the same'.[13] Yet it is precisely that having allowed for 'the great fact of tradition' and going beyond it to what is timeless, that we can discover a fundamental unity which transcends the divisions of culture and tradition.

Fundamental Teachings

In terms of basic teaching there is a wide area of agreement, although the terminology may often differ. First and foremost, both *The Cloud* and Vedanta have, as the heart and centre of their teaching, the idea of a supreme being. The Christian author calls it God, and behind his teaching lies the doctrine of the holy trinity. The Upanishads speak of spirit, of self, of God. God is known as both *Brahman*, the universal lord of all, and as *Ātman*, the indwelling spirit, hidden in the heart of every man. *Brihadāranyaka Upanishad* says unequivocally, 'Self (i.e. *Ātman*) is God. Therefore one should worship Self as Love. Who worships Self as Love, his love shall never perish'.[14] *Brahman* is that same God as the supreme being, of whom the *Katha Upanishad* says 'God is the goal; beyond Him nothing',[15] and the *Aitereya Upanishad* directs, 'His aim is truth; His will is truth. Find Him, know Him'.[16] Thus the follower of Vedanta may worship God within him, in his innermost heart; or he may worship him as everywhere, immanent in his creation; or he may worship him as transcendent, beyond everything. Ultimately, as the real saint discovers, it is all one.

The *Cloud*-author speaks of the soul being 'onyd wiþ God'. Vedanta often refers to this as 'liberation'; the *Geeta* speaks of being 'one with the Everlasting'.[17] The meaning is the same. And both are agreed that the true end and aim of human life is to seek this union. 'Þis is the werk of þe soule þat moste plesiþ God',[18] the *Cloud*-author tells his disciple. And again, 'Þis is the werk . . . in þe whiche man schuld have contynowed ʒif he neuer had synned, & to þe whiche worching man was maad, & alle þing for man, to help him & forþer him þerto'.[19] The *Srīmad Bhāgavatam* says 'The ideal to which all Vedas point, the goal of all sacrifices and Yogas, of all work, knowledge and austerities, the very truth of all religions, is the Lord of Love. There is no other goal but He'.[20] The great sixth-century philosopher and teacher, Shankara, goes so far as to say that the man who fails to seek liberation in God 'verily commits suicide'. 'What greater fool is there', he asks, 'than the man who . . . neglects to achieve the real end

79

of this life'.[21] Again, the *Cloud*-author says that the 'meeke steryng of loue' in the heart is 'þe substaunce of alle good leuyng, & wiþ-outen it no good werk may be bygonne ne eendid'.[22] Shrī Krishna tells Arjuna, 'Spirituality is the real art of living'. Once more, the thought is the same.

It should be stressed that this 'liberation' is not some sort of void in which *I* ceases to exist. 'It is not a state of nothingness, but one of activity, full of freedom and perfection'.[23] It is not a question of losing one's individuality, as westerners often seem to think, rather that the person moves out of his small, selfish, separate ego, and becomes instead gloriously aware of his true self which, shedding all its limitations and imperfections, somehow miraculously becomes 'onyd with God'. The idea is not really in the least unfamiliar to Christians. Herbert Slade, in his *Exploration into Contemplative Prayer*, says that in the experience of contemplation 'the independent ego (is) transcended'.[24] In this state, the person is no longer conscious of any separation between his own self and God, or indeed between himself and all creatures. He has become one with the all. The *Cloud*-author describes it as being 'vtterly spoylid of þi-self & nakidly cloþed in hymself as he is'.[25] He goes on to say:

> Þis siȝt & þis felyng of God, þus in hym-self as he is, may no more be departyd from God in hym-self . . . þen may be departyd God him-self fro his owne beyng, þe whiche ben bot one boþe in substaunce & also in kynde. So þat as God may not be fro his beyng for onheed in kynde, so may not þat soule, þat þus seeþ & feliþ, be fro þat þing þat he þus seeþ & feliþ for onheed in grace.[26]

There are many descriptions in Vedanta literature of souls who have attained this spiritual level. For example, from the *Srīmad Bhāgavatam*:

> Utkala chose the life of renunciation and solitude, realising that the divine Self exists in all human beings, and that all beings exist in the divine Self. His heart found itself united with all things. All his worldly desires were burned in the fire of knowledge. He was filled with great love for God, and enjoyed peace ineffable. He lived in the consciousness of God during his entire life, aware of nothing but the divine *Ātman*, and spent his days teaching words of wisdom and singing the praises of the Lord.[27]

Of this experience of unity, the *Cloud*-author says, 'Trewly I telle þee þat ȝif a soule, þat is þus ocupied, had tonge & language to sey as it feliþ, þan alle þe clerkes of Christendome schuld wondre on þat wisdam'.[28] The same inarticulate wonder comes across in words of the disciple of *The Crest Jewel of Wisdom* upon attaining the supreme reality:

> Thought has ceased, activity of desire has fallen away, through the oneness of the Eternal and the Self, through illumination; I know not this; I know naught other than this; what is it? how great? It is shoreless joy![29]

Christianity, of course, stops short of saying, '*Tat twam asi* – Thou art That'. To say, 'I am God' is, to the Christian, madness and heresy. But it should be understood that when Vedanta says, '*Jīvo brahmaiva nāpara*' – the individual soul is no other than the universal God, Brahman – it does not mean that the ego (*ahankara*), the small, separate, false self is God. Christianity tends not to make a distinction between the limited ego or *me*, and the unlimited, immortal Ātman, the real *I*, the indwelling spirit of God. It is the Ātman—the true, innermost, incorruptible self—of which it is said '*Aham Brahmāsmi*'— I am the Brahman. So when the *Cloud*-author says,

> For þat þou arte þou hast of him & he it is. & þof al þou haddest a biginnyng in þi substancyal creacion, þe which was sumtime nouȝt, ȝit haþ þi being ben euer-more in hym wiþ-outyn beginnyng & euir schal be wiþ-outyn ending, as himself is,[30]

any Vedantist would recognise at once the teaching of his own tradition. The central idea of Vedanta is that the soul cannot be other than the Brahman, because nothing can exist outside Brahman. As the *Cloud*-author says, 'For as noþing may be wiþ-outyn him, so may he not be wiþ-outyn him-self. He is being boþe to him-self & to alle'.[31] And he tells his disciple. 'He is þi being, & in him þou arte þat at þou arte, not only bi cause & bi being, bot also he is in þee boþe þi cause & þi beyng',[32] just as Nārada teaches his pupils, 'He is the Self of all created beings. He is the efficient cause as well as the material cause of the universe. He is the Supreme, the Lord of the Universe'.[33] Nor would Vedanta find any difficulty with the *Cloud*-author's caveat.

> Euermore saving þis difference bitwix þee & him, þat he is þi being & þou not his. For þof it be so þat alle þings ben in him bi cause & bi beyng & he be in alle þinges here cause & here being, ȝit in him-self only he is his owne cause & his owne being.[34]

The *Geeta* expresses the self-same idea. Lord Shrī Krishna tells Arjuna: 'Know thou that my Superior nature is the very Life which sustains the universe. It is the womb of all being; for I am He by whom the worlds were created and shall be dissolved'.[35] But he also says:

> The whole world is permeated by Me, yet My form is not seen. All living

things have their being in Me, yet I am not limited by them. Nevertheless, they do not consciously abide in Me. Such is My Divine Sovereignty that though I, the Supreme Self, am the cause and upholder of all, yet I remain outside.[36]

And again, 'They are in Me, but I am not in them'.[37]

The way in which the *Cloud*-author conceives of God, and his great love of paradox, are very much in keeping with the spirit of Vedanta. For example, to a too literal-minded disciple he says,

> For silence is not God, ne speking is not God; fastyng is not God, ne etyng is not God; onliness is not God ne companye is not God; ne ȝit any of alle oþir soche two contraries. He is hid betwix hem, and may not be founden by any werk of þi soule, bot al only bi loue of þin herte. . . . Chese þee him; and þou arte silently spekyng & spekyngly silent, fastyngly etyng and etyngly fasting; and so forþ of alle þe remenant.[38]

The idea is immediately reminiscent of the Vedic teaching that '*neti, neti* – not this, not this', is all we may say of God. We cannot know *what* God is, only *that* he is. The series of teasing paradoxes may be compared with many passages in the Upanishads. For example:

> The Self is One. Unmoving, it moves faster than the mind. The senses lag, but Self runs ahead. Unmoving, it outruns pursuit. . . . Unmoving, it moves; is far away, yet near; within all, outside all.[39]

Questions about where God is, or what he is, meet with the same paradoxical answers – 'spirit is everywhere, upon the right, upon the left, above, below, behind, in front. What is the world but Spirit'.[40] Our author takes the same idea, but expresses it in its negative sense: 'Bot þus wil I bid þee. Loke on no wyse þat þou be wiþ-inne þi-self. & schortly wiþeutyn þi-self wil I not þat þou be, ne ȝit abouen, ne be-hynde, ne on o side, ne on oþer'. No wonder the poor disciple cries, 'Wher þan . . . schal I be? Noȝwhere, by þi tale!' to which his master gleefully replies, 'Now truly þou seist wel; for þere wolde I haue þee. For whi noȝwhere bodely is euerywhere goostly'.[41] He goes on to play, with much skill and evident delight, with the ideas of nowhere and everywhere, nothing and all. The point is that the 'inner man' sees quite differently from our habitual mode of regarding things from the standpoint of outer sense perception. To find the truth we have to look within, seeing with the eyes of the 'inner man' that what we have been calling *nothing* is in reality *all*. The need to look inward, beyond habitual thinking, to find the truth is expressed in many ways in Vedic writings. The *Mundaka Upanishad* says, 'Truth lies beyond imagination, beyond paradise; great, smaller than the smallest; near, further than the furthest; hiding from the traveller in the cavern'.[42] And in the *Katha Upanishad* we find, 'God made sense turn outward, man therefore looks outward, not into himself. Now and again a daring soul, desiring immortality, has looked back and found himself'.[43] The *Cloud*-author constantly stresses the 'within-ness' of God. For example, he teaches his disciple to try, as he puts it, to hide his longing from God, in order to achieve a deepening of it, a movement inwards: 'For þou wost wel þat alle þat is wilfully helid, it is casten into þe depnes of spiryt'.[44] And he explains that, 'þe more þat þi spirit haþ of goostliness, þe lesse it haþ of bodelines & þe nerer it is God . . . forþi it is more liche vnto hym, when it is in purete of spirit, for he is a spirit'.[45] The direction in which God is to be found is within, in the innermost depth of the soul. The idea of God as being something hidden, the ultimate secret, occurs again and again in the Vedic writings, which commonly use the metaphor of the cavern, meaning the heart. The wise, meditating on God (i.e. in our terms, contemplating him), concentrating their thought, discovering in the mouth of the cavern, deeper in the cavern, that Self, that ancient Self, difficult to imagine, more difficult to understand, pass beyond joy and sorrow'.[46]

The *Cloud*-author, following Dionysius, teaches that God is beyond name. Whatever qualities or attributes we may ascribe to him, 'al it is hid & enstorid in þis litil worde IS'.[47] Over and over again he encourages the disciple not to try to analyse either himself or God. He is simply to offer himself, as he is, up to God as he is: 'þat at I am, Lorde, I offre vnto þee, for þou it arte', he is to say to God, and he is to think 'nakidly, pleinly & boistously þat þou arte as þou arte, wiþ-outyn any maner of corioustee'.[48] All divisions, all 'scateryng & departyng' is strongly discouraged. Naked, simple being in its wholeness is the concept upon which he is to fix his attention – I am, God is. This is very close in spirit to the teaching of Vedanta that God is to be found, not in this or that, but in pure being. Nārada tells King Yudhishtira:

The Ātman alone IS, One without a second. The Ātman alone is Reality. . . . He who follows the path of the contemplative life knows his Self as divine and as one with God. God is the beginning, he is the middle, and he is the end. He is the enjoyer and he is the object enjoyed. He is the high and he is the low. He is the knower and he is the known. He is the word spoken and he is the breath which speaks it. He is the manifest and he is the unmanifest. The man following this path realises that God alone IS, that there is nothing apart from him or beyond him.[49]

The Benedictine, Henri Le Saux, alias Abhishiktananda, brings eastern and western teaching on this point beautifully together:

> Our inner experience of God should be of him as a first person, the one and only I. As long as we try to reach God by forming concepts of him and thereby making him an object, we cannot find him. He is only to be found in the experience of my own I, which is a participation (and not an outward projection) of the *I* of God.[50]

On the uselessness of 'corious lerning' for the attainment of this inner experience – a favourite theme of the *Cloud*-author's – the Vedic scriptures are also eloquent and emphatic. The *Mundaka Upanishad* states: 'The Self is not known through discourse, splitting of hairs, learning, however great. He comes to the man He loves; takes that man's body as His own'.[51] And Shankara comments wrily 'Well uttered speech, a waterfall of words, skill in expounding the scriptures and erudite learning – these merely bring a little personal enjoyment to the scholar – but are no good for liberation'.[52]

How then does a man find God? *The Cloud* teaches: 'By loue may he be getyn & holden';[53] therefore 'Lift vp þin herte vnto God wiþ a meeke steryng of loue'.[54] The author lays great stress on this – love alone can find God. Nor must it be a love tainted with any self-interest – the aspirant must love God for himself alone. In the *Srīmad Bhāgavatam* we find this:

> The highest religion of man is unselfish love of God. If one has this love, one attains to truly divine wisdom. Fruitless is that knowledge which is not love. Fruitless is religion itself, if it have not love. Vain indeed is all struggle for spiritual life if in one's heart there be not love.[55]

The *Cloud*-author stresses love, rather than knowledge, as the way to God. William Johnstone points out that in fact he is dealing with two kinds of knowledge: a lower, conceptual knowledge, the knowledge of 'creatures', and a higher, loving knowledge – a knowing through loving, by which God may indeed be known. The lower knowledge, though it may teach us something of God by analogy, is imperfect. The higher knowledge 'in favor of which it is abandoned is supraconceptual, existential, mystical; it is given by God himself'.[56] Vedanta teaches exactly this; the *Mundaka Upanishad* says:

> Those who know Spirit say that there are two kinds of knowledge, a lower and a higher. The lower is the knowledge of the four Veda, and such things as pronunciation, ceremonial, grammar, etymology, poetry, astronomy. The higher knowledge is the knowledge of the Everlasting.[57]

It is, so to speak, an understood thing in the Vedantic tradition that in deep meditation the soul is fed with this divine knowledge; indeed it is implicity understood that this direct, God-given knowledge, realised within the soul, is the only truly meaningful kind of knowledge; all else, all outward knowledge, is mere information. As the *Cloud*-author says, in comparison with this 'hiȝe goostly wisdom', mere natural knowledge is 'bot feyndid foly formyd in fantome, as fer fro þe verrey soþfastnes whan þe goostly sonne schiniþ as is þe derknes of þe moneschine in a mist at midwinters niȝt fro þe briȝtnesse of þe sonne-beme in þe clerest tyme of missomer day'.[58]

The *Cloud*-author takes considerable pains to expound to his pupil the Church's traditional teaching on the two lives, active and contemplative. We find, again, a parallel statement in the *Geetā*: 'In this world there is a two-fold path, O Sinless One! There is the Path of Wisdom for those who meditate, and the Path of Action for those who work'.[59] And it is similarly taught that no-one has the right merely to abandon his duty in the world and simply refrain from action because it pleases him, or because he thinks inaction superior to action. All obligations must be fulfilled. The important thing is for each person to follow the path that is appropriate for him. It is for the spiritual preceptor to guide his pupils into the right path, according to their disposition. We find exactly the same situation in *A Pistle of Discrecioun of Stirings*, where the young disciple is urged not to rush into taking upon him the way of life and the disciplines which at the moment attract him without the guidance of a properly qualified spiritual teacher. For the *Cloud*-author, as for the followers of Vedanta, obedience to the teacher, or *guru*, is of the greatest importance. Concerning those who misunderstand or criticise seekers following the contemplative path, there is again a very similar attitude. It has, first of all, to be accepted that the truly spiritual person – the real seeker – is something of a rarity. The *Geetā* says: 'One hears of the Spirit with surprise, another thinks it marvellous, the third listens without comprehending. Thus, though many are told about It, scarcely is there one who knows It'.[60] However, the Lord Shrī Krishna instructs, 'A wise man should not perturb the minds of the ignorant, who are attached to action. Let him perform his own actions in the right spirit with concentration on Me, thus inspiring all to do the same'.[61] The *Cloud*-author, for all he may grow impatient with the 'half-mekyd soulys'[62] who refuse to understand, expresses much the same idea when he tells his young disciple that actives have always been critical of those who follow the contemplative path, because they cannot see the point of it: '& þerfore me þinkeþ alweis þat þei schuld be had

85

excused, for whi þei knowen no betir leuyng þen is þat þei liue in þeim-self'.[63]

Beyond the broad classification of active/contemplative, the path of action and the path of wisdom, it is not easy to equate the various divisions and classifications of the spiritual life in the Vedic system with those of fourteenth-century Christendom, though there is plainly – as common sense would say there must be – some correspondence between them. The *Cloud*-author speaks of 'foure degrees & fourmes of Cristen mens leuyng . . . Comoun, Special, Singuler, & Parfite'.[64] The traditional four states of the seeker of God in India are the student – the *brahmachārin* who pursues a life of strict purity and discipline, living in the master's house and serving him while being instructed by him; then the householder, who takes upon him the duties pertaining to life in the world; then the forest-dweller, who, having discharged all his obligations, retires to a life of seclusion and uninterrupted spiritual pursuit; and finally the *sannyāsin*, the renunciate, who, leaving behind him all desires and limitations achieves perfection. The special life, where the disciple becomes a 'seruaunt of þe special seruauntes of his' and learns to 'liue more specialy & more goostly in his seruise'[65] obviously has some affinities with the life of the celibate *brahmachārin*. The life of the householder would of course be what Hilton describes as 'mixed life'. The forest-dweller is analogous to the Christian solitary, and the idea of the perfect life must presumably be similar to that of the renunciate, the perfected soul.

Also taught in Vedanta are three distinct paths to God, which are suited to men of different temperament: *Karma Yoga* – the path of works, in which ritual and sacrament play a very important part; *Bhakti Yoga*, the path of devotion, faith and self-surrender – this is obviously a very strong element in the *Cloud*-author's teaching; and *Jnana Yoga*, the path of knowledge. Of this third path, Srī Bhāratī Krishna Tirthajī told his American audience:

> The third path is the path of absolute illumination, where the person rises above and transcends all possibility of being subject to joys and sorrows. He is called a saint or sage and is at a much higher level than the ordinary run of humanity. He has reached a rung on the spiritual ladder for which very few people would think of competing with him.[66]

This path seems not unrelated to the *via negativa*, and the knowledge or wisdom which is its characteristic is surely none other than that 'souereyn-schining derknes of wisest silence'[67] which may only be reached

86

þorou þe ouerpassyng of þiself and alle oþer þinges, and þus makyng þiself clene fro al worldly, fleschly, & kyndely likyng in þin affeccioun, and fro al þing þat may be knowen by þe propre fourme in þi knowyng [by which] þou schalt be drawen up abouen mynde in affecioun to þe souereyn-substancyal beme of þe godliche derknes, alle þinges þus done awey.[68]

Teachers of Vedanta always point out that these three paths are not to be thought of as exclusive, however. By whatever spiritual path a man may travel, he needs all these three ways, at least to some degree.

Psychology

The world picture of the medieval church is in many ways not unlike that of Vedanta philosophy. In particular, the *Cloud*-author's system of human psychology, which he expounds in considerable detail, has many correspondences with Vedanta. The fundamental division of the two 'principal worching miȝtes'[69] of the soul – the power of knowing, and the power of loving – is fully recognised by Vedanta, which differs however from the *Cloud*-author's teaching in maintaining that God may be found through both; there is a path of knowledge and a path of love. Ultimately, they are held to be indivisible—love is knowledge and knowledge is love— but the aspirant only discovers this when he has almost reached his goal. Certainly, almost all teachers agree that for this age, the age we live in (which, according to the Vedic system of cosmic time, includes the whole Christian era), the way of love is the best and surest path.

In chapters 62 to 66 of *The Cloud*, the author explains the various powers of the soul, which, he says, has three principal powers: mind, reason and will; and two secondary: imagination and sensuality; and these are in a hierarchical arrangement in relation to each other. Mind contains all the other four. Reason is the discriminative faculty; it separates good from evil, truth from untruth. Will is the power which enables the soul to choose goodness and truth, when reason has presented them to it. Imagination deals in 'ymages of absent & present þinges',[70] having the power of picturing what is not immediately physically visible. Sensuality is the power residing in the five senses. Vedanta presents a scheme markedly similar, though not exactly corresponding, to this. Man, according to this system, lives in his body, which is 'like a house to the householder'[71] equipped with five organs of action (hands, feet etc.), five organs of knowledge (ears, eyes etc.), five senses (hearing, touch etc.),—or, as the *Cloud*-author would say five 'bodely' and five 'goostly wittes'—and five breaths, or divisions of

87

prāna, the force of life itself. Then, next in order of subtlety, there is *manas*, the discursive mind, which connects the inner and outer worlds, acting as a sort of messenger to the soul; this seems to have some affinity with 'imagination'. *Buddhi*, the intellect, determines the truth or untruth of what *manas* presents to it, and exercises judgement; and this seems to correspond with both will and reason. Then there is *ahaṅkāra*, the sense of existence, which the *Cloud*-author, though he does not mention it as one of the powers of the soul, nonetheless speaks about a great deal as 'the feeling of thyself'. *Chitta*, sometimes translated as 'mind's mother substance', sometimes as 'soul' and sometimes as 'heart', is the seat of the emotions and of memory, and contains both pure and impure substance. According to its state of purity, it is said to reflect the light of truth, or God, within. All this, *manas*, *buddhi*, *anaṅkāra* and *chitta*, are contained within the *antahkarana*, the inner organ of mind, which appears to correspond with what the *Cloud*-author calls 'mind', which he says 'conteneþ & comprehendeþ in it-self'[72] all the other powers. All these faculties, with the subtle senses, constitute the subtle body of man; his outward body of flesh is the gross body. Vedanta speaks of a third body, a casual or spiritual body, which consists of *avyakta*, the unmanifest, that which exists within in potential, or essence, but is not manifest. This causal body is, as it were, the blue-print for the human being. As the name implies, it is his cause, his essential innermost being, and is immortal. The *Cloud*-author speaks of this causal body in *Privy Counselling*: 'þof al þou haddest a biginnyng in þi substancyal creacion, þe whiche was sumtyme nou3t, 3it haþ þi being ben euermore in hym wiþ-outyn beginnyng & euer schal be wiþ-outen ending, as himself is'.[73]

In the same way that the *Cloud*-author spells out the hierarchy of the soul's faculties, so the *Katha Upanishad* tells us, 'Mind is above sense, intellect above mind, nature above intellect, the unmanifest above nature. Above the unmanifest is God, unconditioned, filling all things. He who finds Him enters immortal life, becomes free'.[74] This passage calls to mind the *Cloud*-author's explanation, in chapter 67, of how the body and senses are 'bineþe þi-self', the 'sotil condicions of þe my3tes of þi soule' are 'wiþ-inne þi-self & euen wiþ þi-self', but God alone is 'abouen þi-self'.[75] His teaching, also, on how the inner faculties should each in turn be obedient to the higher powers, so that there is a hierarchy of control and service, is paralleled in the *Katha Upanishad*:

> Self rides in the chariot of the body, intellect the firm-footed charioteer, discursive mind the reins. Senses are the horses, objects of desire the roads.

. . . When a man lack steadiness, unable to control his mind, his senses are unmanageable horses. But if he control his mind, a steady man, they are manageable horses. . . . He who calls intellect to manage the reins of his mind reaches the end of his journey, finds there all-pervading Spirit.[76]

The Tradition of Spiritual Instruction

There are certain formal and traditional aspects of Vedanta in which similarities with the *Cloud*-author's teaching may be found. One of the most striking characteristics of the literature of Vedanta and the tradition from which it springs is the question – *prashna*. The disciple asks the question, and it is that which draws forth the knowledge and spiritual instruction from the teacher. One finds questions over and over again, sometimes whole rows of them. Without a question, it is held, there can be no answer, no spiritual progress. Thus in the opening verse of the *Kena Upanishad* we find, 'The enquirer asked: "What has called my mind to the hunt? What has made my life begin? What wags in my tongue? What God has opened eye and ear?" '[77], whereupon the teacher begins to instruct him. The *Cloud*-author also works on this principal. The four epistolary works are by implication, and sometimes explicitly, written in answer to the disciple's question. And throughout these works there are passages of imagined dialogue where the disciple puts a question at some crucial point in the exposition, thus providing an occasion for a fuller explanation.

By the same token, enormous importance is given in Vedanta to the tradition of teacher and pupil, or *guru* and disciple. There are many descriptions of the qualifications of a proper spiritual teacher, the main criterion being that he should himself be a knower of God. The *Mundaka Upanishad* recommends for the man who aspires to liberation: 'Let him go to some teacher who lives in Spirit and in whom revelation lives. To such a pupil, humble, master of mind and sense, the teacher can teach all he knows, bringing him to the Deathless'.[78] One is reminded of the *Cloud*-author's frequent gentle reminders to his pupil to 'meek hym to counsel'. It is obvious from a reading of the *Cloud*-author's works, even without the evidence of other contemporary writers, that we are dealing with a well-established tradition of teaching and discipleship, in which the rules are understood and accepted. One finds the same thing in Vedanta. The *Taittiriya Upanishad* puts it forcefully: 'Learning and teaching they are austerity; they are austerity'.[79] In other words, they are in themselves a sacred observance. This is the two-fold spiritual discipline, to be carried out by all men of spiritual life, whatever other duties they may have.

Another tradition which the *Cloud*-author and Vedanta both honour is that of the invocation and dedication to God at the outset of any work. *The Cloud of Unknowing*'s 'preyer on þe prologue', and the opening of the prologue itself with an invocation to the Trinity finds a parallel at the head of all the Upanishads, and indeed of every work of Hindu religion, philosophy, science or art. The blessing of God (sometimes, to be sure, in the form of a particular deity) is always invoked, and the work to be undertaken, its purpose and intention having been stated, is dedicated to him.

Also paralleled is the warning against allowing esoteric spiritual teaching to fall into the wrong hands. All teachers of Vedanta (all genuine ones) insist on the importance of using their teaching responsibly, and on the more powerful parts of it – such as detailed instruction on advanced meditation and spiritual exercises – being given by proper initiation only to qualified pupils by qualified teachers. Thus the lord Shrī Krishna admonishes Arjuna, 'Speak not this to one who has not practised austerities, or to him who does not love, or will not listen, or who mocks'.[80] Sometimes the charge of exclusivity has been laid at the *Cloud*-author's door. But the tradition, and the reasons for it, are as old as man.

Imagery

Even in terms of imagery there are similarities to be found. The metaphor of a cloud obscuring the light of the sun appears in many texts – though always in the context of its being soon to be dispersed. The *Cloud*-author, of course, was used to English weather! Thus we have Patanjali, after explaining a particular yogic exercise, stating, 'Then that cloud that obscures light melts away; and mind becomes fit for attention'.[81] And in *World Within the Mind*, 'The error of egotism is like a dark cloud: it hides the bright disc of the moon of truth in its gloom and causes the shining moonbeams to disappear'.[82] Neither of these uses seem quite the same as that of the English author – a cloud of ignorance is obviously not quite the same as a cloud of unknowing. The metaphor which is more commonly used, and is much closer in concept is that of the 'cavern'; 'Shining, yet hidden, Spirit lives in the cavern'.[83] The metaphor of light and darkness, as one might expect, pervades all the writings. Speaking of the eternal spirit, Shrī Krishna says, 'It is the light of lights, beyond the reach of darkness; the Wisdom, the only thing that is worth knowing or that wisdom can teach; the Presence in the hearts of all'.[84] Sea and storm imagery is also used in a similar way to the *Cloud*-author's. For example, the *Geetā* says, 'As a ship at sea is tossed by the tempest, so the reason is carried away by the mind when preyed upon by the straying senses';[85] to which we may compare, 'For sodenly, er euer þou wite, alle is awey, & þou leuyst bareyn in þe bote, blowyn with blundryng, now heder now þedir, þou wost neuir where ne wheder'.[86]

Practical Teachings

If we turn to matters of practice, we shall again find many points of contact. For example, there is the question of needful preparation for contemplation, to which the *Cloud*-author devotes considerable attention. The disciple must, before he may undertake this 'work', have acquired a degree or self-knowledge; the eager young man of *A Pistle of Discrecioun of Stirings* is as good as told that until he has learnt to know himself, his questions can have little relevance. He must also have a certain calmness or psychological balance, 'For it is ful perilous to streine þe kynde to any soche werk of deuocioun . . . bot it be ledde þerto bi grace'.[87] He must have undergone a considerable amount of spiritual training and ascetic discipline – in fact the *Cloud*-author more or less takes it for granted that his pupil has mastered physical disciplines, and hardly concerns himself with them. He must of course have practised vocal prayer, meditation on the passion etc., and study of the scriptures – all activities for the 'prentice contemplative'—and in general have followed all the ordinances of holy church. Then, having made a full confession of his 'before-done' sins, he must set himself from henceforward to root out sin, and to cultivate virtue. Only then, with the approval of his spiritual counsellor, if by calling and dis-position he is found to be one of those 'þat han forsaken þe worild in a trewe wille, & þerto þat ȝeuen hem not to actyue liif, bot to þat liif þat is clepid contemplatyue liif' he may indeed 'dispose him booldly bot meekly þerto'.[88]

All teachers of Vedanta also lay great stress on the need for proper preparation and rigorous training. Self-knowledge, of course, is the very heart of its teaching, though this is understood more in the sense of coming to know or 'realise' one's true self, rather than the false, sinful self with all its failings. For this, however, it is indeed necessary to conquer sinful impulses. The body and senses have to be brought under disciplined control, and the tendency to entertain never-ending desires for all manner of things other than God has gradually to be overcome. To help with all this, there are a great many

91

ascetic practices enjoined by different teachers—including the chant-
ing of prayers and *mantras*, reflecting on the lives and teachings of the
great masters, and studying of the scriptures. In matters of food, sleep,
etc., a wise moderation is enjoined, very much along the same sort of
lines as the *Cloud*-author teaches. Lord Shrī Krishna says:

> Meditation (i.e. contemplation – the Sanskrit word here is *yoga*, which
> means 'union') is not for him who eats too much, nor for him who eats not at
> all: nor for him who is overmuch addicted to sleep, nor for one who is always
> awake. But for him who regulates his food and recreation, who is balanced in
> action, in sleep and in waking, it shall dispel all unhappiness.[89]

The cultivation of virtue and avoidance of sin are also constantly
stressed, and there are many passages throughout the writings of
Vedanta which deal in great detail with the qualities of the godly and of
the ungodly man. The sixteenth chapter of the *Geetā*, for example,
deals exclusively with this subject. The first two steps of Patanjali's
eightfold path of Yoga consist of two sets of rules, or restraints – five
outward, *yama*, and five inward, *niyama*. These are: doing no harm or
injury, speaking the truth, chastity, non-covetousness, not stealing;
and devotion to God, constant study of the scriptures or repetition of
sacred words, discipline, contentment, and purity – physical, mental
and spiritual. Patanjali says of them, 'These are sacred vows, to be
observed, independent of time, place, class or occasion'.[90] In other
words, they are universal. They would be considered the basic,
ordinary virtues which must have been practised and cultivated by
anyone who would seek God. In the same way, the *Cloud*-author
expects his pupils to have tackled, as best they can, the matter of sin
and virtue. Shankara gives a much more exacting list of qualifications
for one who is deemed fit for the highest spiritual work. First comes
discrimination – *viveka*, conviction of the reality of God, as opposed to
the relative unreality of the ever-changing universe; as for the *Cloud*-
author's disciple, God must be supreme and all other things 'fer put
bac'. Secondly, there is renunciation – *vairagya*, the giving up of
transitory enjoyments, sometimes expressed as 'surrendering the fruit
of one's actions'; this is certainly implied in the decision to pursue the
solitary and contemplative life. Thirdly, there is a list of six virtues as
follows: calmness, or the ability to rest the attention on God – the
Cloud-author's strictures against 'goostly rudenes' are relevant here;
self-control, or the ability to withdraw the senses from their objects;
ceasing to be affected by worldly matters – like his fourteenth-century
English counterpart, the disciple of Vedanta must guard against his
mind being 'ocupied wiþ any bodely þing',[91] forbearance, or being

unaffected by affliction – there are obvious parallels with the *Cloud*-author again here, such as the advice to 'bere þee by meek suffryng'[92] the wild fluctuations in inner state described in *Privy Counselling*; faith; and 'self-settledness', or the constant concentration of the mind and heart upon God, which in itself is the very subject of *The Cloud of Unknowing* and *Privy Counselling*. Fourth, last and most important of the qualifications is *mumukshutā*, the true longing for God, without which very little spiritual development is possible. One is reminded of the *Cloud*-author's statement, 'Alle þi liif now behoueþ algates to stonde in desire, 3if þou schalt profite in degre of perfeccion'.[93]

All of this no doubt sounded as daunting and difficult to Shankara's disciples as the *Cloud*-author's similar instructions to his. But just as the *Cloud*-author teaches that 'þis blinde steryng of loue . . . distroieþ not only þe grounde & þe rote of sinne . . . bot þerto it geteþ vertewes',[94] and that indeed all the virtues are 'sotely comprehendid'[95] within it— from which it follows of course that in the very practice of it the virtues required for its success will be acquired naturally—so in the *Srīmad Bhagavatam* we find this encouraging statement:

Complete transformation of the inner life is necessary; and this is accomplished by the control of the mind and the senses, by the practice of concentration, and by following and living the Truth. The great secret of this complete transformation is the development of love for God. As when the sun rises the dewdrops vanish away, so when love grows all sin and ignorance disappear.[96]

The practice of loving in itself accomplishes the preparation of the soul. It purifies the soul at the same time as leading it deeper within itself. The *Srīmad Bhágavatam* continues, 'Even the most sinful man is purified if he surrenders himself to the God of Love'.[97] One is reminded of the *Cloud*-author's comment that 'oftymes it befalliþ þat somme, þat haue ben orrible & customable synners, comen sooner to þe perfeccion of þis werk þen þoo þat ben none. & þis is þe mercyful myracle of our Lorde'.[98] Later, in answer to the disciple's understandable desire to know how long the work is going to take, he explains that there are some for whom it seems to be easy and natural, because they are 'so sotyl in grace & in spirit, & so homely wiþ God in þis grace of contemplacion':[99] and some for whom a great deal of hard and persistent work is required before they can experience 'þe perfeccion of þis werk'.[100] Vedanta notes the same phenomenon, but explains it differently. Shrī Purohit Swāmi, in his commentary on

Patanjali's *Aphorisms of Yoga*, says this: 'They who have not earned it in their past lives, have to make their effort in the present. Some people attain miraculous powers when they are young, while old men who have tried all their life have hardly got any. The former inherited it as a legacy from their previous life: the latter have just found the path'.[101]

The topic which perhaps exercises the *Cloud*-author more than any other is the control of the mind. Unless the thought processes can be persuaded to cease their activity and become still, contemplation cannot proceed. In the east as in the west, this is the great barrier to spiritual attainment. Discipline of the body is a relatively easy matter. It is the subduing of the mind's ceaseless movement beneath a 'cloud of forgetting', and its concomitant, indifference to worldly desires and attachments, that present the aspirant with his greatest challenge. The *Cloud*-author plainly expects his disciple to find this aspect of the work extremely difficult. He devotes a great deal of attention to ways of dealing with the thoughts that persistently intrude upon the would-be contemplative. For instance, to the thought which would question, and perhaps therefore undermine, the whole basis of his efforts, the disciple is to give a firm, put-down answer: 'Him I coueite, him I seche, & no3t bot him'.[102] Arjuna is expected to encounter similar difficulty: 'O Arjuna! The mind of him who is trying to conquer it is forcibly carried away in spite of his efforts, by his tumultuous senses'.[103] And the answer, in substance, is the same: 'Restraining them all, let him meditate steadfastly on Me'.[104] Again, just as the *Cloud*-author teaches that the fatal mistake is to listen to the thought in the first place: 'Þe cause of þis scateryng is þat þou herddist him first wilfuly, answerdist im, resceiuedist him & letist him allone',[105] so Shankara warns: 'Not a moment's respite should be given to [your enemy] by thinking on the sense-objects. That is verily the cause of its coming back to life, like water to a citron tree that has almost dried up'.[106] The English author's dire warning, in *The Cloud*, chapter 10, of what may happen if the seeker wilfully indulges in thinking – how he may be led, step by step, into mortal sin – is also paralleled by Shankara: 'If the mind ever so slightly strays from [God] and becomes outgoing, then it goes down and down, just as a playball inadvertently dropped on the staircase bounds down from one step to another'.[107] In Vedanta this question of bringing the mind to heel is seen as being central to any kind of spiritual progress. The *Srīmad Bhāgavatam* teaches that 'Mind alone is the cause of bondage or freedom of the soul. By the attachment of the mind to the world we become bound; by the devotion of the mind to God we become free'.[108] Indeed Patanjali states with categorical simplicity that 'Yoga is controlling the activities of the mind'.[109]

Perhaps the most striking resemblance to the practical teachings of Vedanta lies in the *Cloud*-author's apparently highly original instruction on the 'litil worde' which the disciple is to fasten to his heart, 'so þat it neuer go þens for þing þat befalleþ'.[110] As John Main points out in *Word Into Silence*, the practice described in *The Cloud* is rooted in an ancient and venerable Christian tradition, with which the west has all but lost touch.[111] It may well be that the practice was still, in the fourteenth century, in widespread use, and that but for the unusual circumstance of the *Cloud*-author being, for whatever reason, unable to instruct his disciple by word of mouth, and therefore being constrained to resort to letter writing, we should know nothing about it. If the oriental traditions of *namajapa* – repetition of the name of God – and meditation with *mantra* are anything to go by, it would normally have been something which was taught strictly orally. One finds very few detailed or specific references to *mantra* meditation in any of the writings of Vedanta either, but in India of course the tradition is very much alive.[112] In the last twenty years it has been spreading fast in the west also, and indeed has helped to reawaken interest in the Christian church in its ancient traditions of prayer. The kind of spiritual *mantra* that is given for the purpose of meditation, or contemplative prayer, is a rather more precise affair of course than what is implied by the *Cloud*-author's 'Cheese þee wheþer þou wilt, or anoþer as þe list: whiche þat þee likeþ best of o silable'.[113] If the Christian church ever had anything comparable to the extremely precise Hindu science of sound, it must have been lost very early in its history. A *mantra* is a very special word, made up of specific sounds, which has the power to bring about a precise spiritual effect within the person who uses it. It is not simply any word that the person likes or feels would be helpful to him. It is always given to the disciple by the guru who initiates him personally. Nonetheless, in the actual practice the *Cloud*-author is putting forward there is very great similarity with that of *mantra* meditation. The 'litil worde' chosen is to encapsulate all the disciple's thought and emotion, the very essence of his love and desire for God; a *mantra* is similarly concentrated in meaning. The word accomplishes a two-fold purpose. By giving all his attention to it, the disciple prevents the scattering or diversification of his thoughts, thus cutting out distractions; 'Wiþ þis worde þou schalt smite doun al maner þouȝt vnder þe cloude of forȝeting'.[114] It also carries him deeper within himself,

95

closer and closer to the inner silence in which, say the wise, God may be found; 'Wiþ þis worde schalt þou bete on þis cloude & þis derknes abouen þee'.[115] Though a *mantra* may do many things, this is essentially exactly the two-fold effect it is designed to achieve; to cut through the barrier of mental activity, and to take the consciousness deep within, into the silence where it may connect with its own innermost essence and become united with God.

The *Cloud*-author teaches his disciple that while the putting down of thoughts, and in general the work of preparing the soul to receive God is, as it were, his business, yet 'in þinges contemplatyue þe hei3est wisdom þat may be in man . . . is fer put vnder, þat God be þe principal in worching, & man bot only consenter & suffrer'.[116] The actual drawing up of the soul to union is a matter for God's grace. In *The Cloud* the disciple is assured, 'Do on þi werk, & sekirly I behote þee it schal not fayle on hym',[117] for God is 'euermore redy to wirche þis werk in iche a soule þat is disposid þerto'.[118] The teaching of Vedanta is identical to this. Shrī Bhāratī Krishna Tīrthajī Mahārāj, speaking about the need to surrender to God if we would find him, told his audience:

> If you employ an expert driver who knows where to drive you, who knows how to drive you, and who has the will, not merely the will but the eagerness to do anything possible for your speedy attainment of your goal, you shouldn't be interfering and trying to catch hold of the wheel and drive the car according to your own wishes. That would mean danger to yourself and nothing else. The driving has to be given, the wheel has to be handed over to the person having these qualifications.[119]

As far as activity is concerned, here again the attitudes are very similar. The message is that activity *in itself* is indifferent. What matters is the motive for performing it. One acts or does not act according to what may be appropriate. All actions are to be performed for God. 'It is God for whom þou schuldest be stille, 3if þou schuldest be stylle; and for whom þou schuldest speke, 3if þou schuldest speke . . .'.[120] And Shrī Krishna instructs, 'Whatever thou doest, whatever thou dost eat, whatever thou dost sacrifice and give, whatever austerities thou practisest, do all as an offering to Me'.[121] What is more, this very devotion to God and practice of contemplation will of itself teach the soul what is or is not appropriate action.

> Þen þat same þat þou felest schal wel kun telle þee when þou schalt speke and when þou schalt be stille. And it schal governe þee discretly in al þi leuyng withouten any errour, and teche þee mistely how þou schalt beginne

and seese in alle soche doinges of kinde wiþ a grete & souerein dis-crecioun.'[122]

In Vedanta it is taught that the soul gradually learns true discretion – a function of the *buddhi* – through the practice of spiritual disciplines, through meditation, through devotion to God, by all of which means it acquires wisdom.

Both systems also teach that the soul who aspires to God should not become interested in any special powers or spiritual favours. The *Cloud*-author warns against copying 'on ape maner' the outward appearance of holiness observed in others – indeed against spiritual affectation of any kind. He also tells his disciple not to set much store by spiritual 'comforts,' because they are not in fact the goal, but a by-product: '& hereby maist þou see þat we schulde directe alle oure beholdyng vnto þis meek steryng of loue in oure wille. & in alle oþer swetnes & counfortes, bodily or goostly, be þei neuer so likyng ne so holy . . . we schuld haue a maner of rechelesnes'.[123] In the east, as is well known, the masters of yoga attain, through various spiritual practices and techniques, extraordinary occult powers – far beyond anything we know, except perhaps extremely rarely, in the west. Yet the attitude, for the man who desires to find, or to realise, God, is the same as the *Cloud*-author's. Patanjali, having described at some length some of these powers, and their method of attainment, goes on to warn: 'These powers of knowledge are obstacles to illumination'.[124]

The practice of contemplation also begets an attitude of in-difference or detachment with regard to matters which the world considers of high importance. In the *Geeta*, for instance, we find this statement: 'He who desires nothing but wisdom and spiritual insight, who has conquered his senses and who looks with the same eye upon a lump of earth, a stone or fine gold, is the real saint. He looks im-partially on all – lover, friend or foe; indifferent or hostile; alien or relative; virtuous or sinful'.[125] In the same way the *Cloud*-author explains:

In þis werke a parfite worcher haþ no special beholdyng vnto any man by him-self, wheþer þat he be sib or fremmyd, freende or fo. For alle men þink hym iliche sib vnto hym, & no man fremmid. Alle men him þink ben his freendes, & none his foen.[126]

The two aspects of spiritual work which the *Cloud*-author con-stantly stresses–the turning of the mind and heart to God, and, by the same token, the 'forgetting' of all else, are paralleled in Vedanta again and again. The sage Sanatkumara taught King Pritha, 'The following

97

things have been ascertained and declared by all the scriptures of the world to be of the greatest good to mankind'. (We may compare the *Cloud*-author's frequent reassurances that the work is beneficial to others— 'Alle men leuyng in erþe ben wonderfuli holpen of þis werk, þou wost not hou'.[127]) And Sanatkumara goes on to enumerate the two aspects: 'First, to delight in the Self, which is one with God, or to love God. ('Smyte apon þat þicke cloude of vnknowyng wiþ a sharp darte of longing loue'[128]) and secondly to be without attachment to anything else in the universe'.[129] ('& go not þens for þing þat befalleþ'.[130])

There are very many descriptions of the state of contemplation itself in the literature of Vedanta, and many passages of instruction on how to reach it. Krishna tells his beloved disciple, Arjuna:

> Fix thy mind on Me, devote thyself to Me, sacrifice for Me, surrender to Me, make Me the object of thy aspirations, and thou shalt assuredly become one with Me, who am thine own Self.[131]

To the soul who ardently longs for God, he advises:

> Let the student of spirituality try unceasingly to concentrate his mind; let him live in seclusion, absolutely alone, with mind and personality controlled, free from desire and without possessions. . . . With peace in his heart and no fear, observing the vow of celibacy, with mind controlled and fixed on Me, let the student lose himself in contemplation of Me. Thus keeping his mind always in communion with Me, and with his thoughts subdued, he shall attain that Peace which is Mine and which will lead him to liberation at last.[132]

Not so far, surely, from the English author's,

> Lift up þin herte vnto God wiþ a meek steryng of loue; & mene him-self, & none of his goodes, & þerto loke þee loþe to þenk on ouȝt bot on hym-self, so þat nouȝt worche in þi witte ne in þi wille bot only him-self.[133]

and the promise held out at the close of *The Book of Privy Counselling*:

> In þis tyme is þi loue boþe chaste & parfite. In þis tyme it is þat þou both seest þi God & þi loue, & nakidly felist hym also bi goostly onyng to his loue in þe souereyn poynte of þi spirit, as he is in hym-self.[134]

Many thousands of years – no one really knows how long – separate *The Cloud of Unknowing* from the beginnings of Vedanta; a vast gap of culture and tradition stands between them also. Yet in spirit – in the 'souereyn poynte' of the spirit— they seem indeed very close. Perhaps the last word should be given to St Augustine:

> The thing itself which is now called the Christian Religion, was with the ancients, and it was with the human race from its beginning to the time when Christ appeared in the flesh: from when on the true religion, which already existed, began to be called Christian.[135]

NOTES

1. cf. Genesis 1:26.
2. The story is told in *Srīmad Bhāgavatam*, trans. Swāmi Prabhavānanda, Madras, 1972. p. 9. (Hereafter cited as *Srīmad Bhāgavatam*).
3. Psalm 119:129.
4. *The Geeta*, trans. Shri Purohit Swāmi, London 1978, p. 33. (Hereafter cited as *The Geeta*).
5. St. Matthew 5:17,18.
6. Monier Williams, *Indian Wisdom*, Delhi, 1974, p. iv.
7. *Ibid.*, p. xxxiv.
8. His Holiness Jagadguru Shankarācharya Shri Bhāratī Krishna Tīrthajī Mahārāj, *Vedic Metaphysics*, Delhi, 1978, p. 15.
9. For example, St John 14:6.
10. See, for example, Swami Vivekānanda, *What Religion Is*, Calcutta, 1972.
11. Herbert Slade, *Exploration into Contemplative Prayer*, London, 1979, p. 50.
12. *Ibid.*, p. 72.
13. William Johnstone, *The Mysticism of The Cloud of Unknowing*, Wheathampstead, 1978, p. 9.
14. *Ten Principal Upanishads*, trans. Shri Purohit Swāmi and W. B. Yeats, London, 1975, p. 121. (Hereafter cited as *Ten Principal Upanishads*).
15. *Ibid.*, p. 32.
16. *Ibid.*, p. 111.
17. *The Geetā*, p. 40.
18. *The Cloud of Unknowing*, ed. Phyllis Hodgson, Early English Text Society, O.S, 218, London, 1973, p. 16. (All quotations from *The Cloud* are from this edition.)
19. *Ibid.*, p. 19.
20. *Srīmad Bhagavatam*, p. 5.
21. *Vivekachudamani*, (attributed to Shankara Acharya), trans. by Swami Madhavanandu of the Ramakrishna Order, Mayavati 1921, p. 5. (Hereafter cited as *Vivekachudamani*).
22. *The Cloud*, p. 92.
23. K. Bahadur, *The Wisdom of Vaisheshika*, New Delhi, 1979, p. 5.
24. Herbert Slade, *op. cit.*, p. 32.
25. *The Book of Privy Counselling* (ed. Phyllis Hodgson, under the main title of *The Cloud of Unknowing, ed. cit.*) p. 169. (All quotations from *Privy Counselling* are from this edition.)
26. *Ibid.*
27. *Srīmad Bhāgavatam*, p. 65.
28. *Privy Counselling*, p. 153.
29. *The Crest Jewel of Wisdom*, trans. Charles Johnston, London, 1964, p. 73.
30. *Privy Counselling*, p. 144.
31. *Ibid.*, p. 136.
32. *Ibid.*
33. *Srīmad Bhāgavatam*, p. 87.
34. *Privy Counselling*, p. 136.
35. *The Geeta*, p. 47.
36. *Ibid.*, p. 54.
37. *Ibid.*, p. 48.
38. *A Pistle of Discrecioun of Stirings*, in *Deonise Hid Divinite*, ed. Phyllis Hodgson, Early English Text Society, O.S, 231, London, 1958, pp. 71–72. (All quotations from *Stirings* are from this edition.)
39. *Ten Principal Upanishads*, p. 15.
40. *Ibid.*, p. 54.

99

41. *The Cloud*, p. 121.
42. *Ten Principal Upanishads*, p. 55.
43. *Ibid.*, p. 33.
44. *The Cloud*, p. 95.
45. *Ibid.*, p. 89.
46. *Ten Principal Upanishads*, p. 30.
47. *Privy Counselling*, p. 143.
48. *Ibid.*, pp. 136–137.
49. *Srīmad Bhāgavatam*, pp. 152–153.
50. Abhishiktananda (Henri Le Saux), *Prayer*, London, 1977, p. 73.
51. *Ten Principal Upanishads*, p. 56.
52. *Vivekachudamani*, p. 22.
53. *The Cloud*, p. 26.
54. *Ibid.*, p. 16.
55. *Srīmad Bhāgavatam*, p. 9.
56. William Johnstone, *op. cit.*, p. 50.
57. *Ten Principal Upanishads*, pp. 49–50.
58. *Privy Counselling*, p. 146.
59. *The Geeta*, p. 28.
60. *Ibid.*, p. 22.
61. *Ibid.*, p. 30.
62. *Privy Counselling*, p. 149.
63. *The Cloud*, pp. 50–51. The teaching on the nature of action in Vedanta is extremely subtle and does not really correspond with *The Cloud*'s teaching. As Lord Shrī Krishna himself says. 'What is action and what is inaction? It is a question which has bewildered the wise . . . for mysterious is the law of action'. (*The Geeta*, p. 34.) In effect, Vedanta teaches that by offering or surrendering all his actions to God, a man may become free from action, from the iron law of *karma*. He discovers the 'inaction in action' and his actions do not affect or bind him.
64. *The Cloud*, p. 13.
65. *Ibid.*, p. 14.
66. *Vedic Metaphysics*, *op. cit.*, p. 78.
67. *Deonise Hid Divinite*, p. 2.
68. *Ibid.*, p. 3.
69. *The Cloud*, p. 19.
70. *Ibid.*, p. 117.
71. *Vivekachudamani*, p. 33.
72. *The Cloud*, p. 115.
73. *Privy Counselling*, p. 144.
74. *Ten Principal Upanishads*, p. 37.
75. *The Cloud*, pp. 119–120.
76. *Ten Principal Upanishads*, p. 32.
77. *Ibid.*, p. 19.
78. *Ibid.*, p. 52.
79. *Ibid.*, p. 67.
80. *The Geeta*, p. 24.
81. Patanjali, *Aphorisms of Yoga*, trans. Shrī Purohit Swāmi, London, 1975, p. 55.
82. *World Within the Mind* (Extracts from the *Yoga Vasishtha*), trans. H. P. Shastri, London, 1969, p. 34.
83. *Ten Principal Upanishads*, p. 53.
84. *The Geeta*, p. 73.
85. *Ibid.*, p. 26.
86. *Privy Counselling*, pp. 167–168.
87. *Stirings*, p. 67.
88. *The Cloud*, p. 63.

89. *The Geeta*, p. 43.
90. Patanjali, *op. cit.*, p. 53.
91. *The Cloud*, p. 119.
92. *Privy Counselling*, p. 168.
93. *The Cloud*, p. 15.
94. *Ibid.*, p. 39.
95. *Ibid.*, p. 61.
96. *Srīmad Bhāgavatam*, p. 120.
97. *Ibid.*
98. *The Cloud*, p. 64.
99. *Ibid.*, p. 126.
100. *Ibid.*
101. Patanjali, *op. cit.*, p. 36. On the subject of Christianity and re-incarnation see Patrick Blakiston, 'Re-incarnation in Christian Thought', *Wrekin Trust*, No. 71. There are also numerous interesting references to the subject in *Vedic Metaphysics, op. cit.*, and *Autobiography of a Yogi, op. cit.*
102. *The Cloud*, p. 20.
103. *The Geeta*, p. 25.
104. *Ibid.*
105. *The Cloud*, p. 27.
106. *Vivekachudamani*, p. 122.
107. *Ibid.*, p. 127.
108. *Srīmad Bhāgavatam*, p. 42.
109. Patanjali, *op. cit.*, p. 25.
110. *The Cloud*, p. 28.
111. John Main, *Word Into Silence*, London 1980, p. 50.
112. There are, of course, many references to meditation on the sacred word *AUM*—see for example Patanjali, *op. cit.*, p. 38.
113. *The Cloud*, p. 28.
114. *Ibid.*
115. *Ibid.*
116. *Privy Counselling*, p. 163.
117. *The Cloud*, p. 62.
118. *Ibid.*, p. 61.
119. *Vedic Metaphysics, op. cit.*, pp. 269–270.
120. *Stirings*, p. 71.
121. *The Geeta*, p. 56.
122. *Stirings*, p. 75.
123. *The Cloud*, p. 93.
124. Patanjali, *op. cit.*, p. 70.
125. *The Geeta*, pp. 42–43.
126. *The Cloud*, p. 59.
127. *Ibid.*, p. 16.
128. *Ibid.*, p. 26.
129. *Srīmad Bhāgavatam*, p. 70.
130. *The Cloud*, p. 26.
131. *The Geeta*, p. 57.
132. *Ibid.*, p. 43.
133. *The Cloud*, p. 16.
134. *Privy Counselling*, p. 169.
135. St Augustine, *Retractationes*, 1,13.

AUGUSTINE, ANSELM, AND WALTER HILTON

J. P. H. CLARK

THE PRESENT PAPER aims to explore some of the theological background to the contrast which Walter Hilton makes in *Scale* 2 between 'reforming in faith', and 'reforming in feeling'—between bare faith in our salvation, and the illumination of this faith by 'understanding', as our adoption in Christ is increasingly realised.

In Augustine there is a recurrent tension between faith and sight, between belief in God here and now, where our perception of him, and our capacity to respond to him in love, are weakened through Adam's fall, and the open vision of God in heaven. He makes his own the longing, and the anguish, in St Paul's words, which he so often quotes: *Dum sumus in corpore, peregrinamur a Domino; per fidem enim ambulamus, et non per speciem.* (2 Corinthians 5:7). For Augustine, 'the whole life of a good Christian is a holy longing – *sanctum desiderium*.[1] *Species*, the open vision of God, will bring understanding, *intellectus*; in the following passage from *De Doctrina Christiana* Augustine speaks of *intellectus* as belonging, like *species*, to heaven, though he speaks of it elsewhere as in some measure a possibility on earth, just as it is possible even on earth to have some foretaste of the contemplation of God and of eternal things which properly belongs to the life to come. Augustine bases his distinction between faith and understanding upon the old Latin form of Isaiah 7:9, *Nisi credideritis, non intelligetis*, another text which constitutes a *leitmotif* in his writing; he refers to variant renderings of this text:

> So, because understanding consists in eternal sight, faith nourishes us as little children as if with milk while we are cradled in temporal things; yet now *we walk by faith, not by sight*. But unless we have walked by faith, we cannot come to that sight which does not pass away but abides, as, with our understanding cleansed, we cleave to the truth; therefore the one version says, *Unless you believe, you will not abide*, the other, *Unless you believe, you will not understand*.[2]

In his *Tractatus in Iohannis Evangelium*, Augustine expounds the words addressed by Christ to the Samaritan woman. He says that the meaning of Christ's words cannot fall under the cognisance of her five bodily senses of hearing, sight, smell, taste and touch, but only of her understanding. The doctrine of the spiritual senses has its roots already in Origen, and was to have a great future throughout the Middle Ages.[3] Augustine explains that understanding, *intellectus*, is not something separate from the soul, but refers to something in the soul which is proper to man and belongs more particularly to the mind, *mens*, illuminated by the divine light:

> Thus in our soul there is something that is called understanding. This very property of the soul, which is called understanding and mind, is illuminated by a higher light. Now that higher light, by which the human mind is illuminated, is God. For *that was the true light, which illuminates every man that comes into the world.* (John 1:9)[4]

There is a certain interchangeability between *intellectus* and *intelligentia*. Both terms were imposed upon Augustine by the text of Philippians 4:7, *Pax eius quae praecellit omnem intellectum, custodiat corda vestra et intelligentias vestras*, to which he refers in *Ep.* 147.[5] In fact, in various places Augustine uses both terms to refer either to 'understanding' as a faculty within the soul, or else, since he always has a dynamic view of the soul's faculties, to that which is the outcome of this faculty's operation, or of its illumination by God.[6]

Augustine draws regularly on Isaiah 7:9 to show that the humble submission of intellect and will to the truth as revealed by God is the necessary prelude to the illumination of the mind. When he speaks of faith, he has more in mind than simply the intellect's acceptance of facts; to believe, he says, is to think with the assent (of the will).[7] Following St Paul, Augustine sees faith as active through love:

> Understanding is the reward of faith. Therefore do not seek to understand in order that you may believe, but believe in order that you may understand; because, *unless you believe, you will not understand* (Isaiah 7:9). . . . *If anyone will do his will, he shall know concerning the doctrine* (John 7:17). . . . Not just any faith whatever, but *faith that works through love* (Galatians 5:6), let this faith be in you, and you shall understand concerning the doctrine.[8]

A number of passages in Augustine's sermons underline the need to accept God's self-revelation:

> You said, I will understand in order that I may believe; I said, in order that you may understand, believe. The dispute is arisen, let us come to the judge,

let the prophet judge, indeed, let God judge through the prophet. . . . Let the prophet answer, *Unless you believe*, you will not understand.[9]

And, in a passage which Hilton will probably have had in mind:

> If you cannot understand, believe in order that you may understand. Faith goes first, understanding follows, because the prophet says, *Unless you believe, you will not understand.*[10]

Another sermon draws together Isaiah 7:9 with the definition of faith in Hebrews 11:1 to describe the awakening of the interior senses as the light of faith issues in understanding. Augustine holds reason and intuition together; if in some passages he speaks of reason as a property of the mind,[11] he speaks here of reason in the heart:

> The hidden and secret things of the kingdom of God first seek men who believe, that they may make them understand. For faith is a stage of understanding, and understanding is the reward of faith. The prophet says this openly . . . : *Unless you believe, you will not understand.* Therefore also faith itself has a certain light of its own in prophecy, in the Gospel, in the apostolic readings. . . . Therefore *faith is . . . the substance of what we hope for, the conviction of things unseen.* . . . Do not be thankless to him who gave you sight, in order that you may believe what you cannot yet see. God gave you eyes in your body, reason in your heart; arouse the reason of your heart, stir up him who lives within, in your inner eyes. . . .[12]

Faith opens the way to understanding, which gives life to the soul. In his *Tractatus* on St John's Gospel, Augustine comments on John 6:64, *Verba quae ego locutus sum vobis, spiritus et vita sunt*: 'Through faith we are joined to Christ, through understanding we are quickened. Let us first adhere through faith, that there may be something to be quickened through understanding'.[13] And since it is faith which opens the way to Christ's restoring action in us, to the recovery of purity of heart, Augustine delights in Acts 15:9, *Fide mundans corda eorum*, a text which he quotes repeatedly, in many of his works.[14]

As we have seen, *intellectus* may be called a reward of faith;[15] yet it is also a gift freely conferred by God. This is in keeping with Augustine's saying that in crowning our merits, God crowns his own gifts.[16] Augustine assumes an interdependence of faith and understanding in the *Enarrationes in Psalmos* as he describes the work of grace in restoring God's image in us:

> The Apostle . . . says, *Be renewed in the spirit of your mind* (Ephesians 4:23); and indeed understanding is in the mind. Hence again he says, *Be reformed in newness of your feeling* (Romans 12:2). . . . Therefore because of these inner eyes whose blindness consists in not understanding, in order that they may be opened and progressively cleared, *the hearts are purified by*

faith (Acts 15:9). . . . *Unless you believe, you will not understand* (Isaiah 7:9). Therefore our understanding advances to understand, so that it may believe, and faith advances to believe, so that it may understand; and in order that the objects of faith may be more and more understood, the mind advances in the same understanding. But this is not done by our own, as it were natural powers, but by the help and gift of God; just as it is the gift of medicine, not of nature, that a damaged eye receives the power of sight.[17]

We approach God not in a physical but in a moral sense; our spiritual senses are awakened, so that we begin to 'see' God as we grow in purity of heart. We 'feel' his presence as we recover his likeness (*similitudo*, cf. Genesis 1:26), through growth in charity. The following passage draws together many Augustinian commonplaces:

> As those bodies are perceived by the eyes, so [God] is perceived by the mind, and waited on and seen by the heart. And where is the heart by which he may be seen? *Blessed*, he says, *are the pure in heart, for they shall see God.* (Matthew 5:8). I hear, I believe, I understand as far as I can, that God is seen by the heart, and cannot be perceived except by a pure heart. . . . *Draw near to him, and be enlightened* (Psalm 33:6, Vulgate). But in order that you may draw near and be enlightened, let your darkness become displeasing to you. . . . So any human soul draws near, the inner man re-made in the image of God, because he was made in the image of God; he had gone away into unlikeness. For we do not draw near to God, or go away from him, by space and place; if you have become unlike him, you have gone far away; if you have become like him, you are drawing near. . . . In as much as you are drawing near to his likeness, you are advancing in charity, and are beginning to feel God. And whom do you feel? Him who comes to you, or him to whom you are returning? For he never went away from you; God goes away from you, when you go away from God. . . . What you want to see is not far from you. The Apostle says . . . : For in him we live and move and have our being. (Acts 17:28).[18]

While it would be possible to collect almost endless illustrations of Augustine's teaching on the renewal of man's soul, with reference to such texts as Romans 12:2 referred to above, to Ephesians 4:23–24, *Renovamini spiritu mentis vestrae, et induite novum hominem, qui secundum Deum creatus est in justitia, sanctitate et veritate*, and Colossians 3:9–10, *Expoliantes veterem hominem cum actibus suis, induite novum, qui renovatur in agnitione Dei, secundum imaginem eius qui creavit eum*, all of which are used by Hilton in *Scale* 2, 31 when he is describing how '*reforming in feeling*' is effected in the soul so that bodily or sensible feelings are incidental. I have argued elsewhere that, among other works of Augustine, there is an underlying influence especially of *De Trinitate* on Hilton's teaching on 'reforming'.[19] I do not, of course, suggest that all points where Hilton's teaching, or his use of Biblical texts, co-incides with that of *De Trinitate*, the latter is a specific source. But it may be worth noting that in the earlier part of *De Trinitate* we find contemplation implicitly equated with understanding. Having referred to 2 Corinthians 5:7, Augustine goes on:

> Indeed contemplation is the reward of faith, for which reward our hearts are purified through faith; as it is written, *purifying their hearts by faith* (Acts 15:9). But it is shown that hearts are purified for that contemplation, by that saying especially: *Blessed are the pure in heart, for they shall see God.* (Matthew 5:8).[20]

Augustine appeals in Book 7 to the familiar texts of Romans 12:2 and Colossians 3:10 that man who is a created image of the Trinity should be held by faith until God illuminates our hearts so that we come to understanding—once more Isaiah 7:9 is quoted. [21] Book 10 describes the created trinity in man of *memoria, intelligentia, voluntas*;[22] Book 12 speaks of our fall and of the possibility of restoration, referring to Ephesians 4:23 f. and Colossians 3:9 f.[23]. It is in Book 14 that Augustine draws together his teaching on the restoration of man to the *similitudo Dei*, with the transition from faith to understanding. *While we are in the body, we are away from the Lord, and walk by faith and not by sight.* During the time of our earthly pilgrimage the words of Romans 1:17 may be applied to us: *Justus ex fide vivit.* Although we may live according to the inner man (Cf. Romans 7:22), while we live by faith within time, the image of God in us is not yet perfectly renewed; that can only be when we see God face to face. I Corinthians 13:12).[24] In describing the restoration of God's image in us, Augustine again invokes Romans 12:2 and Ephesians 4:23 f.[25] Only in heaven will our adoption in Christ be fully realised as we are conformed to his likeness: *Cum apparuerit, similes ei erimus, quoniam videbimus eum sicuti est.* (I John 3:2).[26] In fact, while we are on earth there can be no final and complete attainment of *intellectus*: echoing Matthew 7:7, *Quaerite, et invenitis*, and recalling again Isaiah 7:9, Augustine says that faith seeks and understanding finds; yet understanding still seeks him whom he finds (or perhaps, has found—the Latin is ambivalent).[27]

Anselm, whose *fides quaerens intellectum* builds on Augustine's teaching, has been called 'the father of scholasticism'.[28] Between Augustine and Anselm a change of emphasis is discernible. For Augustine, the formula *Crede ut intelligas* has an apologetic concern: the receptive attitude of faith is needed in order that one may become a Christian. Faith is indeed a gift of God, and is not reached by a process of intellectual reasoning, though in keeping with his insistence that it is reason which constitutes the *imago Dei* in man,[29] Augustine will use all the resources of his intellect to understand and express the faith which he has received from God. For Anselm, the apologetic aspect is less urgent; his *Credo ut intelligam* is not an exhortation to the unbeliever to believe, but a declaration of his own faith: he seeks a rational insight into the content of the revelation which he has always accepted.[30] True, he will be prepared to enter into controversy when needed, and when he comes to answer Roscelin he will be concerned to show how dialectic is the servant of faith, not a key that unlocks divine mysteries. As a dialectician, Anselm never proposes to render the mysteries of faith intelligible in themselves, but to prove by what he calls 'necessary reasons', *rationes necessariae*, that rational inquiry well conducted ends in supporting them.[31] In his *Proslogion* he shows that for him, no less than for Augustine, the search for understanding is a search at the same time for purity of heart; theology is rooted in the *desiderium Dei*:

> Ah now, Lord God, teach my heart where and how it may seek you. . . . I confess, Lord, and give thanks, that you have created in me this your image, so that mindful of you I may think of you and love you. But this image is so effaced by the wear and tear of vices, so blackened by the smoke of sins, that it cannot do that for which it was made, unless you renew and reform it. Lord, I do not try to enter your height, because in no way do I compare my understanding to it; but I long in some small way to understand your truth, which my heart believes and loves. Nor do I seek to understand in order that I may believe, but I believe in order that I may understand. For I believe this: that unless I believe, I shall not understand.[32]

Anselm speaks of understanding as a mean between faith and the open vision of God in heaven.[33] He repeats Augustine's emphasis on the need for purity of heart arising from faith as the necessary prelude to understanding.

> Some, when they have as it were begun to sprout the horns of a self-confident science, do not know that *if anyone thinks that he* knows *something* (Cf. Galatians 6:3) he has not yet learned in what manner he ought to know; before through the firmness of faith he has his spiritual wings; in their presumption they rise up into the highest questions concerning the faith. So it happens that while they try absurdly to climb by the understanding to those things that first require the ladder of faith, as it is written, *Unless you believe, you will not understand*: they are compelled to descend into manifold errors through the failing of the understanding. . . . Therefore the heart must first be purified by faith, as it is said of God: *Purifying their hearts by faith*; and first through the keeping of the Lord's precepts the eyes must be enlightened, because *the precept of the Lord is clear, illuminating the eyes* (Psalm 18:9, Vulgate); and first by humble obedience to God's testimonies we must become little children. . . .[34]

Anselm's strictures against a presumptuous use of human reason in attempting to explore the mysteries of the faith have in mind the Christological and Trinitarian errors arising from Roscelin's nominalist approach, to which his *De Incarnatione Verbi* is a response. For him, 'understanding' is a personal, lived awareness of the realities of the faith, something that cuts deeper than a detached mental analysis of what we have only heard at second hand:

> For he who does not believe, will not experience; and he who has not experienced will not know. For as much as experience surpasses hearing about a thing, so the science of one who has experience surpasses the knowledge of one who only hears.[35]

If Anselm places living experience above detached academic study of the content of religious belief, he insists, with all the commitment of a monk who sees theological work as a part of his vocation, that we are bound to seek understanding of what we believe. So in *Cur Deus Homo* the disciple Boso observes:

> As the right order demands that we first believe the deep things of the Christian faith, before we presume to submit them to rational discussion, so it seems to me to be negligence, if, after we are confirmed in faith, we do not strive to understand what we believe.[36]

In acceding to Boso's request, Anselm is clear that the theologian stands before God on the same level as every other member of the Church; that he is a learner first, and only incidentally, and instrumentally, a teacher; moreover, that any personal speculation must be kept within the limits of what is believed on the authority of the Church:

> I will try as far as I can, with the help of God and supported by your prayers . . . not so much to show you what you seek, as to seek it together with you, but with that provision with which I want all my words to be received, that if I say anything that is not confirmed by greater authority—although I may seem to prove it by reason—it should not be accepted with any more certainty than as an opinion of mine, until God shows me better by some other way.[37]

Bernard shares with Augustine the use of such key texts as Isaiah 7:9, Matthew 5:8, Romans 1:17, Acts 15:9 and 2 Corinthians 5:7,[38] but his teaching has a different nuance to that of Anselm. Drawing on Origen's exegesis of Lamentations 4:20, he speaks of the 'flesh' of Christ as the 'shadow' under which his divinity is known in the conditions of this life.[39] In a sermon on the Song of Songs, he says:

> So when the prophet says, *Christ the Lord is a spirit before our face, in his shadow we shall live among the gentiles* (Lamentations 4:20), I think that he means that *now we see through a glass darkly*, and not *yet face to face* (I

Corinthians 13:12). And that is so as long as we live among the gentiles; for it is otherwise among the angels. . . . The just man lives by faith (Romans 1:17, the blessed rejoices in sight. . . .

That is a good shadow of faith. which tempers the light to the clouded eye, and prepares the eye for the light; for it is written, *Purifying their hearts by faith* (Acts 15:9).[40]

This passage goes on to describe how at the annunciation the blessed Virgin lived in the shadow of faith.[41] Taking up the same point in a later sermon on the Song of Songs, Bernard again emphasises that illumination of understanding, in its full and proper sense, is reserved for the life to come:

Nevertheless the holy Virgin herself experienced the shadow of faith, she to whom was said, *Blessed are you who have believed* (Luke 1:45). . . . And the prophet says, *Christ the Lord is a spirit* before our face. . . . In shadow with the gentiles, in light with the angels. We are in shadow as long as we walk by faith, and not by sight, (2 Corinthians 5:7) and therefore the just man is in shadow, because he lives by faith (Romans 1:17). But he who lives by understanding is blessed, because he is not now in shadow, but in light. . . . We must first come to the shadow, and thus pass to that whose shadow it is, because *unless you believe*, he says, *you will not understand*.[42]

The same emphasis is found in his third *Sermon on the Ascension*.[43] It was Étienne Gilson who, in his great study of St Bernard's mystical theology, drew attention to Gilbert of Hoyland, the continuator of Bernard's sermons on the Song of Songs; he characterised Gilbert's theology, rightly, as an interesting synthesis of Augustine, Anselm and Bernard. In particular, he pointed to Gilbert's *In Cant.* 4 on Cant. 3:2, *Surgam, et circuibo civitatem*, as a very personal commentary on Anselm's *fides quaerens intellectum*:[44]

That is a good circle performed by the reason: but it is so when reason itself keeps within the rules of faith, and does not exceed faith's limits, reaching *from faith to faith* (Romans 1:17), or from faith to understanding. Understanding, indeed, even if it goes beyond faith, does not consider anything other than what is contained in faith. . . . Faith, so to say, holds and possesses what is true and right; understanding considers this uncovered and bare; reason tries to uncover this. Reason goes to and fro between faith and understanding, reaching out to the latter but governed by the former. . . . That is a good circle, in which *the justice of God is revealed from faith to faith*. That is a good circle, where one is *changed from one degree of clarity to another as by the Spirit of the Lord*. (2 Corinthians 3:18).[45]

Gilbert of Hoyland is certainly behind some of Hilton's teaching in both *Epistola ad Solitarium*, and *Scale 2*, at a number of points.[46] Although there is no evidence that Gilbert is a specific source for

Hilton's teaching on the transition from faith to understanding, for which, as I shall show, Hilton was indebted certainly to Augustine and presumably also to Anselm, it may be worth noting that Gilbert's sermon *In Cant.* 18 repeats Augustine's and Anselm's teaching. Quoting Isaiah. 7:9, Gilbert says: 'The learning of faith marks a stage towards the purity of understanding'.[47] It is suggestive that this very sermon expounds Psalm 80:4, *Buccinate in neomenia tuba*, an unusual text which Hilton uses in his description of contemplative prayer in *Scale* 2, 42.[48] Hilton is not alone among his contemporaries in his familiarity with Gilbert of Hoyland. I have shown elsewhere that Thomas Maldon, O.C., who was prior of the Cambridge Carmelite house from 1369 to 1372, and whose regency may be dated at some point between 1372 and 1378, quotes in his *Lectura in Psalm 118* from a related passage in Gilbert to emphasise that speculation must be determined by the limits of faith, and without actually referring to faith and understanding as such quotes from St Anselm's *Proslogion*, chapter 1, on the soul's search for the God in whom he already believes, but whose consolation eludes him because of the darkness of sin. Maldon is at pains to stress the distinction between the philosophers' search for truth, and the attitude of receptivity and faith which are required in the Christian; his conservative Augustinianism has a number of points of resemblance with Hilton's.[49] While Hilton's higher education was almost certainly in Canon Law rather than in theology as such,[50] there is very strong presumptive evidence that he was educated at Cambridge,[51] and his *Scale* was translated into Latin by Thomas Fishlake, who was BD at Cambridge *c.* 1375,[52] and so has close links with Maldon.

In considering Hilton's works I shall begin with *Epistola ad Solitarium*, which very probably antedates his *Scale* 1.[53] Hilton says that in drawing near to God we must lay a firm foundation of faith, and quotes Hebrews 11:6, *Accedentem ad Deum, oportet credere quia est.* We must have a simple belief in the articles of the faith, especially in the forgiveness of sins.[54] Here, and elsewhere, there are overtones of William Flete's *De Remediis contra Temptaciones*, with its characteristic emphasis on faith as the foundation of the Christian life, and as a habit of the will, which is echoed also in both *Scale* 1, and *Scale* 2, as well as in some of Hilton's other Latin works.[55] From this point Hilton goes on to echo Gilbert of Hoyland on the limits of understanding in relation to faith, while, like Augustine and Anselm, he hopes that a faith which is itself determined by the Church's belief may be rewarded by illumination. The reader is warned to adhere to the Church's faith in

110

Christ in the face of any special or peculiar revelation:

> For then once that foundation is laid, if you feel any unaccustomed impulses or spiritual notions whatever, whether they belong to the understanding as if you had your eye open to penetrate mysteries, or whether they belong to the affection as if you felt fire burning in your inward parts, then you must receive them with humility and prudence, in such a way that you do not entirely cleave to them, nor yet reject them, but immediately turn to Christ and to the Church's faith. . . . Bring into captivity under simple, and as it were stupid faith, every understanding that exalts itself against it (sc. the Church's faith). Nothing should be accepted that is opposed to the ordinance of the Church and to the sayings of the holy Fathers, to the authority of the doctors approved by the Church. And even if you do feel something that is not expressly declared by the Church, nor brought to light by the old Fathers, forsake yourself in this and entrust yourself and what you feel to the Church's faith, and do not obstinately adhere to your feeling as if it were illuminated by the truth, to defend it as if it were truth. Therefore your heart performs a good circle in its spiritual exercise when it begins from the faith of the Church and returns to the same; for thus, according to the Apostle, *the justice of God is revealed from faith to faith*, since *the just man lives by faith* (Romans 1:17); and he who is found approved in this faith, shall perhaps perceive the fruit of faith, that is understanding; though this will be in part as long as *he is away from the Lord* (2 Corinthians 5:6); *Unless you believe*, the Apostle[56] says, *you will not understand*. Therefore believe humbly, in order that you may truly understand. . . .[57]

From echoing Gilbert of Hoyland, Hilton recalls those passages in Bernard which emphasise that on earth whatever understanding we attain can only be partial—that the flesh of Christ must always veil his divinity from our sight in this life.[58] In the following passage there is a suggestion too of the teaching found especially in Bernard on *vicissitudo*—the fluctuating sense of God's presence and absence, with each apparent withdrawal issuing in turn in a deeper sense of union.[59]

> *Believe* humbly therefore, that *you may* truly *understand*; and yet whatever you understand secretly, entrust to the security of faith, choosing rather to sleep meanwhile in the shadow of faith than to be awake in the light of understanding, while this is not yet received in its proper clarity. The prophet says, *Christ the Lord is a Spirit before our face; under his shadow we shall live among the gentiles*. For Christ is light, and faith his shadow. For though Christ may show himself sometimes spiritually to the mind's eye, as truth, goodness, and charity, yet he suddenly hides himself, and then it is useful to rest in the shadow of faith, of his humanity, and this among the Gentiles, not among the angels.[60]

In the same letter, Hilton identifies authentic feeling (*sensus*) with the illumination of the intellect and of the affection—in keeping with

111

Augustine's insistence that contemplation includes knowledge and love together.[61]

> But if you persevere . . . you will feel great liberty and peace . . . , and then with a certain sweet affection you will touch lightly that peace which you have attained, and perhaps with the understanding illuminated you will perceive the sense of your prayer. . . .[62]

Similarly:

> You have conceived Christ through faith, and perhaps he is not yet brought to life in you through the light of understanding, nor formed through the sweetness of charity; therefore work . . . that . . . Christ may be formed and strengthened in you *into a perfect man, into the measure of the stature of the fulness of Christ* (Ephesians 4.13).[63]

In *Epistola ad Solitarium*—at any rate according to British Library MS. Royal 6.E.III—Hilton uses *intellectus* and *intelligentia* variously for 'understanding', as Augustine does.[64]

The emphasis on the transition from faith to understanding can be matched in Hilton's *Epistola de Utilitate et Prerogativis Religionis*, using Isaiah 7:9,[65] and is implied in his *Epistola ad Quemdam Seculo renunciare Volentem*.[66]

In *Scale of Perfection* 1, 9, Hilton again links 'feeling' and 'understanding'. Referring to his third and highest degree of contemplation, that which is 'swetter to þe gostly felyng' in contrast to the 'bodily felyng', he says that it is a 'tastyng & as it wer a syȝt of heuenly ioye', and, quoting Psalm 138:11 (Vulgate), *Et nox illuminatio mea in deliciis meis*, he speaks of 'þe illuminacioun of vnderstondyng in delices of louyng'.[67] In the same chapter he quotes 2 Corinthians 3:18, *Nos autem revelata facie gloriam Domini speculantes, transformamur in eandem imaginem, a claritate in claritatem tanquam a Domini Spiritu*; with 'þe face of our soule vnhiled by openyng of þe gostly eȝe [we pass] fro bryȝtnes of feith in-to bryȝtnes of vnderstondyng, or elles fro clertie of desir in-to clertie of blissed loue'.[68] 'Understanding' here refers to an action of the soul rather than to a faculty of the soul; when in *Scale* 1, 43, Hilton does come to speak of the three faculties of the soul, the *trinitas creata* of *memoria, intelligentia, voluntas* which scholastic theology had distilled from the various patterns meditated by Augustine in *De Trinitate* and elsewhere,[69] he uses 'resoun' rather than 'understanding' for the middle term.[70]

A passage in *Scale* 1, 19, distinguishes between the practice of virtue 'in reason' and 'in affection'. Though this passage does not explicitly refer to the characteristic text of Isaiah 7:9, the Augustinian contrast between faith and understanding, or, as Hilton will say more particularly in *Scale* 2, between faith and feeling, is also present:

> If þou may noȝt fele þis mekenes in þi hert with affeccioun as þou wold, do as þou may; meke þeself in will by þi resoun, trowand þat it schuld be so as I sey þoȝ þou fele it noȝt . . . , and if þou do so, . . . þe vertue of mekenes þat was first in þe naked will, schal be turned in-to felyng of affeccioun. . . .[71]

In *Scale* 1, 45, Hilton speaks of the restoration of man to that conformity to God which had been lost through the fall. He recalls the familiar *reformare* of St Paul (Romans 12:2) and of Augustine:

> . . . þat our soule myȝt be reformed as it wer in a schadue by grace to þe ymage of þe trinite whilk we haden by kynde and after schulen haue fully in blisse. For þat is þe life whilk is verreile contemplatif, vnto bigynne her in þat felyng of loue and gostly knowyng of God by openyng of þe gostly eȝe. . . .[72]

So, if the image of God, or Christ, were reformed in us, 'þou schuldest fynde lyȝt of vnderstondyng & no merknes of vnconyng'. (ch. 53).[73] Both in *Scale* 1, and *Scale* 2, the term 'felyng' may be used in a broad or else in a particular sense. When used of awareness of God and of spiritual things, it may refer either to an awareness that overflows through sensible feelings of devotion, warmth, and so on, or else to that properly supernatural awareness that pertains to the spirit and cannot fall under the cognisance of the senses.[74] In the second book of the *Scale*, 'felyng' is predominantly used in the latter, technical sense.

In *Scale* 2, 4, following Augustine's thought (and St Paul's), Hilton speaks of two kinds of 'reforming' of man's soul: one is 'in fulnes', the other 'in partie'; the former is beyond the scope of this life, and pertains to heaven.[75] These two levels correspond to the familar *fides* and *species*. In turn, the 'reforming' that is accessible on earth is further divided between reforming 'in faiþ only', and reforming 'in faiþ & in felyng'. (ch. 5)[76] the latter is generally simplified to 'reforming in feeling'.

'Reforming in faith' represents bare faith in Christ, without any illumination of the intellect or conscious delight in God's will:

> Þi mynde, þi resound & þe luf of þi soule are so mikel sette in bihaldyng & in luf of erþly þinges, þat of gostly þinges þu felis riȝt litel. Þu felis no reformyng in þi self, bot þu art so vmbilappid wiþ þis blak ymage of synne for oȝt þat þou may do, þat on what syde þu turnes þee, þou felis þi self defoulid & spottid wiþ fleschly stirynges of þis foule ymage. Oþer chaungyng felis þou none fro fleschlynes in-to gostlynes, nouþer in þe priue miȝtes of þi soule wiþ-inne, ne in bodily feling wiþ-outen. (ch. 4)[77]

113

Reforming in faith is sufficient for salvation; even this implies a movement of the will to God, however arid and painful this may be in the face of a previous habit of sin:

> Þaw3 a man fele no þing in hym self bot alle stirynges of synne & fleschly desires, not agayn standand þat felyng, if he wilfully assente not þer-to, he may be reformid in feiþ to þe liknes of God. (ch. 5)[78]

Reforming in faith may be had 'li3tly & in schort tyme', but reforming in feeling may be had only 'þorw lengþ of tyme & mikil gostly trauail'; it 'distroyes þe olde felynges of þis ymage of synne, & brynges in to þe soule new gracious felynges þorw wirkyng of þe holy goost'. (*Ibid.*)[79] Reforming in faith is effected through the sacraments of baptism, and, in the event of mortal sin after baptism, of penance. (chs. 6–8). Although it does not carry the special grace of 'reforming in feeling', it does carry its own proper assurance of salvation – the assurance of faith:

> Of þis reformyng in faiþ spekis seynt Poul þus, *Iustus ex fide uiuit* (Romans 1:17) . . . , þat is, he þat is mad ri3tful be baptem or be penaunce, he lifes in faiþ, þe whilk sufficeþ vn-to heuenly pees, as seynt Poul says, *Iustificati ex fide, pacem habemus ad Deum*, (Romans 5:1), þat is, we þat are ri3tid & reformed þorw faiþ in Crist has pees & acorde made betwix God & vs, no3t agaynst and þe vicious felynges of oure body of syn, for þaw3 þis reformyng be priue & may not wel be felid here in þis liif, nerþeles who so trowes it stedfastly & schapp his werkes besily for to acorde to his trowþ, & þat he turne not agayn to dedly synne, soþly when þe houre of ded comeþ . . . þan schal he fynde it so . . . þus said seint Iohan . . . , *Karissimi, & nunc sumus filii Dei, sed non dum apparuit quid erimus.* . . . (I John 3:2) (ch. 9)[80]

The Augustinian overtones of all this are obvious; so they are when Hilton describes how, as purity of heart is recovered through the ordinary disciplines and means of grace, we attain 'rest in conscience', reforming in feeling, and the illumination of understanding. Here, as elsewhere[81] these various terms are used to describe the different aspects of a single experience:

> Oure lord saide to a man þat was in parlsey when he helid hym þus, *Confide fili, remittuntur tibi peccata tua.* . . . He said not to hym, see or fele how þi synnes are forgifen þee, for forgifnes of syn is don gostly & vnseably þurw3 þe grace of þe holy gost. Bot trow it. Ri3t on þe same wise, ilke a man þat wil come to reste in conscience, hym behouiþ first if he do þat in hym is, trowen with-outen gostly felyng forgifnes of his synnes, & if he first trowe it, he schal aftirward þurw3 grace felen it & vndirstonden it þat it is so. Þus saide þe apostle, *Nisi credideritis, non intelligetis* (Isaiah 7:9). . . . Trowþ gooþ bifore, & vndirstondyng comeþ after.[82] Þe whilk vndirstondyng þat I calle þe si3t of god if it be gracious a soule may not haue bot þorw3 grete

clennes, as oure lord saiþ, *Beati mundo corde, quoniam ipsi Deum videbunt* (Matthew 5:8) . . . , þat is, þei schul see god not with þeire fleschly hiʒe, bot with þe innere hiʒe, þat is vndirstondyng, clensid & illumined þurw grace of þe holy gost for to seen soþfastnes, þe whilk clennes a soule may not felen bot if he haue stable trouþ goand bifore, as þe apostle saiþ, *ffide mundans corda eorum* (Acts 15:9). . . . It is nedful þat a soule trowe first þe reformyng of hym-self, made þurwʒe þe sacrament of penaunce, þaw he see it not, & þat he dispose hymself fully for to lif riʒtwisly & uertuosly as his trouþ askiþ, so þat he may after come to þe siʒt & to þe reformyng in felyng. (ch. 11)[83]

In Hilton we find references at various points to all the five spiritual senses,[84] though in *Scale* 2, especially, it is the sense of spiritual sight to which he returns again and again, and which he identifies with understanding:

If þou mowe not seen it ʒit with þi gostly iʒen, þat þou trowe it.[85] . . . He opneþ þe innere iʒe of þe soule when he lightneþ þe resoun þurʒ touchyng & schynynge of his blissed liʒt . . . þe soule . . . seeþ him in vndirstandynge. . . .[86]
    þis gostly opnynge of þe innere eʒe in-to knowynge of þe godhed I calle reformyng in feiþ & in felynge. Ffor þan þe soule sumwhat feliþ in vndirstandynge of þat þinge þat it had bifore in nakid trowynge. . . .[87]

'Feeling' in fact is an inclusive term, going beyond any one spiritual sense and yet implying something of them all; it implies both knowledge and love, not only understanding but affection:

þei felen . . . graciouse touchynges of þe holy gost in her soules, boþ in vndirstandynge & siʒt of gostly þinges, & in affeccioun of lufe. . . .[88]
gostly felynges are felt in þe miʒtes of þe soule, principally in vndirstandynge & lufe. . . .[89]

We have seen that a basis, or a parallel, for Hilton's use of 'feeling' can be found in Augustine. But *sentire* and its cognates are also characteristic terms in the early Cistercians, whose influence on Hilton, as on so many mediaeval spiritual writers, is pervasive. It is found in Bernard,[90] and in Gilbert of Hoyland,[91] both of whose writings Hilton certainly knew, and also in William of St Thierry,[92] the extent of whose influence on Hilton is more problematic. The term 'felyng' is also found in *The Cloud of Unknowing*, in reference to that awareness of God which is open to the soul in this life in the absence of open vision.[93]

While 'feeling' includes what Hilton tries to express by 'understanding', it is strictly an awareness of God's invisible presence; Hilton refers to 'felynge of his [i.e. Christ's] graciouse vnseable presence',[94] and 'special grace felt þurʒ þe vnseable presence of ihesu'.[95] Christ, risen and glorified, is beyond all that our senses can grasp; yet, as the scholastics would say, he may be known through his effects.[96]

> What þis ihesu is in him self may no soule seen ne heere, bot bi effect of his wirkynge he may be seen þur3 þe li3t of grace.[97]

'Feeling' or 'understanding in *Scale* 2 is above all the realisation of our adoption in Christ, a supernaturally given awareness of the life of grace:

> þis tastyng of manna is a lifely felynge of grace had þur3 opnyng of þe gostly ei3e. . . .[98]

The 'understanding' of *Scale* 1 and 2 clearly represents (together with other elements) the *intellectus* or *intelligentia* of Augustine, the *intellectus* of Anselm. It can hardly be doubted that Hilton knew at least some of the passages in Augustine where the transition from *fides* to *intellectus* is described, though he does not actually name Augustine as a source.[99] Nor does he refer to Anselm in this connection. It is true that, in a different context, he does name Anselm as an authority on the religious life in *De Utilitate et Prerogativis Religionis*,[100] though we must remember that in Hilton's day a number of devotional works were falsely ascribed to Anselm—Thomas Maldon, referred to earlier, speaks of the *Tractatus de Interiori Domo* as Anselm's, under the name of *Libellus de Bona Conscientia*.[101] More significant is the fact that at the beginning of *Scale* 2, 2, the atonement-theory is lifted, without any need of acknowledgement felt, from Anselm's *Cur Deus Homo*,[102] and again that the discussion in *Scale* 2, 4, as to why the complete restoration of the human race did not take place immediately after the Passion, follows Anselm's *De Concordia Praescientiae Dei cum libero Arbitrio*,[103] likewise without referring to Anselm by name.

It is therefore almost certainly to be assumed that Hilton was familiar with Anselm's as well as with Augustine's teaching on *fides/intellectus*. A comparable instance where Hilton shows familiarity with both the characteristic teaching of a mediaeval theologian, and with the roots of this theologian's teaching in Augustine, without referring to the latter in the context, is his treatment of the transition from the 'carnal' to the 'spiritual' love of God in Christ. So *Scale* 1, 35 explicitly refers to St Bernard on this point,[104] while *Scale* 2, 30 shows (without naming sources) the influence of Augustine as well as of Bernard.[105] Indeed, outside Hilton's works, but in a related milieu, something similar may be found in *The Cloud* corpus.[106]

Hilton's concern with faith and with understanding of the object of faith, and his alignment with Augustine and Anselm, is in keeping with other trends discernible in fourteenth-century thought. The scholastic theology of this century was marked by a sharp emphasis on the divergence between natural knowledge accessible to reason and revealed truth. In contrast to the perspective of St Thomas, Neo-Augustinian theologians held that theology could not be considered as a science in the sense of knowledge principles, since it depended on specifically Christian faith; in this intellectual climate those theological truths that could be conceived naturally, such as God's existence, were held to be inevident to man in his actual condition, while those that were beyond reason's comprehension, such as belief in the Trinity and Incarnation, could not even be conceived naturally. The function of reason was to elucidate the meaning and implications of revealed truth, not to provide a natural theology in the thirteenth-century sense of finding natural reasons for revealed truths.[107] Augustine's and Anselm's 'understanding' of faith, stands at a crossroads. On the one hand, the way is open to dialectic—the rational analysis of faith's understanding of itself; and Anselm is indeed a dialectician. But for both of these theologians, 'understanding' also points to an *experience* of the ineffable Christian mystery; and Anselm is clear that dialectic points beyond itself to the mystery, that it bears witness to a supra-intellectual and yet rationally defensible faith.

Fourteenth-century mysticism in Germany, the Low Countries and England stands, of course, in a direct line reaching back to the Fathers through the great thirteenth-century scholastics and the early Cistercians; it is, in varying proportions, a blending of the monastic and scholastic traditions. The wisdom of the monastic tradition, with its appeal to the lived-out experience of the Christian mystery, continued to lead men and women to God even while the optimistic scholastic synthesis of reason and faith sought by the thirteenth century was breaking down. Then, as in earlier centuries, there was the possibility of a true or of a false mysticism; for Hilton, no less than for Tauler or Ruysbroek, whose teaching he can hardly have known, though they stand in part in a common tradition, the validity of religious experience is verified by its conformity with the faith and moral teaching of the Church.[108] Hilton's theology may indeed be conservative, a conscious reversion to old-fashioned traditions; at the same time, in its appeal from faith to faith, it is in keeping with the spirit of his age. Within the limits of faith, Hilton succeeds in showing how the Christian understanding of our fall and redemption both accounts for the grandeur and misery of man, and offers a way of restoration which may, in the context of moral and ascetic theology, be experienced in practice as well as believed by the mind.

ABBREVIATIONS

C.Ch.   Corpus Christianorum, Series Latina, Turnholt, 1953–.

AUGUSTINE

In Ep. Ioann. ad Parthos	In Epistolam Joannis ad Parthos
De Doct. Chr.	De Doctrina Christiana
In Ioann. Ev. Tr.	In Joannis Evangelum Tractatus
Ep.	Epistolae
De Praed. Sanct.	Liber de Praedestinatione Sanctorum
De Lib. Arb.	De Libero Arbitrio
En. Ps.	Enerrationes in Psalmos
De Trin.	De Trinitate
De Gratia et Lib. Arb.	De Gratia et Libero Arbitrio

ANSELM

Prosl.	Prosologion
Ep. de Inc. Verb.	Epistola de Incarnatione Verbi

BERNARD

Super Cant.	Sermones super Cantica Canticorum
Sermo in Asc. Dom.	Sermo in Ascensione Domini

GILBERT OF HOYLAND

In Cant.	Sermones in Canticum Salomonis

PETER LOMBARD

Sent.	Libri IV Sententiarum

WILLIAM OF ST THIERRY

De Nat. et Dig. Amoris	De Natura et Dignitate Divini Amoris
Spec. Fidei	Speculum Fidei and Enigma Fidei

118

NOTES

1. Tota vita christiani boni, sanctum desiderium est. *In Ep. Ioann. ad Parthos Tr.*, 4, 6. Patrologiae Latina, 35, 2008. On the *desiderium Dei* in Augustine, see J. Burnaby, *Amor Dei*, London, 1938, pp. 96f.

2. Ergo, quoniam intellectus in specie sempiterna est, fides uero in rerum temporalium quibusdam cunabulis quasi lacte alit paruulos; nunc autem *per fidem ambulamus, non per speciem*; nisi autem per fidem ambulauerimus, ad speciem peruenire non possumus, quae non transit, sed permanet per intellectum purgatum nobis cohaerentibus ueritati. Propterea ille ait: *nisi credideritis, non permanebitis*; ille autem, *nisi credideritis, non intellegetis. – De Doct. Chr.*, 2, 12, 17, C.Ch., 32, p. 43.

3. K. Rahner, 'Le Début d'une Doctrine des cinq Sens Spirituels chez Origène', *Revue d'Ascétique et Mystique*, 13 (1932), pp. 113–145; 'La Doctrine des 'Sens Spirituels' au Moyen Âge', *Ibid.*, 14 (1933), pp. 263–299.

4. Sic in anima nostra quiddam est quod intellectus uocatur. Hoc ipsum animae quod intellectus et mens dicitur, illuminatur luce superiore. Iam superior ille lux, qua mens humana illuminatur, Deus est. *Erat* enim *uerum lumen, quod illuminat omnem hominem uenientem in hunc mundum. In Ioann. Ev. Tr.*, 15, 19, C.Ch., 36, p. 157.

5. *Ep.*, 147, 18, 45, Corpus Scriptorum Ecclesiasticorum Latinorum, Vienna, 1866— 44, pp. 319 f. The Greek text reads πάντα νοῦν . . . τὰ νοήματα ὑμῶν. (panta noun . . . ta noēmata humōn).

6. For a discussion of Augustine's usage, see E. Gilson, The *Christian Philosophy of St Augustine*, London, 1961, p. 270, note i.

7. Credere nihil aliud est, quam cum assensione cogitare. *De Praed. Sanct.*, 2, 5, Patrologiae Latina, 44, 963.

8. Intellectus enim merces est fidei. Ergo noli quaerere intellegere ut credas, sed crede ut intellegas; quoniam *nisi credideritis, non intellegetis* (Isaiah 7:9). . . . *Si quis uoluerit uoluntatem eius facere, cognoscet de doctrina* (John 7.17). . . . Non qualiscumque fides, sed *fides quae per dilectionem operatur* (Galatians 5:6); haec in te sit, *et intelleges de doctrina. In Ioann. Ev. Tr.*, 29, 6, C.Ch., 36, p. 287. Among very many texts in Augustine on faith as the necessary prelude to understanding, citing Isaiah 7:9, see e.g. *De Lib. Arb.*, 1, 2, 4; 2, 2, 6. C.Ch., 29, pp. 213, 239.

9. Tu dicebas: 'Intellegam, ut credam'. Ego dicebam: 'Vt intellegas crede'. Nata est controuersia, ueniamus ad iudicem, iudicet propheta, immo uero deus iudicet per prophetam. . . . Respondeat propheta, *Nisi credideritis, non intellegetis. Sermo*, 43, 7, C.Ch., 41, p. 511.

10. Si non potes intelligere, crede ut intelligas. Praecedit fides, sequitur intellectus: quoniam propheta dicit, *Nisi credideritis, non intelligetis*. Sermo, 118, 1, Patrologiae Latina, 38, 672. Probably echoed in Hilton, *Scale* 2, 11, cited below.

11. E. Gilson, *loc. cit.*, gives references.

12. Arcana et secreta regni Dei prius quaerunt credentes, quo faciant intelligentes. Fides enim gradus est intelligendi: intellectus autem meritum fidei. Aperte hoc propheta dicit . . . : *Nisi credideritis, non intelligetis*. Habet ergo et fides ipsa quoddam lumen suum in Prophetia, in Evangelio, in apostolicis lectionibus. . . . Ergo *fides est . . . sperantium substantia, convictio rerum quae non videntur*. . . . Ne sis ingratus ei qui te fecit videre, unde possis credere quod nondum potes videre. Dedit tibi Deus oculos in corpore, rationem in corde; excita rationem cordis, erige interiorem habitatorem interiorum oculorum tuorum. . . . *Sermo*, 126, 1–3, Patrologiae Latina, 38, 698–700.

13. Per fidem copulamur, per intellectum uiuificamur. Prius haereamus per fidem, ut sit quod uiuificetur per intellectum. *In Ioann. Ev. Tr.*, 27, 7, C.Ch., 36, p. 273, citing also Isaiah 7:9.

119

14. E.g. *In Ioann. Ev. Tr.*, 68, 3, C.Ch., 36, p. 499, in a context which also includes Romans 1:17, 2 Corinthians 5, 6–8; *Ibid.* 80, 3, p. 529; *En. Ps.* 44, 25, C.Ch., 38, p. 512, with Matthew 5:8; *Ibid.*, 88, 2, 7, C.Ch., 39, p. 1240; *Ibid.*, 109, 8, C.Ch., 40, p. 1608, with Matthew 5, 8; *Ibid.*, 118, 18, 3, C.Ch., 40, pp. 1724 ff. with Ephesians 4:23, Romans 12:2, Isaiah 7:9, etc. (cited below); *Ibid.*, 123, 2, p. 1826, with I Corinthians 13:12, 2 Corinthians 5:6–7. *De Trin.*, 1, 8, 17, C.Ch., 50, p. 51, with Matthew 5:8 (cited below); *Ibid.*, 2, 15, 25, p. 114.

15. In addition to *In Ioann. Ev. Tr.*, 29, 6, (note 8 above), and *Sermo*, 126, 1 (note 12), cf. *De Trin.* 1, 8, 17 (note 20); also *In Ioann. Ev. Tr.*, 22, 2; 48, 1; C.Ch., 36, pp. 223; 413; *Contra Faustum*, 22, 53, Patrologiae Latina, 42, 433.

16. Non Deus coronat merita tua tanquam merita tua, sed tanquam dona sua. – *De Gratia et Lib. Arb.*, 6, 15, Patrologiae Latina, 44, 891, and similarly elsewhere in Augustine.

17. Apostolus . . . dicit, *Renouamini spiritu mentis uestrae:* et utique intellectus in mente est. Hinc rursus ait, *Reformamini in nouitate sensus uestri.* . . . Propter hos igitur interiores oculos, quorum caecitas est non intellegere, ut aperiantur, et magis magisque serenentur, *fide corda mundantur.* . . . *Nisi credideritis, non intellegetis.* . . . Proficit ergo noster intellectus ad intellegenda quae credat, et fides proficit ad credenda quae intellegat; et eadem ipsa ut magis magisque intellegantur, in ipso intellectu proficit mens. Sed hoc non fit propriis tamquam naturalibus uiribus, sed Deo adiuuante atque donante; sicut medicina fit, not natura, ut uitiatus oculus uim cernendi recipiat. *En. Ps.*, 118, 18, 3, C.Ch., 40, p. 1724 f.

18. Vt oculis ista corpora, sic ille mente conspicitur, corde adtenditur et uidetur. Et ubi est cor unde ille uideatur? Beati, ait, *mundi corde, quoniam ipsi Deum uidebunt.* Audio, credo, ut possum intellego, corde uideri Deum, nec posse nisi mundo corde conspici. . . . *Accedite ad eum, et illuminamini.* (Psalm 33:6, Vulgate). Vt autem accedas et illumineris, displiceat tibi tenebrae tuae . . . Accedit ergo utcumque anima humana, interior homo recreatus ad imaginem Dei, quia creatus ad imaginem Dei; quia tanto erat longe factus, quanto ierat in dissimilitudinem. Non enim locorum interuallis acceditur ad Deum, aut receditur a Deo; dissimilis factus, longe recessisti; similis factus, proxime accedis . . . Quantum accedis ad similitudinem, tantum proficis in caritate, et tanto incipis sentire Deum. Et quem sentis? Qui uenit ad te, an ad quem tu redis? Nam ille numquam discessit a te: recedit a te Deus, cum tu recedis a Deo. . . . Non est a te longe quod uis uidere. Apostolus dicit . . . : *In ipso enim uiuimus et mouemur et sumus.* (Acts 17:28). *En. Ps.*, 99, 5, C.Ch., 39, pp. 1395 f. This passage embodies a number of Augustinian commonplaces which are paralleled in Hilton. On the *regio dissimilitudinis*, see E. Gilson, '*Regio Dissimilitudinis* de Platon à S. Bernard de Clairvaux', *Mediaeval Studies*, 9 (1947), pp. 108–130; P. Courcelle, 'Tradition Néo-Platonicienne et Traditions Chrétiennes de la "Région de Dissemblance" ', *Archives d'Histoire Doctrinale et Littéraire du Moyen Âge*, 24 (1957), pp. 5–33, For overtones of this in Hilton, J. P. H. Clark, 'Image and Likeness in Walter Hilton', *Downside Review*, 97 (1979), p. 212.

19. J. P. H. Clark, *art. cit.*, esp. pp. 206 f., 217 f.

20. Contemplatio quippe merces est fidei, cui mercedi per fidem corda mundantur; sicut scriptum est, *Mundans fide corda eorum.* Probatur autem quod illi contemplationi corda mundentur, illa maxime sententia: *Beati mundicordes, quoniam ipsi deum uidebunt.* *De Trin.*, 1, 8, 17, C.Ch., 50, p. 51.

21. Quod si intellectu capi non potest, fide teneatur, donec illucescat in cordibus (cf. 2 Peter 1:19) ille qui ait per prophetam: *Nisi credideritis, non intellegetis.* *De Trin.*, 7, 6, 12, C.Ch., 50, p. 267.

22. *De Trin.* 10, 11, 17,—12, 19; cf. *Ibid.*, 14, 6, 8,—12, 16.

23. *Ibid.*, 12, 7, 12.

24. Quapropter, quoniam sicut scriptum est: *Quamdiu sumus in corpore peregrinamur a domino; per fidem enim ambulamus non per speciem*; profecto quamdiu *iustus ex*

fide uiuit (Romans 1:17), quamuis *secundum hominem interiorem* (cf. Romans 7:22), licet per eandem temporalem fidem ad ueritatem nitatur et tendat aeternam, tamen in eiusdem fidei temporaliter retentione, contemplatione, dilectione, nondum talis est trinitas ut dei iam imago dicenda sit. . . . Non enim semper hoc erit, quod utique non erit quando ista peregrinatione finita qua peregrinamur a domino, ut per fidem ambulare necesse sit species illa succedet, per quam *uidebimus ad faciem. De Trin.*, 14, 2, 4, C.Ch., 50 A, pp. 425 f. This is not the only place where Augustine uses Romans 1:17 to contrast the life of faith with the open vision of God in heaven; cf. *In Ioann. Ev. Tr.*, 68, 3, C.Ch., 36, p. 499; *En. Ps.*, 109, 8, C.Ch., 40, p. 1608. But, as said, it is likely that Hilton knew this part of *De Trin.*

25. *De Trin., op. cit.*, 14, 16, 22.
26. With reference to I John 3:2: Hinc apparet tunc in ista imagine dei fieri eius plenam similitudinem, quando eius plenam perceperit uisionem. *De Trin.*, 14, 18, 24, C.Ch., 50 A, p. 455.
27. Fides quaerit, intellectus inuenit; propter quod ait propheta: *Nisi credideritis, non intellegetis.* Et rursus intellectus eum quem inuenit adhuc quaerit: *Deus enim respexit super filios hominum*, sicut in Psalmo sacro canitur (Psalm 13:2, Vulgate), *ut uideret si est intellegens aut requirens deum. De Trin.*, 15, 2, 2, C.Ch., 50 A, p. 461 f.
28. M. Grabmann, *Die Geschichte der scholastischen Methode*, Freiburg im Breisgau, 1909, Vol. 1, p. 258.
29. e.g. *De Trin.*, 14, 4, 6, C.Ch., 50 A, p. 428.
30. M. Grabmann, *op. cit.*, pp. 274 f.
31. M. Grabmann, *op. cit.* p. 277; E. Gilson, *History of Christian Philosophy*, London, 1955, p. 130.
32. Eia nunc ergo tu, domine deus meus, doce cor meum ubi et quomodo te quaerat. . . . Fateor, domine, et gratias ago, quia creasti in me hanc imaginem tuam, ut tui memor te cogitem, te amem. Sed sic est abolita attritione vitiorum, sic est offuscata fumo peccatorum, ut non possit facere ad quod facta est, nisi tu renoves et reformes eam. Non tento, domine, penetrare altitudinem tuam, quia nullatenus comparo illi intellectum meum; sed desidero aliquatenus intelligere veritatem tuam, quam credit et amat cor meum. Neque enim quaero intelligere ut credam, sed credo ut intelligam. Nam et hoc credo: quia 'Nisi credidero, non intelligam.' *Prosl.*, c. 1, *Opera Omnia*, ed. F. S. Schmitt, Seckau/Edinburgh, 1938—61, Vol. 1, pp. 98, 100.
33. Inter fidem et speciem intellectum quem in hac vita capimus esse medium. *Ep. de Inc. Verbi*, c. 1, ed. Schmitt, *op. cit.*, Vol. 2, p. 3.
34. Solent enim quidam cum coeperint quasi cornua confidentis sibi scientiae producere, nescientes quia *si quis se existimat* scire *aliquid* (cf. Galatians 6:3), nondum cognovit quemadmodum oporteat eum scire, antequam habeat per soliditatem fidei alas spirituales, praesumendo in altissimas de fide quaestiones assurgere. Unde fit ut dum ad illa quae prius fidei scalam exigunt, sicut scriptum est: *Nisi credideritis, non intelligetis*, praepostere per intellectum conantur ascendere: in multimodos errores per intellectus defectum cogantur descendere. . . . Prius ergo fide mundandum est cor, sicut dicitur de deo: *Fide mundans corda eorum*; et prius per praeceptorum domini custodiam illuminandi sunt oculi, quia *praeceptum domini lucidum, illuminans oculos* (Psalm 18:9, Vulgate); et prius per humilem oboedientiam testimoniorum dei debemus fieri parvuli. . . . *Ep. de Inc Verbi*, c.1, ed. Schmitt, *op. cit.*, Vol. 2, pp. 7–8.
35. Nam qui non crediderit, non experietur; et qui expertus non fuerit non cognoscet. Quantum enim rei auditum superat experientia, tantum vincit audientis cognitionem experientis scientia. *Ibid.*, p. 9.
36. Sicut rectus ordo exigit ut profunda Christianae fidei prius credamus, quam ea praesumamus ratione discutere, ita negligentia mihi videtur, si, postquam con-

firmati sumus in fide, non studemus quod credimus intelligere. *Cur Deus Homo*, 1, 1, Commendatio operis, ed. Schmitt, Vol. 2, p. 48. Karl Barth, *Anselm: Fides Quaerens Intellectum*, E. T. London, 1960, p. 21, says: '*quaerere intellectum* is really immanent in *fides*'.

37. Tentabo pro mea possibilitate, deo adiuvante et vestris orationibus, . . . quod quaeritis non tam ostendere quam tecum quaerere; sed eo pacto quo omnia quae dico volo accipi: videlicet ut, si quid dixero quod maior non confirmet auctoritas—quamvis illud ratione probare videar –, non alia certitudine accipiatur, nisi quia interim mihi videtur, donec deus mihi melius aliquo modo revelet. *Ibid.*, 1, 2, p. 50.

38. e.g. *Super Cant.*, 28, 2, 5, *S. Bernardi Opera*, ed., J. Leclercq, C. H. Talbot, H. M. Rochais, Rome, 1957—Vol. 1, p. 195 f., citing Isaiah 7:9, Matthew 5:8, Acts 15:9. *Super Cant.* 41, 2, 2, *Opera, op. cit.*, Vol. 2, p. 29, citing Matthew 5:8, Acts 15:9.

39. J. Daniélou, 'S. Bernard et les Pères Grecs', in *S. Bernard Théologien, Analecta S. Ordinis Cist.* 3–4, Rome, 1953, p. 48 f.

40. Unde ego puto id significatum apud Prophetam, ubi ait, *Spiritus ante faciem nostram Christus Dominus; in umbra eius vivemus inter gentes*; quod scilicet videamus nunc per speculum in aenigmate, et necdum facie ad faciem. At istud sane donec vivimus inter gentes; nam inter angelos aliter. . . . Ergo iustus ex fide vivit, beatus exsultat in specie. . . . Et bona fidei umbra, quae lucem temperat oculo caliganti, et oculum praeparat luci; scriptum est enim: *Fide mundans corda eorum*. *Super Cant.* 31, 3, 8,—4, 9, *Opera, op. cit.*, Vol. 1, pp. 224 f.

41. *Ibid.* n. 9, p. 225, with reference to Luke 1:35.

42. Et sancta nihilominus Virgo fidei et ipsa experta est umbram, cui dictum est, *Et beata quae credidisti*. . . . Et Propheta, *Spiritus*, inquit, *ante faciem nostram Christus Dominus*. . . . In umbra in gentibus, in luce cum angelis. In umbra sumus quamdiu per fidem ambulamus, et non per speciem: et ideo iustus in umbra, qui ex fide vivit. At qui vivit ex intellectu, beatus est, quia non in umbra iam, sed in lumine. . . . Prius est venire ad umbram, et ita ad id, cuius umbra est, pertransire, quoniam *nisi credideritis*, ait, *non intelligetis*.

43. *Sermo in Asc. Dom.*, 3, 3, *Opera, op. cit.*, Vol. 5, pp. 132 f., citing Lamentations 4:20 and referring to Luke 1:35.

44. *La Théologie Mystique de S. Bernard*, ed. 3, Paris 1969, pp. 84 f, note 1.

45. Bonus quidem rationis circuitus: sed quando ratio ipsa intra fidei regulas se continet, et ejus terminos non excedit, *de fide ad fidem* (Romans 1:17), vel de fide ad intelligentiam pertingens. Intelligentia quidem, et si fidem excedit, non tamen aliud contuetur quam quod fide continetur. . . . Fides, ut sic dicam, veritatem rectam tenet et possidet; intelligentia revelatam et nudam contuetur; ratio conatur revelare. Ratio inter fidem intelligentiamque discurrens, ad illam se erigit, sed ista se regit. . . . Bonus circuitus, ubi *justitia Dei* revelatur *ex fide in fidem*. Bonus circuitus, ubi quis *transformatur a claritate in claritatem tanquam a Domini Spiritu*. (2 Corinthians 3:18) *In Cant.*, 4, 2, Patrologiae Latina, 184, 26–27.

46. J. P. H. Clark, 'The "Lightsome Darkness"—Aspects of Walter Hilton's Theological Background', *Downside Review*, 95 (1977), p. 107; 'Walter Hilton and Liberty of Spirit', *Ibid.*, 96 (1978), p. 66.

47. Fidei eruditio ad intelligentiae puritatem gradum praestat. *In Cant.*, 18, 3, Patrologiae Latina, 184, 93.

48. Gilbert, *In Cant.*, 18, 4–5, Patrologiae Latina, 184, 94; cf. Hilton, *Scale* 2, 42, British Library, Ms. Harley 6579, f. 131 ᵛ; E. Underhill's edn., London, 1923, p. 438. Ms. Harley 6579 is being used by Professor S. S. Hussey as the base-text for his edition of *Scale* 2, for the Early English Text Society. For *Scale* 1, the textual tradition is more complicated, and Professor A. J. Bliss is using Ms. Cambridge University Library Add. 6686 for his Early English Text Society edition. In this paper all references to *Scale* 1, will be to C.U.L. Add. 6686. Those to *Scale* 2, to Harley 6579, with cross-references to Evelyn Underhill's edition, which is based on

Harley 6579 throughout, and so is generally reliable (apart from a few minor errors) for *Scale* 2, but not for Hilton's own text of *Scale* 1.

49. J. P. H. Clark, 'Thomas Maldon, O.C.C., a fourteenth-century Cambridge Theologian', at press with *Carmelus*.

50. J. Russell Smith, 'Walter Hilton and a Tract in Defence of the Veneration of Images', *Dominican Studies*, 7 (1954), pp. 184 f.

51. A. B. Emden, *A Biographical Dictionary of the University of Cambridge to A.D. 1500*, Cambridge, 1963, s.v. Hilton, Walter de.

52. A. B. Emden, *op. cit.*, s.v. Fishlake, Thomas.

53. Cf. J. P. H. Clark, 'Sources and Theology in the "Cloud of Unknowing" ', *Downside Review*, 98 (1980), p. 109, note 103. In connection with the judgement given there, it should perhaps be noted that whereas *Ep. ad Solitarium* and *Scale* 2, both make obvious use of Gilbert of Hoyland, *Scale* 1 does not. But this does not in itself mean that *Scale* 1, antedates *Ep. ad Solitarium*; it may well be that Hilton simply felt no need to use Gilbert in *Scale* 1, although he knew his work.

54. Verumptamen, ut secure in hoc exercicio percurres, pone stabile fundamentum, fidem scilicet. *Accedentem*, inquit apostolus, *ad Deum, oportet credere quia est, et quia remunerator, etc.* (Hebrews 11:6). Fides ergo sit firma radix tue opposicionis, ut simpliciter credas articulos fidei, et precipue hunc, scilicet remiscionem peccatorum, quia in hoc solet uanus timor oriri et pusillanimes perturbare, quandoque ex immiscione diaboli. . . . *Ep. ad Solitarium*, British Library MS. Royal 6, E III, f. 121 ʳ, col. 1. All references to *Ep. ad Solitarium* are to this manuscript.

55. The need for faith as the remedy against diabolical temptation to doubt one's salvation is a main theme of Flete's little book. For the influence of Flete on Hilton's account of the life of faith in the midst of spiritual desolation, in *Scale* 1, 37–38, and *Scale* 2, 28, see Clark, 'The "Lightsome Darkness . . ." ', *op. cit.*, pp. 108 f. Flete opens *De Remediis* with Hebrews 11:6, 'Quia, ut ait Apostolus, impossibile est sine fide placere Deo . . .', and speaks of faith as 'petra fundamentalis ecclesie' (MS. Bodley 43, p. 139). Cf. *Ep. ad Solitarium*, f. 121 ʳ, including a ref. to Hebrews 11:6, note in note 54.

De Remediis, p. 141, speaks of faith as a 'habitus voluntatis'. Other passages in Hilton which recall Flete's pre-occupations and emphases include: *Ep. ad Quemdam Seculo renunciare Volentem*, British Library MS. Royal 6, E, III, f. 115 ᵛ, col. 2 – 116 ʳ, col. 1, on resisting doubts as to the reality of absolution: 'firmissime credere debes graciam tibi infusam . . . certissime credere debes . . .'; also f. 116 ᵛ, cols. 1–2; *Scale* 1, 21, C. U.L. Add. MS. 6686, pp. 294, col. 2 –295, col. 1, on faith in the teaching and laws of the Church, and in one's salvation— 'siker trouth . . . with all the will of þin hert'; *Scale* 2, 8, Harley 6579, f. 69 ʳ, Underhill edn., p. 250: 'riʒt as þe proprete of faiþ is for-to trow þat þou sees not . . .', recalling Hebrews 11:6, though this is commonplace anyway; *Scale* 2, 11, f. 73 ʳ, p. 265: 'trow stidefastli þat þei arn forgifen . . .'; *Scale* 2, 21, f. 85 ʳ, p. 305: 'trust sikirly þawʒ þu haue synned . . . here-bifore. . . .

56. Isaiah 7:9 is similarly ascribed to 'the Apostle' in *Ep. de Utilitate et Prerogativis Religionis*, MS. Bodley Lat. Theol. e 26, f. 128 ᵛ; *Scale* 2, 11, f. 73 ᵛ, p. 265.

57. Tunc enim isto fundamento posito, si sencias motus et conceptus spirituales qualescumque (ms: qualiscumque) insolitos, siue pertineant ad intellectum ac si haberes oculum apertum in misteriis perscrutandis, siue ad affectum (ms: effectum) ac si sentires ignem estuantem in tuis visceribus, sic humiliter et prudenter debes recipere vt totaliter eis non hereas, nec tamen recuses, sed statim ad Christum habeas recursum et ad ecclesie fidem. . . . Redige in captiuitatem simplicis et quasi stulte fidei omnem intellectum extollentem se super se aduersus illam. Nichil recipiendum est quod ordinacioni ecclesie et dictis sanctorum patrum, doctorum ab ecclesia approbatorum auctoritati obruat. Et eciam si aliquid sensias quod per ecclesiam expresse nondum declaratur, nec antiquos patres detegitur in

lucem, teipsum in hoc deseras et ecclesie fidei tam te quam illud committe, nec pertinaciter inhereas sensui tuo quasi illuminato a veritate pro illius quasi veritatis defencione. Bonus ergo circuitus cordis tui in exercicio spirituali est quando incipit a fide ecclesie et ad eandem redit; sic enim, secundum Apostolum, *reuelatur iusticia Dei ex fide in fidem*, cum *iustus ex fide viut*, et qui in hac fide probatus inuentus est, forsitan fructum fidei percipiet, videlicet intellectum, *ex parte* tamen quamdiu *peregrinatur a Domino*; *Nisi credideritis*, inquit Apostolus (sic), *non intelligetis*. (f. 121 ʳ, cols. 1–2).

58. See above, notes 40–43, on *Super Cant.* 31, and *In Asc. Dom.*, 3. See also *Super Cant.* 48, *Opera, op. cit.*, 2. pp. 67 f. Mary's fear at the Annunciation is referred to in *Ep. ad Solitarium*, f. 121 ᵛ, col. 1. Ibid., f. 122 ᵛ, col. 1, 'Nam Deus dereliquid (sic) nobis latissimos intelligencie campos in sacra scriptura . . .' finds a parallel in Bernard, *Sermo in Asc. Dom.*, 3, 2 (the remote source for Bernard is Jerome, *Ep.* 148, 14). For Hilton's 'in umbra fidei . . . quiescere' in the following quotation, cf. Bernard *Super Cant.* 48, 6, 8, *Opera*, 2, *op. cit.*, p. 72, 'quiescere in umbra'. Gilbert of Hoyland uses Lamentations 4:20 a in his *In Cant.* 6, 5, Patrologiae Latina 184, 41, without actually citing 20 b, 'sub umbra eius . . .', and with a different emphasis to Bernard; he emphasises, like Anselm, that although illumination in earth falls short of that in heaven, yet it is in a real sense illumination; he goes on to describe the transitory and fluctuating nature of the 'visio': 'Visio haec vel in revelata spiritualiter veritate per intelligentiam, vel in suavitate infusa per gratiam . . . , quamvis futurum juxta modum nondum plena, vicina tamen; vicina qualitate, non aequalitate. . . . Subitanea est et momentanea, repente veniens et repente vadens: et si momentanea est, manent tamen reliquiae cogitationis. . .'.

59. E. Gilson, *La Théologie Mystique de S. Bernard, op. cit.*, p. 166 f. But cf. also Gilbert of Hoyland, *In Cant.* 6, 5, referred to in note 58.

60. *Crede* ergo humiliter ut ueraciter *intelligas*, et tamen quodcumque intellexeris occulte fidei secure committe, eligens pocius dormire interim in umbra fidei quam in luce intellectus dum non (ms: non dum) clara sicut . . . est accipitur, uigilare. *Spiritus*, inquit propheta, *ante faciem nostram Christus Dominus: sub umbra eius uiuemus inter gentes*. Christus enim lux est, fides umbra eius; licet enim Christus quandoque ostendat oculo mentis spiritualiter, uidelicet ut ueritatem, ut bonitatem, ut caritatem; subito tamen abscondit se, et tunc utile est in umbra fidei humanitatis illius uidelicet quiescere, et hoc inter gentes, non inter angelos. (f. 121 ʳ, col. 2).

61. Cf. Augustine, *En. Ps.*, 135, 8, C.Ch., 40, p. 1962: Intellegimus sapientiam in cognitione et dilectione eius quod semper est . . . , matched in Hilton, *Scale* 1, 8, C.U.L. Add. MS. 6686, p. 282, col. 2, Underhill edn. p. 14.

62. Si tamen perseueraueris (ms: persaneraueris), . . . sensies magnam libertatem et quietem . . . , et tunc quodam dulci affectu perstringes illam quietem quam adeptus es, et forsan intellectu illuminato sensum percipies tue oracionis . . . (ff. 121 ᵛ, col. 2–122 ʳ, col. 1).

63. Concepisti Christum per fidem, et forsan nondum uiuificatur in te per intelligencie lumen, neque formatur per dulcedinem caritatis; labora ergo . . . ut . . . Christus formetur et firmetur in te *in uirum perfectum, in mensuram etatis plenitudinis Christi*. (Ephesians 4:13), f. 122 ᵛ, col. 2.

64. See notes 60, 62, 63.

65. Dicit apostolus (sic), *Nisi credideritis, non intelligetis*. Crede ergo prius humiliter, ut postea ueraciter intelligas, et tunc reuera fructum spiritualem sencies in effectu (sic). (MS. Bodley Lat. theol. e, 26, f. 128 ᵛ).

66. Desideras lucem intelligencie, et consciencie quietem. . . . Firmissime credere debes graciam tibi infusam . . . (British Library, MS. Royal 6, E, III, ff. 115 ᵛ, col. 2–116 ʳ, col. 1).

67. p. 283, col. 1, p. 16.

68. pp. 283, col. 2–283, col. 1, pp. 17 f.
69. Augustine, *De Trin.*, *op. cit.*, 10, 11, 17,—12, 19; 14, 6, 8,—12, 16; Cf. Peter Lombard, *Sent.*, I. d. 3 cc. 2–3, Quarrachi, 1916, Vol. 1, pp. 33–36.
70. p. 314, col. 1, p. 100.
71. p. 292, cols. 1–2, pp. 41 f.
72. p. 318, col. 1, p. 109.
73. p. 325, col. 1, p. 128.
74. For sensible 'felyng' in *Scale* 1: e.g. ch. 11, p. 285, col. 1, p. 21; in *Scale* 2, e.g. ch. 29, f. 100 ^{v}, p. 352; for spiritual 'felyng' in *Scale* 1, e.g. *loc. cit.*; in *Scale* 2, *passim*.
75. f. 66 ^{r} p. 238.
76. f. 67 ^{r} p. 241.
77. f. 66 ^{r} pp. 237 f.
78. f. 67 ^{r} p. 241.
79. f. 67 ^{r} p. 242.
80. ff. 69 ^{v}–70 ^{r} pp. 253–4.
81. See especially *Scale* 2, 40, f. 123, p. 416 f; also 2, 41, f. 127 ^{r} p. 426.
82. Cf. note 10 above, with reference to Augustine, *Sermo*, 118, 1.
83. f. 73 ^{v} pp. 265 f.
84. *De Imagine Peccati*, Bodley, MS. Digby, 115, pp. 6 ^{v}–7 ^{r}, refers to the awakening of all five spiritual senses as the image of God in us is restored and we discover the God who was never far from us, citing Acts 17:28. There is a similarity of thought with Augustine, *En. Ps.*, 99.5 (cited in note 18 above), though it would be too much to claim that this passage in Augustine is specifically a source.
    Scale 2, 43, f. 134 ^{r} p. 446 refers to 'þe inly wittes of þe soule. . . .'. There are almost innumerable references to one or other of the spiritual senses.
85. *Scale* 2, 21, f. 85 ^{v} p. 306.
86. *Scale* 2, 32, f. 107 pp. 370–1.
87. *Scale* 2, 33, f. 110 ^{r} p. 378.
88. *Scale* 2, 29, f. 101 ^{v} p. 355.
89. *Scale* 2, 30, f. 105 ^{r} p. 364.
90. *Super Cant.* 74, 1, 1–2, *Opera*, *op. cit.*, Vol. 2, p. 240.
91. *In Cant.* 1, 3, Patrologiae Latina, p. 184, 14. In hac nocte potest Jesus meus magis dulci quodam affectu suaviter sentiri, quam sciri ad purum'. This sermon uses Psalm 138:11, (Vulgate), which is also quoted in *Scale* 1, 9, – but this text is a commonplace anyway. There are, however, clear signs that this sermon (with other sources too) underlies *Scale* 2, 24. J. P. H. Clark, 'The "Lightsome Darkness . . .".' *op. cit.*, p. 107.
92. e.g. *De Nat. et Dig. Amoris*, ed. M. Davy, Paris, 1953, c. 18, p. 94, (uses the commonplace Romans 12:2); c. 37, p. 114: Scripturarum interiorem sensum, et virtutem mysteriorum et sacramentorum Dei ceperimus non solum intelligere, sed etiam quadam . . . experientie manu palpare et tractare, quod non fit nisi quodam conscientie sensu. . . .
    Spec. Fidei, ed. M. Davy, Paris, 1959, c. 3, p. 26, speaks of *intelligere*, citing also Romans 1:17, and presupposing the transition from faith to understanding; c. 63, p. 76, identifies 'feeling' with 'understanding': Mens pro sensu habet intellectum, eo sentit quicquid sentit. Instances could be multiplied in these—and other—authors.
93. *The Cloud of Unknowing*, ed. P. Hodgson, Early English Text Society, O.S, 218, London, 1944, p. 34. 'Felyng' takes the place of clear sight of God in this life.
94. *Scale* 2, 41, f. 129 ^{r} p. 432.
95. *Scale* 2, 41, f. 129 ^{v} p. 433.
96. e.g. St Thomas, *Summa Theologica*, q. 12 a 13 ad 1.
97. *Scale* 2, 43, f. 135 ^{r} p. 449.
98. *Scale* 2, 40, f. 126 ^{r} p. 423.
99. See notes 10 and 82 on a probable echo of Augustine, *Sermo* 118, 1 in *Scale* 2, 11.

100. MS. Bodley Lat. Theol. e. 26, f. 129 ᵛ, referring to 'Gregorious magnus . . . , sanctus Bernardus, uenerabilis Anselmus, Hugo de sancto Victore et specialiter Thomas de Alquino.'
101. J. P. H. Clark, 'Thomas Maldon . . .' *op. cit.*
102. Esp. Lib. 1, c. 20; Lib. 2, c. 8 and 11 ed. Schmitt, *op. cit.*, Vol. 2, pp. 86 f. 120 f. 109 f.
103. q. 3, c. 9, ed. Schmitt, *op. cit.*, Vol. 2, pp. 276 f.
104. p. 306, col. 2, p. 80.
105. Cf. Augustine, *Tr. in Ioann. Ep. ad Parthos* 3, 1–2, Patrologiae Latina, 35.1998.
106. J. P. H. Clark, 'Sources and Theology in *The Cloud* . . .', *op. cit.*, p. 96.
107. See e.g. G. Leff, *The Dissolution of the Mediaeval Outlook*, New York, 1976, ch. 1. In Hilton's Milieu, for Thomas Maldon on the sense in which theology may be called a science, in keeping with the above, see J. P. H. Clark, 'Thomas Maldon . . .' *op. cit.*,
108. J. P. H. Clark, 'Walter Hilton and "Liberty of Spirit" ', *op. cit.*, p. 61–78.

126

CHRIST, THE TEACHER, IN JULIAN'S SHOWINGS: THE BIBLICAL AND PATRISTIC TRADITIONS

RITAMARY BRADLEY

IN THE SHORT VERSION of the *Showings*, Julian of Norwich introduces her account of her revelations with this disclaimer:

> Botte god for bede that ȝe schulde saye or take it so that I am a techere, for I meene nouȝt soo, no I mente nevere so; for I am a womann, leued, febille and freylle. Botte I wate wele, this that I saye, I hafe it of the schewynge of hym tha(t) es souerayne techare. . . . Thane schalle ȝe sone forgette me that I am a wrecche, and dose so that I lette ȝowe nought, and behalde Jhesu that ys techare of alle . . . in alle thynge I lyeve as haly kyrke techis. . . .[1].

Commentators have speculated that this passage may reflect some conflict Julian experienced from prohibitions against women as teachers.[2] Indeed, such prohibitions existed, but there is no precise historical evidence to show that Julian was thinking of such a difficulty. Be that as it may, Julian preserves the concept of Christ, the teacher, throughout both versions of her book. She uses the concept as the basic rhetorical strategy of her accounts, while portraying herself, not as teacher, but as the one taught. At the same time she invites the reader also to take the stance of one learning, according to individual capacity, from Christ, the teacher. In this paper I will show how this rhetorical strategy focused on Christ the teacher appears in the *Showings*. Then I will survey briefly the scriptural and patristic traditions which present Christ, the teacher, as a symbol of the development and fullness of the mystical life. And in a third part I will show how the rich and complex concept of Christ, the teacher, adds to the literary texture of Julian's work.

I. *Christ, the Teacher, in the Texts of the Showings*

By using the concept of Christ as teacher Julian creates a rhetorical strategy which sets her work apart from other writings of its kind. She avoids the method of classical wisdom literature, which portrays the writer as a guide instructing one or more others. Likewise, she circumvents a method widespread in vision literature, in which the visionary simply reports personal revelations. Instead, she creates a dramatic construct built on the relation of disciple to teacher. And, in harmony with her basic purpose—to write for all Christ's lovers—she creates a second rhetorical level, which draws each reader into dialogue with Christ, the teacher, with each one learning according to personal gifts of reason and grace. Though from the beginning Julian perceives a correspondence between the teaching roles of Christ and the Church, this bond grows stronger in her experience as the *Showings* unfold.

Introductions in Both Texts. In the introductory matter and in the accounts of the first revelation, Julian clearly structures her ideas as a dialogue with Christ, the teacher, slowly and explicitly in the short version, sharply and suggestively in the long text. In the short version the concept enters as if by chance: she affirms that Christ 'teches us' as part of the metaphor of Christ as our clothing (S. 4, 5, 212), though how these two ideas fit together is not immediately clear. Not until chapter six—in the passage cited in the opening of this paper—does she say clearly that the revelation is 'a techynge . . . of Jhesu Cryste', intended for all her co-Christians (S. 6, 9, 219). These include those who know no more than the 'common techynge of holy Church', and by implication those with considerable intellectual formation, whose knowledge extends to a broader category, the 'trewe techynge' of that same Church (S. 6, 56, 223). In the following chapter Julian notes that the threefold mode of the revelation—bodily, intellectual, and spiritual—showed forth the 'blyssede techynge of oure lord god' (S. 7, 1, 224).

In the long version in the first chapter Julian identifies the showings as 'techynges of endeless wisdom and loue' (L. 1, 6, 281). In the context of the first revelation she explains that the purpose of all the showings is 'to lerne our soule wisely' to cling to God (L. 6, 1–2, 304). The revelation as a whole is called a 'lesson of loue', which was shown because Christ wills that 'we be occupyed in knowing [and louyng] tylle the tyme comyth that we shal be fulfylled in hevyn' (L. 6, 60–62, 309). The transition to the next chapter is: 'And to lerne vs thys' (L. 7, 1, 310). In what seems to be a re-working of the short text she stresses that her audience extends to those who have only the common teaching of the Church (L. 9, 8, 322) and adds a hope that those will be 'truly taught' (L. 9, 18, 322) who perceive the union between all that has been made and the maker of all. She was taught in the highest of the modes of the revelations that they were intended for all Christ's lovers: 'for I am lerynd in the gostely schewing of our lord god that he meneth so' (L. 8, 33–34, 319–320). She again resolves to accept no showing contrary to what 'the chyrch prechyth and techyth' (L. 9, 21–22, 323).

Short Text: Revelations II–XVI. Words referring to learning, being taught, the teaching of Christ, and Christ, the teacher, occur frequently in the remainder of the short text, after the introduction just surveyed.[3] Then at the end, with a sense of unity in this work of Christ, the teacher, Julian says: 'Alle the blissede techynge of oure lorde god was schewed to me in three partyes, as I hafe sayde before . . .' (S. 23, 57–58, 272).

Long Text: Chapters 10–86. In the body of the long version references to the teaching concept are even more frequent than in the short text, and they contribute more directly to the unity of the whole. There are fifty-eight explicit references to teaching and learning, distributed over thirty-seven chapters.[4]

Some texts refer to the educative process. At times learning unfolds by explanation and rhetorical questioning. Of this process Julian says: 'Thus myghtly, wysely and louyngly was the sowle examynd in this vision' (L. 11, 56–57, 341). In addition, this process goes on until its purpose is achieved, as she says at one point: 'For we be alle in part trobelyd, and we schal be trobeled, folowyng our master Jhesu, tylle we be fule purgyd of oure dedely flesch, and of alle oure inwarde affections whych be nott very good' (L. 27, 18–21, 405–406). And, in this long process, the divine teacher admonishes the disciple to study and reflect, as Julian explains in relation to the parable of the lord and the servant:

> For twenty yere after the tyme of the shewyng saue three monthys I had techyng inwardly as I shall sey: It longyth to thee to take hede to alle þe propertes and condescions that were shewed in the example, though þe thyngke that it be mysty and indefferent to thy syght (L. 51, 86–89, 520–521).

Appropriately Julian clearly labels as a teaching what is conveyed in the most exalted of the revelations, the twelfth, wherein she is shown Christ glorified. She says of this experience: '. . . I was lered that oure soule schalle nevyr reste tylle it come into hym . . .' (L. 26, 4–5, 402).

Likewise, when she calls in doubt the whole of the showings, thinking that she may have raved, Jesus as teacher reassures her, saying: 'But take it, and lerne it, and kepe thee ther in, and comfort the

129

ther with, and trust therto, and thou shalt nott be ovyr com' (L. 70, 37–40, 653).

Again, as the treatise draws to a close, we see how central to the rhetorical unity of the whole were those earlier assertions that Christ is teacher. First, her tensions over any possible conflict between the speaker of the showings and the voice of the Church are resolved when Christ identifies himself both as the one revealed in the visions and as the Church teaching: 'I it am that is alle. I it am that holy church precyth and techyth thee. I it am that shewde me before to the' (L. 26, 10–11, 402–403). Second, this identity between the Christ-teacher and the Church as teacher is set forth as the focal point of relationships for all Christians, in a learning process which finally makes the learner one with the divine teacher:

> God schewde fulle grett plesannce that he hath in alle men and women that myghtly and wysely take the prechyng and the techyng of holy chyrch, for he it is, holy chyrch. He is the grounde, he is the substannce, he is the techyng, he is the teacher, he is the ende [or leryd] and he is the mede . . . (L. 34, 15–19, 431).

Then, recalling the twofold audience which her rhetorical strategy posits, she first says, as though referring to herself: 'Alle this homely shewynge of our curteyse lorde, it is a louely lesson and a swete gracious techyng of hym self, in comforthyng of our soule' (L. 79, 22–24, 274). Next, she explicitly recalls the wider audience, using the key words which refer to instruction: 'And all this lernyng and this tru comfort, it is general to alle myne evyn crysten . . .' (L. 68, 63–64, 646).

Finally, as she had introduced the showings as a 'lesson of love' she fittingly ends with a companion statement in the last chapter: 'Thus was I lerynd, þat loue is oure lordes menyng' (L. 86, 20, 733).

II. *Christ, the Teacher, in Christian Thought*

When Julian cast her showings into a report of a lesson coming from Christ, the teacher, she entered into a tradition with deep roots in Christian thought. The title has its source in accounts of the historical Jesus of the gospels, who was addressed as master and took that title to himself.[5] This biblical concept grew through doctrinal interpretations and scriptural exegesis into a mystical symbol, signifying that those who listen to the teacher, Christ, can become that which he teaches by word and in his person: the disciples can become one with him.

I will trace some of the major links and changes in this tradition of

Christ, the teacher, stressing particularly how it unfolds as a symbol of the contemplative life and mystical union – the senses in which Julian employed it.

New Testament. The texts which appealed to Christian writers when they considered Christ as teacher occur in all the gospels, in several epistles, and at the beginning of Acts. Among texts especially crucial to the mystical tradition are these: 1. Matthew 23: 8–10: 'But be you not called Rabbi. For one is your master; and you are all brethren. . . . Neither be ye called master; for one is your Master, Christ'; 2. John 13:13–14: 'You call me Master and Lord; and you say well, for so I am. If, then, I being your Lord and Master have washed your feet; you ought also to wash one another's feet'; 3. Galatians 3:24–28: 'Wherefore the law was our pedagogue in Christ. . . . But after the faith is come, we are no longer under a pedagogue. For you are all the children of God in faith, in Christ Jesus. For as many of you as have been baptized in Christ have put on Christ. [In Christ] there is neither . . . male or female. For you are all one in Christ Jesus'; 4. Luke 6:40: 'The fully-trained disciple will always be like his master'; 5) John 11:28:' . . . she [Martha] called her sister Mary secretly, saying: 'The Master is come and calleth for thee'. Many other texts were also explored for the meaning and symbolism within mysticism of tutor and teacher or master as applied to Christ.

The Apostolic Fathers. When martyrdom was thought of as the gateway to the mystical life, Ignatius, martyr-bishop of Antioch (writing about 110), called Jesus the 'mouth' by which the Father has spoken,[6] and the teacher for whom the prophets waited. True disciples cannot live apart from this divine teacher.[7] Ignatius, furthermore, invited those disciples to contemplation when he said of the one teacher:

> There is then one Teacher, who spake and it was done; while even those things which He did in silence are worthy of the Father. He who possesses the word of Jesus, is truly able to hear even His very silence, that he may be perfect, and may both act as he speaks, and be recognized for his silence.[8]

The Apologists. One of the first-century apologists, Justin Martyr (111–165) says succinctly that Jesus Christ is a teacher, from God and Son of God.[9] This teacher is 'reason (or the Word, the Logos) who . . . became man and was called Jesus Christ'.[10] Moreover, from this master we have the name of Christians.[11]

Anti-Gnostic Writers. A major witness in the second century to the concept of Christ as teacher is Ireneaus of Lyons. He introduces

131

the thought that the 'true and steadfast Teacher' 'through His transcendent love [became] what we are, that He might bring us to be what He is Himself'.[12] He uses 'Christ as teacher' for his central doctrine, which is at the heart of the experience of such mystics as Julian: namely, that Christ renewed all by recapitulating in himself all that had been interrupted with the fall of Adam. Furthermore, Ireneaeus uses the verb 'to follow' in the sense of a disciple following a master (*magister, doctor*) in possession of the truth.[13]

The Alexandrians. At Alexandria, in the second and third centuries, in the oldest centre of sacred science in the history of Christianity, Clement and Origen developed with considerable fullness the concept of Christ the teacher, adding a depth which influenced later writers. In fact, it is a unifying, central idea in Clement's thought, appearing in minor works, supplying the title to *The Tutor* (or *Pedagogue*), and inspiring a plan for a projected work, which he intended to call *The Teacher*.[14] Clement believed, too, that women as well as men are called to learn from the divine teacher;[15] and the teacher is designated by the feminine names of Wisdom and Mother.[16] Moreover, Clement conjoins teacher with father, mother, and friend, to stress the disciple's participation in the divine nature:

> 'For he that loveth father or mother more than me' the Father and Teacher of the truth, who regenerates and creates anew, and nourishes the elect soul, 'is not worthy of me'. He means, to be a son of God and a disciple of God, and at the same time also to be a friend, and of kindred nature.[17]

Frequently, also, Clement brings out the illumination of the soul by the divine Word who is teacher.[18]

Clement's thought is central, in turn, to that of his pupil Origen. As Jean Daniélou says:

> It might be said that being a *didaskalos* himself, Origen regarded his God as a Didaskalos too, as Master in charge of the education of children, and looked on God's universe as a vast *didaskaleion* in which every single thing contributed to the education of human beings at school there.[19]

Origen makes explicit how this idea applies to the mystical life. In fact, incipient in Origen is the classical notion of the three stages of the mystical life, which he presented as progressions in learning under the tutelage of divine wisdom: '. . . taught of God's wisdom, it [the soul] might say: The things that are hid and that are manifest have I learned'.[20]

In another mystical passage Origen explores the analogy of study:

> If you are eager to study in Christ the exact meaning of this and the other

texts: if, in wishing to pass beyond that knowledge which you have *through a glass and in a dark manner*, you hasten to Him who summons you—you will understand all this as never before, *face to face*, as being friends of the heavenly Father and Teacher. For His friends see things as they are. . . .[21]

The Early Church in Africa. Cyprian (200–258), bishop of Carthage, calls Christ teacher to emphasize that the disciples are all equal – learned and unlearned, men and women.[22] He parallels the title master to that of lord in speaking of Christ, whom he calls 'the Teacher of peace and Master of unity'.[23] Elsewhere he speaks of 'the Lord, the Teacher of our life and Master of eternal salvation'.[24]

Lactantius (c. 250–317), a defender of learning within the Church and, in his old age, an impoverished tutor of the son of Constantine, carries forward the theme of Christ, the teacher, throughout his *Divine Institutes*. He devotes all of chapter twenty-four (Book Four) to the subject. In accord with tradition he designates Christ as 'a teacher, a living law'.[25]

Beginnings of Egyptian Monasticism. Because of the recent discovery of the Christian tract, the 'Teachings of Sylvanus' among the Coptic Nag Hammadi writings, we have a source for Christ the teacher as a concept important to early monks and anchorites. In fact, the text, which may date from the second or third century, could have been written by a forerunner of a monastic community. In any event it was known and used in monastic circles.[26] This Christian Wisdom-piece has many implicit and several explicit passages referring to the divine teacher. For example: 'Accept Christ this true friend as a good teacher';[27] 'Know who Christ is, and acquire him as a friend. . . . He is also God and Teacher';[28] 'The divine teacher is with you always, He is a helper, and he meets you because of the good which is in you';[29] '. . . he is troubled about every one whom he arduously brings to instruction';[30] 'Do not flee from the divine and the teaching which are within you, for he who is teaching loves you very much';[31] 'This teacher is Wisdom your mother, from whom you came into being';[32] she 'became the mother of all'.[33] The tract as a whole, in fact, is addressed to those studying the ideals of the monastic life under divine tutelage.

Cappadocian Fathers. St Basil the Great (died c. 379), the principal founder of monastic life in the Greek Church, developed the theme of Christ the teacher in homilies on the Psalms. Considering the Psalms a chief means for contemplation, he calls them a 'treasury of instructions' and a 'training of the soul'.[34] They are studied under the 'common Director of our lives, the great Teacher' who 'wisely and cleverly sets forth the rewards, in order that . . . we might press on in spirit to eternal blessings'.[35] In a homily advocating the 'contemplation of truth', Basil affirms that Christ taught the beatitudes by deeds as well as by words. He then asks rhetorically: 'Who will teach us the beauty of peace? The Peacemaker Himself, who makes peace and reconciles two men into one new man'.[36] Another Cappadocian, Gregory of Nyssa (died 394), for whom the Christ-teacher concept is not a pervasive theme, nonetheless uses it occasionally. For example, he implies, as Clement of Alexandria had taught, that 'the good tutor is Wisdom',[37] when, in the treatise 'On Virginity' he says: 'He [God] is not fear, nor anger, nor any other emotion which sways the untutored soul, but . . . He is Very Wisdom and Sanctification . . .'.[38]

Cyril of Jerusalem (died 386). Cyril, a contemporary of the Cappadocian fathers, follows the tradition which identifies Christ as teacher for the infirmities of the spirit and physician for the infirmities of the body: Christ, he says, 'adapts himself to our infirmities as . . . the very kindest of physicians or as an understanding teacher'.[39]

St John Chrysostom (died 407). This doctor of the Greek Church presents Christ as teacher, but not in allegorical terms. He takes the view that in the historical sense the function of the law was to prepare human nature for the teacher.[40] Also he develops the text from Matthew (23:10), which stresses that 'one is your Master, and ye are brethren'.[41] In another place he admonishes all to apply the words of Isaias, 'They shall be all taught of God', to the pursuit of the perfect way—conformity to the divine teacher.[42]

Throughout he defines the following of Christ as accepting the instruction of the master and describes Christ's call to holiness in terms of a divine pedagogy.[43]

Latin Fathers of the Fifth Century—Jerome, Ambrose, and Augustine. Jerome repeated that Christ is called teacher, because all things are through him, and because through the mystery of the Incarnation, we are all reconciled with God. But at this time a controversial note arises: why do others—monks, for example—call themselves father or teacher, given the scriptural admonition to the contrary? Jerome does not offer a very convincing answer, but he states that 'We call a man father or teacher to honor his age'.[44]

Ambrose also deals with the problem of why he appropriates to himself the role of teacher, when indeed, 'One is the true Master'.[45] Indeed, he concedes, '. . . in the Gospel and in the Law, he [Christ] first taught us moral instruction, and in His suffering and in His every act and deed . . . the very substance and marrow of wisdom. . .'.[46] Nonetheless, Ambrose accepts for himself the title of master, explaining that unlike the divine teacher he will continue to learn by the act of being a teacher.[47]

Augustine handles this objection that no one on earth, except Jesus, should take the title of teacher by interpreting this injunction to mean that Christ is the only interior teacher, the instructor of minds and hearts.[48] This is the point made in his influential work, *De Magistro*, which translates Matthew 23:9 as: 'There is One in heaven who is the Teacher of all', and uses 'in heaven' as a synonym for the blessed life, found by those who truly know and love God.[49] This interpretation considerably softens the force of the text. Moreover, Augustine allegorizes the scriptural detail that says Christ taught sitting down, saying that this signifies the dignity of the teaching office.[50] In a list of paradoxes he includes the statement that 'the Teacher is beaten with whips', referring to the scourging of Christ and implying that it is the function of the teacher to chastise his pupils, not the other way around.[51] Essentially, however, Augustine uses the notion of the interior teacher as a mystical symbol, parallel to widely-employed symbols of union with the divine. Note, for example, this passage from the *Confessions*:

> I myself will enter into my chamber, and there will I sing a love-song unto thee . . . calling to mind Jerusalem . . . which is my mother, and thyself who are the Ruler of it, the illuminator, the Father, Tutor, Husband, the chaste and strong delight, the lasting joy . . . the One Supreme and true Good. . . .[52]

But by interpreting the references to Christ, the one teacher, as meaning the one interior teacher, Augustine lent his authority to a restricted view of this symbol. What was lost from the patrimony of the apostolic Fathers was the concept that 'you are all brothers', because one alone is the teacher. Thus the hierarchical view of the Christian Church was left intact, whereas equality among Christians, including women, was a muted concept.

St Benedict of Nursia (died c. 547). The father of western monasticism announced in his rule that he was about to 'establish a school for the service of the Lord . . . according to His teaching'.[53] Those who persevered 'according to His teaching until death' will share in his kingdom.[54] That which the monks learn is indeed a contemplative lesson—that is, to put nothing ahead of the love of Jesus, the source of all good.

Gregory the Great (died 604). Like St Basil, Gregory generally refers to Christ as teacher and example in the context of moral instruction.[55] He understands Christ to be 'the historical power of goodness in the world, the teacher and exemplar. . .'.[56] He notes that 'the divine Master, who is Truth Itself', taught at times through his human presence, at other times through inspiration.[57] But the link to the contemplative life is implicit in Gregory's theme that the master is the supreme teacher of humility, even unto death. Gregory's exegesis favors the stress on the interior teacher, as in Augustine. For example, he says that the temple and the house of God, where he teaches, is the mind and conscience of the faithful.[58]

Bernard of Clairvaux (died 1153). Though Bernard opposed the sense in which Abelard called Christ a teacher, the abbot of Clairvaux himself made the idea central to his teaching on contemplation. Monks were in the school of Christ. True disciples heard Christ's teachings in contemplation and heeded them in action, joining the examples of Martha and Mary in the full life of devotion to Christ the teacher.[59] Paradoxically, Christ the teacher was first a pupil, learning not only obedience by mercy, and coming to know by experience what he already knew as God.[60]

William of St Thierry (died 1148). Benedictine mystical theology also transmits the title of Christ, the teacher, through the works of William of St Thierry. He traces our illumination in faith to Christ, the pedagogue,[61] possibly echoing in this the writings of Origen.[62]

St Thomas Aquinas (died 1274). Aquinas devotes a question in *De Veritate* to Christ, the teacher. This *quaestio* centres on Matthew 23:8–10. Thomas argues from that text that though God alone is the one teacher, this means that only God teaches interiorly, citing the authority of Augustine for this view.[63] Thomas might also have received the notion from Albertus Magnus, who writes in the same vein in his mystical theology.[64]

St Bonaventure (died 1274): A full development of the Christ-teacher concept occurs in St Bonaventure's sermon, 'Christus unus omnium magister'.[65] Christ is the one teacher, Bonaventure maintains, in that he teaches all forms of knowledge, ranging from sense knowledge to contemplative wisdom.

Also in his sermon Bonaventure associates a number of images with the basic metaphor of the teacher. With Clement of Alexandria he says that this divine teacher is the mother who feeds her little ones with milk. Also the flesh of the word incarnate is the diadem which crowns Christ, the master, and the true Solomon. This one teacher is the feeding-ground (pasture) of contemplative knowledge, which is twofold in its source: interior, in the Godhead, and exterior, in the humanity of Jesus. Again, the teacher is the door of the sheepfold as well as the pasturing ground. Through that door—the flesh of Jesus—ecclesiastical hierarchies pass, going through the classical stages of contemplation—purgation, illumination and perfection.

Bonaventure cites the authority of scripture to point out that Christ, the one master, is to be honored, listened to, and questioned. He is to be honored because of the dignity of his teaching, revealed in texts from Matthew 23:8–10: 'one is your master, and you are all brothers'; from John 13:13–14, where the true master teaches by the example of the washing of the feet; and from Luke 14:37, where it is said that if one does not follow the master he cannot be his disciple.

Thus, with the addition of some ideas of his own, Bonaventure transmits elements in a long tradition which stressed the concept of Christ as teacher. We turn now to reassess Julian's figure of the Christ-teacher, viewed in the light of this tradition in the thought of a continuous line of ecclesiastical writers.

III. *The Christ-teacher Figure in Julian's Showings: Relation to Tradition*

We cannot, of course, determine if Julian knew any of this tradition in ecclesiastical writings. She would, however, have come upon the concept directly in the scriptures and in all likelihood in art, perhaps in illuminated Psalters.[66] In any case, against the backdrop of this tradition we can reassess her rhetorical strategy and other references to Christ the teacher.

First, there are parallels from other writers to some of her allusions to the Christ-teacher. Like Bonaventure she says that he teaches both interiorly and exteriorly: 'And there fore oure precyous louer helpyth vs with goostely lyghte and tru techyng on dyuerse maner within and withoute. . .'. (L. 71, 7–11, 654–5). With Clement of Alexandria she sees the Christ-teacher as also a mother[67] and as a physician.[68] Like Origen she depicts the stages of contemplation as an educative process, as when she says: '. . . of whych gretnesse he wylle we haue knowynge here, as it were in an A B C. That is to sey that we may haue a lyttle knowyng, where of we shulde haue fulhed in hevyn. . .'. (L. 80, 10–12, 708).

In addition to such parallels (and there are many more), the educator concept also helps make better sense out of some unclear passages. For example, when Julian refers to Christ as our teacher, our

137

shepherd, and our clothing (S. 4, 3–5, 212), we may recall a similar, more explicit, linking of these same ideas in Clement:

> O Instructor, feed us on Thy holy mountain the Church. . . . 'And I will be', He says, 'their Shepherd', and will be near them, as the garment to their skin.[69]

Lastly, the *Showings* bring together in a new synthesis many elements from the tradition, even those that were in conflict. Julian is responding to the teaching of the interior teacher when she says: 'Alle that I say of me I mene in person of alle my evyn cristen, for I am lernyd in the gostely shewyng of our lord god that he meneth so'. (L. 8, 33–4, 319–20). But what she has learned interiorly is that Christ is the one teacher and all others—both men and women—are disciples, without distinction of rank, robe, or dignity. (So said Clement, Origen, and Cyprian, in the pre-Augustinian tradition). Again, the 'lesson of love' has been taught interiorly, but it points to an exterior grounding of all in the one teacher, who is the lesson, the teaching, the reward of those who learn.

Pierre Poiret in his catalogue of mystical writers calls Julian 'Theodidacta, profunda, ecstatica'—taught of God, profound, and ecstatic.[70] That may well sum up her mysticism; and her mysticism leads us to explore, within a long tradition, what it means to be taught of God.

NOTES

1. *A Book of Showings to the Anchoress Julian of Norwich*, ed. Edmund Colledge, and James Walsh, Toronto, 1978, Vol. One, Short Version, 6, 40–52, 222–23. All quotations are to this edition. They will be identified as S (Short Version) and L (Long Version), followed by numbers indicating chapter, line, and page.
2. *Ibid.*, Vol. 1, 222, note 40.
3. These include: 'to lere me atte my vndyrstandynge' (9, 37, 231); 'And that has ben a lernynge to me' (11, 5, 237); 'in this was I lerede' (13, 5, 237); 'And eftyr this techynge' (13, 26, 243); 'I it am that haly kyrke preches the and teches the' (13, 33, 243); '. . . Jhesu in this visionn enfourmede me of all that me neded. I saye nought that me nedes na mare techynge, for oure lorde with the schewynge of this hase lefte me to haly kyrke . . . and wilfully submyttes me to the techynge of haly kyrke with alle myne even-crystenn in to the ende of my lyfe' (13, 46–51, 244); '. . . folowande oure maister Jhesu to we be fulle purgede' (13, 57–8, 244–5); 'Bot in this (I) schalle studye. . . .' (14, 1, 247); '. . . he lered me that I schulde be halde the gloriouse asethe. . . .' (14, 10, 247); 'Here to ere we . . . lered inwardlye by haly kyrke by the same grace' (14, 20–1, 247); 'and þat is the techynge of haly kyrke' (15, 35, 251); 'God schewyd me fulle grete plesance that he has in alle men and womenn that myghttelye and mekelye and wyrschipfullye takes the prechynge and the techynge of haly kyrke, for he is haly kyrke . . . he is the techynge, he is the techare, he is the

ende . . .' (16, 1–5, 252); I assentyd, and þer with I lered . . .' (16, 20–1, 252); '. . . be the techynge of the haly gaste' (17, 36, 256); 'For criste hym selfe is grounde of alle the lawe of crysten menn, and he has tawht vs to do goode agaynes eville. Here we may see that he es hym selfe this charite, and does to vs as he teches vs to do . . .' (18, 15–17, 257); 'In this blyssed revelasionn I was trewly taught . . .' (20, 34, 264); 'And this lernynge . . .' (22, 32–3, 269); '. . . as I am lernede be the schewynge of god' (23, 37–8, 271).

4. These include: 2, 40, 288; 6, 1, 304; 6, 62, 309; 7, 1, 310; 8, 34, 320; 9, 8, 322; 9, 19, 322; 9, 21–2, 323; 10, 68, 332; 10, 74–5, 332–33; 10, 78–9, 333; 10, 84–6, 334; 11, 50–8, 341; 19, 15, 371; 19, 19–20, 371; 25, 19–22, 399; 26, 1–6, 402; 26, 10–11, 402–03; 27, 13–15, 405; 27, 18–21, 405–06; 29, 11–14, 412–13; 31, 1–2, 417; 32, 45–6, 425; 32, 51–5, 426; 33, 4–8, 427; 34, 15–20, 431; 35, 5–6, 432; 35, 9–14, 432–33; 36, 59–60, 440; 37, 5–7, 442; 40, 30–1, 457; 43, 6–8, 475–76; 45, 24–6, 488; 46, 18–21, 492; 46, 21–5, 492; 47, 6–8, 495; 50, 10–13, 511; 50, 35, 512; 50, 37, 512; 51, 76–7, 519; 51, 81–5, 520; 51, 86–7, 520; 51, 115–17, 522–33; 51, 268–72, 539; 52, 59–66, 551; 53, 23–6, 556–57; 56, 609, 570; 60, 34–5, 597; 68, 59–60, 646; 68, 62–5, 646; 70, 38–40, 653; 71, 7–9, 654–5; 71, 10–12, 655; 73, 1–3, 366; 79, 11–12, 703; 79, 22–4, 704; 80, 2–8, 707; 80, 9–11, 708; 86, 20–3, 733.

'Master' is included as teacher in the above list, following the *Middle English Dictionary*, under 'maister'. 'Maister' is the form used in the Short Text (13, 57, 244). It is defined as 'One who directs the formal education of children or youths, a schoolmaster, tutor; also one who gives formal instruction at a higher level'. Uses in these senses are cited from *Ancrene Riwle*, Lydgate, Langland, and Wiclif.

5. See *Modern Concordance to the New Testament*, ed. Michael Darton, Garden City, New York, 1976, pp. 618–20. John McKenzie says that 'The Aram [Aramaic] title, my master, was used for a teacher of the Law; it is attested for NT times only in the NT; but it appears in post biblical Judaism and must have been coming into use at this time. The term or the Gr [Greek] equivalent is often used by those who address Jesus in the Gospels. . . . Honorific titles are rejected because the disciples are all brothers—there is one Father, God, and one teacher, the Messiah'. *The Jerome Commentary*, ed. Raymond Brown et al, Englewood Cliffs, New Jersey, 1968, 2, p. 102. See also ch. 7, 'Didache as a Constitutive Element of the Written Gospel', in David M. Stanley, *The Apostolic Church in the New Testament*, Westminster, Maryland, 1965, p. 204: 'The Gospels mention the fact of Jesus' teaching more frequently than they do that of His preaching; and, what is more significant, they multiply examples of this teaching'; and p. 208: 'From Luke we know that Christ's teaching of His own went on during the postresurrection period: it was mainly an opening of their minds to understand 'the Scriptures' (Luke 24:25).

6. *Ignatius to the Romans*, Ante-Nicene Fathers, American Edition, ed. A. Cleveland Coxe and A. Menzies, Grand Rapids, Michigan, 1951–1965, 1, ch. 8, p. 77.

7. *Ignatius to the Magnesians*, *Ibid.*, 1, ch. 9, p. 62.

8. *Ignatius to the Ephesians*, *Ibid.*, 1, ch. 15, p. 55–6.

9. *Dialogue with Trypho*, Ante-Nicene Fathers, *op. cit.*, 1, ch. 108, p. 253: '. . . those who confess Him to be Christ, and a Teacher from and Son of God'.

10. *First Apology*, *Ibid.*, I, ch. 5, p. 164.

11. *Ibid.*, ch. 12, p. 166. Other uses are in ch. 4, p. 164; ch. 13, p. 166; ch. 19, p. 169. Though not clearly in the mystical tradition in their references to Christ as teacher, other Greek Apologists (Aristides, Tatian, Theophilus, Hermias, and Melito of Sardis), focus on Christ as 'above all the teacher of a new morality or a true philosophy'. J. Gonsales, *A History of Christian Thought*, Nashville, Tennessee, 1970, 1, 121.

12. *Irenaeus against Heresies*, Ante-Nicene Fathers, *op. cit.*, 1, preface to Book 5, p. 526. Also in ch. 1 of Book 5 he says: 'Again, we could have learned in no other way than by seeing our Teacher, and hearing His voice with our own ears, that, having become imitators of His works as well as doers of His words, we may have

139

communion with Him, receiving increase from the Perfect One . . .' Related references are in Book 4, ch. 1, p. 463; and in ch. 5, p. 467.

13. Simone Deléani, *Christum Sequi. Étude d'un Thème dans l'oeuvre de saint Cyprien*, Paris, 1979, p. 71.

14. John Ferguson, *Clement of Alexandria*, New York, 1979, p. 59. 'God's instrument in teaching is the collection of the scriptures. . . . He calls for his many hearers to be gathered (if our manuscripts are correct) 'into one love'. . . . So the many separate voices blend in a single choir under one conductor, and their song is 'Abba, Father', the first word of a child'.

15. *The Instructor*, Bk. 1, ch. 4: Ante-Nicene Fathers, *op. cit.*, 2, p. 211: '. . . the virtue of man and woman is the same. For if the God of both is one, the master of both is also one . . . common to them are love and training'.

16. *Ibid.*, Bk. 1, ch. 4, p. 210: '. . . the good Instructor, the Wisdom, the Word of the Father. . .'. In relation to Matthew 23:37, Clement says: 'Thus are we the Lord's chickens; the Word thus marvellously and mystically describing the simplicity of childhood' (Bk. I, ch. 4, p. 212). And again: 'As nurses nourish new-born children on milk, so do I also by the Word, the milk of Christ, instilling into you spiritual nutriment' (Bk. 1, ch. 6, p. 218). Also: '. . . the milk was this child fair and comely, the body of Christ, which nourishes by the Word the young brood, which the Lord Himself brought forth in throes of the flesh, which the Lord Himself swathed in His precious blood. . . . The Word is all to the child, both father and mother, and tutor and nurse' (Bk. 1, ch. 6, p. 220). Likewise: 'He who has regenerated us with His own milk, the Word . . .' (Bk. 1, ch. 6, p. 221); and also in other passages.

17. *The Miscellanies*, Bk. 3, ch. 9, Ante-Nicene Fathers, *op. cit.*, 12, p. 445.

18. *The Instructor*, Bk. 1, ch. 7, Ante-Nicene Fathers, *op. cit.*, 2, p. 223. See also: 'Clement d'Alexandrie', *Dictionnaire de Spiritualité*, vol. 2, part 1, col. 952.

19. Jean Daniélou, *Origen*, trans. Walter Mitchell, New York, 1955, p. 276. Also pp. 277–78: 'All the bitter-seeming things God sends turn out to be educative as well as medicinal. God is a healer and a Father, a kind and not a cruel master'.

20. *Commentary on the Song of Songs*, Bk. 3, ch. 12, Andrew Louth, The Origins of the Christian Mystical Tradition, Oxford, 1981, p. 59.

21. *Exhortation to Martyrdom*: Ancient Christian Writers, e. J. Quasten and J. C. Plumpe, Westminster, Maryland, 1946–, No. 19, p. 153. See related passages, such as: *Commentary on John*, Bk. 1, ch. 23: Ante-Nicene Fathers, *op. cit.*, 9, p. 309: 'He declared Himself in these words to be their Master and Lord: You call Me Master and Lord, and you say well, for so I am'; p. 314: 'Christ as Teacher and Master. . . . It is plain to see how our Lord is a teacher and an interpreter for those who are striving towards godliness . . .'; p. 319: 'From an activity of another kind He is called Shepherd and Teacher. . .'.

22. *On the Lord's Prayer*, Bk. 4, ch. 28: Ante-Nicene Fathers, *op. cit.*, 5, p. 455: '. . . the Word of God, our Lord Jesus Christ, came unto all, and gathering alike the learned and the unlearned, published to every sex and every age the precepts of salvation'.

23. *On the Lord's Prayer*, Bk. 4, ch. 8: Ante-Nicene Fathers, *op. cit.*, 5, p. 449.

24. *Of Works and Alms*, Bk. 8, ch. 7: *Ibid.*, pp. 477–78.

25. *The Divine Institutes*, trans McDonald Book 4, ch. 25, Fathers of the Church, Washington D.C. 1964, 49, 308. Other references are on pp. 268, 272, 300, 304, and 312.

26. Introduction to 'The Teachings of Sylvanus', trans. Malcolm L. Peel and Jan Zandee, *The Nad Hammadi Library in English*, New York, 1977, pp. 346–47.

27. *Ibid.*, pp. 349–50.

28. *Ibid.*, p. 357.

29. *Ibid.*, p. 352.

30. *Ibid.*, p. 359.

31. *Ibid.*, p. 348.

32. *Ibid.*, p. 350.
33. *Ibid.*, p. 360.
34. *Exegetic Homilies*, trans. Way. 10: Fathers of the Church, *op. cit.*, 1963, 46, p. 151.
35. *Ibid.*, pp. 154–55.
36. *Exegetic Homilies*, 16: *Ibid.*, p. 256.
37. See note 16. See also John Ferguson, *Clement of Alexandria*, New York, 1974, pp. 68–105.
38. Nicene and Post-Nicene Fathers, 2nd Series, ed. P. Schaff, Grand Rapids, Michigan, 1961, 5, p. 362.
39. *Catechetical Lectures*, 10:3–5: Library of Christian Classics, 4, ed. W. Telfer, London 1954, pp. 133–34. See also Clement of Alexandria, *The Instructor, op. cit.*, Bk. 1, ch. 2, p. 210.
40. *Discourses Against Judaizing Christians*, 7: Fathers of the Church, *op. cit.*, 5, 185: 'Then I said, Behold I come. When was "then"? When the time was ripe for perfect instructions . . . the loftier lessons which surpass the nature of man we had to learn through the Lawgiver himself. . . . John said, "For the Law was given through Moses; grace and truth came through Jesus Christ". (John 1:17). And this is the highest panegyric for the Law, namely that it prepared human nature for the Teacher'.
41. *On the Gospel of Matthew*, Part III, ch. 18: Library of the Fathers, ed. E. B. Pusey et al., Oxford, 1838–61, 3, p. 966: 'For what saith He? *But be ye not called Rabbi.* Then follows the cause also; *For one is your Master, and all ye are brethren,* and one hath nothing more than another. . . . And again He adds, *Neither be ye called guides,* for One is your guide, even Christ'. John also, in the same section, upbraids teachers generally for violently seizing the teacher's chair and loving their long robes, cautioning them: 'Be ye not called Rabbis'.
42. *Homilies on Philippians*, 12: Nicene and Post-Nicene Fathers 1st series, ed. P. Schaff, Grand Rapids, Michigan, 1956, 13, p. 240: 'Thou hast Him who is truly a Teacher, whom alone thou shouldst call a Teacher. . . . Take not heed, then, to thy teacher, but to Him and to His lessons . . . thou hast a most excellent model, to it conform thyself'.
43. See Saint Jean Chrysostome, in 'Imitation du Christ', *Dictionnaire de Spiritualité*, vol. 7, part 2, cols. 1568–1570.
44. Commentaire sur S. Matthieu, Tome II, *Sources Chrétienne*, Paris, 1979, pp. 167–78.
45. *Three Books on the Duties of the Clergy*, Bk. 1, ch. 1: Nicene and Post-Nicene Fathers, 2nd series, *op. cit.*, 10, 1.
46. *Letter to Simplicianus*, trans. Beyenka, Fathers of the Church, *op. cit.*, 1954, 26, 309.
47. *Three Books on the Duties of the Clergy, op. cit.*, p. 1.
48. *Confessions*, trans. Roger Hudleston, Chicago, 19, Bk. 2, ch. 8, p. 335: 'So in the Gospel he speaketh through the flesh, and this did sound outwardly in the ears of men, that it might be believed and be sought for inwardly and might be found in the eternal Truth, where all disciples are taught by that good and only Master'.
49. *The Teacher*, trans. Russell, ch. 14.46, Fathers of the Church, *op. cit.*, 1968, 59.
50. *The Lord's Sermon on the Mount*, Bk. 1: Ancient Christian Writers, *op. cit.*, 5, 13.
51. *Sermons for Christmas and Epiphany*, Christmas: Ancient Christian Writers, *op. cit.*, 15, 156.
52. *Confessions, op. cit.*, Bk. 12, ch. 16, p. 381.
53. *St Benedict's Rule for Monasteries*, trans. Leonard J. Boyle, Collegeville, Minnesota, 1948, p. 2.
54. *Ibid.*, p. 8.
55. Reinhold Seeberg, *Text-Book of the History of Doctrines*, trans. Charles E. Hay, Grand Rapids, Michigan, 1977, 2, p. 20–21.
56. *Ibid.*, p. 21.

57. *Dialogues*, trans. Zimmerman, 1, Fathers of the Church, *op. cit.*, 1959, 39, 8–9.
58. *Homilarum in Evangelia*, Lib. 2, Homily 39, Patrologiae Latina, 76, col. 1298.
59. Jaroslav Pelikan, *The Christian Tradition, The Growth of Medieval Theology* (600–1300), Chicago and London, 1978, 3, pp. 147–48.
60. Bernard of Clairvaux, *Steps of Humility*, Cambridge, 1940, p. 88: 'This same teacher of the Gentiles teaches this again when He states that He was tempted in all things as we are without sin, in order to become merciful'.
61. *Speculum Fidei*, Patrologiae Latina, 180, col. 373: 'Sit ergo interim auctoritas paedagogus noster in Christo Jesu, ut per humilitatem credendi a gratia mereamur illuminari'.
62. Jean Déchanet, quoted by F. Ruello, *Recherches de Science Religieuse* 68 (1980), 144.
63. *De Magistro, Quaestio* XI, *De Veritate, Quaestiones Disputatae*, Rome, 1949, pp. 223–33.
64. *Super Mysticam Theologiam, Capitulum Primum, Opera Omnia*, Aschendorff, 37, part 2, p. 456: '. . . ipsa [divina veritas] est magister interior, sine quo frustra laborat magister exterior, at dicit Augustinus'.
65. Sermo IV, Sermones Selecti, *De Rebus Theologicis*, Opera Omnia, Quaracchi, V, 567–71.
66. See Emile Male, *L'Art Religieux du XIIIᵉ Siecle en France*, Paris, Librairie Armand Colin, 1910, pp. 211–13; and also Meyer Schapiro, ed., *Late Antique, Early Christian and Mediaeval Art*, New York, George Braziller, Inc., 1979, plates 9 and 17.
67. This function of the Christ-Mother is analyzed by Jenifer P. Heimel, *'God is Our Mother': Julian of Norwich and the Medieval Image of Christian Feminine Divinity*, Diss., St John's University, 1980, pp. 70–71.
68. *The Educator*, trans. Wood, Book 1, ch. 1, Fathers of the Church, *op. cit.*, 1954, p. 210.
69. *Ibid.*, Book 1, ch. 9.
70. *Bibliotheca Mysticorum Selecta*, Amsterdam, 1708, p. 236, (cited in Colledge and Walsh, *op. cit.*, Volume One, p. 14).

The author wishes to acknowledge the assistance received through a Mellon Fellowship at the University of Iowa for researching the materials used in the writing of this article.

142

PSYCHOTECHNOLOGICAL APPROACHES TO THE TEACHING OF THE *CLOUD*-AUTHOR AND TO THE *SHOWINGS* OF JULIAN OF NORWICH

DANIEL J. ROGERS

A BASIC TENET OF Christian thought, explicitly stated by Thomas Aquinas in his opening question of the *Summa Theologica* and much in evidence in the writings of Julian and the author of *The Cloud of Unknowing*, is that grace does not destroy nature but perfects it.[1] It is more than evident to us today, of course, that spiritual growth is dependent upon one's physical and mental well being and that these, in turn, have been shaped in part by one's multifaceted inheritance of life. The converse has also been evidenced throughout time, namely, that in a variety of ways one's spiritual development influences all the other dimensions of one's experience.

That apparently obvious but, in fact, profound interplay is now receiving increased attention from a number of perspectives, one of them being developed within the medical profession. While instruction in our western colleges of medicine has normatively been based on the biomedical model, significant changes have begun to occur in the philosophy of medical education. One outstanding proponent of a substantial modification of the biomedical model is a physician and professor of medicine who for years has fostered a broader, more encompassing concept which he calls the biopsychosocial model.[2] Others, though in agreement, say that this, too, is inadequate. Recently some medical schools—I know of at least two of prominence in the United States—are proposing that this alternative and highly desirable model is in itself insufficient because it fails to provide adequately for the spiritual and, at times, overtly religious dimensions of life which interplay in the development of both illness and wellness. Efforts in those institutions are being made to modify the basic medical model, therefore, into what is being called a bio-psycho-spiritual-social health model.[3] But the change is slow to take root.

143

Meanwhile, many more limited but nonetheless encouraging approaches to the care and development of the whole person are at work in medicine. I have been in touch with one such programme, having had the good fortune recently to spend a sabbatical year in the College of Medicine at the University of Iowa, a highly regarded and progressive yet traditionally oriented medical centre. My purpose in doing so was to study in concrete ways the endless interplay of body, mind, and spirit that I was convinced goes on with us all. Here was an opportunity for me to focus, in context, on that part of the triad of which I had had least formal study, viz., the body. At the University of Iowa as Visiting Fellow in the Department of Anaesthesia, I joined the staff of the Pain Clinic to undertake research and, as a member of a closely-knit team consisting primarily of medical personnel, to work with patients suffering from severe chronic, benign pain.

Simultaneously, however, due to the kindness of Iowa's Valerie Lagorio of the Department of English, I was able to update my studies of the fourteenth-century English mystics. As the year progressed, I came to acknowledge the many ways in which my clinical work was helping me to understand more fully the teaching and practice of the mystics.

In this paper, the focus will be on three of the varied modalities of treatment we employed in the Pain Clinic. I have labelled them psychotechnologies because, broadly speaking, they are at once applied sciences and creative therapeutics dealing with the psyche.[4] In this paper, then, relaxation therapy, guided imagery, and, more briefly hypnosis will be related to two major works of the English mystics, *The Cloud of Unknowing* and Julian of Norwich's *Showings*.

The Relaxation Response

& þis abilnes is not elles bot a stronge & a deep goostly sorow. Bot in þis sorow nedeþ þee to haue discrecion on þis maner: þou schalt be ware in þe tyme of þis sorow þat þou neiþer to rudely streyne þi body ne þi spirit, bot sit ful stylle, as it were in a slepyng slei3t, al forsobbid & for-sonken in sorow.[5] (*The Cloud* ch. 44)

God will be knowen, and him liketh that we rest in him; for all that is beneth him sufficeth not us; and this is the cause why that no soule is restid till it is nowted of all things that is made. Whan he is willfully nowtid, for love to have him that is all, then he is abyl to receive ghostly rest' (*Showings* ch. 5).

In the past decade, attention has been increasingly given in medical circles to a phenomenon associated with the altering of consciousness known through the ages in various cultures and now called the relaxation response. A substantial article on the subject, whose senior author is a physician and professor at Harvard Medical School, was published in *Psychiatry* in 1974. Its introductory abstract should be of particular interest here; it states:

In the Western world today, there is a growing interest in nonpharma-cological, self-induced, altered states of consciousness because of their alleged benefits of better mental and physical health and improved ability to deal with tension and stress. During the experience of one of these states, individuals claim to have feelings of increased creativity, of infinity, and of immortality; they have an evangelistic sense of mission, and report that mental and physical suffering vanish. Subjective and objective data exist which support the hypothesis that an integrated central nervous system reaction, the 'relaxation response', underlies this altered state of conscious-ness. Physicians should be knowledgeable of the physiologic changes and possible health benefits of the relaxation response.[6]

The authors state, in summary, that the response 'consists of changes opposite to those of the flight or fight response'. Its major elements, they say, 'are consistent with generalized decreased sympa-thetic nervous system activity and are distinctly different from the physiologic changes noted during quiet sitting or sleep'. The technique of eliciting the response usually involves the use of four basic factors: 1. the use of a mental device to provide a constant stimulus, (e.g., a sound, word, or phrase repeated silently or audibly, or fixed gazing at an object, the purpose of the procedure being to shift from logical, externally oriented thought. 2. a passive attitude in which one dis-regards passing thoughts and concerns about how well one is per-forming the technique; 3. minimal work for the muscles, aided by comfortable posture, and 4. an environment of decreased stimuli conducive to quiet. Also, the authors note, the assistance of a trained instructor usually facilitates the process.[7]

One of the reasons for a pain clinic's interest in the relaxation response has to do with a discovery in the 1970s that the human body can produce at least seven different natural pain-killing substances, collectively known as endorphins. There is reason to believe that when the relaxation response is present, the pituitary gland may more effec-tively produce this opiate-like substance which can electrically stimulate specific morphine receptors, particularly in certain areas of the brain, and thus bring about an appropriate elimination of pain sensations.[8] I mention this fact to reinforce the statement made earlier about how profoundly body, mind, and spirit interact.

The article just mentioned begins with a brief history of 'subjective writings' that attest to the existence of the relaxation response. The authors begin their extended discussion of how various religions of west and east have made use of this response by citing *The Cloud of Unknowing*. Considering the purpose of the article, the authors cannot be expected to discuss *The Cloud* in depth. It is worth noting, however, what they do single out. Here is the heart of their comment, mostly concerned with the use the *Cloud*-author makes of the basic elements of the relaxation response listed above.

> *The Cloud* . . . discusses how to attain an altered state of consciousness which is required to attain alleged union with God. . . . The anonymous author states that this goal cannot be reached in the ordinary levels of human consciousness, but rather by the use of 'lower' levels. These levels are reached by eliminating all distractions and physical activity, all worldly things including all thoughts. As a means of '. . . beating down all thought', the use of a single-syllable word, such as 'god' or 'love', should be repeated. . . . There will be moments when '. . . every created thing may suddenly and completely be forgotten. But immediately after each stirring, because of the corruption of the flesh . . . [the soul] drops down again to some thought or some deed. . .'. An important instruction for success is '. . . do not by another means work in it with your mind or with your imagination . . .'.[9]

That, of course, hardly does justice to what the *Cloud*-author has to propose, but it does tell us that, for all the differences in purpose and motivation, medical authorities recognize a similarity between the state of someone practising prayer in accord with the *Cloud*-author's direction and the state of one experiencing the relaxation response when using one or another clinical technique. It is my contention that this commonality ought to be pursued further to better determine whether or not and perhaps how the two practices may shed light one upon the other, to the betterment of the person engaged in either practice.

Guided Imagery

Closely related to relaxation therapy is guided imagery, a technique I wish to consider at length. Though images have traditionally been thought of as products of that mental faculty called the imagination, for therapeutic purposes they are more specifically associated with processes which typically occur in the right or non-dominant hemisphere of the brain and so are distinguished from verbal and mathematical processes. While the cognitive and rational tends to be exalted in western society, an interplay of the imaginal with the verbal is required if we are to progress very far toward the realization of 'full human development'.[10]

The use of guided imagery as a therapeutic aid is quite recent. One physician, David Bresler, who uses imagery in the treatment of chronic pain, writes: 'By creating and utilizing personalized mental images, guided imagery enables an individual to make contact with the deepest levels of his body, psyche, and soul. Images are the language of the unconscious mind, and when properly programmed, they are able to mobilize, to a remarkable degree, the body's intrinsic ability to heal itself'.[11]

The following brief explanation of that mobilization of inner ability, provided by Bresler in his handbook for people in pain, may also help us to appreciate more fully the experiences of Julian and the *Cloud*-author. He writes:

Because the experience of pleasure and pain are related to autonomic nervous system functioning, I insist that my patients learn how to communicate more directly with their ANS [automatic nervous system], using the higher-order language of the unconscious mind—the language of imagery and symbolism. It is a difficult process for many people, simply because they have been preoccupied with their conscious mind for so long. However, like other habits, this one can be broken by creating a new habit incompatible with the old.

An important first step is to practise dissociating yourself from the thoughts of your conscious mind. . . . Observe your conscious mind, allow yourself to be aware of its thoughts, but choose not to identify with them.

One way to achieve this type of dissociation is to allow yourself to relax, using the Conditioned Relaxation exercise. Not only can this exercise be an effective tool for easing tension and the pain that accompanies it, but it is also a means for quieting down the dominant, rational, verbal part of your nervous system. By relaxing the muscles controlled by the somatic nervous system, you quiet the conscious mind so you can get in touch with your nondominant self, and take fullest advantage of the power of your imagination.

Once you're relaxed, then spend a few minutes simply daydreaming. If you carefully pay attention to the images, and not to random verbal thoughts, you will find yourself gaining access to your right hemisphere— your intuitive, creative, instinctive side.

Both in the therapeutic techniques which he uses in the clinic and in related exercises adaptable for home use and presented in his handbook, Bresler guides the patient in the use of images. And so he adds:

As you become more familiar with your right hemisphere . . . you may find it to be the source of the following benefits:

Through the language of the right hemisphere, you may uncover new insights and new information that will lead to improvement not just in your pain problem, but in your entire life.

You may also discover unconscious misconceptions that need to be corrected in order for the healing process to occur. For example, you may find that your right hemisphere is brimming with negative expectations which, in turn, are responsible for many or most of your negative experiences. These inappropriate expectations must first be identified before they can be changed.

Finally, you may be able to actively promote the healing process through the language of the right hemisphere. Keep in mind that the autonomic nervous system, which regulates pain and pleasure, is controlled by the unconscious mind. By communicating effectively with the right hemisphere, you may be able to produce dramatic changes in your body.[12]

But too often the idea that imagery is the language of the unconscious is ignored by either therapist or patient or both. Results may be much compromised when the procedure is seen as not merely something that is willed but, unfortunately, as something that is primarily if not totally a conscious and deliberate step-by-step procedure of manipulation, management, or control.

In contrast, the *Cloud*-author's engagement of the will in the work he commends seems quite compatible with the development of right-brain activity. It is the will, he says, that allows one to do this work instinctively in even the shortest time, for time 'is neiþer lenger ne schorter, bot euen acording to one only steryng þat is wiþ-inne þe principal worching miȝt of þi soule, þe whiche is þi wille' (*The Cloud*, ch. 4). The work is easily and speedily accomplished 'when a soule is holpen wiþ grace in sensible liste. . . . Bot elles it is hard & wonderful to þee for to do. Lette not þerfore, bot trauayle þer-in tyl þou fele lyst' (*The Cloud*, ch. 3). The will, then, furthered by the grace to desire the work—a grace experienced intuitively rather than cognitively—makes use of imagery as a language of the unconscious, persisting until the desire is felt.

The use of a technique to achieve an altered state of awareness through relaxation frequently provides an opportunity for the person to tap the unconscious, as some would say, or, as others would have it, to mobilize an altered dimension or state of consciousness in which the image functions with special efficacy.

While images are regularly perceived to be visual, they may also be auditory, kinaesthetic—rarely olfactory—or an integration of these forms.[13] Both Julian and the *Cloud*-author, in fact, seem to make use of a visual frame of reference most of the time. Patients who do not 'try' but rather allow themselves to experience images report using all of the kinds of images just mentioned, though they too most frequently refer to images as visual. Patients can 'see' their disease, illness, or pain, for example. They are also able to visualize their recovery or desired state of health.[14] They can also use images to concretize and personify aspects of their inner self that can provide them with useful information about what may be required before they get better.[15]

Julian distinguishes images that are visual, verbal, and those not sense-perceived. She carefully delineates three varieties of visions, 'be bodily sight and by word formyd in my understonding and be gostly sight' (ch. 9). Because the latter seems not to rely on images at all it will be given special attention shortly. Useful at this point, however, is a logically prior distinction made by the *Cloud*-author, that between using the image effectively and in accord with nature and using it 'aȝens cours of kynde', the latter being the case when 'þei feyne a maner of worching, þe whiche is neiþer bodily ne goostly'. This he calls 'fantasie, or any fals ymaginacion, or queynte opinion', the result of 'a proude, coryous & an ymaginatiif witte' (ch. 4).

Just as a patient can get carried away when using his imagination without guidance, so the *Cloud*-author warns his disciple against this same indulgence, indicating that such a preoccupation may keep him from responding to a simpler urging toward God himself. In other words, thoughts, memories, imaginings can get between the soul and God (*The Cloud*, ch. 5).

Nevertheless, in urging his disciple to get beyond such limitations, and stressing that he not strain to see anything, the *Cloud*-author implicitly guides him not to literally see but, rather, to imagine a cloud of forgetting as well as a cloud of unknowing through which, on occasion, some ray of the light of divine presence may penetrate. So, he explains, do not take the notion of the cloud literally—lest he expect 'þat it be any cloude congelid of þe humours þat fleen in þe ayre'—for such is imagined 'wiþ coriouste of witte'. In keeping with the dictum he has just made use of in a related matter, that 'God, þat is þe rewler of kynde, wil not . . . go before þe steryng of kynde in a mans soule' (ch. 4), he now directs his disciple to discontinue meditation if he feels called by God to do so, and to strive for 'a naked entent directe vnto God', for that 'suffiseþ inouȝ' (ch. 7). Yet for many, that ideal may prove too inaccessible, in which case a verbal, auditory image, such as the simple word 'GOD' or 'LOUE' will suffice. In recommending this direction to his disciple, however, he makes use of visual suggestions, thus providing the disciple, in effect, with an exercise in guided imagery:

þis worde schal be þi scheeld & þi spere, wheþer þou ridest on pees or on werre. Wiþ þis worde þou schalt bete on þis cloude & þis derknes abouen þee. Wiþ þis worde þou schalt smite doun al maner þou3t vnder þe cloude of for3eting . . . (ch. 7).

In other words, he makes use of images even as he instructs his disciple to get beyond them. They are simply means to get in touch with that natural yet grace-inspired urge—a grace that would not take him beyond his God-given potential—to devote himself to this work. In urging against a left-brain, analytic activity, he personifies cognitive effort as being a ' "tempter" or antagonist of God':[16]

& 3if he profre þee of his grete clergie to expoune þee þat worde & to telle þee þe condicions of þat worde, sey him þat þou wilt haue it al hole, & not broken ne vndon (*The Cloud*, ch. 7).

The repetition of the single word, then, has more to do with a verbal image than with an analytical exercise.

Besides making use of corporal and verbal images, Julian presents us with a third use of the image, at once subtle, simple, and sophisticated. In explaining this type of vision which Julian calls 'gostly sight', Molinari identifies it as 'a vision granted freely by God himself without direct and intrinsic connection with any sense-experiences. It is exclusively concerned with purely spiritual objects . . . which are not described in detail'.[17] For an extended example of such a vision allegedly lacking a sensory connection, he refers us to Julian's ghostly sight of the blessed Virgin. Julian perceives Mary not in physical, external detail, but in terms of abstracts such as 'hey and noble and glorious and plesyng to hym above al creatures' (ch. 25). But how does she become aware of this ghostly vision? It is given her, she says, by Jesus when 'our gode lord lokyd downe on the ryte syde and browte [it] to my mynde' (ch. 25).[18]

Here Julian envisions the Lord looking down his side—the short text suggests he looked into his pierced side; here Julian visualizes it as the right side, a detail not in the gospel accounts of the Passion—and his doing so occasions her to consider the blessed Virgin not as being presented to her visually but as being understood by her in the abstract terms mentioned above. This relationship of the visual with the abstract is an important and recurrent practice of Julian's which enriches her experience immensely.

The chairman of the Psychosynthesis Research Foundation of Florence, Italy, Roberto Assagioli, hypothesizes that what we call the creative experience involves a 'shifting between right and left hemisphere modes of cognition. That is, intuitive ideas emanating from the right hemisphere [which may include visualization as well as various forms of non-analytic meditation] must then be analyzed by the left hemisphere in order to deduce the parts contributing to the whole'.[19] Julian seems to be engaged in this type of correlated operation of the hemispheres and in her effort to communicate her awareness to us in writing probably furthers that operation. In this regard authors from the University of Southern California School of Medicine explain:

> Visual imagery alone is valuable, but visual imagery synthesized and integrated with conceptualization, by, for example, sharing our inner experiences with others verbally, gives us greater contact with our experiential process. . . .[20]

Here, then, is an example of the enhancement resulting from a synthetic use of both hemispheres of the brain.

Granting that Julian was living in grace and so was responsive to the promptings of the Holy Spirit, I find it reasonable to suggest that Julian uncovered, whether intuitively or by assistance from spiritual writers and counsellors, what it was she had to do to cooperate in developing her intense experience of Christ's Passion. Once that had been accomplished, she was suddenly rid of her intense illness, the better to contemplate over the years the significance of the revelation.

It is my present thinking that Julian's description of the various forms of her showings offers no contradiction to, but in fact reinforces and is reinforced by what we now know of the use of imagery in therapeutic settings. Further, as therapists consider ways in which to make the exercise more effective, they might well learn of this subtle but real distinction, repeatedly illustrated in these two writers, between a contrived, 'unnatural' or artificial effort to curiously imagine something, and a deeper, simpler, and more profoundly motivated activity which encourages the non-analytic spirit of man to operate, once the body and mind are disciplined enough and relaxed enough, and, in tune with this desire of one's spirit, making it a desire of the whole person, an action proceeding to wholeness and unity.

Julian thus encourages us to make use of several kinds of knowledge, including a knowledge of God and a knowledge of ourselves— 'that we knowen ourselfe, what we arn be him in kinde and grace' (ch. 72). It is this self-knowledge, more available to us in our own day than ever, that may help us appreciate how her showings, a gift of God 'in grace', were able to actually take form 'in nature'.

Since images may arise 'in nature' even without our conscious volition, Robert R. Holt distinguishes between an 'image' and a 'presentation', the former term being used 'when we are speaking about a phenomenal content of a sensory or quasi-sensory nature', the latter 'when we are speaking about the same meaning as mediated by (encoded in) a brain process without awareness'.[21]

I find here a possible clue to the explanation of what natural means God may have been using in his showings to Julian, for in Holt's further comment on these 'presentations' which may become images he explains:

> At all times, presentation-forming programs must be under the control of motive systems of some kind, and there is good reason to suppose that in many if not all people unconscious motive systems over which there is little if any voluntary control are forming and processing sensory presentations a great deal of the time, possibly always. Granted the right set of internal and external conditions, some of these may become conscious images of a passive or unbidden kind.[22]

Holt explains, however, that 'people seem to differ considerably in their abilities and proclivities to construct conscious mental images from this matrix of presentations, whether actively or passively', and that 'only a good deal more research' will enable us to account fully for these differences.[23] Here again, I see grace not destroying nature but perfecting it.

Though we have not as yet widely attempted to correlate such study with the writings of authorities on the Christian mystical experience, the need to do so and the possibility of doing so are matters worthy of consideration. For, as Molinari explains, Julian is already speaking of a lesser form of infused contemplation rather than acquired contemplation 'when she speaks of the "beholding which is not shewing" '. But even there 'the infusion from God . . . is not necessarily felt or perceived' while the concomitant activity of the soul remains a conscious and dominant activity.[24] Even in that phase of infused contemplation, the individual still profits from activity which disposes one for God's grace and thus furthers its effect.

As for the *Cloud*-author, we see there this same movement toward God quite in keeping with the deepening of consciousness that guided imagery may provide. For, in speaking of the 'Common' and the 'Special' stages of the active life, he says that in the latter the person lives 'more from the depths of himself . . . becoming, therefore, *more fully human*' [italics mine].[25]

Once 'þe grete rust of his boistous bodelynes be in grete party rubbid awei', subsequent 'clepying' and 'drawyng' by the Spirit will be 'þe rediest & þe sekerist witnes þat may be had in þis liif' (*Privy Counselling*, p. 161). Even here, at these higher levels of spiritual development, the *Cloud*-author guides by using imagery that is both visual and kinaesthetic. The same will be true for the disciple as he adapts this counsel using 'his concience' and his spiritual father or 'counseil' (*Privy Counselling*, p. 161).

And though the evil one will be in an anguish of curiosity, not appreciating what the disciple is about, the latter remains deeply relaxed: 'Bot no force þerof, for "þou schalt gracyously rest" in þis louely onheed of God & þi soule' (*Privy Counselling*, pp. 147–48).

The author's purpose, then, has been to assist one from that early and appropriate position of 'beholdyng of þe Passion of Criste' (*Privy Counselling*, p. 159) to a point where he would 'forgete alle þinges bot þe blynde felyng of þi nakid beyng', and, finally, to forget even that: 'þat þou schuldest forȝete þe felyng of þe beyng of þi-self as for þe felyng of þe beyng of God', for 'God is þi beyng' (*Privy Counselling*, pp. 155–56).

We might well conclude our discussion of imagery by recalling Morton Kelsey's comment regarding the suspicion that images are only for beginners and not for the spiritually proficient:

> Imagination and the body are not to be treated like first-class offenders as St John of the Cross and St Teresa suggest in their less careful passages. None of us is really filled with the Spirit of the loving God until both imagination and body are cooperating and at one with that love as in Jesus Christ. No wonder Christianity was called 'the way'. It is the process of becoming, again and again, forever. And in this process images are the recurring guideposts upon the way.[26]

Hypnosis

Of the psychotechnologies under consideration here, the last is hypnosis, perhaps the most misunderstood of the three. Though my experience with clinical hypnosis has been relatively limited, the potential value of relating hypnosis to the mystical experience, past and present, seems to me to be so promising that I want to provide a brief account of my growing awareness of this interplay.

Popular conceptions of hypnosis continue to be, for the most part, misconceptions. This being the case, one physician—a gynaecologist, obstetrician and surgeon—who has made extensive use of hypnosis has, until recent years, shied from the explicit use of the term hypnosis. When colleagues or patients inquired about the nature of his procedure he generally replied, to the satisfaction of the questioner, that it

153

was a form of relaxation therapy. It is only in recent years that hypnosis has achieved acceptance as a legitimate modality of treatment.[27] But even now its effectiveness is greatly limited for the average patient unless he or she is open minded when hearing the term used and then receives a careful explanation of its nature and employment.

Not until I had studied hypnosis at the University of Iowa's College of Medicine, under a psychiatrist experienced in its use, was I ready to value its possible presence in the mystical experience. My subsequent understanding of hypnosis, and particularly of auto-hypnosis, has helped, for example, to reinforce for me, rather than detract from, the authenticity and significance of Julian's experience. I found, in short, that hypnosis may well have assisted Julian both to dispose herself for God's grace-filled action and to cooperate in that divine activity as it progressed.

The model of therapeutic hypnosis I was presented with features five components:[28]

1. concentration on a neutral or pleasant device; 2. a sense of quietude; 3. muscular relaxation; 4. decreased defensive awareness or passive cooperation and 5. therapeutic suggestions.

A hypnotic induction, then, consists of making use of all five of these features while any subsequent deepening of this state consists simply of making further use of the same five components.

The purpose of hypnosis is succinctly put by Milton Erickson, a pioneer in medical hypnosis.

> The technique in itself serves no other purpose than that of securing and fixating the patient's attention. . . . There is then the opportunity to proffer suggestions and instructions serving to aid and to direct the person in achieving the desired goal or goals.[29]

The point is important enough to restate: the patient's attention is thus focused and heightened rather than suppressed in some sort of sleep-like state, the suggestion that it is a sleep-like state being unfortunate and inaccurate.[30]

As the following statements will indicate, the professor mentioned above was careful to demystify the subject from the outset. Hypnosis, he explained, is a means to facilitate changes that we already desire. In hypnosis, one cannot be forced to act in ways contrary to one's desires. In fact, all hypnosis is ultimately self-hypnosis.[31] Therefore a trance-like state is not necessary. Actually, a deep hypnotic state is not always desirable for therapeutic purposes;

rather, lighter degrees of hypnotic awareness are often more useful. It is not a form of sleep but rather an altered state of relaxed and heightened awareness. Many people experience hypnotic states without ever realizing the fact. On the other hand, a person who wants to be hypnotised and tries to bring it about is the one most likely to fail.

I came to realize that I had experienced a form of hypnosis when, driving an automobile, I had questioned whether or not I had yet driven through a particular town I knew to be on the way.[32] Again, I realized that I had experienced a form of hypnosis when using a typewriter, not consciously thinking of what keys I was pressing. I also discovered that the two groups of professionals most frequently making use of hypnosis but without being aware of their doing so are clergymen and teachers. I read and heard discussed countless reports of how vicariously and effectively hypnosis could be used for the anaesthetic relief of pain as well as an adjunct procedure in surgery— all, at times, with dramatic results. I began to realize, further, that I had probably been making use of it myself even as I worked with patients in providing relaxation therapy and guided imagery.

But when I discovered how various patients had made effective use of hypnosis even without having been trained in its use, and without even having been aware that they had used the technique[33]—it was then that I began to consider the possibility of its presence in Julian's practice and teaching as well as in the *Cloud*-author's orientation.

I can appreciate, however, the position that Molinari and others have taken in accounting for the nature of Julian's visions since these scholars apparently see only two alternatives, allowing no room for hypnosis or auto-hypnosis to play a favourable role. Either they suggest that Julian was mentally disturbed—something Molinari finds unacceptable—or they conclude that her visions were a gift from God, presumably by means of direct intervention. Here is the rationale Molinari presents for establishing only the two above alternatives. He writes:

In fact, if it were established that Julian's illness was merely the result of neurotic or hysterical dispositions, this might be taken as depreciating the value of her spiritual teaching, especially as the 'shewings'—on which Julian's doctrine is mainly based—began immediately after the crisis of her sickness, when she was suddenly released from it. Hence we must ask whether the sights form part of and result from a neurotic sickness or whether their origin and nature has to be explained by a special intervention of God.[34]

155

Once having linked the neurotic and the hysterical to the undesirable alternative of the two, he soon adds hypnosis to the list as a third element, thus suggesting that hypnosis is both a pejorative term and an undesirable act or state. But in addition Molinari finds it helpful to introduce the unlikely, not to say unnatural, possibility that God, being himself unlimited, may use such pathological conditions to produce consequences of positive spiritual value which, for all their external appearance, resemble undesirable consequences of a pathological condition. He writes:

> there is no theological principle from which it would follow that an extraordinary divine activity on the psychological and physiological apparatus of the recipient must produce phenomena intrinsically different from those associated with hypnotism, hysteria, neurosis, and the like.[35]

It is unfortunate that Molinari here juxtaposes hypnosis (a valuable therapeutic tool) with neurosis (a broad term covering a variety of functional disorders), with hysteria (one specific psychoneurotic disorder), and with his imprecise tag 'and the like'.

Perhaps the linking of these terms is a matter he simply and inappropriately presumes to be factual. The link is implied even in this passage Molinari has cited from a critic with whom he disagrees; though that critic's word in translation from the French is autosuggestion, not auto-hypnosis, the sense is retained when that critic questions:

> Have we not sufficient matter to recognize in this ecstasy a pathological character; that is to say do not the circumstances of the ecstasy strengthen the hypothesis of auto-suggestion (leaving Julian's good faith intact), this hypothesis being already suggested by the perfect correspondence between the anchoress' desires and their realization?[36]

Yet, ironically, on the same page Molinari chides yet another critic for what, he says, is 'a less [than] cautious employment of technical terms such as "state of hypnotism" '.[37]

I gather, then, that neither Molinari nor the commentators he surveys has yet given careful consideration to the possibility that hypnotism may have played a positive role in facilitating Julian's spiritual development. Whether in the external or internal events prior to or connected with her illness—as, for example, the visit of her curate in her illness who sets the crucifix before her and suggests an alternative position for her eyes, already fixed heavenward[38]—or in the series of subsequent showings or in her affective reflections upon them in the years that followed—not to mention her reading[39] and participation in religious observances[40]—in all these a hypnotic factor is either possible or, given the facilitating conditions, likely.

Conclusion

In this new age, when the frontiers of exploration move to the interior landscapes of consciousness,[41] no less awesome than our probes into outer space, it is time to reassess our commitment to and the scope of our pursuit of scholarship in the work of the medieval mystics. The above discussion of a few specific potentials, inherent in the human condition throughout time, channelled by Julian and the *Cloud*-author, among many others, and more recently made the focus of inter-disciplinary efforts within the theoretical and applied sciences as well as the humanities – this discussion has, I hope, served only as an identifiable tip of an iceberg. It is granted that these developments must be part of and thus subsumed under further considerations beyond the scope of this paper, considerations that would relate the restoration and furthering of 'health' and 'wholeness' of the individual[42] to a 'salvation-health linkage within a larger understanding of the destiny of the whole people of God'.[43] But within that context, as man becomes the focus of an integrative bio-psycho-spiritual-social study, the concluding words of Valerie Lagorio's paper at the 1980 Exeter Symposium may well sound a clarion call for the initiation of additional avenues of interdisciplinary research involving the medieval mystics. Her closing words are germane as conclusion to this paper as well:

> It is hoped that the foregoing comments have limnèd the research potential residing in the English mystics, as well as their continental contemporaries – a potential which summons scholars from a myriad of disciplines, and one which is indeed relevant for today's world.[44]

NOTES

1. Q. 1, article 8, reply to obj. 2.
2. George L. Engel, 'The Need for a New Medical Model: A Challenge for Bio-medicine', *Science*, 196 (April 8, 1977), 129–36 and 'The Clinical Application of the Biopsychosocial Model', *The American Journal of Psychiatry*, 137 (1980), 535–44.
3. Elisabeth McSherry, 'The Way Spiritual Health Care Could Be: The Course of Human Spiritual Development and its Implications for Total Health Care', *Proceedings, First National Conference on the Third Dimension of Integrated Health Care: A Public Seminar on Basic Health Policy*, California, May 17, 1980.
4. Psyche: 'a designation for the soul in the most general sense, in contrast to the

157

material body, or *soma* (*Encyclopedia of Psychology*, ed. H. J. Eysenck *et al.*, New York, 1972). 'In modern psychiatry the psyche is regarded in its own way as an "organ" of the person. The psyche, like other organs, possesses its own form and function, its embryology, gross and microscopic anatomy, physiology, and pathology'. *Psychiatric Dictionary*, ed. Leland E. Hinsie and Robert Jean Campbell, 4th ed., New York, 1970.

5. Unless otherwise noted, reference will be made to *The Cloud of Unknowing* and *The Book of Privy Counselling*, ed. Phyllis Hodgson, Early English Text Society, O.S, 218, London, 1944, and to Julian of Norwich, *A Revelation of Love*, ed. Marion Glasscoe, Exeter, 1976, the latter cited as *Showings*.

6. Herbert Benson, John F. Beary, and Mark P. Carol, 'The Relaxation Response', *Psychiatry*, 37 (February 1974), 37.

7. Benson, Beary, and Carol, *op cit.*, p. 38.

8. David E. Bresler, *Free Yourself From Pain*, New York, 1979, pp. 29, 221–23.

9. Benson, Beary, and Carol, *op. cit.*, pp. 38–39.

10. Barbara L. Forisha, 'The Outside and the Inside: Compartmentalization or Integration?' *The Potential of Fantasy and Imagination*, ed. Anees A. Sheikh and John T. Shaffer, New York, 1979, pp. 1–9.

11. Bresler, *op. cit.*, p. 189.

12. Bresler, *op. cit.*, pp. 354–55. For a detailed, medical presentation see David E. Bresler and Ronald L. Katz, 'Chronic Pain: Alternatives to Neural Blockade', in *Neural Blockade in Clinical Anesthesia and Management of Pain*, ed. Michael J. Cousins and Phillip O. Brindenbaugh, Philadelphia, 1980, pp. 651–78.

13. Forisha, *op. cit.*, p. 5

14. See, e.g., O. Carl Simonton *et al.*, *Getting Well Again*, Los Angeles, 1978, regarding the use of imagery in treatment of patients with advanced stages of cancer and other illnesses.

15. So Bresler *op. cit.*, pp. 396–427, recommends an exercise which enables the patient to discover one or more inner guides who may communicate with them. But many outside of the clinical situation recognize the value of such direction. See, e.g., Willis W. Harman (Professor of Engineering, Stanford University and Director of the Institute of Noetic Sciences), Keynote Address, Conference of the Association for Transpersonal Psychology, Asilomar, California, August, 1979.

16. *The Cloud of Unknowing*, ed. Ira Progoff, New York, 1957, p. 74.

17. Paul Molinari, *Julian of Norwich*, New York, 1958, p. 41.

18. Molinari, *op. cit.*, p. 39. A similar movement from the visual to the abstract occurs in chapter 13, for example:

> And after, or God shewid ony words, he sufferd me to beholden in him a conable tyme, and all that I had sene, and all intellecte that was therein as the simplicite of the soule migte take it. Than he, without voice and openyng of lippis, formys in my soule these words. . . .

19. Evelyn Virshup and Bernard Virshup, 'Visual Imagery: The Language of the Right Brain', in *Imagery: Its Many Dimensions and Applications*, ed. Joseph E. Shorr et al., New York, 1980, p. 108, referring to Roberto Assagioli, *Psychosynthesis*, New York, 1965.

20. Virshup and Virshup, *op. cit.*, p. 109. And they add '. . . and [so gives us] more tools to make effective impact on our world'.

21. Robert R. Holt, 'On the Nature and Generality of Mental Imagery', in *The Function and Nature of Imagery*, ed. Peter W. Sheehan, New York, 1972, p. 10.

22. Holt, *op. cit.*, p. 29.

23. Holt, *op. cit.*, p. 28.

24. Molinari, *op. cit.*, pp. 141, 143. Until the time of John of the Cross, he explains, there is no clear-cut distinction between acquired and infused contemplation.

25. Harvey D. Egan, 'Mystical Crosscurrents', *Communio*, 7 (1980), 8, citing William Johnston's translation of *The Cloud*, New York, 1973, p. 59, of 'a man is wiþ-inne

him-self & euen wiþ him-self'. Once reaching 'þe hiȝer partie of contemplatiue liif', however, man may not advance 'bi kynde' (ch. 8); thus the *Cloud*-author employs the Thomistic distinction between nature and grace.

26. Morton T. Kelsey, *The Other Side of Silence*, New York, 1976, pp. 159–60.

27. 'Many medical schools in the United States now have courses for students and postgraduates on hypnotic theory and techniques, and hypnosis is recognized by the American Medical Association as an accepted therapeutic technique. . . . There are hypnosis societies in England, Sweden, Japan, and Australia as well. Similar societies under the name of "sophrology" exist in Italy, Spain and Brazil. A search of the medical literature between 1974 and 1978 has revealed more than eight hundred published scientific papers dealing with hypnosis'. David B. Cheek, reprinted from 'Health for the Whole Person',' in *The Institute of Noetic Sciences Newsletter*, 9 (1981), 17.

28. Conrad Swartz, Department of Psychiatry, College of Medicine, University of Iowa, January 9, 1981.

29. Cited by Eric Greenleaf, 'Active Imagining', in *The Power of Human Imagination: New Methods in Psychotherapy*, ed. Jerome L. Singer and Kenneth S. Pope, New York, 1978, p. 173.

30. 'One theory about hypnosis was held by some of the old-timers such as Liebeault and Bernheim, and advanced by the great Pavlov. This was the principle that hypnosis is a form of sleep. A hypnotized person whose eyes are closed certainly looks as if he is asleep, and the lethargy displayed also indicates it. Of course this theory does not hold because there is always awareness while the subject is in hypnosis. Also, the sleep pattern shown with encephalography is not present, nor is the patelar reflex (the knee jerk when the knee is tapped). This is present when one is awake, but lost during sleep'. (L. M. LeCron, *The Complete Guide to Hypnosis*, New York, 1971, pp. 8–9, in Center for Integral Medicine, eds., *Clinical Hypnotherapy; Workbook*, vol. 1, Pacific Palisades, California).

    Hypnosis, however, can be used to induce sleep. So 'Platonov (1959) in a psychophysiologic treatise on psychotherapy and hypnosis, describes how he has used suggestive "sleep" for achieving positive therapeutic effects in thousands of patients', William S. Kroger and William D. Fezler, *Hypnosis and Behavior Modification: Imagery Conditioning*, Philadelphia, 1976, p. 47. But this is another matter, as are the various therapeutic uses possible for the state of awareness 'Between Wakefulness and Sleep: Hypnagogic Fantasy', see Peter McKellar, in Sheikh and Shaffer, *op. cit.*, pp. 189–97.

31. Authorities agree on this point. 'A patient must be made aware that all hypnosis is essentially self-hypnosis and that his improvement is due to his own actions and responses, not those of the therapist's. In our opinion, a patient's best interests are served when he assumes responsibility for his own care, rather than being continually dependent on a therapist' (Bresler and Katz, *op. cit.*, p. 667).

32. Griffith W. Williams, 'Hypnosis in Perspective', *Experimental Hypnosis*, ed. L. Lecron, Secaucus, New Jersey, 1952, p. 5.

33. 'Many patients from the psychiatric clinics fall spontaneously into hypnotic states. But people who are sound in body and mind can also spontaneously fall into such states without suggestion'. Georgi Lozanov, *Suggestology and Outlines of Suggestopedy*, New York, 1978, p. 180.

34. Molinari, *op. cit.*, p. 23.

35. Molinari, *op. cit.*, p. 26.

36. P. Renaudin, *Quatre Mystiques Anglais*, p. 60, as cited in Molinari, p. 23.

37. W. Inge, *Studies of English Mystics*, p. 58, as cited in Molinari, p. 23.

38. Ch. 2, short text; ch. 3, long text. A current text notes:

    Rodriguez (1960) makes full use of a religious approach in conjunction with hypnotherapy. Today, many clergymen, especially those who are also psychologists, are employing hypnotherapy with astonishing success. Since they are already a sort of father-confessor to many of their parishoners, they are in an enviable position to help them because of well-established faith. Pastoral counselling has made rapid strides recently, and it is only a matter of time until there will be more clergymen making use of hypnotherapy (Kroger and Fezler, *op. cit.*, p. 47).

39. 'The hypnotic qualities of literature are well known. Many critics have called attention to the fact that not only is the form hypnogenetic, as in music, but the content of literature may also be used for this purpose' (Williams, *op. cit.*, p. 6).

40. 'Much that is conducive to self-hypnosis in religious practice will similarly pass unnoticed. Consider the darkened interior of the church, the hush, the brightly illuminated altar as a point of fixation, the nature of the music – these and the ofttimes monotonous chant of the priest or minister, together with other factors, furnish ideal conditions for the trance'. Williams, *op. cit.*, p. 5.

41. See, for example, the provocative survey of Marilyn Ferguson, *The Aquarian Conspiracy: Personal and Social Transformation in the 1980s*, Los Angeles, 1980, and her serially published *Brain/Mind Bulletin*, reporting on frontiers of research, theory and practice, and *Leading Edge Bulletin*, regarding 'frontiers of social transformation', both published by Interface Press, Los Angeles.

42. 'Overall, our data give no support to the still widely held assumption in the psychological literature that persons who have intense spiritual experiences are more or less pathological personality types. On the contrary, the correlation of indices of personality flexibility with spiritual experiences suggests that study of such phenomena may, as Maslow has suggested, be richly rewarding in adding to our understanding of personality growth and maturity'. Eugene Thomas and Pamela E. Cooper, 'Coincidence and Psychological Correlates of Intense Spiritual Experience', *The Journal of Transpersonal Psychology*, 12 (1980), 84.

Psychiatrist David H. Rosen, an instructor of future psychiatrists in California, writes: 'Faith and hope are measures of our maturity, a process of going forward humbly and selflessly'. 'Physician, Heal Thyself', *Clinical Medicine*, 80 (1973), 27.

43. Leroy T. Howe, 'Where Are We Going in Pastoral Care?', *The Christian Century*, 98 (1981), 1162.

44. Valerie Lagorio, 'New Avenues of Research on the English Mystics', in *The Medieval Mystical Tradition in England*, ed. Marion Glasscoe, Exeter, 1980, p. 243.

THE MYSTICAL EXPERIENCE OF JULIAN OF NORWICH, WITH REFERENCE TO THE EPISTLE TO THE HEBREWS (ch. IX). SEMIOTIC AND PSYCHOANALYTIC ANALYSIS

BERNADETTE LORENZO

(trans. Yvette Le Guillou)

'AND THUS WAS I lernyd to my vnderstandyng that *sekyng is as good as beholdyng*' (10, 74–75) said Julian of Norwich, a fourteenth century English anchorite. Through her writings, we are proposing to find out how she lived through the psychic and spiritual evolution as described in Hebrews, 9:1–11:

> . . . the first covenant had also ordinances of divine service, and a worldly sanctuary. For there was a tabernacle made; the first, where in was the candlestick, and the table; and the shewbread, which is called the sanctuary. And after the second veil, the tabernacle which is called the Holiest of all; . . .
>
> But Christ being come, an high priest of good things to come, by a greater and more perfect tabernacle . . .'

these three tabernacles can represent the journey of a soul seeking God through suffering and love.

THE FIRST TABERNACLE

We have no biographical data about Julian. Her family and her youth are totally unknown. Our psychoanalytic reading cannot therefore be historical, it will be structural. As a geologist, observing vegetation, can say which type of soil it grows on, so the psychoanalyst, attentive to the psychic and spiritual work visible through her writings, can discover the structure of Julian's personality.

Words used repeatedly by Julian, insistant images refer to the primitive character of the first tabernacle. Readers will have noticed that Julian with all her might wants 'to see': '. . . ioyeng in that I saw, and desyeryng as I durste to see more . . .' (8, 20). The frequent recurrence of the verb 'to see' is such and her demands for knowledge are so urgent that her psychic structure bears distinct marks of the oral phase.'[1] (The urge to see is originally connected with the oral phase, witness such expressions as 'devour with your eyes'; 'I can't stand the sight of him, he makes me sick').

Information through images naturally leads to knowledge. The function of seeing is so important for Julian that she constantly indicates the way she sees: 'by bodely syght', 'by gostely syghte' (73, 2 & 4). Her expression 'by bodely syght' clearly shows she is talking about sensorial images, perceptive hallucinations, either external as when the crucifix hanging in her room comes to life or within herself as with the phantasmagoria of dream. 'By gostely syghte' seems to refer to direct intuitive knowledge, a light shed into her intelligence. About this particular way of reaching knowledge, she says: 'I haue seyde some dele, but I may nevyr fulle telle it' (73, 7). Sometimes, the vision is blurred. In those cases, the content of the vision is much more relevant to psychoanalysis than to theology. The same is true of a vision connected with her maternal imago.[2]

THE MATERNAL IMAGO

'One tyme my vnderstandyng was lett down in to the sea-grounde, and ther saw I hilles and dales grene, semyng as it were mosse begrowyng with wrake and gravell'. (10, 21–23). The poorness of those submarine depths is well worth noting: seaweeds suggest infertile soil; gravel is an image of the past, a vestige of worn away rocks. In this type of dream; many people are in their own elements. Julian, on the other hand, uses an expression full of ambivalence; she has to call up for almighty God's protection against the danger involved by this predicament:

> 'Then I vnderstode thus: that if a man or woman wer there vnther the brode water, and he myght haue syght of god, so as god is with a man contynually, he shoulde be safe in sowle and body, and take no harm' (10, 23–26).

Mystical life, by going through the psychic organism, shakes its foundations and brings about states of deep regression. These are necessary to allow both a de-structuring and a re-structuring of the psyche in mystical life. Julian, who feels this adds: 'This secounde shewyng was so lowe and so little and so symple, that my spirytes were in great traveyle in the beholdyng, mornyng, dredfull and longyng; for I was some tyme in a feer wheder it was a shewing' (10, 32–34). What her imagination has here produced is a pre-natal image, that of being steeped in the water of being as it were wrapped in it, together with the vague feeling of some undefined danger. Now in Julian's terminology, the notion of 'wrapping' is omnipresent. She constantly seeks a second skin, a wrap, a kind of confinement. In her narrative of this vision fraught with psycho-analytic meaning, Julian immediately makes associations on a depressive key. In it, she sees: 'It was a fygur and a lyknes of our fowle blacke dede, . . .' Could these typically Christian words betray the unknown and unbearable existence of a fundamentally destroying aggressiveness, here levelled at the maternal imago? Soon comes to the surface the picture of a 'bashed' face: 'the brownhead and the blackhead, rewlyhead and leenhead' of this image, that of Veronica's veil (vernacle) which Julian associates with herself: 'it was the ymage and the lyknes of owr fowle blacke dede' (10, 59–60). When she mentions Mary, the maternal image 'par excellence', Julian wishes to see her 'by bodely syght', but in vain. She can only see her through her intellect. She can only see with her bodily eyes what is connected with the masculine imago. Moreover, while she excels at describing faces, Christ's or the devil's, she does not do so with Mary. She can, however, interiorize some aspects of Mary, see her at three different stages of her life: at the time of Incarnation, at the foot of the cross, in heavenly glory. She is dazzled by what she sees. Mary, after Jesus, is the most beautiful object of contemplation.

HER RELATIONSHIP WITH THE BODY

The subjects that bear excessive marks of primitive stages, either foetal or oral, have a deep urgent need for strong and extreme sensations, imperatively they have to feel they have a skin, a limit, but this is unreachable, extremely distant, it can only be got at through excessiveness. That is why Julian will put in this most unusual request to God: that he should send her a severe illness that would lead her to the border of death, which she would not however cross. 'I desyred to haue all maner of paynes, bodily and ghostly, that I should haue if I should haue died, all the dredys and temptations of fiendes and all maner of other paynes, saue the out passing of the sowle' (2, 26–29). This psychic intensity is felt by Julian and she expresses it in every context, even in her theological considerations. When she thinks about the inexorability of original sin, she writes: 'Thys steryng [of wonder] was much to be forsaken; and nevyrthelesse mornyng and sorow I made therfore withouȝte reson and dyscrecion' (27, 10–11). Verbs suggesting a limit abound in her writings, as for example: 'The number of the words passyth my wytes and my vnderstandyng and alle my myghtes, . . . the joy that I saw in the shewyng . . . passyth alle that hart can thynk or soule may desyre' (26, 11–15). This urge of going further than a limit that escapes you has a complementary impulse: that of being enveloped, confined, hidden. This psychological feature is the key-note of Julian's relationship vith her God. 'but in his goodnes is all the hole' (6, 10) . . . 'For as þe body is cladd in the cloth, and the flessch in the skynne, and the bonys inþe flessch, and the harte in the bowke, so ar we, soule and body, cladde and enclosydde in the goodnes of god' (6, 41–44).

She is 'embosomed' or perhaps more suggestively 'enwombed' and can think of no mediator between God and herself. 'For till I am substantially vnyted to him I may never haue full reste ne verie blisse; þat is to say that I be so fastned to him, that ther be right nought that is made betweene my god and me' (5, 19–22). This is an axiom of spiritual theology, but it is carried too far since the saints themselves are not to settle in that particular space: 'Then saw I verily that it is more worshipp to god . . . that we feaithfully praie to him selfe of his goodnes . . . then if we made all the meanes that hart maie thinke. . . . We praie to god for . . . his holie passion, . . . his sweete, mothers loue . . . his holie crosse, . . . 'the blessed companie of heaven'. 'For if we make all these meanes, it is to litle, and not ful worshippe to god (6, 5–21). Other mystics on the other hand have mentioned the presence of saints as of as many companions and brethren. So with Teresa of Lisieux who in 1896, wrote: 'My heart melted with joy and gratitude, not only for the saintly woman who had visited me, also for all the blessed ones who dwell in heaven'.[3]

Julian's psychic structure will naturally show in her knowledge of man her anthropology: 'for oure kyndely wille is to haue god and the good wylle of god is to haue vs' (6, 57–58). This vocabulary is found in other mystics, but on a different register, that of eros, connected with the genital phase.[4] We would like to stress the fact that in our anchorite's writings all her images are akin to images which in psycho-analysis, suggest that the subject is enbosomed, enwombed, merged into someone else, therefore pregenital images. Julian's eroticism is different from that of Teresa of Avila receiving a javelin from a cherub or Teresa of Lisieux asking for snow on the occasion of her taking the habit: 'How thoughtful of Jesus. Anticipating the desires of his little bride, he gave her snow. . . . What mortal, however powerful, could make it fall from heaven to charm his beloved?' Julian is, as far as her libido is concerned, fixed at a pregenital stage.

We have found it interesting to note that the cultural background of the Christian faith will enable her to keep clear of border-line states,[5] leading to regression, to disintegration even. Her sound theological training gives her the spiritual means to achieve what merging and safety she needs. She will take nothing else; nothing or hardly anything connected with the genital phase and its eroticism. Other Christian mystics have found in mystical union the satisfaction of needs created by the way their psyche worked, but of those needs exclusively. A case in point is Marguerite-Marie Alacoque, in her teens, a victim to extremely sadistic situations, who escaped masochistic annihilation by finding in a vision of the crucified Christ, the image of her own suffering and a fellow-sufferer.

Julian's theological elaboration of the motherhood of God has its roots in existential reality. Julian had to elaborate it so as to weave in herself the skin, the limit that would enable her to become an adult. This theology of a Mother-God is particularly well suited to our times when so many children while receiving many materials gifts from their mothers still miss their warmth of affection and suffer from their spiritual barrenness. The idea of the Word as a mother calls forth images of boundless and infinite fondness which might suit young people nowadays; psychologists such as Reich or Marcuse have fostered the development of regressive fantasies centred on the archaïc mother through rejection of the father and also of the adult mother. Julian is so tense that this can be detected in her perception of her own corporeal time. She frequently uses the word 'suddenly'. Something suddenly erupts in her, coming from the depths of her unconscious. A new desire or a new image spring up unexpectedly. The *id* has the better of her more rational thinking, shattering the boundaries of logical structures.

We have just studied the symbol-making function of her body with regard to limits, that is to say of the skin as it is experienced symbolically. What about her own anatomy? She mentions her eyes, describes their movements with infinite precision. Her heart is mentioned once, in a compressed turn of phrase including both her anatomical heart and the heart as the seat of the will: 'Then was I holpen to be set vpright, under sett with helpe, for to haue the more fredom of my hart to be at god's will, and thinkyng on god while my life laste' (3, 18–20). She also mentions her back only by the way, as it will help her to see better.

Seriously ill people complain with accuracy about an organ or a limb, they describe the evolution of a pain. Julian is at death's door and can only give general indications about her biological body: 'Then was my bodie dead from the miedes downward, . . . after this the over part of my bodie began to die . . .' (3, 17–18 & 33). No limb or organ is mentioned, it is as if the representation or image of her own body had left in her a notion of something rough-hewn, beyond her awareness. She is however able to make distinctions elsewhere, in a transposed manner, as for example in the careful analysis she makes of the colours of Christ's blood and her keen philosophical and theological elaborations. Lost as she is in her pre-genital stage, aware of only parts of her body, she nevertheless has enough resources and strength to derive joy from intelligence and contemplation and meet the experience of existential integration she has hitherto lacked.

Similarly, her apprehension of other bodies in her visions is incomplete. She only sees faces when she is in anguish and ignores the rest of the body. She admirably describes the faces of: Christ suffering his Passion (7), Veronica's vernacle (headcloth) (10), the Fiend (67).

THE PATERNAL IMAGO[6]

Basic imagoes undergo cleavages. Julian's paternal imago proves to be very much split: as in the case of children, the division is very pronounced. Her relationships with Christ and God the Father on the one hand give us indications of her positive paternal imago; on the other hand her contacts with the demon betray her negative paternal imago. It is all black and white. Of course, these basic psychoanalytic indications in no way impair the theological content of her visions. When these revelations are over, she again suffers in her body as her illness reappears, and feels depressed. She has forgotten all her visions totally, she has unconsciously repressed the realization of her most cherished desires: '. . . but as a fole I lett it passe oute of my mynde' (66, 28–29). She is overwhelmed by guilt: 'A, loo how wrechyd I was! This was a grett synne and a grett vnkyndnesse . . .' (66, 30–31). Then, in this vulnerable and weak state, she is submerged in threats of the negative paternal imago:

> Ande in my slepe at the begynnyng me thought the fende sett hym in my throte, puttyng forth a vysage fulle nere my face lyke a yonge man, and it was longe and wonder leen. I saw nevyr none such; the coloure was reed, lyke þe tylle stone whan it is new brent, with blacke spottes there in lyke frakylles, fouler than þe tyle stone. His here was rede as rust . . . (67, 1–7).

If we compare the pictures she gives of her positive and negative imagos we find them both very fine, symmetrical and reversed. Red is omnipresent and varies from bright red (on Christ's face) to brown red

166

(on Veronica's Vernacle) and the tile or rust red of the devil. Good or bad, divine or diabolical, these faces of the masculine imago bear the mark of blood. Blood that so often appears in Julian's visions.

> He grynnyd vpon me with a shrewde loke, shewde me whyt teth and so mekylle me thought it the more vgly. Body ne handes had he none shaply, but with hys pawes he helde me in the throte, and woulde have stoppyd my breth and kylde me but he myght not. (67, 7–11).

A head without a body or hands refers to pre-genital angst; teeth and claws to the early sadistic oral phase, all the more so as the devil will come back and will in the course of one night destroy Julian's self-esteem: 'and all was softe whystryn. And I vnderstode nott what they seyd, and alle this was to stere me to dyspere . . .' (69, 6–8). The word 'throat' occurs twice. The throat is what we swallow by, where the relationship with the powerful breast takes place, where the mother's insistence on feeding, the baby's rejections, chokings and spasms are experienced. So the devil's face, a partial object, and paternal imago, comes into contact with the part of her body expressing the relationship with the imago of the feeding mother. This combination is related to both pregenital anguish and hysterical components where anguish is very often felt in the throat.

Another instance of reversed symmetry can be noted in her paternal imago of the roof and the tile: 'I saw the bodely syght lastyng of the (plentuous) bledyng of the hede. . . . The plentuoushede is lyke to the droppes of water that falle of the evesyng of an howse after a grete shower of reyne, that falle so thycke that no man may number them with no bodely wyt' (7, 13–14, 22–24). Whereas with the devil's colour 'was reed, lyke þe tylle stone whan it is new brent. (67, 5). The 'evesyng' (roof) suggests the tile and vice-versa. Both are in the higher part of the house. The house is a representation of the personal body and of the family as a bodily structure; this appears in the dreams and modelling of people in analysis. What about the roof, the head, the chief, in Julian's history? We do not know. But she sees heads without bodies all bearing marks of blood. She herself feels the danger of losing her head: 'I had ravyd to day' and feels the need of being reassured about this by God: 'Wytt it now welle, it was no ravyng that thou saw this day, . .'. (70, 33–34). This conjunction of red and roof, both in the negative imago and in the positive imago paternal, underlines the interference between the good and the bad father, the devil and God.

Her reaction against the problem involved in the notion of 'head' will be to stretch her mind to the outmost in organizing her theological thinking. Other phases of this revelation in sixteen scenes are calmer, more adult and concern the second and third tabernacles. However the data connected with the first tabernacle subsist and are the very web of the personality. Their destruction would bring about a complete collapse. The believer therefore has to make a sublimation by crossing the second tabernacle, that of adult maturation.

THE SECOND TABERNACLE

The second tabernacle looks like adult age: 'which had the golden censer and the ark of the covenant overlaid round about with gold, wherein was the golden pot that had manna, and Aaron's rod that budded, and the tables of the covenant'. (Hebrews 9:4). This religious symbolism can also be a psychological one, that of masculine and feminine sexuality (the rod and the pot) with an image of expansion (the censer). The writing already shows a sublimation, the development of thought, of knowledge. Then inner worship stands uppermost and sheds on the whole the beauty of the sacred: 'And over it, the cherubims of glory shadowing the mercyseat' (Hebrews 9:5).

Because she was disappointed with herself, Julian asked for a serious illness: 'And this ment I for (I) would be purgied by the mercie of god, and after liue more to the worshippe of god by cause of that sicknes (2, 29–31). She is entering the second tabernacle through pain and a fight with thanatos or the death instincts at odds with the life urges deep in ourselves. Teresa of Avila also had wished to break away from the inner tragedy of her adolescence through a serious illness, this led to catatonia; for four days she was like a living corpse; she was then only 23. Only those who were a prey to despair in their youth can be led to wish for such a state. Julian must have experienced great disappointments with herself and others, have accumulated a crushing feeling of guilt to wish for such a radical 'purification'.

THE SEMIOTIC SQUARE

To study (1) illness as an event in her life, (2) her contemplation of Christ's face, we have devised analytical tables and condensed the whole in a semiotic square. The semiotic square is a logical diagram, based on the binary system A, B, that is to say on contrasting pairs: black-white, day-night. This simplistic view of language structures will be corrected by the psychoanalytic consideration of what lies in-between, in other words of what goes on existentially between A and

B. 'Ours is the realm of what lies in-between' Freud said. Where is Julian? Where does he stand exactly between the zero of death and the unreachable absolute totality of life?

To find it out, we have built our semiotic square on the two fundamental poles of existence: life-death. B is death: Then went I verily to haue passed' (3, 35). A is life, the truest, that belongs to the future: Christ himself says so in the sixteenth revelation 'But take it, and lerne it, and kepe thee ther in, and comfort the ther with, and trust therto, and thou shalt not be over come' (70, 38–40). Between the two peaks A and B, between life and death, are Julian's waverings or more deeply her ambivalence. Does she want to live? Does she want to die? 'Frely without anie sekyng, a wilfull desyre to haue of gods gyfte a bodily sicknes. I would that that sicknes were so hard as to the death. . . . For I desyred to haue ben soone with my god and maker (2, 20–22, 32–33). 'And yet in this I felt a great louthsomnes to die' (3, 7). Now this is the realm of what lies in between, between death that she dreads and yet desires, and a generous life she cannot yet assume. To pole A, along the diagonal, corresponds its mathematical opposite non-A (A); to the pole indicating life, corresponds non-life (life); different from death, it represents the domination of death instincts:

'And anone my sycknes cam aȝene, furst in my hed, with a sownde and anoyse. And sodeynly all my body was fulfyllyd with sycknes lyke as it was before . . . and as a wrech mornyd hevyly for feelyng of my bodely paynes, and for fautyng of comforte gostly and bodely' (66, 11–15).

In this illness which has hardly anything to do with organs and is simply a general discomfort, her anatomy appears to have lost its vitality. Her body then becomes intensely manifest elsewhere: through time and space in which she seeks her own identity. Time: Julian does not say she has suffered for seven or eight days: she says: three days + three nights + one night + two days + two nights + one night. . . . This is a real breaking-up of time. Space is also broken up, through the organs that perceive it: the eyes to be set upright', I had set vp my eyen', my eyen was sett vpright into heauen', I ascentyd to sett my eyen in the face of the crucyfixe' (3, 21–26). These coporal precautions are accompanied by a quasi-magical thought: 'For my thought I might longar dure to looke even forth then *right vp*' (3, 27).

This operation is akin to obsessional mecanisms of measurement and caution; serious illness will reawaken this kind of psychic protection. Moreover, this particular way of finding one's biological body through measurements of time and space is especially connected with the abstractedness where pregenital space and time emerge. These processes save her from disintegration.

To pole B, along the other diagonal, corresponds its mathematical opposite: non-B($\overline{B}$). To the pole figuring death, corresponds its opposite: non-death ($\overline{death}$). Julian seems to be dying or even dead, but what she writes shows that even then wishes suddenly appear. Although seriously ill, she remains entirely bent on her desire: to see Christ's passion. What she wants to see is more important than what she endures. Through this long vision when her body is that of a dying woman, impressions of love and comfort reach her heart and her intelligence: 'sodenly all my paine was taken from me' (3, 35–36); this was most comfort to me that oure goode lorde, that is so reverent and dredfulle, is so homely and so curteyse' (7, 32–33).

What goes on between the $\overline{A}$ and $\overline{B}$ poles of the square, between non-life and non-death? What can this 'in-between' represent? Julian is in an abstractedness (trance), morbidity reaches her conscious mind, 'I had ravyd to day', but, at the same time, she experiences ecstasy which is equally a kind of abstractedness: 'I saw with bodely sight . . . a parte of his passion' (10, 34). She is introduced into the state of ecstasy by the hallucination of the crucifix coming to life in front of her. So this is not a vision in an empty field of perception, but in psychiatric terms, a hallucination supported in space by a concrete object, as when Teresa of Lisieux saw the statue of the Virgin come to life and smile to her.

What help is the semiotic square? Its advantage in the end is to bring to the fore the psychic difference between ambivalence and paradox. In her exhausting discussion with herself, Julian was ambivalent between her desire of death and her sense of guilt on one hand and her feeling 'of louthsomnes to die' on the other hand. Ambivalence is a defensive process where incompatible motivations come into play. Positive component A and negative component B of the semiotic square are indissolubly linked. The subject is compelled to say both yes and no regardless of his or her psychic balance. The word 'paradox' in psychoanalysis attempts to define a state of normality, a condition of human existence which is life and death. To live out paradox, it is necessary to have elaborated in oneself a deep feeling of trust and safety. This is only possible if the mother was reliable[7] or if, through transfer, the believer finds reliability in God and can introject it. The true mystic has not only been able to go beyond ambivalence, he has also managed not to erase paradox. Julian has taken stock of what she can let die in her and of what she wants to live with Christ. That is why her writings show such astonishing determination. So at the borders of non-life and non-death, there spring symbol and mystery.

THE INSTINCT (IMPULSE) TO SEE BLOOD

Julian did not want to die before being totally impregnated with Christ's Passion:

> And in this sodenly I saw the reed bloud rynnyng downe from vnder the garlande, hote and freyshely plentuously and liuely (4, 12). The grett droppes of blode felle downe . . . lyke pelottes, semyng as it had comynn ouȝte of the veynes, and in the comyng ouȝte they were brown-rede, for the blod was full thycke; and in the spredyng-abrode they were bryght-rede . . . not wythstonding the bledyng contynued tylle many thinges were sene and vnderstondyd, the feyerhede and the lyuelyhede continued in the same bewty and lyuelynes . . . (7, 14–21). And one tyme I saw how halfe the face, begynnyng at the ere, over ȝede with drye bloud, tyll it closyd in to the myd face (10, 6–8).

All these notations refer to the way the vision of blood[8] resonates in her. The phrases 'I saw, to see, my sight' come again and again, stressing the visionary phenomenon she has so much wanted in her body: 'I should desyer the second wound . . . that my bodie might be fulfilled with mynd and feeling of his blessed passion' (3, 43–45). She herself endures the most acute corporal and psychic suffering in her compassion with Christ, thus realizing her plan to know something of the incomprehensible compassion of Mary and of his disciples. 'Thys shewyng was quyck and lyuely, and hidows and dredfulle and swete and louely' (7, 30–31).

Is this insistence on the contemplation of blood voyeurism or sadism? A sado-masochistic person is driven to the most narrow form of narcissism, seeks to inflict pain to get pleasure, to torment people for a deviated affective and libidinal pleasure. The instinct (impulse) to see is extremely developed in Julian. Yet, unlike the masochist, she disinvests her own suffering, loses interest in her illness and begins to suffer Christ's pains. Will she then, as is the case in the sado-masochistic relationship, exhaust her drive, fall a prey to anguish, debase herself, dissociate?

First, we have to notice that the blood she contemplates is shown in superimposition, on top of other images that follow one another as in a dissolve (a film technique whereby the last images of a sequence gradually fade out while the first images of the next sequence gradually appear. 'And in the same shewing sodeinly the trinitie fulfilled my hart

171

most of joy, . . . , In this he brought our ladie sainct Mari to my vnderstanding' (4, 9, 28). And in this he shewed a little thing, the quantitie of an hasel-nott, lying in þe palme of my hand, as me semide, and it was as round as a balle . . . It [was] all that is made' (5, 9–13). Also, as blood 'rynning downe' flows abundantly, she uses the language of praise: 'And I sayd: Benedicite, Dominus. This I sayd for reuerence in my menyng, with a mightie voyce, and full greatly was I stonned for wonder and marvayle that I had (4, 16–18). The paradox is lived through totally. She was watching with the greatest possible attention. So many mothers, so many husbands and wives do not have the strength to live out this paradox: death and love:

> How myght ony eyne be more then to see hym that is alle my lyfe, alle my blysse and alle my joy suffer? Here felt I stedfastly that I louyd Crist so much aboue my selfe that ther was no peyne that myght be sufferyd lyke to that sorow that I had to see hym in payne' (17, 59–63).

As the vision progresses, safety and strength are two constant themes. She gets them on more than one occasion and this enables her to assume the paradox: love and pain. The two components, safety and strength, are totally absent from sadomasochistic language.

As she contemplates the martyred Christ, she discovers an unexpected dimension in a body which has lost all human appearance; she discovers divinity. This is for her the source of new psychic and spiritual strength: 'In which shewyng I understodd vi thynges. . . . The thurde is he blessydefulle godhede that ever was and is and schalle be alle myghty, alle wysdom and all loue' (8, 3–8). In this experience, blood is no longer associated with crushing and destruction; it is the meeting-point with transcendental life: divinity.

Blood is life when it is not seen. When it is shed or seen, it announces death. Even in transfusion when it gives life, it is linked with death, for death would probably occur if it were not given. In its symbolism, blood condenses the two opposites life and death. When she sees Christ's blood, Julian calls forth images of rain, showers, all suggesting blessings as they bring overabundant life:

> Not with standyng the bledyng contynued a whyle, tyll it myght be seen with avysement. And this was so plentuous to my syght that me thought if it had ben so in kynde and in substance, for that tyme it shulde haue made the bedde all on bloude, and haue passyde over all about (12, 8–12).

This mode of expression belongs to a lover, but the image is foetal, water is replaced by blood 'for there is no lycour that is made that lykyth hym so wele to yeue vs' (12, 16–17). For her, blood represents Jesus in the totality of his two natures: human and divine. And later: 'And ouyrmore it flowyth in all heauen, enjoying the saluacion of all mankynd that be ther and shall be, fulfylling the number that faylyth' (12, 29–31). Her erotic vocabulary will not go beyond this. She never says 'I' in strongest moment of love: 'and of the vertu of this longyng in Crist we haue to long aȝene to hym' (31, 42–43). For her, Christ's love is always connected with the sufferings of his humanity. She is unable to see this divine love without locating it in the pains of the man-God. 'And theyse be the workes of Cristes manhed, wher in he enjoyeth (31, 29–30). And Jesus cannot express his love otherwise: 'It is a joy, a blysse, an endlesse lykyng to me that evyr I sufferd passion for the' (31, 30–32). She is shy of saying 'I' which would correspond to the 'you', and brings in her fellow-humans. 'We be his blysse, we be hys meed, we be hys worship, we be his crowne' (31, 33–34).

THE THIRD TABERNACLE OR THE SANCTUARY

'Destroy this temple, and in three days I will raise it up' (John 2, 19). Jesus was speaking about his body. The third tabernacle[9] is the body of Christ. The times of narcissistic suffering, of solitary grief are over. Here now comes eros agape, love embodied in Christ. Entry into the third tabernacle[10] is best tested by the mystic's ability (or any believer's) to suffer Christ's own sufferings, to live on his joys, and therefore have the strength of carrying his or her fellow-humans. It is worth pointing out that when sublimation is successful, escaping the snares of idealization, the desirable elements of the first tabernacle are met again in the third, in a transcended way. Thus Julian will find again the maternal clothing of the first tabernacle in that she will be embosomed or enwombed by divinity.

EROS IN THE THIRD TABERNACLE

Catherine of Siena, who lived at the time of Julian, describes her vision of the heart of Jesus: 'As the fire of desire was increasing in me, I wondered at the sight of Christians and Infidels entering the wound on the side of Jesus Crucified and through the gate of desire and love, I entered Christ with them.' Julian herself writes:

> Wyth a good chere oure good lorde lokyd into hys syde and behelde with joy, and with hys swete lokyng he led forth the vnderstanding of hys creature by the same wound in to hys syd with in; and ther he shewyd a feyer and delectable place, and large jnow for alle mankynde that shalle be savyd and

rest in peese and in loue. And ther with he brought to mynde hys dere worthy blode and hys precious water whych he lett poure out for loue. And with the swete beholdyng he shewyd hys blessyd hart clovyn on two' (2, 3–10).

The body of Christ is assimilated to a temple. Julian is asked by the vision to move 'in her understanding'. She enters Christ's body through the wound made by the spear. Re-entering the body, but is this regressive? This vision may mean the return to a foetal state: place, blood, water, in the breast of Christ-mother. The human values are not destroyed: in Christian mystical life, man has a right to his roots, to his history; the constituents of the first tabernacle are transposed here.

In the third tabernacle, Catherine and Julian will open out in joy and share with others through their writings; this is not at all emprisonment or psychic regression. Just as this vision leads Julian to consider the motherhood of Christ, an image of the maternal imago crops up. 'And with thys chere of myrth and joy our good lord lokyd downe on þe ryght syde, and brought to my mynde where our lady stode in the tyme of hys passion, . . . so he shewyd her than, hygh and noble and glorious and plesyng to hym aboue all creatures' (25, 3–5, 29–31).

In the sixteenth revelation, she is in a state similar to Teresa of Avila's seventh dwelling. All her contemplation is now fixed on God, her creator living in her. Images of light spring up as with the mystics who have reached deep union: 'For in mannes soule is his very dwellyng. And the hyghest lyght and the bryghtest shynyng of þe sytte is the glorious loue of oure lorde god (68, 33–36). Spatial comparisons help her to understand her own soul: she sees it as an extremely vast world, a blessed kingdom, a glorious city:

in myddes of that cytte (sitts) oure lorde Jhesu, very god and very man, a feyer person and of large stature, hyghest bysschope most solempne kinge, wurschyp fullest lorde. And I saw hym clothyd solemply in wurschyppes (68, 5–9). And this was a synguler joye and blysse to me that I saw hym syttyng; for the truth of syttyng shewde endless dwellyng (68, 50–51).

Therefore, in a few hours, the sixteen revelations have led Julian through all the phases of psychic and spiritual life. The partial images of the dark moments are replaced by, the complete figures of the luminous moments. She has received a sort of programme for the forty years she has yet to live. A resolute lover, she wanted to see with all her might. She saw twice in images and more often in the secret of her inner light. Psychoanalysis is not indifferent to the fact that inner contemplation leads to knowledge. Indeed these revelations had three

174

goals: the knowledge of God (exercising the function of the sacred), of ourselves, of our ontological reality, of our present state. Julian was given this threefold knowledge: she kept it and transformed her existence with it, for she had heard these words from the divinity:

I loue the and thou lovyst me, and oure loue shall nevyr be depertyd on two; . . . I kepe the full sykerly (82, 18–21).

BIBLIOGRAPHAL REFERENCES

Sainte Therese de l'Enfant Jesus, *Histoire d'une âme*, Paris, 1972, p. 217.

Bernadette Lorenzo, *La dévotion mariale de quelques figures féminines du XIIIème au XVème siècle: Projection de la psyché ou réalité théologale?* in Acta Congressus Mariologici-Mariani Internationalis, Romae, Anno 1975 celebrati Pontifica Academia Mariana Internationalis, Romae, 1980.

Raymond de Capoue, *Vita S. Catharinae Senensis* et *Legenda Major*. Acta S. S. Avril Tome 3, Paris, 1866.

D. W. Winnicott, *Playing and Reality*, London, 1971.

A Book of Showings to the Anchoress Julian of Norwich, ed. E. Colledge, J. Walsh, Toronto, 1978.

R. Maisonneuve *Le petit livre des révélations de Julienne de Norwich, selon le manuscrit Amherst Additional 37790*, Paris, Ed. du Parvis.

Meunier (Dom G). *Révélations de l'amour divin à Julienne de Norwich, recluse du 14ème siècle*, Paris, 1925.

Bernadette Lorenzo, Le destin des pulsions agressives et le masochisme dit chrétien à travers les textes de Marguerite-Marie Alacoque, in *Le coeur transpercé de Jesus; expérience, sources, théologie*, Symposium de Paray-Le-Monial, 1980.

Roland Maisonneuve, *L'univers visionnaire de Julian of Norwich*, Doctoral Thesis, Sorbonne, Paris, 1979.

Henri Faure, *Hallucination et réalité perceptive*, Paris, 1969.

Sigmund Freud, *Essais de psychanalyse appliquée*. T. F. Paris. Gallimard. 1933. (comme modèle pour l'analyse profonde des textes).

Georges Dumas, 'Comment aiment les mystiques chrétiens', *Revue des Deux Mondes* 35 (1906).

J. G. Gunderson and J. E. Kolb, 'Discriminating features of border-line patients', *American Journal of Psychiatry* 7 (1978).

Psychanalyse à l'Université *Les états-limites*; p. 71–73, tome V, n° 17, 1979 Paris Ed. Replique. 9, Rue Dupont-des-Loges. 75007.

A. J. Greimas, *Sémantique structurale*, Paris, 1966.

Groupe d'Entrevernes, *Signes et paraboles, sémiotique et texte évangélique*, Paris, Seuil, 1977, (voir carré sémiotique).

Sémiotique et Bible, *Bulletin d'études et d' échanges*, publié par centre pour l'analyse du discours religieux (CADIR). Lyon. 25, Rue du Plat. (voir carré sémiotique).

NOTES

1. Oral stage: a psychoanalytic term defining the first infantile stage of psychosexual development. Feeding provides elective significations through which is expressed and organized the relationship with the object (a thing or a person).

175

2. Maternal imago: an idealised figure that works as a structure, as a pattern, exercising a dominating influence, in later life, on fantasies and behaviour.
3. The saint who visited Teresa of Lisieux was the Venerable Anne de Jesus, Anne de Lobera, the founder of Carmel in France.
4. Genital stage: the adult stage of psychosexual development where the partial phases of the earlier stages are fused, under the dominance of the genital erotic stage.
5. *Border-line*: generally refers to individuals who are near the border of depersonalization.
6. *The paternal imago:* see 'maternal imago'; of course, the images and affects dominated by parental imagoes obey the law of sexual desire: daughter-father, son-mother, etc.
7. *Reliable*: a concept developed by D. W. Winnicott.
8. My special field of research in spiritual theology is precisely on how women have experienced mystical life through their bodies, this includes their problems or attitudes in relation to blood.
9. *The third Tabernacle*: The true tabernacle is defined in Hebrews 9:11–12, 'But Christ being come . . . by a greater and more perfect tabernacle, not made with hands, that is to say, not of this building; . . . 'by his own blood, he entered in once into the holy place.

   This passage deals with the human psyche for it is about the body of Christ and its mystery of suffering and glorification. The sanctuary or Holy Place is defined in Hebrews 9:24, 'For Christ is entered . . . into heaven itself now to appear in the presence of God for us'.
10. *Entry into the third tabernacle* and into the sanctuary. The passage has a spiritual connotation which is closely akin to psychoanalytic data: 'The Holy Ghost this signifying, that all the way into the holiest of all was not yet made manifest while as the first tabernacle was yet standing' (Hebrews 9:8). All the components are there, but sublimated and transcended.

SEMIOTIC SQUARE

TO DIE OR TO LIVE?

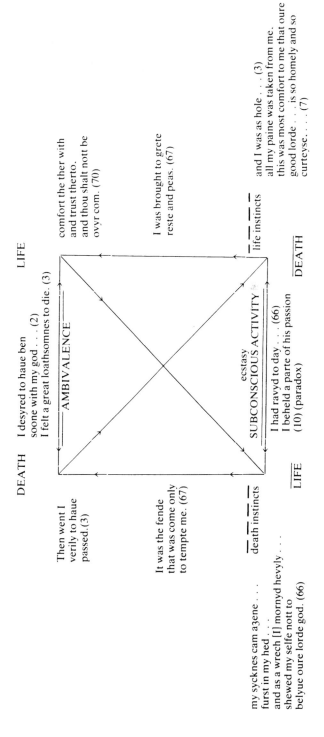

LIFE

DEATH

I desyred to haue ben
soone with my god . . . (2)
I felt a great loathsomnes to die. (3)

comfort the ther with
and trust therto.
and thou shalt nott be
ovyr com. (70)

AMBIVALENCE

I was brought to grete
reste and pees. (67)

Then went I
verily to haue
passed. (3)

ecstasy SUBCONSCIOUS ACTIVITY

I had ravyd to day . . . (66)
I beheld a parte of his passion
(10) (paradox)

It was the fende
that was come only
to tempte me. (67)

death instincts

LIFE

life instincts

DEATH

and I was as hole . . . (3)
all my paine was taken from me.
this was most comfort to me that oure
good lorde . . . is so homely and so
curteyse. . . . (7)

my sycknes cam aȝene . . .
furst in my hed . . . .
and as a wrech [I] mornyd hevyly . . . .
shewed my selfe nott to
belyue oure lorde god. (66)

A TEXT	THINGS	her BODY	her SPACE	her TIME	her PSYCHE and her spirit	VERSUS Life	VERSUS Death
(Ch. 3) Thus I indured		I indured			I indured		
till day				till day			↕
and by then							+
was my bodie dead		my bodie			was dead		+
from the miedes downward		miedes downward					
as to my feeling		my feeling			my feeling	+	
Then was I holpen					I holpen		
to be set vpright		to be set vpright	vpright			+	
undersett with help						+	
for to haue the more fredom					more fredom		
of my hart to be at god's will		hart			hart . . . at god's will		+
. . . I had set vp my eyen		my eyen					
and might not speake		not speake			not speake		
. . . my eyen wes sett		my eyes	were set			+	
vpright into heauen			vpright		into heaven	+	
. . . but nevertheles I ascentyd					I ascentyd	+	
in the face of the crucyfixe	crucyfixe	my eyen	to sett				↕
if I might					if I might		↕
and so I dide					so I dide		↕
For my thought					For my thought	+	
I might longar dure		I might dure		longar	I might dure	+	
to looke even forth		to looke	even forth			+	+
then right vp			right vp			+	+
After this				After			
my sight began to eyle		sight began to feyle				+	
and it waxid as dark	as dark					+	
aboute me			aboute me				+
in the chamber	chamber		in the				
as if it had ben nyght				as nyght			↕
saue in the image of the crosse	crosse						
wher in held a comon light	light					+	
All that was	All					+	
beseid the crosse	crosse		beseid				
was oglye and ferfull to me					was oglye and ferfull to me		+
as if it had been much					had been much		+

B TEXT	THINGS	her BODY	her SPACE	her TIME	her PSYCHE and her spirit	VERSUS Life	Death
occupied with fiendes			occupied		ffiendes		+
After this				After this			
the over part of my bodie		part of my bodie			the over part		+
began to die		began to die			began to die		+
se farforth that vnneth							+
I had anie feeling		anie feeling			anie feeling		
My most payne was shortnes of breth		shortnes . . . breath			my most payne	+	
Then went I					went I		
verily					verily		+
to haue passed					to haue passed		
And in this							
sodenly				sodenly			
all my paine was taken from me		my pain			was taken from me		
and I was as hole		as hole			I was as hole	+	
and namely in þe over						+	
parte of my bodie		the over parte				+	
as ever I was befor				as ever . . . befor		+	
(Ch. 66) And at the ende				at the ende			
alle was close					alle was close		
and I saw no more		I saw no more			I saw no more		
And soone				soone			
I feelt		I feelt			I feelt		
that I should life longer		I should life longer		longer			+
And anone my sycknes		my sycknes			came aȝene		
cam aȝene		came aȝene					
furst in my hed		in my hed					
with a sownde		a sownde			a sownde		
and anoyse		anoyse			anoyse		
and sodeynly				sodeynly		+	
all my body		all my body					
was fulfyllyd		fulfyllyd			fulfyllyd sycknes		
with sycknes lyke as it was before		sycknes		before			+
as a wrech					as a wrech		
I mornyd hevyly		mornyd hevyly			mornyd hevyly		

| C TEXT | Her PSYCHE | | CHRIST'S BODY | CHRIST'S | CHRIST'S |
	Versus life	Versus death	(soma)	nous	Names
(chap. 3) I should desyer	désyer				
. . . that my bodie	my bodie				
might be fulfilled	fulfilled				
with mynd and feeling			feeling	mynd	
of his blesed passion			his passion		
(chap. 4) in this sodenly	sodenly				
I saw	I saw				
the reed bloud		+	reed bloud		
rynnyng downe		+	rynnyng downe		
from vnder the garlande			from . . . the garlande		
hote and freyshley			hote and freyshley		
plentuously and liuely			plentuously and liuely		
as it was in the tyme that the garland of thornes	+			tyme (his) (condensation)	
was pressed on his blessed head			blessed head		
(chap. 7) The grett droppes of blode			grett droppes of blode		
were browne rede			browne rede		
and . . . bryght rede			bryght rede		
The feyerhede	+		feyerhede	feyerhede	
and the lyuelyhede	+		lyuelyhede		
continued in the same bewty and lyuelynes			continued in the same		
this was most comfort to me	most comfort to me				
that oure good lorde					good lorde
that is so reverent and dredfulle	so reverent	dredfulle		reverent dredfulle	
is so homely and so curteyse	homely and so curteyse			homely. curteyse	
(chap. 10) And after this	after				
I saw with bodely sight	bodely sight				
in the face of the crucifixe	the crucifixe		(face of the crucifixe)		
that hyng before me	before me	+			
a parte of his passion			a parte of his passion	passion	

D TEXT	Her PSYCHE Versus live	Versus death	CHRIST'S BODY (soma)	CHRIST'S nous
dyspyte, spyttyng		+	spyttyng	dyspyte
and solewing and buffetyng		+	solewyng, buffetyng	solewing
and manie languryng paynes			languryng pains	paynes
mo than I can tell	mo than I can tell			
and offten chaungyng of colour		+	chaungyng	
And one tyme	one tyme			
I saw how halfe the face	I saw how		halfe the face	
begynnyng at the ere			begynnyng at the ere	
over3ede			over3ede	
with drye bloud		+	with drye bloud	
tyll it losyd in to the myd face			to the myd face	
(chap. 16) I saw the swete face	I saw		the swete face	swete
as it were drye			as it were drye	
and blodeles with pale dyeng			blodeless	pale dying
and deede pale.			deede pale	
langhuryng		+	langhuring	langhuring
and than turned more deede in to blew	and than	+	more deede into blew	
and after in browne blew	and after	+	browne blew	
as the flessch turned more depe dede	as	+	flessch . . . deepe dede (his lips)	depe dede
. . . This was a peinfulle chaungyng to se	to se	peinfulle	a peinfulle chaungyng	a . . . chaungyng
this depe dying		+	this depe dying	depe dying
And also thys nose clongyn to geder and dryed	also		nose clongyn. dryed	
to my syght	to my syght			
and the swete body		+	the swete body	swete
waxid browne and blacke		+	browne. blacke	
all chauyngyd and turned ou3te of þe feyer		+	chaungyd and turned ou3te of þe feyer	of feyer
fressche and liuely coloure of hym selfe		+	fressche and liuely coloure of hym selfe	

THE DYNAMICS OF THE SIGNANS IN THE SPIRITUAL QUEST

GUY BOURQUIN

I

THE WORD *signans* should first be defined in its relation to two other words: *sign* and *signatum*, corresponding to two different modes of designation, viz. 'pointing to' and 'standing for'. A sign is that which points to something else. Now 'pointing to' does not mean 'explaining' but 'showing the way towards'. That which is pointed (or referred) to is the referent. Also a sign is something created by somebody for somebody else. It therefore does not exist *per se* but in relation to an agent (or user), a referent and a recipient (or experiencer). A more elaborate definition of the sign could be: that which is made by somebody (agent) to show somebody else (recipient) the way towards something (referent).

The sign has a double allegiance: to its referent and to its recipient. The operation of directing the recipient to the referent requires a more or less important degree of mediation. The referring (or pointing to) value of a sign may not be immediately apprehensible and thus has to be represented. This is where the standing for element comes in. The representation is achieved through a substitute (or series of substitutes). The substitute is a vicarious element apearing instead of the primary one. A distinction between 'vicarious' and 'primary', 'representative' and 'represented', 'that which stands for' and 'that which is stood for', thus appears within the sign, making it a complex Janus-like entity with one face (the *signatum*) looking towards its referent and the other (the *signans*) towards the recipient:

$$\text{referent} \longleftarrow \underbrace{\begin{array}{l} \textit{signatum} \\ \textit{signans} \longrightarrow \text{recipient} \end{array}}_{\text{sign}}$$

The referent/*signatum* relation is one of 'pointing out', the *signatum*/

signans one of substitution or re-placement, the *signans*/recipient one of apprehension. As to the recipient/referent relation, 'experiencing' or 'understanding' or 'knowing' seem, for all their vagueness, the most appropriate terms.

The above diagram applies in a variety of situations, the most obvious—and least original—ones occurring on the conscious, inter-personal communication level, when the referent is an already well-known world of shared knowledge, the semiotic organization itself a socially established code and transparency and expectancy prevail throughout. The first difficulties arise when parts of the referent are not already known to the recipient and some explaining has to be done: the sign organization here acquires a didactic function based on analogy (pointing to the already known in such a way as to induce or infer the unknown). The next more original step is the creative activity of the research-scientist or of the poet. Both are set on altering the *status quo*, discovering or thinking up new relational spaces through an intense exploitation of the virtualities of the pointing function: their fundamental ambiguities, the unconscious associations which proliferate when not kept under strict rational control. A dialectical give-and-take is established between sign and space in which the artist appears not only as a space-creator but also as a sign-producer, an opener of new space-building virtualities, a reveller in a world of symbols beyond which he sometimes does not even care to go. The true poet is perhaps more of a symbol-taster than of a space-creator.

II

All this raises the more general problem of the fundamental relation of man—whether individual or species—to his own environment. Man's awareness of himself as something different from his own surroundings is the most perplexing issue in psychology and philosophy. What does 'being aware' mean? What is the objective value of that awareness? Is all that man thinks, feels, senses, perceives, experiences, a reflection of naked reality or sheer delusion? Is there even such a thing as reality?

The most radical approach to the problem in contemporary psychology—that of Lacan's neo-Freudian school—on the one hand postulates reality—of which man is a mere component—and on the other claims it to be irretrievable, unknowable. Reality is at once present and absent, here and elsewhere, at work within man and ungraspable. One of Freud's main discoveries, somehow glossed over

183

by his followers but sharply re-emphasized by the Lacanian school, is that the unconscious part of the psyche, although organized along different principles from the conscious part, is just as remote, as estranged from reality, as is the conscious part.

The psyche is, in fact, organized into a sign system, i.e. a network of symbols pointing to something irrecoverably out of reach. That inward symbolic space—as Janus-like as any sign organization—is itself subdivided into *signatum* and *signans*. The *signatum* is a complex of tentative unexplained, unanalyzed intimations sent from the body into the psyche but as mysterious as the reality to which they are somehow related. Moreover, the *signatum – signans* relation is just as elusive as that between the signatum and reality. The mediation of the *signans* is achieved through a never-interrupted creation of substitutes for an ever-vanishing *signatum* in a desperate attempt to recapture its fugitive presence. Something gradually builds itself up which stands for what paradoxically turns out to be utterly unrepresentable, irrecoverably elsewhere. The psyche is thus entangled in a web of symbolic representations (*signantia*) cut off from what they are supposed to represent (i.e. the unpredictible *signata*). Standing for other *signantia* in an endless chain of representations is all that a *signans* ever manages to achieve. The chain stops short on the verge of the *signatum* because one link is always missing, the very link which could bridge the gap between the ultimate *signans* and the actual *signatum*. The symbolic chain is therefore an empty chain, tied to nothing, ending nowhere.

Yet man is part of reality and so immersed in it, so pervaded by it, so oned with it that it becomes impossible for him simply to step aside and take the hints let dropped. Even the unconscious part of the psyche fails to represent them unambiguously. The hints (i.e. the pointing *signata*) are the only possible way for reality to manifest itself, but what is manifested is not its 'whatness' but 'its being here'—and such manifestations are perceived only negatively like pointless, meaningless disruptions.

Reality is concealed by the very signs which are supposed—if not to unveil—at least to point towards it. This failure is due to the internal arrangements within the sign organization—the inability to maintain a transparent relation between *signans* and *signatum* because of the shiftiness, the instability, of the latter (viz. the hints let dropped). The *signans*, in its strangeness and opacity, is all that is left for man to be 'aware' of. Man's awareness, whether conscious or unconscious, is therefore doomed to develop in a closed vacuous world of symbol

184

patterns severed from, yet undermined by, and uninterpretable environment. Man's awareness is nothing but an awareness of *signantia*.

III

One may wonder what the above approach may have in common with the process of man's awareness of God as exemplified in the Christian theological tradition. God is everything, the ultimate explanation of everything, the only true reality. Man is a part of that reality—unconsciously so. God is in the same mysterious relationship with the soul as is the soma with the psyche. Just as the soma manifests itself indirectly within the psyche through the enigmatic *signantia* it delegates into it, even so God's presence is manifested to the soul through intimations which man should call up and decipher. God, like reality, is both within man and elsewhere. He is, in fact, elsewhere within man, and that other place has to be found out so that the soul may fully coincide with it, fully inhabit it. The 'finding out' is the spiritual quest and is just as strenuous, just as near-impossible as is the re-capturing of the somitic reality underlying the psyche. The symbolic web of *signantia* which is the texture of the unconscious part of the psyche is paralleled by the divinely-ordained patterning of man's soul.

What the quest of the psyche and that of the soul have in common is the way they both deal with the original *signans/signatum* dialectics they both have to reckon with. In neither case is the situation the straightforward one of a crystal-clear *signatum* mirroring itself in a transparent *signans*, as is the case in ordinary sign systems. In both cases the *signatum* (the pointing process) is unknown—worse: unknowable—and the *signans* (the substitution activity) enigmatic, ambiguous. In other words, the semiotic process does not necessarily have anything to do with explaining a way or clarifying. And, more often than not, man is left with one tangible, if ambiguous, phenomenon to wrestle with: the *signans*.

Wrestling with the signans seems to be the common lot of all serious spiritual seekers in the Christian tradition.

a. The Christian mystery is essentially semiotic. Not in the edulcorated sense of its being a message conveyed to man, but in the pregnant sense of its being an epiphany enigmatically forced upon man and paradoxically requiring man's active participation in its fulfilment. Viewed semiotically the Christian mystery is the manifestation of God to man, of the creator to the creature, of the infinite whole to the finite part. Diagrammatically:

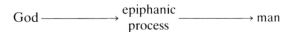

Being essentially semiotic, the epiphanic process is expected to point towards a referent and to be apprehended by a recipient, i.e. to be both God-pointing and man-oriented. The God-pointing man-oriented epiphanic entity is the Word of God.

The Word is that part of God's mystery which delegates itself into the epiphanic process, that part of God which is signified (i.e. turned into a sign) and through which God's mystery is pointed out: 'No man has seen God at any time; the only begotten Son, which is in the bosom of the Father, he has declared him' (John I:18). Now, being 'declared' does not mean being 'clarified'. A sign may be just as opaque as that which it is supposed to point towards. It may be apprehended, but not necessarily 'comprehended', 'received': 'He was in the world . . . and the world knew him not. He came unto his own and his own received him not . . . The light shineth in the darkness; and the darkness comprehended it not (John I:10–11).

The word of God is not a sign essentially, *per se*, but only in so far as God's creation is concerned. The Word (the Son) is co-extensive, co-eternal with God: 'In the beginning was the Word, and the Word was with God, and the Word was God' (John I:1). As a sign—i.e. as the epiphanic entity—the Word is the wholeness of God wholly attending to its own epiphany, the wholeness of God signifying itself (making itself sign) so as to be apprehended by man, the wholeness of God pointing the way towards its own unattainable infinity. This is a semiotic process of a very special sort indeed, wherein a sign is the very thing it purports to point to or, conversely, wherein the referent is a sign unto itself. Diagrammatically:

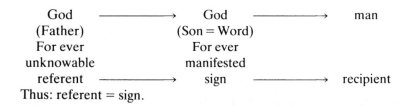

Thus: referent = sign.

The uniqueness of that semiotic process not only appears in its referent-oriented function but also in the way the internal components of the sign (i.e. *signatum* and *signans*) are related to each other. In non-theological semiotic processes, the signans usually belongs to an altogether different order of reality from that of the signatum. Moreover—according to Lacanian psychoanalytical approach and to literary semiotic theorists—the presence of the *signans* implies the absence of the *signatum*, the *signans* thus enjoying a certain amount of autonomy. Not so in the epiphanic process: 'The Word was made flesh, and dwelt among us . . . And of his fulness have we all received' (John I:14, 16). The 'Word made flesh' is Christ, whose terrestrial life is the *signans* of God's everlasting manifestation, i.e. the visible substitute of the invisible epiphanic *signatum*. But this *signans* is no ordinary envoy or ambassador: it is the very thing it purports to stand for or, conversely, the *signatum* is a *signans* unto itself. Diagramatically:

God (Father) → *Signatum*: God (as everlastingly
                                    manifested)
                   Signans: God (as man-orientedly →   man
                                    manifested)
referent   →   sign: God (Son)   →   recipient
           Thus referent = *signatum* = *signans*
           Father = Son = Word = Christ
           God = God = God = God

Throughout the stages of the epiphanic process the referent is present, in no danger of being eliminated. Substantially, Christ is the Word, the Word is the Son, the Son is the Father, although, phenomenally (or, rather, *semiotically* or epiphanically), Christ is the terrestrial substitute of the Word, and the Word the 'declarer' of the Father. These are what might be termed the 'semiotic modes of being' of the deity. Nothing is ever lost of the divine essence, the divine presence:

I am the way, the truth and the life: no man cometh unto the Father, but by me. If ye had known me, ye should have known my Father also: and from henceforth ye know him, and have seen him. Philip saith unto him, Lord, shew us the Father, it sufficeth us. Jesus saith unto him, Have I been so long time with you, and yet hast thou not known me, Philip? he that hath seen me hath seen the Father . . . The words that I speak unto you I speak not of myself: but the Father that dwelleth in me he doeth the works (John 14:6–10).

Now Christ is the arch-*signans*, the arch-substitute, and as such the originator (the matrix) of countless derived *signantia*. The most immediate substitute for historical Christ in the uninterrupted chain is the Paraclete (the Holy Spirit), a second envoy sent from the Father 'in the name of Christ', whose role is to ensure the perpetuation of the divine epiphany throughout the ages:

> And I will pray the Father, and he shall give you another Comforter, and he may abide with you for ever; Even the Spirit of truth; whom the world cannot receive, because it seeth him not, neither knoweth him: but ye know him; for he dwelleth with you, and shall be in you . . . The Comforter, which is the Holy Ghost, whom the Father will send in my name . . . (John 14:16–17, 26).

This is where man, the ultimate receiver of the epiphanic process, has to be brought into the picture. The chain of substitutes is definitely man-oriented, but the second substitute is more specifically destined to the responsive creature, to him who has been reacting positively to God's manifested presence:

> Judas saith unto him, not Iscariot, Lord, how is it that thou wilt manifest thyself unto us, and not unto the world? Jesus answered and said unto him, If a man love me, he will keep my words: and my Father will love him, and we will come unto him, and make our abode with him. He that loveth me not keepeth not my sayings: and the word which ye hear is not mine, but the Father's which sent me. These things have I spoken unto you being yet present with you. But the Comforter, which is the Holy Ghost, whom the Father will send in my name, he shall teach you all things to your remembrance, whatsoever have I said unto you (John 14:22–26).

So far, each substitute in the derivational chain is just another mode of being of the deity. Yet the participation of man in the derivational process is openly called for (God will *inhabit* him who participates). The participation can take on a variety of forms, the most complete one being for man to enter the epiphanic process through turning himself into a substitute for the lowest *signans* in the divine chain, i.e. the Paraclete. By so doing, man ceases to be a mere passive receiver and becomes the instrument of the manifestation of God.

Historically, that part of the epiphanic process materializes differently according to whether it takes place before or after the incarnation of Christ (the 'enfleshment' of the Word). A distinction is here to be drawn between what happens 'under the law' (i.e. before Christ) and 'under grace and truth' (i.e. since the advent of Christ). Before Christ the Old Testament relates the deeds of God's heralds and harbingers (from Abraham to Moses to the Prophets to John the Baptist): these are not the Word's substitutes, but only his human indirect manifestation. Theirs is a designative (pointing) function, not

188

a substitutive one. In other words, they are human, full-fledged signs both essentially and phenomenally distinct from the essence of the divine they are pointing to. They are human signs whose referent is another sign, the everlasting divine sign—the Word. The divine sign is here mediated through a human sign process. Diagrammatically:

referent ← sign
(God)   (Word)

referent   ←   sign   →   man
                                (Old Testament,
                                  harbingers)
    God   man   man

The Incarnation of Christ subverts the above system based on a two-level twice-repeated sign-referent relationship. The divine plenitude will, henceforward, both assume and subsume the human side of the epiphanic movement, altering the lower-level, man-oriented referent-sign relationship into a *signatum-signans* one integrated into the sign of the higher order. When Christ appears, the Old Testament harbingers of God disappear. The very verses of John's gospel which explain the epiphany of the Word are symptomatically interspersed with references to the older, vanishing system, i.e. John the Baptist (cf. John 1, *passim*). The status of man in the epiphanic process is henceforth radically altered. The displacement of John the Baptist by Christ is no ousting of man out of the semiotic process. On the contrary, man is promoted on to a higher level: his witnessing of God is no longer to take place on a separate semiotic level ('under the law') but within the divine sign, within the Word itself ('under grace'). Christ does not act as captor but as a donator. The arch-Signans is a generator of substitutes which he himself subsumes both pheno-menally and essentially. Any human witness of God has to liken himself to God ('*eritis tanquam dei*'), i.e. imitate Christ and thus be subsumed by the Paraclete (Christ's everlasting earthly substitute) and become not a harbinger or herald, but a manifestant, an evidencer, a perpetuator of God's presence, 'manifesting forth his glory' through having become a visible part of that glory. God's epiphany 'under grace' is not delegated but shared by all imitators of visible Christ. Any such imitator is the substitute of the arch-*signans*, the co-*signans* of the Word and can be said to be semiotically divine, not the essence of the divine, but its epiphanic mode of being. Man is then no longer a mere receiver: he has become a co-donator.

Thus both referent and recipient are the sign which is supposed to relate them to each other, the difference being that God is the whole of the sign (both *signatum* and *signans*) whereas man is only the *signans* and, even more restrictively, the phenomenal part of the *signans*. Diagrammatically:

referent ←————— signatum
God   *God*

signans ————————→ experiencer
essence, *God*
                                            man
phenomenon, *man*

The *signans* thus appears to be the only place where man can be said to be substitutable for God, to be in relation to the mysterious essence of God, to be God. Nevertheless, man is no nearer to a full understanding of God for being included in his epiphany. Once again, 'manifesting' or 'showing forth' does not mean elucidating. What is manifested is the unfathomable mystery of God's glory. Man is left not with a knowledge of what God is but with the fulness of his enigma. As a *signans*, he is expected to assume, share, shine forth the ambiguity of the enigma.

b. The epiphanic *signans* is a most complex affair, a universe of its own. It is essentially made up of *historical* and *mystical* Christ (i.e. Jesus of Nazareth and the Paraclete). The network of derived *signantia* develops along two main lines corresponding to two interacting human approaches to the divine *signans*: viz. interpreting and experiencing. Neither exists in isolation; each requires a certain amount of the other. Besides they are both subdivided: the former into symbolical and catechetic, the latter into contemplative and imitative. Here again the evidencing of God requires a certain amount of interaction between symbolic and catechetic on the one hand, contemplative and imitative on the other. Both the symbolic and the catechetic modes of interpreting have been initiated by Christ (the sacraments and sacramental life—the teaching of the gospel and of the apostles), then relayed by man (the liturgical network and literary and iconographical art—the writings of the Church Fathers, Church dogmas, homiletic literature). The contemplative and imitative components of the experiencing process also interact and are often complementary within one and the same individual. The acme of spiritual life is no doubt the bringing together of the four components and their merging into one another, i.e. man as the relay of a mysterious epiphany, of a fulness of love that passes all understanding, in which he is both giver and receiver. The more epiphanous the spiritual seeker, the deeper the mystery he shines forth.

The saints and the martyrs are the supreme evidencers of a mystery whose essence is the person of Christ, his life, his spoken word, his suffering and death, his mysterious resurrection. The terrestrial life of Christ has always been felt to be the ultimate enigmatic source of the four components. More particularly, the somatic element has received especial emphasis: the suffering body of Christ appears not only as the fountain of sacramental life and symbolism but also as a mysterious phenomenal reality betraying a no less mysterious essence. The deeper the fascination of the mystery, the more intense the scrutiny of the minutest details of Christ's terrestrial manifestation, in particular of his passion and death on the cross. As the physical place where the body of Christ is outrageously manifested forth to the world, the cross represents a metonymic shifting of the divine *signans* and is, as early as the primitive Church, the symbol of Christianity ('in hoc signo uinces'). Late medieval Devotio Moderna mysticism dwelt on the last moments of Christ's passion and made them the focus of religious meditation: the holy face, the holy wounds, the precious blood, the sacred heart, the holy rood thus came under intense scrutiny. Oneing oneself with God, i.e. evidencing the mystery of God meant becoming literally co-crucified with Christ, blessed with the *stigmata* of Christ's passion (e.g. Francis of Assisi), the identification with Christ operating not only in the mystic's soul but also in his flesh.

IV

Most late-medieval English religious writings show a similar concern with the visible part of the enigma. Neither *Piers Plowman* nor the religious drama nor the prose mystics try to rationalize away the enigma. On the contrary, all are, in their several original ways, conducive to a deepening of the mystery rather than an elucidation of it. The emphasis is laid now on God manifesting himself now on man manifesting God either to his own inner self or, more often, to his own fellow-creatures.

a. The *signans/signatum* relationship within the soul of man is tentatively and subtly analyzed in *Piers Plowman*. In Passus A.I., the

Dreamer, having just heard Holychurch praise Truth as 'tresour triȝest on erþe', further enquires about its manifestation within the soul. Holy church answers:

> It is a kynde knowyng þat kenneþ in þin herte
> For to loue þi lord leuere þanne þiselue; . . .
> For in kynde knowyng in herte þer comsiþ a miȝt,
> And þat falliþ to þe fadir þat fourmide vs alle,
> Lokide on vs wiþ loue, & let his sone deiȝe . . .[1].

The God-given 'might' man can become aware of is an aptitude to imitate the life of Christ. Man has within himself Christic potentialities. Christ is historically outside but potentially within every human soul. The deciphering of the soul's potentialities goes therefore hand in hand with a meditation of Christ's life of love: any progress in the understanding of the outward manifestations of Christ is a progress in the understanding of the inward virtualities of the soul. Here lies the dual enigmatic *signans* man has experientially to discover.

Piers Plowman as a whole can be looked upon as a masterly and elaborate exposition of the enigmatic duality of the spiritual quest, i.e. of the simultaneous deepening of God's life on earth and man's experience of self-oblivion and other-centered love. In fact, the quest in *Piers Plowman* is more than dual, it is *mutual*: man and God are seeking each other experiencing each other. This mystical phenomenon is built into the poem's fabric, into the polysemy of its keywords, the ambiguity of its allegorical pattern, and even the mode of its allegorical growth. The word 'truth' in the *Visio*, for instance, brings man and God together by referring simultaneously to God's presence in man's soul, man's spiritual quest, the terrestrial pilgrimage of Christ, God's fidelity to man and his mysterious presence in the world, man's fidelity to God through the imitation of Christ, etc. The Dowel, Dobet, Dobest triplet, on the other hand, appears throughout many passus of A and B as an elusive empty form which the Dreamer clings to in a desperate attempt to wring some spiritual clue out of it. Then, as the poem's allegorical pattern develops, the three words, at another level of its architectonics, symbolize God's progress in the experiencing of the life of man, culminating in Christ, himself also ambiguous as both a historical phenomenon and a permanent irresistible upsurge. Dobest is the symbol word for the merging of God's and man's natures, the dynamics of their mutual exploration within the epiphanic process. But the merging also arises in the poem out of the mystical growth of the character of Piers (from plowman in A.VI to 'procurator and reeve' of the Paraclete in B.XIX through various identifications with

Christ in the Dobet passus) and, even more so,—paradoxically enough—out of the ultimate displacement of Piers by Liberum Arbitrium in the C-Text.

In many ways, *Piers Plowman* is an expanding of the liturgical approach to Christian symbolism. The labyrinthine web of liturgical connotations is re-designed into a pattern 'rich and strange'. The complexity of the Christian *signans* is thus amply set out. The purpose of *Piers Plowman* is not to offer an interpretation of it but simply to bring out its fundamental ambiguity – and to suggest that the deep meaning of a quest does not consist in rendering the *signans* unambiguous but, on the contrary, in intensifying its polysymbolic ramifications, thereby deepening the underlying mystery: there is no ending to the explorations of the epiphany of the godly within man.

Exploring means finding new paths, new phenomena, new symbols, new mysteries, a more and more complex, intricate organization of the network of *signantia* viewed as mysterious intimations from beyond, strange messengers with no clearly worded message, but whose very 'being here' testifies to some meaningful—though unapproachable—reality. *Piers Plowman* thus clearly stands out as a literary experiment in ambiguity—creative ambiguity—and as a subtle and deeply orthodox enrichment of the enigma of the Word of God.

The true mystical approach to the Word of God is perhaps epitomized here. The true mystic is not he who attempts to solve the enigma, but he who deliberately enters into it, not in order to conquer but to be conquered by it, absorbed in it, he who loses himself in it, settles in it, revels in it. Other cases in point than *Piers Plowman* are the religious drama and the prose mystics.

b. In the mystery plays the Christian enigma is properly acted out before a large audience by actual human beings. This special relationship brings out in an original way the ambiguity of the Word of God as *signans*: man ambiguously mimics for himself the myth of his own condition. The actor enters into the terrestrial life of Christ and of Christ's precursors, and a whole community in various ways contributes to the staging of the Word of God. The human actor ironically re-enacts the process of God's humanization, which mystically underlies the process of man's regeneration. Man's godliness and God's manliness are thus intertwined and fused. What *Piers Plowman* achieves through the multi-level polysemy of the Dowel, Dobet, Dobest trilogy (man's progress within God and God's progress within man) is here brought about by the necessities of the genre.

The genre visibly has a few notable peculiarities, fully relevant to the present study. In the drama, the Word of God is materialized, visualized into gestures and speeches. Many events of the life of Christ (or Christ's precursors) are dwelt upon at considerable length with a wealth of realistic details: Noah's ark, the Nativity scenes, the scourging of Christ, and several other episodes of the Passion. Such goings into detail and apparently trivial additions were once looked down upon as undignified and futile. And yet—however paradoxical this may sound at first— they are in perfect consonance with the most genuine mystical approach to the Christian *signans*. Unable to contemplate God 'facie ad faciem', the mystic is left with the enigma of the *signans* to pore upon and scrutinize. Being the only tangible link of man with the divine, the enigma is what one turns to when one is in need of God. The intensity of the scrutiny magnifies the minutest details, causing them to stand out and obliterate the more general— often too obvious—outlines. The more mystical the contemplation, the more the visionary eye focuses upon apparently unimportant spots as if they were more pregnant substitutes for the ungraspable *signatum*. The mystic's is a poetical, not a prose, *signans*. The difference between the two is that, in the former, everything—for want of a strictly defined co-respondent in the signatum—is felt to be potentially important. In the Mystery Plays, the coarser scenes— whether realistic, burlesque, comical or sadistic—should therefore be read not as artistic blemishes or weaknesses or mere digressions, but as precious evidence of something mysteriously at work within the very process of writing.

The mystery-plays dramatize the historical development of the epiphanic process, i.e. the moving of God and man closer and closer to each other until they are undistinguished in Christ's humanity, the *signans* of the Word. The morality-plays go one step further than the mystery-plays by showing that the presence of Christ on earth can be made permanent by man himself: every withdrawal of God's manifestation is caused by man and can be reversed by man. *Everyman* aptly illustrates the contribution of man to the semiotic pattern. Everyman is 'summoned' into the epiphanic process not through his own death but through the ambiguity of Christ's death. The character of Good Deeds embodies the inward illumination of Life-in-Death (man's life in Christ's death) or man as the 'spouse of Jesus', as a part of his shining glory. Good Deeds is the epiphanic element in Everyman, which shines forth Christ from the very moment Everyman begins to act 'in remembrance of Christ's passion'.

c. The spelling out of the details of Christ's passion characterizes most prose mystics, particularly Julian of Norwich and Margery Kempe. Although poles asunder from each other, they shared the same aptitude to scrutinize the *signans* so intensely as to become immersed in its enigmatic complexity.

We shall only deal here with the case of Margery Kempe, an interesting illustration of an ambiguous relationship with the Passion and death of Christ. Margery's vivid imagination calls up scenes of Christ's life and adds to them a variety of details. Her soul is the place where contacts with God are said to happen—where God the Father proposes to her, then 'takes her by the hand' and utters the ritual words of the wedding ceremony in front of the second and third persons of the Trinity, the Virgin, the angels, the saints, the martyrs, the whole celestial court. Margery's soul is not only the Tabernacle of God, but also the place where she also invites other creatures in order to bring them in a privileged relation with God. God thanks her for such initiatives:

> 'And also, dowtyr, þu clepist my Modyr for to comyn in-to þi sowle & takyn me in hir armys & leyn me to hir brestys & ȝeuyn me sokyn . ... and also þu clepist . . . al þe court of Heuyn in-to þi sowle for to wolcomyn me . . .'.[2]
> 'þu hast bathyd me in þi sowle at hom in þi chambre . . . þu hast herberwyd me & my blissyd Modyr in þi bed', (here referring to Margery's capacity as 'handmaiden of the Virgin').[3]

Margery thus re-enacts—with herself as an additional protagonist—scenes of the terrestrial life of Christ, which she amplifies with a wealth of down-to-earth personal and other details and with celestial overtones. *Illud tempus* here becomes indistinguishable from her everyday life. She, in a way, works out her own liturgy, with herself *in medias res*, sometimes in conjunction with the liturgical celebrations she happens to be attending: on a Good Friday ritual ceremony, she has a vision of the Passion of Christ within her soul. The outside world offers her countless spiritual stimuli: she is once moved to thoughts of Christ by the sight of a poor mother and her little boy and the sadness of the mother merges itself into the sadness of the Virgin at the moment of the Passion. Through the filter of Margery's sensitiveness, the world becomes a direct partaker of the epiphanic process.

The more Margery reads God into the world outside, the more she becomes the bearer, the manifestant of God to other people. Her body relays the suffering body of Christ. Her weeping and crying are the acting out of her painful identification with the arch-*Signans*, her permanent assumption of the Virgin's *planctus*. Christ himself refuses her request that he should send her crying in private: he, on the contrary, desires of her that her tears should be public so that they may improve other creatures. She has truly become the phenomenal *signans* of Christ who uses her as he thinks fit:

> I ȝyf þe sum-tyme smale wepyngys & soft teerys for a token þat I lofe þe & sum-tyme I ȝeue þe gret cryes & roryngys for to makyn þe pepil aferd wyth þe grace þat I putte in þe in-to a token þat I wil þat my Modyrs sorwe be knowyn, . . . (five more 'tokens' are enumerated).[4]

Margery's spiritual drama is semiotic. Her drama is made up of what happens to God on behalf of man, what happens to herself on behalf of God, what happens to God and to her for the sake of each other. By fully assuming—both in her soul and in her body—many episodes, whether homely or noble, sweet or painful, of Christ's life, Margery partakes of the epiphany of the Word. Although perhaps not the type of woman the Church would care to canonize, she is nevertheless, technically at least, a signal link in the never-ending chain of Christic *signantia*.

d. The *Cloud of Unknowing* illustrates a radically different approach to the semiotics of God's epiphany. The emphasis is laid on the impossibility for man to know God: '. . . loue may reche to God in þis liif, bot not knowyng'[5]. The danger of setting one's mind on anything beneath the unapprehensible deity is again and again pointed out in paradoxical phrasings:

> . . . wher anoþer man wolde bid þee gader þi miȝtes & þi wittes bodiliche wiþ-inne þi-self, & worschip God þere—þof al he sey ful wel & ful trewly, ȝe! & no man trewlier & he be wel conseiuid—ȝit for feerde of disseite & bodely conceyuyng of his wordes, me list not byd þee do so. Bot þus wil I bid þee. Loke on no wyse þat þou be wiþ-inne þi-self, & schortly wiþ-outyn þi-self wil I not þat þou be, ne ȝit abouen, ne be-hynde, ne on o side, ne on oþer. 'Wher þan', seist þou, 'schal I be? Noȝwhere, by þi tale!' 'Now trewly þou seist wel; for þere wolde I haue þee. For whi noȝwhere bodely is euerywhere goostly . . . & þof al þi bodely wittes kon fynde þer noþing to fede hem on, for hem þink it nouȝt þat þou doste, ȝe! do on þan þis nouȝt, elles þat þou do it for Goddes loue. & lete nouȝt, þerfore, bot trauayle besily in þat nouȝt with a wakyng desire to wilne to haue God, þat no man may knowe. For I telle þee trewly þat I had leuer be so nowhere bodely, wrastlyng wiþ þat blynde nouȝt, þan to be so grete a lorde þat I miȝt when I wolde be euerywhere bodely, merily pleiing wiþ al þis ouȝt as a lorde wiþ his owne. . . . Reche þe neuer ȝif þi wittys kon no skyle of þis nouȝt; for whi I loue it moche þe betir . . . What is he þat clepiþ it nouȝt? Sekirly it is oure utter man, & not oure inner. Oure inner man clepiþ it Al . . .'[6]

Things material and spiritual alike have to be by-passed, left behind. A 'cloud of forgetting' has first to be raised. The *signans* no longer seems to be in the position of something to be entered into or scrutinized or conquered, but of something to be broken through and 'overpassed'. Even the symbolic network of God's presence appears as an obstacle to the pure merging of the mystic into the 'nowhere' of the cloud of unknowing. The liturgical *signantia* which were the props of Margery's and Julian's mystical experience of God are no longer considered here as things to be scanned and scrutinized at all costs but rather as retarding elements preferably (though perhaps not obligatorily) to be avoided. The soul, as a result, hangs in a vacuum, apparently in between the Word as *signans* and the Word as *signatum*, having access to neither.

Yet *The Cloud* clearly distinguishes between 'knowing' and 'love'. The phrase 'loue may reche to God in þis liif' in the above quotation is at least as important as the second part of the sentence: 'bot not knowing'. Though intellectually in a vacuum as regards perceiving or understanding the *signatum* of the Word, the human soul nevertheless reaches God with the 'darts of longing love' which she sends towards him through the cloud of unknowing. One may therefore suppose that, by so doing, man is somehow mysteriously relayed by the epiphanic dynamics, more particularly by the 'essential' mode of the *signans*, which would mean that his unflinching quest of the divine has made him become at least the 'phenomenal' mode of that very *signans*. In other words, when he tries to pierce through the mystery of the *signatum*, man, because of his loving kindness, has already become a part of what he fails to understand, i.e. a part of that 'love that passeth all understanding'.

V

From whichever position it is approached by the spiritual seeker, the divine is apprehended as a manifestation of something for ever elusive yet shareable. The sharing may be attained through entering the manifestation process, i.e. through becoming a part of the sign, more particularly an element of the chain of *signantia*. The epiphanic process is a process of love: eternal love for ever shining forth superabounding love upon such human creatures as accept to become, in their turn, the reflectors of its radiance.

NOTES

1. Langland, *Piers Plowman: The A Version*, ed. G. Kane. London, 1960, p. 198, ll 126, 130–1, 139–141.

2. *The Book of Margery Kempe*, ed. Sanford B. Meech and Hope Emily Allen. Early English Text Society, O.S, 212, London, 1940, p. 210.
3. *Ibid.*, p. 214.
4. *Ibid.*, p. 183.
5. *The Cloud of Unknowing*, ed. P. Hodgson, Early English Text Society, O.S, 218, London, 1944, Ch. 8, p. 33.
6. *Ibid.*, ch. 68, pp. 121–2.

MYSTIC'S FOOT: ROLLE AND AFFECTIVITY

VINCENT GILLESPIE

I

'. . . our erected wit maketh us to know what perfection is, and yet our infected will keepeth us from reaching unto it'.

Philip Sidney, *A Defence of Poetry*

IT MAY SEEM odd to begin a paper on affectivity in the fourteenth century with a quotation from a protestant courtier poet of the sixteenth. Yet Sidney's words echo a debate about the nature and justification of imaginative literature in general and poetry in particular which had crystallised by the thirteenth century.[2] The essence of the debate was whether poetry could properly be described as a human or divine science. One view was that Aristotle had demonstrated that poetry, and indeed all literary endeavour, was a skill that had been developed from within man's own capabilities. The opposite view was that it was a divine science, the product of inspiration. It had been validated by God in Scripture through deliberate exploitation of literary genres (chronicles, elegies, love songs, psalms) and the strategic use of literary tropes (allegory, metaphor, etc.) by the inspired human writers who had given form and shape to God's word. The identification of the literary qualities of scriptural writing had been one of the major developments of the Franciscan school of theological thought in the University of Paris in the thirteenth century building on the work of the school of Laon. Thinkers such as Alexander of Hales and, most notably, Bonaventure evolved a highly influential theory of aesthetics based on the premise that literature had been sanctioned by God, that it was one of the major strategies employed in the didactic edifice of the Bible, and that modern writers could do no better than to model themselves on biblical precedent when they came to make their own contributions to the literature of the faith.[3] However, much of what the Franciscans made explicit, and indeed practised in their own contributions to the vernacular literatures of Europe, had been implicit in earlier thought, particularly in Augustine's central discussion of the problem in *De Doctrina Christiana*.

Yet the argument about whether poetry should be entrusted to the divine sciences or the human sciences was only one manifestation of a much larger, more traumatic, discussion precipitated by the re-introduction of Aristotelian logic into the Paris schools. The application of reason, the introduction of new methodologies, to the study of older disciplines such as grammar, brought rapid advances in sophistication and new and significant insights into the workings of language and the nature of meaning. But particular problems were presented by the application of these new techniques to a specific set of words bound together by a particular grammar: the inspired discourse of the Bible. Given that the divine author of the text had revealed truth in an avowedly mysterious way, and given that man's reason, for all its new found technical virtuosity, was a profoundly limited instrument in the search for absolute truth because it was constrained to operate from within the body of a fallen man, how possible was it to apply scientific methods of analysis to the sacred Scripture, and how amenable would Scripture be to those methods? To formulate the question in the way the thirteenth-century thinkers put it: was sacred Scripture a science? In the 1240s that question was the first to be asked at the outset of the Paris theology course.[4] In reply, a theory of pragmatic affectivity was formulated, which filtered down in the course of the next century to influence all areas of devotional and didactic activity.

The problem of how to apply the new learning to the old texts was the more urgent because the thirteenth century had seen the development of theological modes of thought and areas of reasearch to which the newly rigorous procedures were peculiarly suitable. Although the reading of the *sacra pagina* remained the basis of the theology course, new and more speculative discussions developed about matters that simple reading could never solve. Texts such as the *Sentences* of Peter Lombard mark the move away from the Bible as the sole focus of interest, and as commentaries on the *Sentences* began to proliferate, the systematisation of doctrine threw up areas of uncertainty and confusion which the new logic could do much to clarify. *Quaestiones* were formulated as a means of setting forth the problem and dissecting its implications. These *quaestiones* often produced solutions of direct pastoral relevance. This branch of the study of the faith could truly be called theology.[5]

Yet the application of reason to the *donnée* of Scripture could seem to undermine faith: as William of Auxerre, citing Gregory, pointed out in c. 1220, 'fides non habet meritum ubi humana ratio prebet experimentum'.[6] What was needed, and what (this being the thirteenth century) was forthcoming, was a distinction. The great masters of both the Dominicans and the Franciscans agreed on a distinction between theology and Scriptural exegesis (thus allowing the more speculative areas of endeavour to continue), and between human science (the study of cause and effect) and divine science (the study of the cause of causes). Whereas human science had sought knowledge for its own sake (*scientia ut scientia*), divine science sought knowledge as a means of gaining wisdom (*scientia ut sapientia*). Not only were the ends different, but also the means used were forcefully contrasted. Thus Alexander of Hales contrasted the methods of *scientia* (*definitivus, divisivus, collectivus*) with the modes used by Scripture (*praeceptivus, exemplificativus, revelativus, orativus*), and went on to point out that the latter modes were literary and, above all, affective.[7]

This prominence given to the affective modes of Scripture led inevitably to discussions and analyses of how the affective faculty within man worked and in particular how it could be worked on by literary means. Because the Bible was essentially literature, Aristotelian ideas were regarded as inapplicable: 'omnis modus poeticus est inartificialis sive non scientialis'.[8]

As Andrew Louth has pointed out, the distinction between *sapientia* and *scientia* was not a new development in the thirteenth century, but rather a re-classification in a more systematic way of division found in much patristic writing. Augustine had seen the distinction, but it was the affective theologians of the twelfth century in particular who had emphasised the importance of feeling and compunction in the search for wisdom.[9] Bernard, with his usual facility for encapsulating concepts in memorable phrases, had said that 'Instruction makes us learned but feeling makes us wise'. He emphasised the pseudo-etymology of *sapientia* (going back to *sapor* or taste) as part of his distinction from knowing. In the thirteenth century, Robert Kilwardby distinguished between what he called metaphysics, dealing with first causes and appealing to the intellectual part of the man, and sacred Scripture, which he describes as teaching of the true so as to lead to the good (*verum ut bonum*) which he says 'pertinet ad motionem affectus. Et haec proprie dicitur sapientia a sapore, quia facit cognitionem secundum gustum'. Alexander of Hales wrote

'Theologia igitur, quae perficit animam secundum affectionem movendo ad bonum per principia timoris et amoris, proprie et principaliter est sapientia'. In the fourteenth century Langland defines his concept of kynde knowyng, which seems close to *sapientia*, thus:

> 'a kynde knowynge that kenneth in thyn herte
> For to loven thi Lord levere than thiselve',

thus stressing that love is an essential and fundamental part of this higher knowing.[10] The difference between knowledge and wisdom is very effectively brought about in *Disce Mori*, an English vernacular text of the early fifteenth century, which demonstrates clearly the way that the academic discussions of *sapientia* had percolated into the mainstream of popular piety. In the course of its lengthy exposition of the *Pater Noster*, it defines wisdom and lists the ways in which the gift of wisdom from the Holy Spirit works on the soul of man:

> Sapience is called a sauoury science for whan a man hath this gifte and grace he tasteth and knoweth the swetnesse that is in god by the gifte of understonding. A man knoweth god like as a man knoweth goode wyne whan he seeth it faire and clerer in a verre. But by the gifte of sapience a man knoweth as he knoweth the wyne by the drinking . . .

The nice play on words in this definition of wisdom—'a savoury science'—encapsulates the difference from the other sciences:—it is a knowledge which is also a sensual encounter—an 'experience'.[11] What concerned the theologians and writers of the Middle Ages was how the individual soul could be brought to this state of wisdom; how they could be moved away from sin to a firmer relationship with God; and perhaps most difficult of all, how knowledge of the laws and doctrines of the Church could be catalysed into a profound yearning to embrace God through those same laws. Although it could be assumed that most Christians knew what was required of them in terms of moral rectitude and spiritual orientation, just as they would know wine if they saw it in a glass, the problem was bridging the gap that existed in fallen man between perceiving the true and embracing the good. As Sidney's formulation puts it, the erected wit saw the road to truth, but the infected will diverted man into a cul de sac of sin. To see how they set about solving that problem we need first to look briefly at the basic psychology involved.

II

The complexities of medieval discussions of the powers of the soule, the nature of sense perception and the relationship between wit and

202

will are such that I do not wish to venture into them here.[12] So in attempting to explain how the affective faculty was thought of, I will restrict myself to the simpler discussions. In any case, like so many philosophical debates, the detail generated by the scholastic analyses of motivation conceals a fairly simple division between the powers of the intellect and the powers of the will, which is more frequently present in a crude form in the affective literature of the fourteenth century. All impressions received through the senses are processed by the intellect which, according to Robert Grosseteste, in this first look verifies what has been received. The mind then satisfies itself about what is attractive or noxious (presumably by reference to known ethical, religious or social absolutes) and then the affection (*affectus*) 'yearns to embrace what is attractive or withdraws within itself in flight of what is noxious'.

Thus, theoretically, once the intellect has verified the data by reference to what it knows of the true, the *affectus* yearns towards the good or away from the bad.[13] Or so it would be if man was not a fallen creature. As a result of the fall, the will has been corrupted, and it runs after the joys of the world instead of resolutely fixing itself on the good. The role of affective literature is to regain the attention of the *affectus*, by winning it away from the proximate things to which it has become attached and focussing it firmly on absolute good, to enable the intellect to penetrate more deeply into its understanding of absolute truth, which it knows to be desirable but from which it is constantly distracted by the dissipation of the will. Thus John Trevisa's translation of the *De Proprietatibus Rerum* describes the division in the make-up of man:

> If þe soule by resoun turneþ toward god, he is by schyned, mendid, and Imade perfite; And ȝif he turneþ by affecciouns toward creatures, he is Imade derk, corrupt apeired.[14]

A recurring image of this odd relationship between the *affectus* and the reason takes the image of the soul journeying towards heaven as being like a man walking along a road. One foot is ever ahead, eager to complete the journey and clear about which direction to take, and this is the foot of the intellect (*pes intellectus*); the other foot is always dragging behind and is reluctant to follow its partner, and this is the foot of the affections or the will (*pes affectus*).[15] Augustine had used the image several times. In his commentary on John 13:6, for example, which deals with Christ washing the feet of the apostles at the last supper, Augustine says that feet are like affections which become

203

dirtied with the dust of sin and need to be washed daily. His commentary on Psalm 94 takes up this image and explicitly links the affections with morality. If we are immoral we journey away from God, but if we live good lives we journey towards him. 'Pedes enim nostri in hoc itinerere affectus nostri sunt'.[16] Although the original, primarily moral, force of Augustine's use of the image becomes blurred, the contrast between the two feet is repeated very often throughout the Middle Ages and becomes a popular way of exemplifying the conflict apparent to many thinkers between a knowledge of the truth and a voluntary acceptance of that truth through embracing the good by an act of will. Several vernacular texts use the image. The ascetical treatise *The Doctrine of the Hert* has an extended discussion of the *pes affectus*, including this exposition:

> He haþ ȝeve to þi feet schoes of iacynte. By þis iacynte, þe whiche is like to a clere colourid firmament, þou schalt undirstond heuenly desire wheraftir þi foot þe which is þi gostly affeccion schuld be arayed. Therfor, Sister, meke to þi foot of þi gostly affeccion a scho of alle Heuen as pought Y myȝt sey þus to þe: Araye alle þin affeccion with heuenly desires þat Holy Chirche may se of þe as Salamon seith of þe kyngis douȝtir of Heuen: Quam pulcri sunt pedes tui in calciamentis filia principis. He seith: O kynges douȝtir, how faire ben þi fete of gostly affeccion in schoes of heuenly desires.[17]

Here the shoes of heavenly desires are clearly intended to protect the feet from the dust and dirt of the earth, and from sin. In Hilton's *Scale of Perfection*, it occurs as part of his discussion of the value of prayer for the contemplative:

> For he who can not run lightly in the way of contemplative prayer, because the feet of his knowledge and love are lamed by sin, needs a firm staff to lean on. This staff is the vocal prayer ordained by God and the Church for man's assistance (1.27).[18]

The vernacular translation of the Carthusian Guigo II's *Scala Claustralium*, known as *A Ladder of Foure Ronges*, goes further than these sources with the statement that 'By a fote in Holy Wrytte is love vndirstonde'.[19]

No doubt Rolle would have concurred with this statement, as his two commentaries on the Psalms miss few opportunities to emphasise the affective meaning of the foot image. Several of the many references to feet in the Psalms are explained by the various glosses gathered together in the *Glossa Ordinaria*, but Rolle is far more systematic than the *Glossa* and than his major source, the Psalter Commentary of Peter Lombard (a *catena* of other patristic writings on the psalms).[20] On at least seven occasions Rolle interprets references to feet as meaning the affections or the will when there is no such reading in Lombard. Thus at Psalm 25:12, his Latin commentary has:

> *Pes meus* id est, affectus et amor meus *stetit in directo* id est, perseuerauit usque ad mortem supernam *et* tuum amorem solummodo appetando propter quod *in ecclesiis* id est, in coelo vbi sunt multe mansiones *benedicam te domine* laudabo sine fine.

Similarly the reference at Psalm 35:12 to 'pes superbiae' evokes this comment in the English psalter: 'The fote of pride is a proude will or thoght that beris man fra god til the devel'. The end of affectivity is clearly spelt out in Psalm 17:34:

> *Qui perfecit pedes meos* id est perfectos fecit affectus meos in ipsum *sicut cervorum* id est vt transcendam spinosa et umbrosa implicamenta huius secula *et super excelsa* id est super coelestem habitationem *statuens me* id est figens intentionem meam, vt conversatio mea in coelis sit.

Psalm 39:2/3 stresses the moral elements in affective reformation:

> *Et statuit supra petram* id est, firmitatem virtutum *pedes meos* id est, affectus meos, non super arenam *et direxit gressus meos* id est, actiones meas, ad supernam intentionem erexit, vt prosperarer in spiritualibus non in corporalibus.

As this last quotation suggests, because the *pes affectus* is generally associated with the will, and with the search for the good (rather than the search for the true which is initially the role of the intellect), literature which attempts to rectify the affective disorders to which the human will is prone is generally involved in the first instance with the basics of morality and the foundations of virtuous living. As Alexander of Hales had said, theology which perfects the soul 'per affectionem', moves it to good principally by means of fear and love. Of course, the fear of the Lord is the beginning of wisdom, and it is wisdom (*sapientia*) which was seen as the final end of the affective and poetical writing in the Bible. Bonaventure went so far as to say that because this affective moving of the will to good and away from evil was the function of Scripture, it was therefore divided into two testaments, the simple difference between them being that the Old Testament dealt with fear and the New Testament with love.[21] As Bernard had written in his *Sermons on the Song of Songs*, 'We first taste God when he makes us fear him, not when he instructs us'. Similarly he writes 'knowledge of God is one thing and fear of God another. What confers wisdom is not knowledge, but fear that touches the heart'.[22] Bonaventure, the great literary theoretician of Biblical studies evolved from the basic premise of the affective force of Scripture, a doctrine of the *multiplex modi* of the Bible, a way of explaining the vast range of styles and techniques which literary examination of the text had brought to light. Working from the well known list of attributes of human science (*definitivus, divisivus, collectivus*) contrasted with divine science as manifested in the Scriptures (*praeceptivus, exemplicativus, revelativus, orativus,* etc.), he explains that the *affectus* is moved more effectively by example than by argument, by devotion more than by definition and so on (incidentally invoking a didactic tradition going back to Gregory). The Bible must use a range of different modes of expression to coincide with the range of different motivations to be found in human nature.[23] His principle seems to be that the Bible is able to please all of the people at least some of the time, and that the different types of discourse and levels of literacy artifice are part of the affective strategy of the work's final cause, God, the divine author. If the Old Testament works on the level of fear (in general terms which seem to include within them respect for the precepts of the law, i.e. the Commandments, and therefore to include within them general moral exhortation and the literature of the good Christian life which is the essential foundation for an effective reformation of the will), then the New Testament works on the level of love, and in particular aims to foster love for the person of Christ, particularly in his human nature.

As far as it is discernible in the theological discussions we have considered, the standard progression of the reforming process in the will takes the following shape. The raw material must be present in the intellect through education in the basic beliefs of the Church. The will must be affectively moved to accept those teachings. Then the will must be won over away from carnal desires to love of spiritual things, perhaps by way of the human nature of Christ as a bridge between the carnal and the spiritual. Once this has been achieved, further insight into the nature of the true can continue without the interruptions of the fickle and fleeting will. This insight will be a combination of knowledge and feeling. The affective response is a concentrating of the carnal elements of the rational soul to allow the natural tendency of the will towards good (*synderesis*) to assert itself. This natural tendency is the counterpart of conscience in the intellect. An affective response allows the intellect and the will to act in harmony, and this concentration or focussing results in new insights and a more rigorous striving for illumination and truth.[24]

Christ as an affective focal point offers many advantages. In his human nature, he can attract to himself (by virtue of the compassion we feel for his sufferings) the very carnal affection which it was the desire of affective writers to overcome, thus liberating the will to support the intellect in its search for truth. By virtue of his dual nature, Christ could lead the reformed affections into a more rarified and purified form of devotion, indeed into the higher levels of contemplation to which only the most rigorously disciplined and purged wills allowed access. Once the initial reformation of the will had been achieved, the subsequent stages of contemplative ascent were able to proceed. Thus burning love for God in Christ becomes the most resounding cliché of devotional literature. For Rolle, it was central not only to his own mystical experience but also to the affective strategies in his writings for others.

III

Lovers and madmen have such seething brains,
Such shaping fantasies, that apprehend
More than cool reason ever comprehends.
The lunatic, the lover and the poet
Are of imagination all compact'.
A Midsummer Night's Dream V.I. 4–9.

Rolle would have been well aware of the popular views of affectivity, and his study of scriptural and theological writers at Oxford, and perhaps after, could have led him to become familiar with the more complex formulations of the role of the *affectus* in man's psychological make-up.[25] His works demonstrate a comprehensive understanding of the ways in which an affective response could be generated. Again and again throughout the Latin and vernacular works, the same basic premises are enunciated: man's will is corrupt, it must be reformed through a rejection of carnal affections and an acceptance of the love of Christ, a yearning love of Christ will lead to a further kindling of love as a gift from God, this new kindled love will fix our intellects and the eye of our soul on the contemplation of God and will help us to achieve wisdom. These processes are well summarised at the opening of the *Emendatio Vitae*:

We are not turned to god wiþ goyng of oure bodili feet.
but þoruȝ chaungyng of oure affeccioun *and* oure maneres.
þanne turne we us to god. whanne we reise up þe scharpnesse of oure mynde unto him (cap. 1).[26]

This turning of our affections to God, which he describes in *Desyre and Delit* as a spiritual circumcision 'when all oþer besynes and affeccyons and thoghtes are drawen away oute of his saule, that he may hafe tryste

207

in Goddes lufe', is not achievable through rational or intellectual decision.[27] It has to be willed as well as decided upon. Rolle makes this quite clear in the prologue to the *Incendium Amoris*, where he offers the book not to philosophers, sages and theologians, bogged down in argument, but to 'the simple and unlearned, who are seeking rather to love God than to amass knowledge. For he is not known by argument, but by what we do and how we love'. Paraphrasing St Paul, he emphasises that 'Knowledge without love does not edify or contribute to our eternal salvation; it merely puffs up to our own dreadful loss' (cap. 5).[28] Similarly, in a passage which brings together several of the concepts enunciated in the academic discussions of affectivity, he stresses that the freedom of the will is an awesome responsibility which carried with it awesome consequences:

> All the time your love is not wholly directed towards your Maker you are making it plain that you are loving one of God's creatures beyond what is honest and lawful. It is not possible for a rational soul to be without love while it is alive. It follows that love is the foot, so to speak, by which after its pilgrimage on earth it will be carried either up to God or down to the devil.

He makes it plain that he understands many of the aesthetic assumptions of the theologians in this comment:

> Nothing is loved, except for the good it contains or is thought to contain, whether real or apparent. This is the reason why those who love physical beauty or temporal wealth are deceived or, one could say, tricked. For in visible and tangible objects there does not really exist either the delight that superficially appears, or the glory that is supposed, or the fame that is pursued (cap. 23).[29]

This is why he was so vehement in his denunciations of worldly love, for 'no one can be united to God perfectly while he is held by a liking for the created and worldly' (cap. 10).[30]

He followed Bonaventure and many others in believing that the way to perfection and wisdom was through Christ. In the prologue to the *Itinerarium Mentis in Deum*, Bonaventure had referred to St Francis's vision of a six-winged seraph, which he had allegorised as six stages of illumination by which the soul passes into peace 'by ecstatic revelations of Christian wisdom'. But he had started with a firm and unequivocal statement of the need for affective reform: 'The way, however, is only through the most burning love of the crucified'. Even in the fourth stage (the reformation of the image of God in man), he affirmed that the reformation takes place 'in affective experience rather than in rational consideration'. He had written in the prologue that 'one is not disposed to contemplation which leads to mental elevation unless one be with Daniel a man of desires' (Daniel 9:23). But desires are kindled in us in two ways: either by a flash of apprehension (i.e., illumination as a direct free gift) or by the cry of prayer which makes one groan with the murmuring of one's heart, and, in particular, the cry of prayer through Christ crucified. Bonaventure stressed this affective approach lest anyone should believe that it 'suffices to read without unction, speculate without devotion, investigate without wonder, examine without exultation, work without piety, know without love'. Once again the contrast between the techniques of human science and this 'savoury' science which is the search for wisdom are implicit in this list of opposites. Even the rhetorical *diminutio* with which he concluded the prologue exploits this divide between knowledge and wisdom. He claims that the intention of the author was 'the exercise of the affections rather than the erudition of the intellect'.[31]

The same message, that the most potent affective force is meditation on the sufferings of Christ, is found in the ascetical text *The Doctrine of the Hert*, although there it is presented in terms that are so forceful in their imagery as to be affective in themselves. Christ in his Passion has provided a cleansing bath of water and blood and a healing bath of sweet tears:

> for to entre into þis bath is noþing ellis but for to drenche þin affeccions and þi thouзtes in Christis passion consideryng both the shedyng of His blode and watir also þe wetyng and wepyng of His body þat wolde God þou woldist dygh only þi fote in His blode as David seith: Intinguantur pes tuus in sanguinine. He seith: Wold God þat þe fote of þin affeccion were made rede in þe licore of his precious blod.[32]

This ingenious use of Psalm 67 reinforces *A Ladder of Foure Runges*: 'By a fote in Holy Wrytte is love vndirstond'.

Christ and his sufferings hold a central place in Rolle's affective strategy. In addition to the lyrics and *Meditations on the Passion*, he is constantly encouraging his reader to speak, pray, meditate on the Passion of Christ 'þat the mynde of Jhesu Christe passe noght fra his thoght'.[33] But central as the Passion may be, it is not the event itself, but rather the ways in which it is presented which are most illuminating about his view of affectivity. Throughout his writing career he seems to have experimented with different ways of structuring his material, not merely in terms of the articulation of the sense, but also the small scale devices of sentence-structure, verbal play and rhythm. Two recent articles have highlighted different aspects of this concern.[34] Alford's study of Biblical *imitatio* in his writings has illustrated the way in which he creates 'a network of submerged biblical texts, joined by association and transformed by substitution and amplification'. Rolle exploits the 'literature of reminiscence' with the intention of provoking a response that is potentially greater than the paraphraseable content of the material.[35] Alford reminds us that Rolle's Latin works show strong influences of academic commentary styles, and that the *Melos Amoris* is overtly in postill form. Not only is he providing an authoritative justification for his arguments as he develops them by imitating Biblical styles, but he is invoking other contexts and associations and providing the raw material for the kind of meditative exercise he is advocating even as he describes it. Perhaps even more important than this technique is the use he makes of rhetorical tropes and artful syntactical structures in his writing to highlight meanings and to suggest associations which the letter of the text is unable to articulate. In a remarkable recent article, Smedick has illustrated the way in which the punctuation of manuscripts of *The Form of Living* highlights a kind of rhythmical segmentation which 'does not necessarily coincide with the demands of syntax or of delivery. . . . As in verse so in prose with some verse-like properties, metre or rhythm may both reinforce or cut across sentence patterns and units of delivery'.[36]

What both articles illustrate is that Rolle was capable of deliberate manipulation of the responses of the audience at the less conscious levels of perception. The subtleties of the rhythmical manipulation of parallel phrases in *The Form of Living* can be compared with the almost grotesque verbal patterning of the *Melos Amoris*, although it has been suggested that in that work Rolle was attempting to create a kind of four stress alliterative line comparable with the vernacular form. The aspirations towards verse of parts of the *Melos Amoris* were recognised by at least one reader, who created the *Carmen Prosaicum* from some of the most highly patterned sections of the longer work.[37]

It is in his use of verse that Rolle was able to exploit the affective properties of form most fully, and it is not accidental that he uses the term *canor* to describe a central part of his own mystical experience in terms of harmony, melody, and joyful singing. For, despite his repeated contrast between earthly song and heavenly song, his use of this vocabulary to describe his experience has interesting implications for his own verse. Thought turns to song, words to singing, harmony and melody abound; the description of *canor* is founded on strict and formal ideas of order, rhythm and harmony; those things which the medieval aesthetic theorists had decided were fundamental to beauty.[38] But if the perception of divine beauty is expressed, however inadequately, in terms of literary activity, and indeed in terms of a particularly highly ordered and disciplined kind of discourse, the fact that the earthly kind of discourse used to describe that experience fails to do justice to it is less important than the fact that it is more appropriate to describe it than any other kind of human activity, literary or otherwise. To put it simply; earthly song is clearly flawed, but because of the order which it manifests in itself, it is closer to heavenly song than other kinds of speech. Rolle's use of literary devices such as alliteration, rhythm and verse, then, are an attempt to enact the order which he has perceived to be at the heart of his spiritual experience.

The medieval mind was highly conscious of rhythm and structure. Underhill spoke of it as 'more sharply aware of the part which rhythmic harmony plays in the worlds of nature and grace.' Rhythmical discourse could be said to celebrate within itself, and to enact, that order and rhythm which the Christian firmly believed underpinned the universe. This had been an aesthetic principle from Augustine through Boethius. Duns Scotus had written 'Omne ens est ordinatum' and Alexander of Hales had re-emphasised the Augustinian view of the universe as a supreme symphony, a tableau of perfect harmony. These so-called sapiential aesthetics influenced the Franciscan theory of art. Bonaventure in the *Itinerarium* discussing the link between the beautiful and the good had written:

> Since, therefore, all things are beautiful and in some way delightful, and beauty and delight do not exist apart from proportion, and proportion is primarily in number, it needs must be that all things are rhythmical (*numerosa*). And for this reason number is the outstanding exemplar in the mind of the Maker, and in things it is the outstanding trace leading to wisdom. It causes Him to be known in all corporeal and sensible things while we apprehend the rhythmical, delight in rhythmical proportions, and through the laws of rhythmical proportion judge irrefragably (cap. 2.10);

and had referred to 'that art productive, exemplifying and ordering given to us for looking upon God'.[39]

If number is the exemplar in the mind of the divine maker, it is hardly surprising that earthly makers should wish to exemplify that rhythm in their own works, by using the ordering art given to us for looking at God, especially when attempting to describe the experience of looking at God. Thus, that form of discourse which is most *numerosus* is the most appropriate for discussing transcendent themes. Perhaps it was the realisation that the gap between this world and the next could in some sense be bridged by the spark of affective response generated through the 'ordering art' of literature which encouraged Rolle to use the term *canor*, rooted in earthly literary activity, to describe his own profound experience.

IV

Rolle's account of his first experience of *canor* describes how it was preceded by a long period of affective yearning which he describes as *calor*.[40] This experience of heat was itself induced by or coincided with a time when he was 'delighting in the sweetness of prayer or meditation'. Like his experience of song, his first awareness of heat was during a visit to a chapel, and what is particularly interesting about his account of heavenly song is that it is preceded by a period of formal prayer (paralleling the prayer and meditation preceding the sense of heat):

> While I was sitting in that same chapel and repeating as best I could the night-psalms before I went into supper, I heard, above my head it seemed, the joyful ring of psalmody, or perhaps I should say, the singing. In my prayer I was reaching out to heaven with heartfelt longing when I became aware, in a way I cannot explain, of a symphony of song, and in myself I sensed a corresponding harmony at once wholly delectable and heavenly, which persisted in my mind. Then and there my thinking itself turned into melodious song, and my meditation became a poem, and my very prayers and psalms took up the same sound.[41]

Rolle distinguishes two aspects of his prayerful activity in the chapel. One is the repetition of the psalms, and the other (clearly an integral part of the devotion) is his prayer 'reaching out to heaven with heartfelt longing'. He is using the liturgical discipline of the office as an affective devotional trigger and as a meditative framework for his yearning. Thus, the sense of heavenly song is linked in some way with his own formal canonical prayer, and this link cannot be explained simply with reference to the metrical form of the psalms acting as a kind of incantatory subconscious rhythm, although this may play some part in the overall effect.[42]

Rolle's view of the centrality of the psalter is mapped out in the prologue to his English Psalter Commentary where he stresses the considerable spiritual benefits accruing to those who say or sing the psalms 'in lovynge of Jhesu Crist':

> þai drop swetnes in mans saule and helles delites in þeire thoghtes and kyndelis þaire willes with þe fire of luf, makand þam hate and brynnand within, and faire and lufly in Cristes eghen. And þam þat lastes in þaire

devocioun he rayses þam in to contemplatif lyf and ofte syth in to soun and myrth of heuen.[43]

The effects he describes resemble those he experienced in the two chapel experiences recounted in the *Incendium*; heat and burning leading to 'soun and myrth'. Reworking his own experience from the *Incendium* for the vernacular *Form of Living*, he assigned the experience of song to the highest degree of love, which he calls 'singuler', probably borrowing the terminology from Richard of St Victor:

þan þe sange of lovyng and of lufe es commen, þan þi thoght turnes intil sang and intil melody, þan þe behoves syng þe psalmes þat þou before sayde.[44]

Elsewhere in the vernacular writings, he recommends the efficacy of praying the psalms and other formal prayers of the Church, 'For thorow gode thoghtes and hali prayers þi hert sal be made byrnand in þe lufe of Jhesu Criste'.[45] His interest in the psalter is of course understandable: apart from standing at the centre of the liturgical worship of the Church in the canonical hours, the psalter had long been valued for its literary qualities and, parallel to these literary qualities, for its affectivity. The link between these two is made explicit in Gilbert de la Porree's Commentary on the Psalter, the preface to which shares Rolle's central emphasis on the psalms as evoking a burning love of Christ through reformation of the affections and the will:

Intendit enim propheta non solum de christo quae proponit docere verum etiam ad docendo affectum carnalium hominum ad eandem laudere trahere. Unde enim metrice scripsit et diversis loquendi generibus opus ornavit.

Restating the Augustinian view, Gilbert describes the psalms as a *liber hymnorum*: 'Hymnus est laus dei cum cantico. Canticum verum est mentis exultatio habita de aeternis prorumpens.'[46] Rolle, probably echoing Peter Lombard (who uses the same definition), also classifies and describes the work in these terms:

þis scripture es called boke of ympnes of Crist. Ympne es lovyng of God with sange . . . Sange es a gret gladnes of thoght of lastand thinge and endeles joy, brestand in voyce of lovynge.[47]

Rolle's experience in the chapel bears out Gilbert's contention about the affective force of the psalter and provides some explanation for his enthusiasm for it in meditative contexts. But the description of the psalter as a *liber hymnorum* also draws attention to the fact that literary analysis of poetical books of the Bible served to emphasise the similarities between them and other types of literature. Thus the *liber hymnorum* proper, the office hymns of the Church, attracted a commentary or *Expositio* which in some versions bears a marked similarity to commentaries on the psalter.[48] David, for example, assumes central importance in both genres; as author or compiler of the psalms and as the first author of hymns: 'Hymnos primum David prophetam condidisse ac cecinisse manifestum est'. Similarly both genres are seen as being the product of a combination of divine inspiration and human workmanship. Like the psalms, the hymns are primarily designed to praise God: 'Item ymnus est canticum laudantium . . . ; proprie ymni sunt continentes laudem dei.'[49] Like the psalms, the hymns are metrical and often affective, and, through the praise they offer to God, attain the status of prayer: 'laus vero divina oratio est'.[50] The implications of this were far-reaching. It was possible for Rolle and his contemporaries to see all literary productions which fulfilled these criteria as belonging, however loosely, to the same genre: 'Carmina autem quecumque in laude dei canuntur, ymni vocantur'.[51] The influence of this doctrine on the religious lyrics of the Middle Ages has long been recognised: it provided a further impetus to the Franciscan aesthetic of vernacular verse, for example. It may not be unreasonable to see similar aesthetic assumptions underlying Rolle's attitude to 'song' in its earthly and spiritual manifestations.

In *The Form of Living*, the discussion of the third and highest degree of love contains the famous, and perhaps faintly patronising contrast between the song enjoyed by the spiritual lover and ordinary singing:

> swa þat þe saule es anely comforted in lovying and lufying of God, and til þe dede com es syngand gastly til Jhesu, and in Jhesu, and Jhesu, noght bodyly cryand wyth mouth – of þat maner of syngyng speke I noght, for þat sang hase bath gude and ill; and þis maner of sang hase nane.[52]

But the contrast Rolle establishes is not only one which is based on the corruptness of some earthly song, but also on the sublimity of the spiritual experience which he describes metaphorically as song. Thus, later in the same chapter of *The Form*, he emphasises that this sublimity overpowers the other song:

> Wha hase it, hym thynk al þe sang and al þe mynstralcy of erth noght but sorow and wa þartil.'[53]

This is not so much a rejection of earthly song as an attempt to emphasise the transcendence of the other experience: he wishes to stress that it is different in kind by describing it as being different in degree.[54] It is, of course, one of his recurring ambitions in the Latin epistles to attempt to describe the nature of the transcendant experience which transformed his life. He is repeatedly caught in the linguistic incapacity trap—the inability of a fallen language to articulate and express an experience of perfection and beauty which persistently refuses to allow itself to be categorised in terms of human sense perception as articulated by the limited potential of either Latin or the vernacular.[55] Just as Richard of St Victor had taken the scriptural account of Elisha and the minstrel and built upon it a spiritual reading stressing the importance of song or melody, so Rolle extends the musical metaphor to offer some poor formulation of his own experience. Yet he is aware of the dangers in such a proceeding; not only the problem of reductiveness in his description, but also the problem of what might be called guilt by association. As he says in *The Form*, earthly song has both good and bad aspects. Elsewhere he is concerned to distinguish between the secular song or poetry, which merely corrupts the will and enflames the carnal affections, and song or poetry which is intended to serve a spiritual purpose. The contrast is made in the *Melos Amoris* between the coarseness of certain 'carnal' songs and the affective purity of singing with the intention of converting to Christ:

> Sed et cantum carnalium concito calcaui,
> Ad Christum conuertens quod cantabatur,
> Ut currerem constanter ad brauium beatum
> Et ardens apparerem in oculis amati
> Integro amore.[56]

This kind of conversion is essential if the lover is to progress towards the gift of spiritual song but is a very early stage in the progression; the substitution of one kind of sensuous stimulation with another. The rejection of song and noise, and the search for isolation which the more advanced contemplative is encouraged to make, are achieved only when these stimulations have done their work and have triggered the yearning in love which leads to heat and song and sweetness. Thus the *Contra Amatores Mundi*, stressing the differences between love of God and love of the world, emphasises the way in which the contemplative enjoying spiritual song will avoid earthly music at such times, and the *Incendium Amoris* contains a similar comment:

And while this is happening he will sit alone, mixing as little as possible with those who sing psalms, and deliberately not singing with the rest.[57]

Yet Rolle emphasises throughout his descriptions that the experience of *canor* is not likely to be achieved by many would-be contemplatives and that the majority will find the earlier disciplines too daunting or extremely lengthy. Thus, although he was fascinated by the experience of *canor* and attempted, perhaps under pressure from friends, to articulate his experiences, he also .recognised, particularly in his vernacular works, that the audience for which he was writing would need some sort of assistance in the form of 'good' earthly song, even if he had been able to move beyond it himself.[58] He had found the psalms to be a useful affective spur to more profound meditation in his own spiritual life, and the lyrics which survive in his works, or which, circulating separately, have been attributed to him, illustrate the way in which he attempted to serve the needs of his audience in this respect. The issue has sometimes been clouded because in some of his writings he attempts to articulate and describe the spiritual *canor* which so obsessed him by using lyric forms. But his use of them is carefully controlled. Thus in *The Form of Living* he ends his description of the highest grade of love with a *cantus amoris* which he introduces: 'ymang other affeccions and sanges þou may in þi langyng syng þis in þi hert til þi Lord Jhesu'.[59] This appears to contradict all his statements on the inability of man to describe or capture the song; here he appears to be doing just that. But he says that the song or lyric is to be sung in the heart 'when þou covaytes hys comyng and þi gangyng'. Thus it is meant to function not as an account of the song, but rather as an affective trigger to be employed when desirous of achieving the state of song; in this it parallels the 'minstralcy' of Richard St Victor. Similarly, the *cantus amoris* at the same point in the *Ego Dormio* is prefaced by the comment: 'Now I write a sang of lufe, þat þou sal delyte in when þow art lufand Jhesu Criste', where the poem itself seems to describe the context and diagnose the spiritual state in which Rolle envisages its use:

I sytt and syng of luf langyng þat in my breste is bredde
Jhesu, Jhesu, Jhesu, when war I to þe ledde?
Ful wele I wate, þou sees my state; in luf my thoght es stedde.
When I þe se, and dwels with þe, þan am I fylde and fedde.[60]

The lyrics found in sections describing the highest state of love are at the head of a hierarchy of lyric writing in the works. It has been suggested that this use of lyrics in the vernacular treatises is 'intended to serve the function of crystallising Rolle's recommendations', but it is hard to see them merely as mnemonic summaries when they appear to be providing meditative paradigms appropriate to the level of advancement under discussion.[61] Thus in *Ego Dormio*, the first degree of love is founded on moral rectitude: obeying the Commandments, avoiding the deadly sins and being 'stabyl in þe trowth of hali kyrke'.[62] This is the lowest form of spiritual life; anyone entering into it is still liable to be tempted by the pleasures of the world and flesh. Moral reformation has not yet turned into a fully committed love of Christ. It is, therefore, highly appropriate that it should be concluded by a lyric explicitly meditating on the transience of earthly pleasures. The second degree, to follow Christ in poverty, requires a rejection of earthly affections, including love for members of one's family. This is the point of affective reformation where the *affectus* is moved away from carnal loves towards spiritual loves, by means of meditating on the crucified humanity of God in the person of Christ, thus achieving the first progress towards wisdom: 'For als sone as þou feles savoure in Jhesu, þe wil thynk al þe worlde noght bot vanyte and noy for men sawles'.[63] This section ends with a *Meditacio de passione Christi*, which again enacts within itself the process of spiritual development needed to be able to progress to the highest degree. It starts with a standard recapitulation of the sufferings of Christ leading to an affective desire to receive the fire of love from Christ and to see the suffering face transfigured in joy. Rejection of earthly pleasure becomes impatience to leave ('How lang sal I be here?'), and the lyric ends with an eager anticipation of the heavenly song which, in this version of his schema of ascent, is the preserve of the next and highest degree: 'Whan mai I negh þe nere, þi melody to here?' Rolle is explicit that this form of meditation is valuable: 'If þou wil thynk þis ilk day, þou sal fynde swetness þat sal draw þi hert up'.[64] The third degree of love is similarly provided with meditative paradigms. Yet it is not only in the formal expositions of doctrine that this strategic use of verse is found. The *Meditations on the Passion* are interspersed in one text with lyrics and in the other with rubrics recommending the recitation of the *Pater Noster* and *Ave Maria*, incidentally illustrating the similar functions Rolle thought formal prayer and lyric meditation served.

Thus Rolle was aware of different functions which might be performed by the lyrics included in the longer works. He also seems to be aware that the efficacy of such paradigms depends largely on the responsiveness of the individual user.[65] But in general he makes little distinction between those lyrics to be said or sung 'in lufand of Jhesu Criste' and the psalms which he was saying when he first experienced spiritual song; he regards them as similarly effective in provoking an affective response. Just as the different lyrics included in the vernacular texts serve a variety of different functions, so the psalms have a variety of different effects: both forms of literary activity manifest the *multiplex modi* traditionally found in Scripture. This is emphasised in the prologue to the English Psalter:

> Þe sange of psalmes chace fendes, excites aungels tille oure help, it dose away synne, it quemes God, it enfourmes parfitnes, it dose away and destroys noy and angere of saule and makes pees betwix body and saule, it brings desire of heuen and despite of erthly thinge.
> Sothely þis shinand boke es a chosen sange bifore God, als laumpe lyghtenand oure lyf, hele of a seke hert, huny till a bitter saule, dignite of gastly persones, tunge of prive vertus.[66]

Related claims are made for the name prayer, which is frequently part of Rolle's recommended meditative programme, perhaps not surprisingly when we remember that the psalms are to be prayed 'in lovynge of Jhesu Criste':

> If þou thynk Jhesu contynuly, and halde it stabely, it purges þi syn, and kyndels þi hert; it clarifies þi sawle, it removes anger and dose away slawnes; it woundes in love and fulfilles in charite; it chaces þe devel and puttes oute drede; it opens heuen and makes a contemplatif man.[67]

As Rolle says, there is no need of many books when the principles of affectivity have been achieved: 'halde lufe in hert and in werke, and þou has al þat we may say or wryte.'[68] The moving of the soul to love is an art that can be learned—an art that Rolle believed he had mastered:

> When I am awake I can try to warm my soul up, though it is numb with cold. For I know how to kindle it when the soul is settled in devotion and how to raise it above earthly things with overwhelming desire.[69]

It is this art, I would suggest, that Rolle is practising in his lyrics and in the submerged rhetorical devices of his other works, for, as Grosseteste had said, 'to Rhetoric especially belongs the setting in motion of our affections, the rousing up of torpid spirits, the correction of the unruly, the encouraging of the faint-hearted, the assuaging of the truculent'.[70]

V

The Song of Love Longing to Jesus exemplifies the ways in which Rolle is capable of manipulating the *pes affectus*. It is a complete drama of the process of conversion and affection, brought about through an intense concentration on the figure of Christ.[71] The poem opens with a formal request for Christ to help in the process of reforming the will:

Send wil to my hert to covayte þe.
Reve me lykyng of þis land, my lufe þat þou may be (11. 2–3).

This is, in miniature, the basic premise of all the longer treatises, and by the third stanza of the poem progress has clearly been made by the implied protagonist:

þi wil es my ȝhernyng; of lufe þou kyndel pe fyre,
þat I in swet lovyng with aungels take my hyre (11. 11–12).

In the *Incendium Amoris*, he writes that one of the effects of this love is that 'the will of man is united with the will of God in a remarkable friendship'.[72] Earlier in the same work he writes:

Before he can experience even a little of God's love, he must really be turned to him, and, in mind at least, be wholly turned from every earthly thing. The turning indeed is a matter of duly ordered love, so that first he loves what he ought to love and not what he ought not and, second, his love kindles more toward the former than the latter.[73]

These processes are clearly being invoked in a concise way by this lyric, and it may not be too fanciful to see the formal statement of intent to reform which the verse provides as part of this process of duly ordering which the verse itself enacts. Certainly the affective force is initially achieved here not by the usual invocation of the Passion sufferings, but rather by the invocation of the name 'Jhesu' in the first line of each stanza in the first section of the poem with an allusive and reflexive reference to his suffering ('Thyrl my sawule wyth þi spere') to allow the reader to invoke his own personal images of the Passion within the framework. The structure of each stanza is intended to make it flexible in a meditative context. Each line is a sense unit, each stanza operates on mono-rhyme, the lines often break into two units around the central caesura and there are considerable syntactical similarities between the various units and sub-units creating a sense of pattern, order and harmony which is so important for the overall effect. The requests for the gift of compunction and affective yearning ('Wounde my hert within and welde it at þi wille'.) give way to an enactment of the state of love-longing, which is simultaneously a description of the new state and of the way in which the poem itself should or could be used at this stage ('My sang es in syghyng, whil I dwel in þis way'). The lyric should not be regarded as imprisoned in its form; it is meant to provoke as well as to provide an ordered framework for the meditation and 'loving'. This much is implicit in Rolle's comment in *The Form* when, having provided a paradigm prayer to be said 'in þi hert' at mealtimes, he comments:

> Or if þou have other thoghtes þat thou has mare swetnes in and devocioun
> þan in þese þat I lere þe, þou may þynk þam. For I hope þat God will do
> swilk thoghtes in þi hert als he es payde of and as þou art ordaynde for.

Here again the concept of 'ordaining' stresses the difficulty of making absolute rules in meditative procedure and the multiplicity of possible responses to any particular strategy.[74] In this light it is perhaps interesting that in the lyric under discussion, the formal Passion narrative (based on the traditional liturgical *Candet nudatum pectus*) does not appear until the love-longing has been achieved, and even this is framed by the much more abstract liturgical and sacramental idea of the crucified Christ as 'aungels brede'. This invocation of a traditional hymn reminds us of the literary tradition within which Rolle is working, as well as relating the lyric to the orthodox doctrinal mainstream. By the end of the poem the speaking voice has acquired a teaching authority urging others to follow in the affective path of the lyric: 'Gyf al þi hert til Christ þi qwert, and lufe hym evermare' (1. 48). The love-longing as given way to some new understanding of the mystery of the crucifixion ('aungels brede'), a development well attested by the affective theorists we have already discussed.[75] By virtue of this new understanding or wisdom, the protagonist is able to direct the attention of others and to add his own authority to the received wisdom on the subject, providing a logical framework for a poetic experience which sets out to defy logic.

Other lyrics attempt to work by a process of free association. The *Song of the Love of Jesus*, for example, creates many of its effects by a display of rhetorical virtuosity in varying the position of the word 'love' in any given line, creating an elaborate pattern of expectation, denial and response, and an almost hypnotic and dazzling variety of meditatively provocative formulations of the concept.[76] Like the prose treatises from which much of its material derives, the lyric implies a framework of meditative progression through the three degrees of love. Unlike the prose works, it does not articulate the stages explicitly, but rather invokes them through allusion and implicit structure. It invites the reader to enact the stages of ascent through a variety of different strategies. The basic knowledge is presumed to be present, and is reformulated as the premises of the literary experience which follows:

> Luf es lyf þat lastes ay, þar it in Criste es feste;
> For wele ne wa it chaunge may, als wryten has men wyseste (11. 1–2).

By rehearsing the concept, the literary protagonist is led to assert it at the end of the poem: 'Ihesu es lufe þat lastes ay, til hym es owre langyng' (1. 93). But the assertion is not achieved simply by the provision of paradigmatic or provocative material, as it is in the *Song of Love Longing*, which is actually subsumed within this lyric in two manuscripts as part of the affective strategy.[77] Rather, the poem posits a variety of relationships between poem and reader. Initially, the protagonist is placed in a position of student, neophyte-lover (If þou wil luf þus as I say (1. 4)), subordinate to the authority of the poem's opening statement (als wryten has men wyseste). This posited role of receptivity continues for the first three stanzas, which provide the raw material for what is to follow in the form of cryptic definitions of love. These involve the reader in the processes of the poem by implicitly requiring him to explicate the enigmatic relationships existing between the apparently unrelated and potentially paradoxical formulations. They invite such explication by the syntactical parallelism, which implies some conceptual or philosophical harmony between them not necessarily apparent at a superficial level of perception. In the third stanza, the tutorial relationship dissolves into one of joint quest, as the use of *us* and *owr* further implicates the reader in the process of investing the experience of the text with meaning, while stressing the homogeneity of the concept under construction by retaining the prevailing syntactical formulation:

> Luf us comfortes and mase in qwart, and lyftes tyl heven ryke.
> Luf ravysches Cryste inmtyl owr hert; I wate na lust it lyke (11. 15–16).

The concept of *raptus*, traditional in mystical contexts, is overtly contrasted with carnal desire ('lust'), restating in a more formal way the audacious and potentially sexual definition of love (luf copuls god and manne).[78] In both cases however, the implicit sexuality of the relationship is minimised, either by ambiguity or denial through contrast. It is for the second phase of the poem to activate this potential. As in the previous lyric, the lifting of the heart towards heaven coincides with an implied shift of perspective on the part of the protagonist.

The next stage of the lyric involves the enactment of the process of reformation. Following a stanza of exhortation and instruction (different from the authoritative statements of the first movement of the poem), the lyric has four stanzas in the first person which dramatise the renunciation of the pleasures of the world and the request for the gift of *calor* which in the treatises mark the first grade of love:

221

Þi lufe es ay lastand, fra þat we may it fele.
Þarein make me byrnand, þat na thyng gar it kele.
My thoght take into þi hand, and stabyl it ylk a dele,
þat I be noght heldand to luf þis worldes wele (11. 25–8).

Although the sense of community with the interlocutor of the poem is preserved in the first person plural of the first line, clearly the initiative has passed to the protagonist.

This marks the end of the first phase. The second opens with a restatement of the need for reformation, which appears to presuppose that the reformation has taken place in the interstices of the text and the protagonist's response to it; that is, in the affective response of the reader to the calculated campaign of seduction against him. The second stage, as throughout Rolle, is focussed firmly on the love of Christ (For now lufe þow, I rede, Cryste, as I þe tell (1. 45)). This is a reassertion of the interlocutor's control over the reactions of the protagonist; a restatement of the relationship posited at the beginning of the first phase (If þou wil love þus as I say). The pattern is repeated. The anaphorical formulations of love are resumed in the same form as before, and restate the same truths. Thus in the first phase, the contact is stressed (luf copuls god and manne), a formulation of the 'remarkable friendship' mentioned above. In the second phase, this is repeated, but no longer as an abstract external truth. Now it is internalised and personalised in affective and passionate terms of achievement:

In luf be owre lykyng, I ne wate na better wane,
For me and my lufyng makes bath be ane (11. 55–6)[79]

The effects of an intense concentration of the will on Christ are evoked through the concept of *canor* which would be experienced outside the literary framework of the poem, and again this is described in permissive rather than didactic terms: 'If þou wil lufe, þan may þou syng til Cryst in melody' (1. 67). Significantly, it is at this point in the poem's strategy that the *Song of Love-Longing* is inserted in two manuscripts. As we have seen, the affective force of that poem works without the provision of a narrator/interlocutor figure, and its inclusion here marks the true emancipation of the reader. The movement from knowledge to understanding which it enacts merely repeats in microcosm the pattern of its new context. Even without the interpolation, the lyric firmly stresses the change from provision to performance, from the permissive tones of the narrator quoted above to the actual fulfillment of his prophecy:

[I] sygh and sob, bath day and nyght, for ane sa fayre of hew.
Þar es na thyng ma hert mai light, bot lufe, þat es ay new (11. 69–70).

The narrator is dispensed with, and the reader is required to assert in his own person and with his own will the teachings of the first stage of the poem. Significantly, for the first time in the poem, the first person narrative of the protagonist achieves the syntactical pattern of the poem's opening definitions:

Lufe es fair, þare it es fest, þat never will be calde.
Lufe us reves þe nyght rest, in grace it makes us balde (11. 82–3).

The achievement of the poem's strategy, to bring the reader to a fuller understanding of God through affective reformation, is thus enacted in the very form of the poem itself. All the protagonist's previous references to love have been displaced from the opening position in the line, graphically illustrating the 'disordered' affections from which he is assumed to be suffering. The harmonising of his expression with the earlier authoritative statements made earlier not only makes a philosophical point, but also works aesthetically by fulfilling the subconscious desire for a literary fulfillment of the pattern established early in the lyric. As Rolle says in *The Form of Living*, 'luf es perfeccion of letters'.[80]

The last stanza is simultaneously a resolution of the potential paradoxes of the first phase of the poem (Christ harmonises all disharmonies; all things are made one in him; God is love; love was his meaning), and a formal statement of the centrality of Christ: each line proceeds from and derives its meaning from his name. It also implicitly calls to mind Rolle's own devotion to the name prayer, and the affective responses which he stressed it was capable of generating.

Jhesu es lufe at lastes ay, til hym es owre langyng:
Jhesu þe nyght turnes to þe day, þe dawyng in-til spryng (11. 93–4).

Towards the end of the poem, we find the comment 'In lufe lacyd he hase my thoght, þat I sal never forgete' (1. 79). Apart from the parody of secular love-lace invoked by the juxtaposition of the words (and perhaps illustrating the way spiritual love is more potent than secular love, stressed in the introduction to the poem's second phase),[81] this phrase admirably describes the strategy of the poem with its weaving and twisting of sense and meaning throughout the poem, set against basic rhythmical and syntactical patterns which admirably dramatise the search for resolution in the love of God.

As Smedick has shown, similar patterns can be found in the prose works, where the larger scale of the syntactical undertaking allows for even greater variations. One very obvious example is the *Meditations on the Passion* with their stylised rhetorical sense units and heavy alliterative and rhythmical patterning, not to mention the use of anaphorical openings to each new phase of the meditation, and of course the strategic use of verse to highlight moments of particular intensity. The dramatic gesture of taking the 'rode fote in my armys' described in the Meditations I symbolises the intensity of response which is intended and the action represents the submission of the will to Christ and the placing of the affective foot on the right road.[82]

NOTES

1. I am grateful to Mrs P. T. Ingham and Mr. M. B. Parkes who read early versions of this paper and made many helpful comments and suggestions. For the remaining errors and inaccuracies I must bear responsibility.
2. The background to this debate and the development of Biblical and theological poetics are described in E. R. Curtius, *European Literature and the Latin Middle Ages*, tr. W. R. Trask, London 1953, ch. 12; A. S. D. Fowler, *Protestant Attitudes to Poetry 1560–90*, unpublished D. Phil. thesis, Oxford, 1957, pp. 64–75 and *passim*; C. G. Osgood, *Boccacio on Poetry*, Princeton, 1930, pp. 36–47.
3. M. D. Chenu, *La Théologie comme Science au XIIIe Siècle*, 3rd ed., Bibliothèque Thomiste, 33, Paris, 1957, pp. 33–57, 93–100; U. Köpf, *Die Anfänge der theologischer Wissenschaftstheorie im 13. Jahrundert*, Beitrage zur historischen Theologie, 49, Tübingen, 1974, pp. 107–12 and 266–7; A. J. Minnis, 'Literary Theory in Discussions of *Formae Tractandi* by Medieval Theologians', *New Literary History*, 11 (1979–80), 133–45. My debt to Dr Minnis will be apparent throughout the first section of this paper.
4. Chenu, *op cit.*, pp. 37–52; Köpf, pp. 125–54.
5. B. Smalley, *The Study of the Bible in the Middle Ages*, 2nd ed., Oxford, 1952, pp. 66–75; for an example of pastoral *quaestiones*, see G. Lacombe, 'The *Quaestiones* of Cardinal Stephen Langton', *New Scholasticism*, 3 (1929), 1–18, 113–58; 4 (1930), 115–64.
6. Chenu, *op cit.*, p. 34.
7. Chenu, *op. cit.*, pp. 40–41; Minnis, *op cit.*, 134; A. J. Minnis, *Medieval Theory of Authorship: Scholastic Literary Attitudes in the Later Middle Ages*, forthcoming, will discuss many of these points in greater detail.
8. Alexander of Hales, cited Chenu, *op cit.*, p. 40, n.1.
9. A. Louth, 'Bernard and Affective Mysticism', in *The Influence of St Bernard*, ed. B. Ward, Oxford, 1976, pp. 2–10, esp. p. 3; *The Origins of the Christian Mystical Tradition*, Oxford, 1981, pp. 132–58, esp. pp. 153–4. On compunction, see, e.g., *The Prayers and Meditations of St Anselm*, tr. B. Ward, Harmondsworth, 1973, pp. 53–6; J. Leclercq, *The Love of Learning and the Desire for God*, tr. C. Misrahi, 2nd revised ed., New York, 1974, chs. 4, 6, 9.
10. Bernard, *In. Cant. Sermo*, 23, quoted Louth, 'Bernard', *op cit.*, p. 4; *Robert Kilwardby: Quaestio de Natura Theologia*, ed. F. Stiegmüller, *Opuscula et Textus*, Series Scholastica, 17, Münster, 1935, p. 49, cited Minnis, *op cit.*, p. 134; Alexander of Hales, *Summa Theologica*, Introd., art. I. quoted Chenu, *op cit.*,

p. 94, cited Minnis, *op cit.*, p. 134; *William Langland, The Vision of Piers Plowman: A Complete Edition of the B-Text*, ed. A. V. C. Schmidt, London, 1978, I, 143–4, (p. 14). On the link between kynde knowynge and *sapientia*, see M. C. Devlin, 'Kynde Knowyng as a Middle English Equivalent for 'Wisdom' in *Piers Plowman* B', *Medium Aevum*, 50 (1981), 5–17. For a general account of medieval views of Wisdom, see E. F. Rice, *The Renaissance Idea of Wisdom*, Harvard Historical Monographs, 37, 1958, pp. 1–29.

11. Oxford, Bodleian Library Ms. Laud. Misc. 99, fol. 179 ʳ. On *Disce Mori*, see P. S. Jolliffe, *A Check-list of Middle English Prose Writings of Spiritual Guidance*, Pontifical Institute of Mediaeval Studies, Subsidia Mediaevalia, 2, Toronto, 1974, A.6 (p. 64). W. Riehle, *The Middle English Mystics*, tr. B. Standring, London, 1981, pp. 108–12 discusses the use of metaphors of taste and feeling in English mystics.

12. I hope to discuss these matters in greater detail elsewhere.

13. The paraphrase is taken from D. A. Callus, 'Robert Grosseteste as Scholar', in *Robert Grosseteste, Scholar and Bishop: Commemorative Essays*, ed. D. A. Callus, Oxford, 1955, p. 16. The text of Grosseteste's *Introitus* (otherwise called *De Artibus Liberalibus* or *De Utilitate Arcium*) is printed in L. Baur, *Die philosophischen Werke des Robert Grosseteste Bischofs von Lincoln*, Beitrage zur Geschichte der Philosophie de Mittelalters, 9, Münster, 1912, pp. 1–7. A more general account of the term *affectus* is found in C. Morris, *The Discovery of the Individual 1050–1200*, London, 1972, pp. 76–9.

14. *MED* s.v. affeccioun.
Richard of St Victor's influential *Benjamin Minor*, translated into the vernacular as *A Tretyse of þe Stodye of Wisdom þat Men Clepen Beniamyn*, printed in *Deonise Hid Divinite*, ed. P. Hodgson, Early English Text Society, O.S, 231, London, 1955, contains a fascinating analysis of the differences between reason and affection: 'þorow reson we knowe, and þorow affeccioun we fele or loue. Of reson springeþ riȝt counselles & goostly wittes, and of affeccioun springeþ goostly desires and ordeynd felynges'.

15. The *pes affectus* is referred to by Riehle, *op cit.*, p. 68; S. Wenzel, *The Sin of Sloth: Acedia in Medieval Thought and Literature*, Chapel Hill, 1967, pp. 67–8, 108–9, lists some of the occurences of the image in moral handbooks and exegetical treatises, including works by Hugh Ripelin of Strasbourg and Richard of St Victor which may well have been known to Rolle. Thomas Gallus and Thomas Cisterciensis also use the image, see *Rudolf von Biberach: Die sieben strasenzu got*, et. M. Schmitt, Spicilegium Bonaventurianum, 6, Quaracchi, 1969, p. 136* (cited Riehle, *op cit.*, p. 190 n.11).

16. *Sancti Aurelii Augustini, In Johannis Evengelium Tractatus CXXIV*, Corpus Christianorum, Series Latina, 36, 1954, p. 468; *Enarrationes in Psalmos LI – C*, 39, 1956, p. 1331. The image may have begun in Plotinus, see Louth, *Origins, op cit.*, pp. 40–1.

17. *The Doctrine of the Hert*, ed. M. P. Candon, unpublished Ph.D. thesis, Fordham University, New York, 1963, p. 64; Oxford, Bodelian Library Ms. Laud. Misc. 330, fol. 27 ᵛ. In another striking image, this text urges affective reformation: 'Therfor, sister, ȝif þou wilt be trewly fled fro þe world, cut away fro þin hert þe iessis of worldly affeccions þe whiche letteth þe fliȝt of contemplacion to Godward'. (p. 57, fol. 22 ʳ). The work is a translation from a Latin treatise of the thirteenth-century. The foot image is also found in the *Book to a Mother*, ed. A. J. McCarthy, Studies in the English Mystics, 1, Elizabethan and Renaissance Studies, Salzburg, 1981, p. 143. A moralisation of the toes of the *Pes affectus* is found in sermon 14 of *Middle English Sermons*, ed. W. O. Ross, Early English Text Society, O.S, 209, 1940, pp. 77–83.

18. *Walter Hilton, The Scale of Perfection*, tr. G. Sitwell, London, 1953, p. 40.

19. Printed in *Deonise Hid Divinite*, ed. Hodgson, *op cit.*, p. 115, 23. The comment

225

occurs in an expansion of the original text undertaken by the translator.

20. On Rolle's Psalter Commentaries, see H. E. Allen, *Writings Ascribed to Richard Rolle, Hermit of Hampole, Modern Language Association* Monograph Series, 3, New York, 1927, pp. 165–92. Quotations from the Latin Psalter are from *D. Ricardi Pampolitani [sic] Anglosaxonis Eremitae . . . in Psalterium Davidicum . . . Enarratio*, Cologne, 1536. References to the English Psalter are from *The Psalter or Psalms of David and Certain Canticles with a Translation and Exposition in English by Richard Rolle of Hampole*, ed. H. R. Bramley, Oxford, 1884. Rolle departs from Lombard in making an 'affective' interpretation of feet at Psalm 25:12; 30:7–8; 55:12–13; 65:8; 90:12; 93:18; 114:8.

21. *De Latitudinae Sacrae Scripturae, Breviloquium, prologus*, in S. Bonaventurae Opera Omnia, Quaracchi, 1882–1902, 5, 1891, pp. 202–3.

22. *In Cant. Sermo* 23, quoted Leclercq, *op cit.*, pp. 266–7.

23. *De modo procedendi ipsius sacrae Scripturae, Breviloquium, prologus*, Opera, *op. cit.*, 5, 206–7. On the *Multiplex Modi*, see Minnis, *op cit.*, 134–42, esp. pp. 134–6, who discusses the development of the idea in Alexander of Hales and his disciples. An interesting parallel with these views is found in Richard of St Victor's *Benjamin Major (The Mystical Ark)* (Bk 3, cap. XXII-III) where he stresses the diversity of human affections: 'But who would suffice to enumerate all the qualities of human affection? Who would suffice to explicate all the modes of its changes? There are almost as many varieties of affections as there are differences of things'. See *Richard of St Victor: The Twelve Patriarchs, The Mystical Art, Book Three of the Trinity*, tr. G. A. Zinn, The Classics of Western Spirituality, London, 1979, pp. 252–5, Patrologiae Latina, 196, pp. 131–2.

24. cf., e.g., R. P. Prentice, *The Psychology of Love according to St Bonaventure*, Franciscan Institute Publications, Philosophy Series, 6, New York/Louvain, 1951; E. Gilson, *The Philosophy of St Bonaventure*, tr. I. Trethowan and F. J. Sheed, London, 1938, chs. 12 and 13. The distinction between conscience and *synderesis* was not always clearcut in medieval thought: this view is characteristic of the Franciscan tradition.

25. On Rolle's learning, see Allen, *op cit.*, pp. 78, 144, 157; J. A. Alford, 'Biblical Imitatio in the Writings of Richard Rolle', *English Literary History*, 40 (1973), 1–23; M. Jennings, 'Richard Rolle and the Three Degrees of Love', *Downside Review*, 93 (1975), 193–200; G. Liegey, 'The *Canticum Amoris* of Richard Rolle', *Traditio*, 12 (1956), 369–91. On his career at Oxford see A. B. Emden, *A Bibliographical Register of the University of Oxford to A.D. 1500*, 3, Oxford, 1959, 1586–7. As Allford *op cit.*, (p. 7) points out, the office prepared for the eventuality of Rolle's canonisation remarks on his preference for sacred rather than secular learning during his student career: 'Desideravit plenius et perficudius imbui theologicis sacrae Scripturae doctrinis, quam phisicis aut secularis scientie disciplinis', *Officium de Sancto Ricardo de Hampole*, ed. G. G. Perry, Early English Text Society, O.S, 20, Oxford, 1867, p. 10.

26. Oxford, Bodleian Library Ms. Digby 18, fols, 7 $^\text{v}$ – 8 $^\text{r}$ (cf. Allen, *op. cit.*, p. 240). This is a Version 1 translation of the text. For Richard Misyn's translation, see *The Fire of Love and The Mending of Life or the Rule of Living*, ed. R. Harvey, Early English Text Society, O.S, 106, London, 1896, p. 106: 'Not with goynge of feytt to goyd we ar turnyd bot with chawngis of our desyrs and maners . . .'.

27. *Desyre and Delit*, printed in *English Writings of Richard Rolle, Hermit of Hampole*, ed. H. E. Allen, Oxford, 1931, pp. 57–8, p. 57, (herafter *English Writings*).

28. *The Fire of Love: Richard Rolle*, tr. C. Wolters, Harmondsworth 1972, pp. 46, 58 (hereafter *FL*). Chapter 5 of the *Incendium Amoris* discusses this distinction in detail: 'An old woman can be more expert in the love of God—and less worldly too—than your theologian with his useless studying' (p. 61). The Latin text is printed in *The Incendium Amoris of Richard Rolle of Hampole*, ed. M. Deanesly, Publications of the University of Manchester, Historical Series, 26, Manchester, 1915, where

these quotations are found on pp. 147, 157, 160 (hereafter *IA*). The same ideas are expressed in the Canticle commentary: 'non enim quis est quia multas litteras didicit, set quia voluntatem suam voluntati divine in omnibus conformavit', *Richard Rolle's Comment on the Canticles*, ed. E. M. Murray, unpublished D. Phil. thesis, Fordham University, New York, 1958, pp. 132, xxiii.

29. Ch. 23, *FL*, *op cit.*, p. 116; *IA*, *op cit.*, p. 210.
30. Ch. 10, *FL*, *op cit.*, p. 74; *IA*, *op cit.*, p. 172.
31. *The Mind's Road to God: St Bonaventura*, tr. G. Boas, The Library of Liberal Arts, New York, 1952, pp. 4–5, 29; Opera, *op cit.*, 5, 295–6, 306.
32. Ed. Candon, *op cit.*, p. 60; Ms. Laud. Misc. 330, fol. 25 ᵛ.
33. *The Commandment, English Writings*, *op cit.*, p. 78, c.f., *English Writings*, pp. 62, 67, 80 etc.; *Emendatio Vitae*, ch. 8 (Misyn, *op cit.*, pp. 119–21); *The Contra Amatores Mundi of Richard Rolle of Hampole*, *op cit.*, ed. P. F. Theiner, University of California English Studies, 33, 1968, pp. 68, 87–9, etc.
34. Alford, '*Imitatio*'; Smedick, L. K., 'Parallelism and Pointing in Rolle's Rhythmical Style', *Medieval Studies*, 41 (1979), 404–67.
35. Alford, '*Imitatio*', *op cit.*, 12. On the literature of reminiscence, see Leclercq, *op cit.*, pp. 89–96.
36. 'Parallelism and Pointing', *op cit.*, 412. Smedick points out (405) that 'Parallelism has a special suitability for meditative texts . . . Memory is aided, attention focussed, and the effect of incantation produced through the reiterative style'.
37. G. Liegey, 'Richard Rolle's Carmen Prosaicum, an Edition and Commentary', *Medieval Studies*, 19 (1957), 15–36, p. 21.
38. On *canor*, see *Contra Amatores Mundi*, cap. 4, ed. Theiner, *op cit.*, pp. 78–83; *Comment on Canticle*, ed. Murray, *op cit.*, pp. xvii, 129, 205, 209–10 etc.; *The Melos Amoris of Richard Rolle of Hampole*, ed. E. J. F. Arnould, Oxford, 1957, pp. 4–5, 135–47, etc.; Liegey, *op cit.*, 31–6; *FL, IA op cit., passim; English Writings, op cit.*, pp. 4–5, 46, 63, 69, 90, 103, 105–6, 108; Allen, *Writings Ascribed, op cit.*, pp. 72, 200, 473–4, etc.; S. de Ford, 'Mystical Union in the *Melos Amoris*', in *The Medieval Mystical Tradition in England*, ed. M. Glasscoe, Exeter, 1980, pp. 173–201, esp. pp. 185–90. On medieval aesthetics, see E. de Bruyne, *Etudes d'Esthétique Médiévale*, 3 vols., repr. Geneva, 1975 (orig. ed. Bruges, 1946), esp. 3, pp. 30–71, 189–226 and 2, pp. 203–54.
39. E. Underhill, *Mysticism*, London, 1960 (orig. ed. 1911), p. 77; de Bruyne, *op cit.*, 3, 3, 6; *The Mind's Road*, tr. Boas, *op cit.*, p. 20, Opera, 5, p. 302. On the influence of Franciscan aesthetics on vernacular literature, see D. L. Jeffrey, *The Early English Lyric and Franciscan Spirituality*, Lincoln, Nebraska, 1975, chs. 2 and 3. On the importance of number in medieval aesthetics see S. Manning, *Wisdom and Number*, Lincoln, Nebraska, 1962, ch. 1, esp. p. 31 'for the medieval man a definite correlation existed between a poet's numbers and the wisdom of his subject matter'; R. A. Peck, 'Number as Cosmic Language', in *Essays in the Numerical Criticism of Medieval Literature*, ed. C. D. Eckhardt, Lewisburg, 1980, pp. 15–64; E. Reiss, 'Number Symbolism and Medieval Literature', *Medievalia et Humanistica*, New Series, 1 (1970), 161–74. I am not, of course, suggesting that Rolle had a particular numerological key to his works (although there is a certain trinitarian pattern), but rather that he was aware that 'versification . . . is based on number, proportion and harmony—which in turn lead man's thoughts to God, so that the contemplation of his skill could lead ultimately to the same goal as the contemplation of his subject matter: to an apprehension of the perfect order which is God himself' (Manning, *op cit.*, pp. 30–1).
40. Ch. 14, *FL*, *op cit.*, p. 89, *IA*, *op cit.*, p. 185. On *calor* in general, see Allen, *Writings Ascribed, op. cit.*, pp. 84–92; de Ford, *op. cit.*, pp. 183–5.
41. Ch. 15, *FL*, *op cit.*, p. 93, *IA*, *op cit.*, pp. 189–90. The final sentence in the Latin reads 'Nam cogitacio mea continuo in carmen canorum commutabatur, et quasi odas habui meditando, et eciam oracionibus ipsis et psalmodia eundum sonum

edidi'. Misyn, *op cit.*, has 'Forsoth my toyth continuly to myrth of songe was chaungyd, end als wer loveynge I had þinkand, and in prayers and salmys sayand þe same sounde I scheuyd' (p. 36). Rolle's description of his experience was clearly valued by his successors: it achieved a circulation independent of the main text (Allen, *Writings Ascribed, op cit.*, pp. 209, 222–3). A vernacular metrical version is preserved in the important Northern Carthusian Compilation British Library Add. Ms. 37049, and is printed by F. M. Comper, *The Life and Lyrics of Richard Rolle*, London, 1928, pp. 315–6. Richard of St Victor's *The Mystical Art, op cit.*, (Book 5, Chs. 17–18) has a lengthy and powerful exposition of the means of recovering 'exultation of the heart' by meditation:

> And so, when by such effort the inner affection of the heart is released with full devotion in the magnificence of divine praises, what is this other than that (if I may speak in this manner) an air hole is opened, by which an emanation of celestial sweetness and an abundance of divine pleasantness is spouted into that small chamber of our heart? (p. 339).

Citing the example of the prophet Elisha, who used a minstrel to regain the gift of prophecy, he writes:

> In an ordinary state of mind, a sweet harmony is accustomed to gladden the heart and to recall its joy to memory for it. Without doubt the more strongly anyone's love affects his soul, certainly the more deeply the harmony that is heard touches the affection. The more profoundly he is touched by affection, the more effectively he is renewed with respect to his longings. Therefore, what else is it proper to feel about the prophetic man [Elisha] except that for him an external harmony brought back to memory that interior and spiritual harmony, and the melody that was heard called back and raised to customary joy the mind of the one listening? (p. 340).

He offers a 'spiritual' interpretation of the event, which invites comparison with Rolle's own experience:

> However, what does it mean to summon a minstrel of this sort except to regain exultation of the heart by provident meditation and to awaken devotion of the heart by recollection of divine kindnesses and promises? Here without doubt we cause a minstrel to sing when on account of great dancing of the heart we shout in divine celebration and while rising up in thanksgiving we reecho in divine praises with a great shout of the heart from the innermost parts of ourselves (p. 341). Patrologiae Latina, 196, 189–92.

42. The value of the Psalter in contemplative life is well attested. Evagrius of Pontus said that the singing of psalms 'calms the passions and brings tranquility to the unruliness of the body' (quoted Louth, *Origins, op cit.*, p. 106); *The Doctrine of the Hert* makes similar claims (ed. Candon, *op cit.*, p. 79, Ms. Laud, Misc. 330, fol. 34 ʳ). Its use in the eremitic life is exemplified by Christina of Markyate, see *The Life of Christina of Markyate*, ed. C. H. Talbot, Oxford, 1959, p. 93.

43. *English Writings, op cit.*, p. 4; *Psalter*, ed. Bramley, *op cit.*, p. 3.

44. *English Writings, op cit.*, p. 106; Jennings, 'Rolle and Three Degrees', *op cit.*, 193–200.

45. *Ego Dormio, English Writings, op cit.*, p. 66; cf. clso p. 118. Allen discusses Rolle's attitude to the Psalter in a note on the prologue to the English Psalter (*English Writings*, pp. 121–2).

46. Gilbertus Porretanus, *Prologus Commentarii in Liber Psalmorum*, in Préfaces de la bible latine, ed. D. de Bruyne, Namur, 1920, p. 111. Gilbert's commentary was popularly called the *media glosatura*, coming between the glosses of Anselm of Laon and Peter Lombard (who was a major source for Rolle's work on the Psalter).

47. *English Writings, op cit.*, p. 6; *Psalter*, ed. Bramley, *op cit.*, p. 4.

48. On the *Expositiones Hymnorum*, see H. Gneuss, *Hymnar und Hymnen in englischen Mittelalter*, Buchreiche der Anglia Zeitschrift für englische Philologie, 12, Tübingen, 1968, pp. 194–206.

49. The *Expositio* prologue from which these quotations are taken is printed by Gneuss, *op cit.*, p. 265. For the importance of David as prototype Christian poet, see n.1.

50. *Biblia Sacra cum Glossa Ordinaria*, Antwerp, 1617, 3, col. 424. The comment is taken from Nicholas of Lyra's Psalter commentary, incorporated into the *Glossa*. He points out that the Psalter operates 'per modum laudis'. Nicholas died in 1340, Rolle in 1349.

51. Gneuss, *op cit.*, p. 265.

52. Ch. 8, *English Writings*, *op cit.*, p. 106. Rolle frequently doubles praising (lovying) and loving (lufyng).

53. *Ibid.*

54. Cf. *Incendium Amoris*, Ch. 33: 'It is not an affair of those outward cadences . . . nor does it blend much with those audible sounds made by the human voice, and heard by physical ears; but among angel melodies it has its own acceptable harmony' (*FL*, *op cit.*, p. 147, *IA*, *op cit.*, p. 239).

55. The problem is central to Riehle's account of the English mystics, esp. p. 1, pp. 104–27; see also J. A. Burrow, 'Fantasy and Language in *The Cloud of Unknowing*', *Essays in Criticism*, 27 (1977), 283–98.

56. Liegey, 'Carmen Prosaicum', *op cit.*, p. 19; *Melos Amoris*, ed. Arnould, *op cit.*

57. *Contra Amatores Mundi*, ch. 4, ed. Theiner, *op. cit.*, pp. 78–83; ch. 32, *FL, op. cit.*, p. 146, *IA, op. cit.*, p. 237; cf. also ch. 31, *FL*, p. 141, *IA*, p. 233, and ch. 33, *FL*, pp. 147–8, *IA*, pp. 238–40. The *Melos Amoris* contains similar comments, see Allen, *Writings Ascribed*, *op cit.*, pp. 124–5.

58. Allen, *Writings Ascribed*, *op cit.*, pp. 200–1; see also note 65 below.

59. Ch. 8, *English Writings*, *op cit.*, p. 107.

60. *English Writings*, *op cit.*, pp. 70–1.

61. M. A. Knowlton *The Influence of Richard Rolle and of Julian of Norwich on the Middle English Mystics*, De Proprietatibus Rerum, Series Practica, 51, The Hague, 1973, p. 51.

62. *English Writings*, *op cit.*, p. 63.

63. *English Writings*, *op cit.*, p. 67.

64. *English Writings*, *op cit.*, pp. 67–9.

65. cf. *Emendatio Vitae*, ch. 8: 'I myȝte ȝeue þee meditacioun, but whiche are moost spedeful to þee I knowe not, for whi I se not þin inner affecioun' (Ms. Digby 18, fols. 25ᵛ – 26ʳ); Misyn, *op cit.*, p. 120. He goes on to say that other men's words may, nevertheless, be useful at a preliminary stage.

66. *English Writings*, *op cit.*, pp. 4–5; *Psalter*, ed. Bramley, *op cit.*, pp. 3–4.

67. *The Form of Living*, ch. 9, *English Writings*, *op cit.*, p. 108. The description in *The Form* (pp. 109–10) of the effects of love seems to combine both traditions. The account of the name prayer in the Canticle commentary contains a similar list (ed. Murray, *op cit*, p. 158). The section circulated independently (Allen, *Writings Ascribed*, *op cit.*, pp. 66–8, 73–6).

68. *The Form of Living*, ch. 9, *English Writings*, *op cit.*, p. 108.

69. *Incendium Amoris*, prologue, *FL*, *op cit.*, p. 46; *IA*, *op cit.*, pp. 146–7.

70. Callus, *op cit.*, p. 16. Cf. also Bonaventure's comment in the *itinerarium* that rhetoric 'makes us skillful in persuasion or stirring the emotions' (*The Mind's Road*, tr. Boas, *op cit.*, p. 27, Opera, 5, 305).

71. Index of Middle English Verse 1715, English Writings, *op cit.*, pp. 41–3; W. E. Rogers, 'Image and Abstraction: Six Middle English Religious Lyrics', *Anglistica*, 18 (1972), 69–81, discusses this lyric in detail and suggests in passing (pp. 80–1) a careful numerical patterning, although he fails to point out the obvious numerological significance of beginning the Passion narrative at line 33.

72. Ch. 17, *FL*, *op cit.*, p. 101, *IA*, *op cit.*, p. 196.

73. Ch. 1, *FL*, p. 48, *IA*, p. 148.

74. Ch. 7, *English Writings*, *op cit.*, p. 104. See also note 65 above.

75. See above. A similar process is found in Julian of Norwich. The *panis angelorum* image is discussed by Rogers, *op cit.*, pp. 77–9.

76. Index of Middle English Verse 2007, *English Writings*, *op. cit.*, pp. 43–7. *Religious*

Lyrics of the XIVth Century, ed. C. Brown, 2nd ed. rev. by G. V. Smithers, Oxford, 1952, provides (pp. 270–1) a list of the source passages in *Incendium Amoris* for 11. 1–60. Manning, *op cit.*, pp. 58–9, discusses the stanzaic progression of this lyric. R. Woolf, *The English Religious Lyric in the Middle Ages*, Oxford, 1968, ch. 5, has an important discussion of the lyrics and their context.

77. The interpolated copies are London, Lambeth Palace Library, Ms. 853, and Longleat 29. The latter is printed by S. Wilson, 'The Longleat Version of "Love is Life",' *Review of English Studies*, New Series, 10 (1959), 337–46. Wilson's argument that the Longleat version (which breaks the resulting verses into three distinct poems, each ending with Amen) is textually superior, may well be correct, although it has no bearing on my argument here as the divisions merely provide an external articulation of a movement implicit in the poem.

78. Rolle discusses the use of *raptus* in mystical contexts in *Incendium Amoris*, ch. 37, *FL*, *op cit.*, p. 166, *IA*, *op cit.*, pp. 254–5.

79. Cf. *Incendium Amoris*, ch. 17 'And when he has got it a man rejoices, for joy is caused only by love. Every lover is assimilated to his beloved: love makes the loving one like what he loves', *FL*, *op cit.*, p. 100, *IA*, *op cit.*, p. 195. Bonaventure also claims that love transforms the lover into the beloved, see Prentice, *The Psychology of Love*, *op cit.*, p. 54 ff.

80. Ch. 10, *English Writings*, *op cit.*, p. 109.

81. *MED*, s.v. 'luflace'.

82. *English Writings*, p. 25. Cf. *A Book to A Mother*, ed. McCarthy, *op cit.*, p. 143: 'And so þou maist go to him and clepe him to þe and holde his fet as þe Maries diden, lenger and bettur þan þei deden bodiliche . . . For ȝif þou weshe clene þi fet, þat ben þine affecciouns, wiþ þe lore of þe foure Euangelistes, þat Crist clepiþ a welle of springinge water, þanne þine fet ben his and þi spirit is on wiþ him; and so þou maist holde his feet algate ȝif þou wolt make þi affecciouns accorde wiþ his'.

THE ORGANIZATION OF *THE SCALE OF PERFECTION*

MICHAEL G. SARGENT

AMONG THE MORE important questions with which the modern critic of medieval literature must deal is the difference between his own concept of literary form—of the set of principles and methods of organization according to which a work is written—and that of the author. Certainly part of the difficulty of discerning the form of the literature which survives to us, in the copies in which it survives, lies in the difference in method, and indeed intention, in publication before the advent of print. To a large extent, the question of the shape and order of Chaucer's *Canterbury Tales*, for example, or of the number of authors of *Piers Plowman*, depends on a process of manuscript publication which began at a stage at which the modern critic, or even the author himself, might consider the work incomplete. But it is at least equally important that many medieval works were written according to different organizing principles than those which are common in more recent literature. Recognizing this difference, a number of critics have sought to explain the forms of medieval literature by comparison with the organizational principles of medieval architecture. In particular, Robert Jordan, in *Chaucer and the Shape of Creation*,[1] has pointed out that the way in which the structural elements of Chaucer's poetry are made visible and prominent, rather than being hidden away behind the surface of the narrative, can be compared with the prominence of structural elements in the gothic cathedral. John Leyerle, in a related essay,[2] has compared the ambivalence of structural and decorative elements—of what the visual arts term figure and ground—in Dante with that of the great west windows which according to the light, appear either as roses of stained glass or as wheels of carved stone. And in a recent modernization of *The Scale of Perfection*, M. del Mastro has compared Hilton's constant returning to a small set of themes with the upward progress of a spiral staircase.[3]

In fact, the writing of major devotional prose underwent a

231

transition in the later medieval period, related closely to the increasing prominence of the vernacular and the rise of the *devotio moderna*. Where the older, monastic devotion may be most aptly described by the classic triad of reading, meditation and prayer, its primary literary form was the scriptural commentary, which tended to emphasize the pondering—the rumination, to use the common metaphor[4]—of the Latin words of the text itself, and the association of texts in a verbal memory constantly reinforced by the singing of the divine office. The modern, vernacular devotion, on the other hand, was marked by its independence of the Latin text of the scriptures and the singing of the office; it was characterized rather by individual meditations on the life, and particularly the passion, of Christ, and the literary forms employed by vernacular writers of the late thirteenth and fourteenth centuries (even excluding visionaries) tended to be more experimental. Viewed in this light, Richard Rolle appears less innovative than he is usually considered: as John Alford pointed out in the essay 'Biblical *Imitatio* in the Writings of Richard Rolle',[5] the verbal memory and association of scriptural texts was the predominant organizational feature of even those of Rolle's works, such as the *Incendium Amoris* and the *Melos Amoris*, which do not belong to the *genre* of biblical commentary.

Walter Hilton, however, seems to have derived his organizational methods from those of scholastic exposition: in consideration of any question, he distinguishes its parts, defines their relationship to each other and to the question as a whole, and proceeds to treat them one by one. To a reader well-enough acquainted with scholastic philosophy, this type of organization is quite familiar, as is Hilton's tendency to return to the same themes, which had promted del Mastro's analogy with a staircase repetitively returning to the same position at higher levels. For it is a commonplace of scholastic writing that a particular argument or observation can recur several times in the course of the proof or disproof of the several articles and sections of a question, and that in proceeding with the discussion of the articles and sections of a major question, it is occasionally necessary to revert to the question itself—if only to keep the end in view. That Hilton knew how to argue a quodlibetal question was established some years ago by Joy Russell-Smith, in her discussion of the attribution to Hilton of a tract *De Adoracione Ymaginum*.[6] On the other hand, the oft-repeated statement that the manuscript descriptions of Hilton as 'Magister' prove that he held a doctorate in theology is simply false. Nicholas Orme cautions rather that the title was so freely applied in the later middle ages that it did not necessarily imply graduate status at all.[7] Further, the opinion derived from the late, derivative continental textual tradition of Thomas Fishlake's Latin translation of the *Scale* that Hilton gained this doctorate at Paris is equally improbable. Russell-Smith's hesitancy to condemn outright a textual tradition with Carthusian connections is of course understandable, given the reputation of the order; but the interest that they may have taken in the transmission of a text by no means proves the authority of the text itself, in the lack of corroborating evidence; and in this case, there simply is no such evidence.[8] The fact remains, without going to extremes, that Hilton must have had an education, was relatively well-read in the Latin sources of medieval devotional literature, and seems to have been familiar with scholastic methods of exposition. It is the purpose of this paper to discuss his use of those methods in the first book of *The Scale of Perfection*. Although it is true that, as S. S. Hussey reports, Hilton seems in *Scale* II 'largely to discard categories in favour of analogies',[9] it would also be possible to show some of the same organizational methods in the second book, if time and space allowed.

The question of the organization of *Scale* I is complicated by the fact that three manuscripts, British Library MS. Harley 6579, the famous Landon Charterhouse copy, the Chatsworth *Scale*, annotated by James Grenehalgh of Sheen Charterhouse, and All Souls' College, Oxford, MS.25, which belonged to Rose Pachet, an early sixteenth century prioress of Syon (hereafter H, Ch and As), all contain, at least in part, a different system of chapter divisions than the other thirty-eight substantially complete manuscripts of this book. This different system of chapter divisions seems to represent an attempt to re-organize the same chapters into longer units, rather than a radically different division of the whole; and comments will be made during the course of this discussion on the alternative division of the material. Finally, chapter titles will be ignored: their origin is problematic, their authority dubious, and their descriptions occasionally misleading.

The first chapter of *Scale* I serves as an introduction to the whole. Hilton addresses his text to a 'ghostly sister in Jesus Christ', apparently, as is common in such works of spiritual counsel, to a woman under his direction. He begs her to hold herself content in her vocation and to progress steadfastly in the spiritual fulfillment of her physical enclosure: that is, that as she is shut off from contact with the outside world, so she should turn her heart from the attraction and repulsion of earthly things, *and conform herself inwardly to the likeness*

233

of God by meekness and charity and other spiritual virtues. This is the recurrent theme of the *Scale*, and we may note that it is with the same theme that he will later begin the second book. The manuscripts of the OQ tradition, as described by Rosemary (Birts) Dorward,[10] including Cambridge University Library. Additional MS.6686 (hereafter C), probably the most authoritative single copy of *Scale* I, end this first chapter with the distinction, drawn from Gregory the Great, between the active and contemplative lives. The manuscripts of the N tradition, on the other hand, make this the first sentence of the second chapter, thus reducing the symmetry of the descriptions of the active and contemplative lives in chapters two and three.

The active life, Hilton points out, lies in love and charity shown outwardly; he distinguishes between the necessary works of the active life: the fulfillment of the commandments and the performance of the seven corporal and spiritual works of mercy, which are appropriate to everyone according to his ability, and the optional works, such as fasting, keeping vigil or other penances, which are done in order to make the body more subservient to the will of the spirit, rather than for their own sake. Hilton suggests that these latter are a good help in the early stages of the contemplative life, and thereby completes his discussion of the active life. This tendency to make the necessary distinctions, then to dismiss those subjects not appropriate to his audience, which we see repeated, for example, in the discussion of the proper activities of the contemplative life in *Scale* I.15, may be taken as evidence both of Hilton's analytical method of organization and of the fact that he was writing for a particular case—that the 'ghostly sister' of the introduction was not merely a convenient fiction.

The next eleven chapters of *Scale* I (the next five in the variant H system) comprise the description of the contemplative life. The first of them, chapter three in both systems, opens with a definition of the contemplative life parallel to that of the active life: where the active life lies in love and charity shown outwardly, the contemplative life lies in *perfect* love and charity *felt inwardly*. Hilton exhorts his disciple to follow this life by whatever means seem best; but states that before discussing the appropriate means, he intends to describe the end, the contemplative life, to which they are directed. The distinction drawn here, of course, is that between formal and final causality. It is interesting to note, before going on, that these two chapters on the active and contemplative lives make up a symmetrical whole, and that in the variant system found in Ch and As, they are treated as a single chapter.

The fourth chapter distinguishes the first of three parts of contemplation: the knowledge which can be achieved by the natural means of reason, authority and reading of scripture. He points out that this knowledge is in itself morally neutral, and is good or bad only according to the measure of meekness and charity. The next three chapters, which form one chapter in the variant system, deal with the second part of contemplation, or affection without understanding. Chapter five defines it by examples; chapter six distinguishes a lower degree of affection in the evanescent fervor felt even by active men and women; and chapter seven distinguishes a higher degree in the continual delight in prayer and the divine service felt by those who have long since ceased to live in the world.

Chapter eight deals with the third, or perfect, part of contemplation, in which the soul, being first reformed by virtues to the image of Jesus, is ravished out of all earthly affections, the mind illumined to see by understanding the truth which is God, and the soul for the time united and conformed to the Trinity. He states that although the beginning of this part of contemplation can be attained in this life, the fullness of it is reserved for the bliss of heaven. The next chapter distinguishes between the second part of contemplation, which Hilton terms 'burning love in devotion' and the third, or 'burning love in contemplation'. Here he also introduces a series of cautions: that no one can receive the higher gift unless he is first reformed by virtues to the likeness of Jesus; that in this life the gift of the third part of contemplation is given only from time to time; and that although by a special grace it may be given to those leading an active life, the full use of it is reserved to solitaries and contemplatives. These two chapters on the third part of contemplation form one, the sixth, in the variant system in H; it is joined to the preceding chapter on the second part of contemplation in the Ch system, and continues onward another chapter in As.

Having described the second and third parts of contemplation as species of 'burning love', and having cautioned his disciple on the conditions necessary for the reception of these gifts, Hilton proceeds in the next four chapters, one chapter in the H system, to warn against a piety based on external sensations—a disruption of the flow of his argument, and probably directed against an over-literal or over-enthusiastic reading of Richard Rolle on the part of his disciple. He refers specifically in chapter ten to such physical sensations, seemingly spiritual, as sounds in the ears, savours in the mouth, smells at the nose, or any perceptible heat, as it were a fire glowing or warming the breast or any other part of the body. He points out that these sensations are in themselves simple and secondary; they may be either good or evil, but being possibly either good or evil, cannot be themselves the highest good. He warns that these sensations can be caused as well by the devil as by a good angel, and that in their manner of external feeling they cannot be easily distinguished by anyone who has not experienced both. In chapter eleven, he suggests, as a means of distinguishing, that any light, or sound, or savour, or heat, or physical pleasure or apparition of an unnatural order which stirs one to withdraw from contemplation of God, from prayer and meditation on one's self and one's faults, from desire of virtues and of spiritual knowledge and love of God, to set the attention wholly on the sensation itself, that sensation is evil, and of the enemy. If the opposite, then it is of God. Where this chapter states its argument in terms of aversion from true contemplative activity, the twelfth gives the reverse argument, in terms of attraction: that Jesus is bound to the soul in proportion to the good will and desire of that soul for him. Whatever lessens that desire loosens the bond; whatever strengthens the desire tightens the bond—and this, not physical sensation, is to be sought for its own sake. The thirteenth chapter extends this exhortation to complete the section of the *Scale* defining the end of contemplative life.

The fourteenth chapter forms the structural transition by which Hilton proceeds from the consideration of the *end* of the contemplative life to the consideration of its *means*, a discussion which he had postponed at the end of chapter three. At that point, as again at the beginning of chapter fourteen, he marked the division of his material: 'Nevertheless, before I tell you. . . . Now that I have told you . . .'. Hilton also points out two degrees in the virtues which are necessary to reform the soul to God: in the first degree, a man may have virtues in reason and will, but not yet in affection; in the second, by grace and constant exercise, he comes to love the virtues in themselves—to have them in affection. In the first of these degrees, he may achieve the second part of contemplation described before; without the second degree, however, he shall never come to the third part of contemplation. This distinction is the first statement of the distinction between reformation in faith, and reformation in faith and feeling which is one of the dominant themes of *Scale* II.

Hilton opens his discussion of the means of the contemplative life in chapter fifteen with the well-known statement of the traditional occupations of contemplative life: reading, meditation and prayer. Again, his dismissal of the inappropriate is a sign of the particular occasion for which he wrote. 'Reading,' he says, 'you cannot well do, so you will have to occupy yourself the more with prayer and meditation.' A number of critics have baulked at this passage: it is suggested that Hilton meant that his disciple could not read well, or could not read Latin, or that no English version of the Bible—or at least not all of it—was available to her. Although in fact a lack in her ability to make out the words on a page, in English or Latin, or in the availability of appropriate reading material could have presented difficulties, this is probably not Hilton's point. In the monastic tradition, reading, meditation and prayer were aspects of a single, continuous act; and this passage, like the latter half of the treatise *On the Mixed Life*, shows that Hilton was concerned to find appropriate contemplative exercises for a reader for whom the traditional exercises were inappropriate. The remainder of chapter fifteen is taken up with an encomium on meditation and prayer; he says that by meditation she will see her lack of virtues—the stirrings of sin, boiling up out of her heart like water from a putrid well (an image that becomes important later), so that she may neither see nor feel cleanly the love of Jesus— and she will see the virtues which she lacks. In prayer she will desire and obtain those virtues, without which she cannot be contemplative. We may note finally that these two transitional chapters form one, the eighth, in the variant system, and that (perhaps to redistribute the lengths because of the relative shortness of chapter thirteen) the divisions between the thirteenth, fourteenth and fifteenth chapters are differently placed in the N textual tradition.

The sixteenth chapter continues the discussion of the means, or occupation, of the contemplative life, treating the foundation of that occupation in meekness, sure faith and a whole intention to God. This is occasionally considered a disruption, or at least another postpone-ment, of the discussion of means. In fact, it is not: we have noted earlier that the means or occupation can be considered the formal cause of the reformation of the soul in contemplation; and any consideration of formal causality must first determine the point at which the action can be said to begin. Hilton then goes on to discuss meekness: he counsels his disciple first to consider that she has been shut up alone in her house not because of her holiness, but rather her inability to lead a sinless active life—much less contemplative. But lest she become therefore discontented with her vocation, he cautions that the purpose of this consideration is rather that she should come by exercise and the grace of God to true, heartfelt humility, only the beginning of which can be achieved in this life. Here he gives himself as an example: that he feels himself so far from those things that he has spoken that he can only cry mercy; and exhorts her to do so herself, or better, according to the grace that God gives her. It is interesting to note that at this point in the text of the Rosenbach copy of the first printing of the *Scale*, James Grenehalgh has put a 'W.H.' monogram in the margin, similar in form to those that he made for himself and Johanna Sewell at Syon, and the note, 'auctor de seipso.' Grenehalgh was apparently much impressed by Hilton's personal humility; and opposite three texts on humility in *The Cloud of Unknowing* in Douce MS.262, he commented, 'O Hilton sanctissime, magna erat humilitas tua', 'compilatoris humilitas prout in Scala eiusdem & ceteris tractatibus', and 'a diuino Waltero disce hic humilitatem'.[11] Thus began the tradition that Walter Hilton wrote *The Cloud of Unknowing*.

The latter half of *Scale* I.16 deals with true meekness as it relates to others. Hilton argues that since the end of contemplative life is the knowledge and love of God, whatever thwarts that end should cause the greatest displeasure. Thus one's own venial sins should be more displeasing than all the sins of other men, which, as they could not hurt the contemplative, should not be judged by her. This long discussion of humility forms one chapter in all systems.

At the beginning of chapter seventeen, Hilton interrupts the course of his argument to take up the objection that it is an act of charity to reprove men for their faults, and to judge them for their amendment. The formula with which he introduces this passage, 'But now you say . . .' introduces several other interruptions of the argument at later stages—including the probably authorial additions in *Scale* I.44 (the Holy Name passage) and I.70 (the Charity passage). Hilton's manner of treatment of these interruptions, his use of this formula to introduce them, and the fact that two of them seem to have been added when the text of *Scale* I was already in circulation, suggests the possibility that we are dealing here with the real objections and queries of the first reader—or readers—of this book. Hilton's answer to the objection concerning the charitable duty of reproof is that this duty belongs primarily to active men, particularly to prelates and curates who have spiritual authority and care (he uses the technical term 'cura') over others, and not for any joy derived from reproving others, but for the good of their souls; it belongs to active men without such spiritual authority and care only in cases of mortal sin which may not well be corrected by another, and where there is belief that the reproof will have good effect. The manuscript evidence on this sentence is divided between the reading just given and one in which the distinction is rather between the actives, who by definition have authority and care of others, and contemplatives, who by definition do not. The text in C, on the other hand, originally began the second part of the distinction correctly, 'but other men who are active and have no cure'; but the 'no' has been erased, apparently also by a scribe who mistook the meaning. In fact, the duty of contemplatives in this matter had already been retreated: they were bound to reprove only in cases of great need, in which a man would perish without their reproof. Hilton probably means 'perish' here in the literal, and not the moral sense; so that the distinction below becomes that between those actives who are duty-bound to reproof in all cases, and those who are duty-bound only in cases of mortal sin—and there, too, only where there is hope of amendment.

Having stated the negative side of the contemplative's duty in meekness to other men—that she was not to judge them—Hilton goes on in the seventeenth chapter to state the positive side—that she was even to esteem them higher than herself. Using the text, 'Whoever humbles himself shall be exalted, and whoever exalts himself shall be humbled' (Luke 14:11) as a transition, he returns to the point of departure for this discussion in the fifteenth chapter: that she is to practise this meekness in reason and will until by exercise and grace she comes to the fullness of it, and other virtues, in feeling. The importance of meekness in Hilton's scheme becomes fully apparent here: using Augustine and Gregory as authorities, he points out that it is the foundation and the preservation of all other virtues. The nineteenth chapter states even more strongly the position that if she will exercise herself to have such meekness in will alone, she may come to have it in feeling by the working of grace; but if she will not have it in will, she will not come to it, or to any other virtues, in feeling. The twentieth chapter points out that the sin of heretics and hypocrites is that they do not have such meekness either in will or in feeling; rather, they judge others, and esteem themselves holier. To exemplify this, Hilton gives an exposition of the gospel account of the publican and the Pharisee. He then recapitulates the teaching of this chapter, using the objection formula, 'But now you say, "Wherein did this Pharisee trespass?" ' leading to an exhortation on the necessity of meekness and the conclusion of the discussion. These five chapters on meekness are made one chapter, the ninth, in the variant system.

The second point of the foundation of contemplative life, sure faith, occupies chapter twenty-one (chapter ten of the variant system). Hilton states first that his disciple should believe in all the articles of the creed and the sacraments of the church; and that if she feels tempted against any of them, she is not to fear, but to consider the creed of the church to be her faith, and not the thoughts to which she is tempted. Again, the distinction between a virtue held in will and one felt in affection underlies this teaching. Second, she is to love and worship the laws and ordinances of the church on faith and morals, and to assent to them even when she might consider them unwise. Third, she is to have steadfast hope in salvation, in spite even of personal temptations to despair or diabolic testimonies of damnation.

The third point of the foundation is stable intent, or a 'whole will and desire only to please God'—which is charity. J. P. H. Clark has pointed out that Hilton draws a set of distinctions in this chapter parallel to those describing virtual intention:[12] that she is not to set any time after which she will cease trying to please God, in order to return fresher to her labours later, nor can she have it constantly in her will only to please God—this is simply not possible; but that she is in all things to attempt to please God. She is to use discretion in eating, drinking and sleeping, in bodily penances, prayers and devotions. In all of these, she is to keep the mean; but not in destroying sin and desiring virtues and the knowledge and love of God. This description of intention occupies a single chapter in both systems.

The next chapter, the twenty-third (the eleventh in the variant system) is purely structural. Hilton points out that he has now described the end and the beginning of the contemplative life, and exhorts his disciple to meekness, faith and whole intent to God. He ends by re-introducing the two means of contemplative life, prayer and meditation.

Prayer, he says in the twenty-fourth chapter, is profitable and useful in destroying sin and receiving virtues, not because one can tell God in prayer what grace is needed, but because prayer is a precondition for the proper reception of such grace. He suggests that at this point his disciple might wish to know how she should pray, where she should set her intention in prayer, and what forms of prayer were best to use. On the first point, he says that when she first rises to pray, she will feel herself lethargic or preoccupied with the physical concerns, temptations and business of the world; and it is then that she is to stir herself by prayer to devotion.

In the next chapter, he continues this theme by pointing out that she is not to set her intention in any mundane concerns, but to draw it in from such concerns, and direct it upward to God, whom she can not properly conceive physically, nor yet in imaginary physical likeness.

The text of this chapter is somewhat confused by the Christocentric additions found in some manuscripts: Hilton seems to have been speaking of the simple intention of a recollected mind; the additions, which focus the attention on the manhood of Christ, tend to obscure this. The manuscripts of the N tradition also obscure the division of the material, putting the discussions of how to pray and intention in prayer together into the twenty-fifth chapter, and leaving only the opening paragraph of prayer in the twenty-fourth. Hilton ends his discussion of intention with the comparison of prayer, by which desire rises directly to God, and the natural upward motion of fire. This simile seems once more to recall the teachings of Richard Rolle, and Hilton spends the next, short chapter warning that not everyone who speaks of the 'fire of love' knows what he is talking about, and specifically that although the body may feel itself warmed by a sympathetic reaction to the warmth of devotion, the fire of love itself is in no way physical, nor can be felt by any physical sense.

In the twenty-seventh chapter, Hilton turns to the third of the questions he had posed concerning prayer: what kind were best to use. He distinguishes three kinds, of which the first is vocal prayer ordained by God (as the Lord's prayer), by the Church (as matins, evensong and the hours), or by devout men (as prayers to God, Mary and the saints). He points out that since his disciple was a religious, and bound by custom and rule (presumably *consuetudo* and *regula*) to say the hours—her duty in this respect was primarily to say the Lord's prayer—that she should do so as devoutly as she could. Second, in the matter of private prayers and devotions, he suggests that in the beginning it is best to use whichever of such inspired prayers as the Lord's prayer, the psalms and the hymns of the Church she finds the greatest help to devotion, for until the soul is cleansed of former sins, it is too much attracted to worldly thoughts and physical loves, and too prone to errors and fantasies to stand on its own. The twenty-eighth chapter develops this thought into a criticism of those who presume to leave off ordained vocal prayer when they first feel themselves touched by devotion. This entire series of five chapters introducing the subject of prayer and treating the first of its three kinds forms one chapter, the thirteenth, in the variant system.

The second manner of prayer, the discussion of which comprises the next three chapters (one chapter, the fourteenth, in the variant system) is vocal prayer without set form. In the twenty-ninth chapter, Hilton describes it as the spontaneous expression of the emotion that the contemplative feels at the time. The thirtieth chapter points out that this kind of prayer belongs to the second part of contemplation as described earlier; it is short-lived in its fervor, but great in its effect. This he exemplifies in the next chapter, commenting on the text of Jeremiah, 'And it was made in my heart as a glowing fire shut up in my bones; and I fell, unable to bear it' (Jeremiah 20:9). That is, that this fire of love burns away all fleshly loves in the soul, filling the faculties of mind, reason and will with such grace and spriritual sweetness that it seems even to make the body tremble; and because it cannot long be born, God tempers this grace, withdrawing it and allowing the heart to fall into an easy sobriety. Whoever can pray thus, he concludes, will gain more of virtues in a short time than in all the penance he might do otherwise, and whoever has this gift should therefore be discreet in the other penances he undertakes.

The third manner of prayer Hilton describes in the thirty-second chapter as prayer only in the heart, without speech, in great peace and rest of body and soul. It is proper to the higher degree of the second part of contemplation, particularly in that it is not achieved without either long physical and spiritual travail, or the sharp blows of love just described; and the affection is turned into a spiritual savour, so that those who have it may pray nearly continually, loving and praising God unimpeded by idle thoughts and temptations. The next chapter gives again the impression of a real reader's objections to his teaching. 'But now you say', he reports, that she finds his teaching too high for her in this manner of prayer, for whenever she attempts to fix her attention on God alone in prayer, she finds herself so distracted that she can feel neither savour, nor rest, nor devotion in it. He answers that it is true that he spoke of greater things than he himself could do, but rather of what he and she should do, and advises her not to upbraid herself nor to blame God if she does not come easily to this kind of devotion, but simply to attempt it, trusting in God's grace. These two chapters on the third manner (one chapter in the variant system) conclude the discussion of prayer.

In the thirty-fourth chapter, Hilton begins to treat the subject of meditation. He points out that there is no set rule to follow in this, for meditations are in the free gift of God, and given to different souls according to their state and disposition; further, as they grow in virtue and state, God increases both the love and the knowledge that they find in meditation. He proposes next to describe several types of meditation, so that his disciple may choose whichever she thinks would be better to work at. In the beginning of his conversion from a sinfull life, he says, a man is usually drawn to think on his sins with such compunction and tears that no matter how truly he may be confessed, he would not, but for the mercy of God, feel himself forgiven. The purpose of this is twofold: first, that by the pain of conscience in this life, the pain of purgatory may be lessened; and second, that if a man will receive any special gift of the love of God, he must first be cleansed by compunction for his sins. After this, he is often given meditations on the humanity of Christ, as on his birth or his passion, or on the compassion of Mary.

Using a meditation on the passion of Christ for an example, Hilton proceeds in the next chapter to point out that if such a meditation of the humanity of Christ is given, with devout affection answering to it in the heart, the contemplative may know that it does not arise out of his own working, nor the feigning of an evil spirit, but of the grace of the Holy Spirit; for it is an opening of the spiritual eye (an image that becomes more prominent later) into the humanity of Christ and, as St Bernard called it, a physical love of God. It is also a great help in destroying sins and gaining virtues, and thus eventually to the contemplation of Christ's divinity. In the thirty-sixth chapter, Hilton also points out that this kind of meditation is not given to a man whenever he wants it, but according to God's gift. To some, it is given nearly continuously; others are so tender in their affection that their hearts melt in devotion at the mere mention or thought of the passion; to others the gift is given at first plenteously, then withdrawn for various reasons—for pride that they may feel in it, or that they may be tried and tempted by the fiend and thus disposed to even greater knowledge and love of God. Further, Hilton points out in the thirty-seventh chapter, one must suffer many temptations first, particularly when devotion is withdrawn for a time, and the devil interposes strong temptations to carnal sins such as lechery and gluttony, to spiritual sins such as disbelief or despair, self-hatred or accidia, or for the contemplative, even diabolic apparitions. He is then doubly pained, both for the temptation and for the loss of devotion, and further tempted to despair of his vocation. These four chapters on the first stages of meditation form one chapter, the sixteenth, in the variant system.

Having raised the subject of temptation as an aspect of the withdrawing of meditation on the humanity of Christ and a preparation, if withstood, for the reception of greater graces, Hilton proceeds in the thirty-eighth chapter to describe the remedies, or consolations, which are useful against such temptations. He suggests that his disciple should not consider them a reproof or forsaking by God, but rather as a trial; and that although such temptations may try the soul, they cannot harm it without assent. She should not worry too much about them, nor strive against them, for that will merely make them more tenacious; she should perhaps tell them to some wise and experienced man, and follow his counsel, but definitely not to some ignorant secular, whose unwise advice might bring her to despair. Finally, Hilton returns to the idea that God allows such temptations only as a chastisement in an exposition on the text of Isaiah that God has deserted her and punished her only for a little while, that he may gather her to himself in mercy (Isaiah 54:7); he ends the chapter with an exhortation similar to that ending his reply to her on distractions in prayer, that she is to stand firm in hope and to pray, for she shall truly spring up as the day-star in gladness and true confidence in God (Job 11:17). In the next chapter, Hilton repeats the second point of consolation against temptation: that God allows such temptation in order to try the contemplative and bring her into the right way, where he will take her to himself and show her the secrets of his knowledge and understanding of righteousness. Again here, Hilton ends by exhorting his disciple not to fear too greatly if she is so tried, but to stand firm as he has said, or do better if she can.

The next three chapters form the transition to another, perhaps higher, type of meditation, that by which the contemplative enters into her own soul in order to know what it is, and come thereby to the knowledge of God. The fortieth chapter treats of the disengagement of the earlier gift: Hilton says that although it is not necessary for everyone to move on to other types of devotion, and is even harmful for those who feel true devotion in one type to attempt another, yet after the soul has been tried by the withdrawal of meditation on the humanity of Christ, or even without such a trial, it is not good to fall into idleness, but rather to begin a new game and a new travail. He points out that she is not to leave off the former gift too soon or too late, but only at the time when God offers the appropriate grace of devotion. The forty-first chapter reinforces particularly the idea that one is not to attempt to deceive one's self into working after a gift which one does not have, for different gifts are given to different men.

In the forty-second chapter, however, Hilton goes on to say that meditation on one's own soul and its powers is one work which is useful to come to contemplation: for in it one will find the worth and the dignity that the soul should have by nature in its creation and the misery that it has fallen into by sin, and thus come to desire to recover its former dignity. The description of this three-fold movement dominates the remainder of *Scale* I; the third part of it is the primary theme of *Scale* II. One will find the inner ground of sin, Hilton continues, in a false, misruled love of one's self, according to St Augustine, and delight in the things of this world, from which one must withdraw one's attention in order to find the image of God. This is a difficult work, but by it one is able to destroy the tendency to sin within one's self, where before one could attempt only to withstand the temptation to sin from without. This series of five chapters forming the transition from meditation on the humanity of Christ to meditation on the soul as the image of God, is one chapter, the seventeenth, in the variant system.

Following the Augustine tradition, Hilton states in the opening of the forty-third chapter that the soul is a life created as a trinity of faculties: mind, reason and will, in likeness of the uncreated Trinity of Father, Son and Holy Spirit. By original sin, however, it was corrupted into a foul, dark and wretched trinity of forgetting and ignorance of God, and misdirected love of one's self. This corruption is the result of original sin alone, regardless of personal sin, even venial sin, and is redeemed by the passion of Christ alone. Therefore, he counsels his disciple in the next chapter, if you think that I have spoken too high for you before, for you cannot accomplish what I have described or will describe, I will fall down as low as you wish, both for your good and my own. That if she will only cry mercy and ask salvation by virtue of Christ's passion, then without doubt she, or any Christian souls who ask mercy and forgiveness and humble themselves to the sacraments of the church, will be saved and come to the bliss of heaven. It is at this point that the Holy Name passage occurs, introduced by the objection formula, 'But now you say . . .'. She is worried by what she finds written in some men's books (usually, again, referred to Rolle) that unless she feels drawn in devotion to the name of Jesus, she will never come to the bliss of heaven. Hilton points out, in an extended exposition of the literal meaning of the name of Jesus, 'healer' or 'health', that just as anyone who truly desires to be whole is devoted to that which is signified by the word 'health', so anyone who truly desires to be saved is devoted to that which is signified by the name of Jesus.[13]

The forty-fifth chapter replies to the argument stated immediately before the interruption, that it is by virtue of the passion of Christ that one is redeemed from original sin; Hilton points out to his disciple that she should not therefore become reckless in her living, but more anxious to please God and recover in hope at least a likeness of that dignity which all men lost, and be reformed in soul by grace at least to a shadow of that image of the Trinity which was, and will be in the bliss of heaven. This work, which is true contemplation and the opening of the spiritual eye, can not be fulfilled in this life, but she is to attempt it as she can. These three chapters on the natural dignity of the soul before the fall, and upon its redemption through the passion of Christ, form one, the twentieth, in the variant system.

The next three chapters (again, one chapter in the variant system) comprise a Christo-centric exhortation. Hilton begins the forty-sixth chapter by telling his disciple to seek for what she has lost; that anyone who had ever a sight of the dignity which the soul had by kind and will have by grace would never rest until he came to it again. And because her inner eye is not yet opened to see fully what it is, he tells her in one word what she should seek, desire and find: Jesus. In the text here, as in the preceding Christo-centric addition, he is not speaking of devotion to the name itself, which can be painted on a wall, or written in a book, or formed by the lips or feigned in the heart, but that which the name signifies: all goodness, endless wisdom, love and sweetness, her joy, her worship and everlasting bliss, her God, her Lord and her salvation. By whatever prayer or devotion gives her the greatest desire for him, she will best feel him and find him—not that she should rest there; for even there she has found only a shadow of him, and not himself. In the next two chapters, Hilton points out that this desire is greater than any other occupation or affection; that she is to seek, like David, desire by desire; that she is to seek, like the woman who lost a drachma, lighting her house with the lantern of the word of God and the lantern of reason, sweeping out the house of her soul with the broom of the fear of God and washing it with her tears, until she finds the drachma, the penny, Jesus, that she had lost. At which she may well call together her friends to rejoice with her. It is interesting to note that these two chapters form a traditional exercise in scriptural exposition: seven texts are elicited in succession, of which the first two deal with the ideas of desire and volition, the next three are linked by the word 'to seek' and the last two by the word 'lantern'.

This method of exposition continues into the next section as well: the forty-ninth chapter proceeds from the idea of seeking Jesus to the question of where he is hidden, using the texts, 'Truly you are a hidden God' (Isaiah 45:15) and 'The kingdom of heaven is like a treasure hidden in a field' (Matthew 13:44). He is hidden, Hilton says, in the soul; he sleeps spiritually in the soul, as he slept physically in the boat on the Sea of Galilee while his disciples cried out to him in the storm. The fiftieth chapter takes this image further, saying that truly she sleeps more often when she should be crying out to him than *vice versa*;

and the idea that she should hear him calling out to her suggests the verse, 'Hear, O daughter, and see, and bend your ear toward me, and forget your people and the house of your father'. (Psalm 44:11). Hilton then develops the idea of forgetting from the latter half of the verse to point out that she should seek to be oblivious to the unrestful din of vain thoughts and physical desires crying out for her attention, and to bring love of virtues and full charity into her heart in their place; for as long as the image of God is not reformed in her, he will be far from her and she will not hear him. Therefore, he continues in the fifty-first chapter, she should array herself in his likeness, in meekness and charity, which are his special livery. The argument of this chapter, too, is made through a series of scriptural references, in this case, to those things which identify the lovers of Jesus: 'Whoever loves me, is loved by the Father, and I will manifest myself to him' (John 14:21); 'Learn from me, for I am mild and meek of heart' (Matthew 11:29); and 'This is my commandment, that you should love one-another' (John 13:34 ff.). This set of three chapters, which form the twentieth chapter in the variant system, ends the discussion of the recovering of the image of God in the soul. Hilton summarises these nine chapters at the beginning of the fifty-second:'Now have you heard a little what your soul is, what worship it had and how it lost it; I have also told you that something of this worship may by grace and busy travail be recovered again in part, in feeling'.

Virtually all of the remainder of the first book of *The Scale of Perfection* deals with the second part of meditation on one's own soul, pointed out in the forty-second chapter: the recognition and eradication of the image of sin which prevents one from seeing the image of God. The first part of this discussion is almost an exact parallel to that preceding: Hilton has exhorted his disciple to seek the image of Jesus within her soul by introversion; here he tells her to recollect herself from all external concerns, and particularly when she does not feel devotion, to seek Jesus within herself, and she will find instead a dark and painful image of her own soul without either light of knowing or feeling of love. This image, this shadow, this 'body of sin and body of death' as St Paul called it (Romans 6:6), is covered and dressed in the seven deadly sins (the reverse of Hilton's image of meekness and charity as the livery of God); it is a stinking well out of which spring many streams of sin, just as from the image of Jesus, if it were reformed in the soul, would spring sparks of desires, clean affections, wise thoughts and honesty of virtues. He then proceeds from the effects of the image of sin to the consideration of its nature. Perhaps, he tells his disciple, she wonders what this image is like: it is like nothing. If she recollects her powers and looks within, she will find nothing—a lack of love and of light—just as sin is nothing but a privation of good. If she were reformed, her introspection would find Jesus: she would find light of understanding and not the darkness of ignorance; she would find love and affection, and not pain and bitterness. This darkness, this negation, is the image of which he speaks. Nevertheless, Hilton says in the fifty-fourth chapter, if she will find Jesus, she must work and sweat a while in the pain of this nothingness; she must suffer and abide a while in this darkness, and arise out of it in busy prayer and fervent desire to God, as if she would bear it down and go through it. She shall hate and loath this nothingness as the very devil of hell; she shall despise it and burst through it—for within it is hidden the image of Jesus. The entire purpose of his writing, he points out, was to stir her to this work, if she feels called to it in grace. Finally, he shows that this nothingness is the image of the first Adam, the earthly man, which we have carried in sin heretofore; and that we will hereafter bear the image of the heavenly man, Jesus, the second Adam. Even St Paul found the image of sin heavy and burdensome, for he says, 'Who shall deliver me from this body and image of death?' and answers himself, 'The grace of God through Jesus Christ' (Romans 7:24–25). These three chapters comprise the description of the image of sin in itself; they form one chapter (the twenty-first) in the variant system. The version paraphrased here corresponds to that found in C; the many additions (particularly the Christo-centric) and omissions in the confused textual evidence on these three chapters would seem to demonstrate a good deal of misunderstanding—some, perhaps, wilful—of Hilton's teaching on this clear, but difficult, point. It is also interesting to note that the work of the Christo-centric annotator of H has been particularly prominent in the past few chapters. Of eighty-two additions to the text in *Scale* I, eighteen occur in the exhortation to seek the lost image of Jesus in the soul in chapters forty-six through forty-eight; none in forty-nine through fifty-one; but twelve in fifty-two through fifty-four. Better than a third, then, of the Christo-centric annotations to the ninety-two chapters of *Scale* I occur in the six chapters on the image of Jesus and the image of sin. The annotator breaks off at this point; he makes only ten more annotations to *Scale* I, all in the last half-dozen chapters.

The next chapter, the fifty-fifth (the twenty-second in the variant system), forms the transition from the consideration of the dark image of sin in itself to the discussion of its effects, the seven deadly sins.

Hilton begins with a short summary, leading to a recurrence of the objection formula, 'But now you say, "How may this be so?" ' She wishes to know how he can portray the state of her soul in such bleak terms. Hilton replies, developing the metaphor of the foul spring of sin, that although she has stopped the external actions, the sins themselves, unless she eradicates their source in the dark image of sin, she will be like the man who stops up a poisonous well in his garden, only to find that he has thereby poisoned the garden itself.

The next eight chapters deal with the sin of pride: Hilton begins the fifty-sixth with the Augustinian definition of pride as a love of one's own excellence or honour. The greater is her love of her own excellence, he warns his disciple, the more of that sin is in her. She replies, again in the objection formula, 'But you say that you cannot escape such stirrings of pride, for you feel them often against your will, and thus consider them no sin, or at most venial'. He agrees that the temptation in itself is no sin, but a grace and a privilege to all Christians, although to those who are without the Christian faith, all such stirrings are mortally sinful. Even for Christians, however, such stirrings of pride may be turned into delight, and accordingly as their delight is set in such stirrings, they may be mortally or venially sinful—although he cannot give a strict rule for distinguishing the two.

Pride is a mortal sin, Hilton continues in the next chapter, when the heart chooses it as its only end, rest and delight, as it were its god. His disciple objects, 'But now you say, "What fool would choose pride for his god?" ' He replies that there are two manners of pride: physical and spiritual. The former is the sin of those worldly men who set all their value in secular honour, choosing it instead of God. She pursues the question, 'But now you say, "Who would choose love of honour instead of God?" ' He replies that anyone who is so enamoured of honour that he transgresses the commandments of God or the duty of love and charity to his fellow Christian, or would be willing to do so, is guilty of this sin, even if he could not admit to it as such. The next two chapters deal with the spiritual form of the sin of pride, that of heretics and hypocrites. The fifty-eighth chapter points out that the heretic sins in valuing his own opinion of God over the teaching of the Church, and rests in this conceit. Having thus rendered himself incapable of correction, the heretic sins mortally. The fifty-ninth chapter attributes the mortal sin of pride in hypocrites to their choosing to perform corporal and spiritual good deeds not for their own sake, but for the pride which they feel in the performance of them. Such hypocrites are so ravished in the delight of spiritual pride that they will for that reason perform great acts of devotion and penance, not choosing sin for the sake of sin, but good for the sake of vain joy in themselves, which they mistake for true joy in God. Again, the disciple objects, 'But now you say that there are very few, or none,' who could make such a mistake. Hilton replies that there are indeed many who do not consider themselves hypocrites, but are; just as there are many who fear that they are hypocrites, but are not.

Having discussed the deadly forms of the sin of pride, Hilton proceeds in the sixtieth chapter to describe the venial sin of spiritual pride. This occurs particularly when a man or woman is disposed to contemplative life, is enclosed or enters a religious order, and feels the stirrings of vain glory and delight at the time, but either does not perceive it, or reproves and withstands it when he does. For this temptation, if withstood, these servants of God gain in grace and receive a special reward in heaven. He develops this point in the next chapter in comfort, as he says, of his disciple or any other who has chosen the enclosed life. He points out that there are two rewards in heaven: the first, the sovereign and principal reward of the knowledge and love of God, belongs to all the saved, according to their measure of charity when living on this earth. As this reward does not vary according to state or degree of life, but according to charity simply, it is possible for a secular lord or lady, a knight or squire, merchant or plowman, man or woman, to rank higher in this than some priest or friar, monk or canon or anchoress. On the other hand, there is a secondary reward—a distinction or halo—for special good deeds, of which the Church specifically names three: martyrdom, preaching and celibacy. And so it is of other special good works, as entry into religion, the strictness of the religion, enclosure, and particularly election as a bishop or prelate. The sixty-second chapter closes the discussion with an exhortation to meekness and charity, for it is only according to their measure that the sovereign reward of heaven is given, to which the special reward given to such as anchoresses and religious is only secondary.

In the sixty-third chapter, Hilton closes his discussion of pride by returning to the theme of the dark image of sin which, he says, he had almost forgotten at this point. If she will know how much pride she has, he tells his disciple, let her see whether it pleases her for men to praise her or her living, or angers her to hear herself calumniated. If so, then she has the stirring of pride—not the sin itself, but the tendency, with which the motivation of all her good works is mixed and therefore less pleasing to God. She must learn to guard her heart against not only the deliberate assent to the sin of pride, but so much as she can, against the unconscious, involuntary tendency to it. The theme of guarding the heart will recur later. This series of chapters forms one chapter, the twenty-third, in the variant H system. In the related texts in Ch and As, it is joined to the single chapter (fifty-five in the standard system, twenty-two in H) on the dark image of sin considered as a foul spring in the soul.

The next seven chapters treat together of the sins of envy and sloth; as in the preceding treatment of pride, Hilton discusses first the nature of the sin and second how his disciple is to find the tendency in her soul. He tells her first to reverse the image of pride and examine it: she will discover in it two members, wrath and envy, with all their branches of hatred, suspicion, false judgement, despite, false accusation, backbiting, anger at those that despise her, gladness at their discomfort, and fierceness against sinners and others that will not do as she thinks they ought, with desire for their punishment. This latter is a form of wrath particularly dangerous to the contemplative, and Hilton devotes the sixty-fifth chapter to pointing out that it is relatively easy to perform great penances and travails, compared with the difficulty of learning to love the sinner while hating the sin. This is the special gift of charity, and the only good work which can be accomplished by charity alone, and not for sinful reasons. The next chapter develops this idea, pointing out that the same good works may be done in charity by a good man, but for sinful reasons by a worldly man, a heretic or a hypocrite, and only God will know the difference. For this reason, he continues in the sixty-seventh chapter, we should be unwilling to judge the actions of any man, whether good or bad, but be willing to esteem them well, saving only heretics and ex-communicates, who have removed themselves from the bond of charity, and with whom she should have nothing to do. He concludes the discussion in the sixty-eighth chapter by returning to the idea that the charity which loves the sinner while hating the sin is the most difficult of good works: that except for those who are perfectly humble, no one can know surely whether he is in charity. One can, in fact, perform what are considered works of charity—he uses the example here of reproving sinners for their amendment—for uncharitable reasons. However, since his disciple might thus be moved to despair, Hilton goes on to say that although it is the most difficult of works to accomplish by one's own travail, it is the easiest for God to give, if she will only exercise herself in meekness. He points out specifically that if she has imperfect meekness only in will, but not affection, she will have imperfect charity—which is yet sufficient to salvation—but it is best if she can come to perfect meekness, and thus to perfect charity. These five chapters on the image of envy and wrath form one chapter, the twenty-fifth, in the variant H system.

In the next two chapters, Hilton describes to his disciple how she is to find the tendency to envy and wrath in her own soul. He tells her in the sixty-ninth chapter to see how often she is moved to melancholy, bitterness or impatience against God or her fellow Christians; as many such movements as she feels, so much less is the image of Jesus reformed in her. Not, again, that these movements are sinful in themselves, but that they are the source of sin. He goes on in the next chapter to point out that it is not enough to search out these feelings when she is at rest: she should look particularly for them whenever someone says or does anything against her. He proceeds thus to the doctrine that she is to love her enemies, exemplified by the love shown by St Stephen, when he prayed for those who stoned him, or by the forgiving love of Jesus for Judas, his betrayer; and that she is to love her fellow Christians in accordance with Christ's commandment. It is at this point that the second of the objection passages occurs, apparently added by Hilton after the first book of the *Scale* was in circulation: 'But now you say, how shall you love the bad as well as the good?' He replies that, according to St Augustine, she is to love her neighbour, as she loves herself, either *in God*, when he is in the state of grace, and she thus loves the goodness of God in him, or *for God*, when he is in sin, and she loves him not as he is, but that he might become good. These two chapters on the discovery of the tendency to envy and wrath in one's self form one chapter, the twenty-fifth, in the variant H system. The division of the discussion in Ch and As is different: the sixty-fourth through sixty-seventh chapters in the standard system are made one chapter there, and the sixty-eighth is joined to the sixty-ninth and seventieth to form a second.

The discussion of the sin of covetousness occupies a single long chapter in all systems. Hilton begins by reverting to the theme of the dark image of sin: she is to lift it up and examine it to see if it is not covered in great part by greed for earthly things, although never in great degree. She has, in fact, renounced earthly things; but if she still feels desire for the small things that she is allowed, and pain and anger in their loss, she is no less guilty of this sin than any worldly person, merely a poor merchant—she has traded the sin of greed for great things for the sin of greed for small things. This he applies particularly to those who have taken up voluntary poverty, although he does not single out any particular orders or states, for every state has its good and bad followers. But the greed for few and simple things is most harmful to them, for the difference between pure love of God and the love of God mixed with love of even one other thing besides is greater than that between simply lesser and greater degrees of greed, in consideration of the lessening of their reward in heaven. Yet he points out finally that if even greed for one thing besides God impedes such men and women from the spiritual knowledge and love of him, then all the more are those who live in the world harmed by their constant acquisitiveness. But he says that since he is not writing for a secular audience at this time, he will say no more; this much he did say only so that if they saw what they did, they might not do so. This is one of the two indications in *Scale* I that Hilton even considered that such people might read this work.

In the next six chapters, which form one chapter, the twenty-seventh, in the variant system, Hilton deals with the fleshly love of one's self found in the physical sins of gluttony, sloth and lechery. His disciple immediately objects: 'But now you say', that since she *has* to eat, drink and sleep, and cannot do any of them without pleasure, it appears to her that this pleasure is no sin. To this, Hilton replies that if she does not eat or drink beyond measure, nor take more delight in it than nature demands, but does it rather for the sake of spiritual delight, she certainly does not sin. St Paul could do this, and St Augustine, who says that God has taught him to take food as a medicine; but Hilton is forced to admit that he himself has not yet learned to separate the need for food from the pleasure of eating. He goes on, however, to point out that since the ground of gluttony and sloth is in natural necessity, and not in the dark image of sin, it is difficult for anyone who is not in mortal sin spiritually to sin mortally in these; truly those who are in mortal sin already can sin mortally by gluttony, for they fall to at their meals as an animal to carrion; but those who have a general will, a virtual intention, to God, whatever their specific intention in eating, drinking or sleeping, seldom sin more than venially. Hilton ends by pointing out that in this case, since the ground of sin is in natural necessity, his disciple is to fight against the sin, but not to attempt to eradicate its ground, as with the spiritual sins which are grounded rather in the dark image of sin in the soul; but since the sin of lechery is not grounded in necessity, she should seek to destroy its ground as well.

Nevertheless, he continues in the seventy-third chapter, she should not attempt to do this by physical travail, but spiritual: by prayer and spiritual virtues. For just as the spiritual sins of pride, envy, wrath and covetousness are not grounded in natural necessity, and are destroyed only by meekness and charity, so also lechery and improper delight in food and drink can be destroyed by these spiritual virtues, rather than by attempting to eradicate by mortification the needs which we have by nature. Further, and for the same reason, it is more important to eradicate the ground of spiritual sin in the soul than to combat physical sin by great penance. Although this is not the common opinion, Hilton states that it is the teaching of scripture and the doctors, if properly understood. On the other hand, he continues in the seventy-fourth chapter, he does not excuse those who fall into the physical sins of gluttony and lechery; it is his intention rather to point out to his disciple that some sins are more dangerous to her than others are. Nevertheless, any sin, even venial sin arising out of natural necessity, should be avoided—although, again, not by the attempted eradication of the necessity. Finally, he says in the seventy-fifth chapter, the physical pain and discomfort of extreme mortification can hinder spiritual occupation in prayer and meditation as often as help.

In the seventy-sixth chapter, Hilton recapitulates his teaching on combating the physical sins of gluttony and sloth: that his disciple is to attempt to keep the mean in food, drink and sleep. She is not to be too concerned by the temptation to take more than is necessary, nor too depressed by the thought that perhaps she has done so at one time or another. She is rather to exercise herself in meekness and charity, by which she will accomplish more in a year against these sins than one could in seven years of constant striving against them, flagellating one's self daily from sunrise to evensong. In the seventy-seventh chapter, he recapitulates the entire section: again, she is to strive simply to come to meekness and charity, by which even the physical sins of gluttony, lechery and sloth will be overcome. He says that he has spoken more on this point than he had planned: in fact, we may note that the organization of this section might have been clearer, and less repetition been required, if he had separated the treatment of the sins of gluttony and sloth, which have their ground in physical necessity, from that of lechery, which does not. He concludes by pointing out that she can see somewhat by what he has said of the dark image of sin, which lies like a chasm between herself and Jesus.

In the next five chapters, Hilton completes his description of this image. When he first raised the subject of the perversion of the soul from an image of the Trinity into an image of sin in the forty-third chapter, Hilton pointed out that so long as the soul was not reformed, none of the five senses could safely be used to enjoy any creature of God spiritually, for the senses were perverted to vain lust and delight. In the seventy-eighth chapter, he reverts to this theme, saying that the senses are five windows through which the soul goes out to seek its delight in vanity, and which must therefore be stopped up, and only opened when necessary; for it is because she is unable to see the beauty of her own soul, covered up with the image of sin, that her attention is drawn outward through the senses. This idea is repeated in the next chapter, in an exposition of a verse from the Song of Songs: 'O fair one among women, if you do not know yourself, go out and walk after the steps of the flock of your fellows, and your kids' (Song of Songs 1:7). The reverse motion, that of going in, is described in an exposition of another verse in the next chapter: 'The king led me in to a wine cellar' (Song of Songs 2:4). By this, Hilton exhorts his disciple to recollect the powers of her soul from outward attention.

In the next three chapters, he takes up a series of objections. 'But now you say', the eighty-first chapter begins, that she already does as he says: she is in fact shut away from seeing and hearing worldly things. Yet unless she keeps her attention from imagination of worldly things, he replies, she has gained nothing. She can, for example, see him in imagination, although not physically; and she is as capable of giving her attention to other things as well. She pursues her question: 'But now you ask', whether it is really so great a sin to pay attention to worldly things either in sense or in imagination. He answers that he would rather that she did not ask such a question at all, for whoever wishes truly to love God should not be interested in finding out acceptable degrees of evil, but rejecting all evil. Nevertheless, he continues in the eighty-second chapter, her desire requires him to say more in answer to this question than he had originally intended. He makes the point in an exposition of the parable of the man who gave a great feast, from which various guests excused themselves (Luke 14:16–20): concerning the guest who failed to come because he had bought five yoke of oxen, Hilton says that these represent the five senses, which are beastly in kind. Used properly, they are not subject to reproof, but if used for vain delight or worldly pleasure, so that she rests in them as in her god, then they are evil. She shall not, according to St Paul, follow her lusts, nor wilfully sample delights (Romans 13:14, conflated with Ecclesiasticus 18:30): a man or woman already in mortal sin will not fail to sin in this. Although in fact he says that he does not believe this of her, Hilton points out that she can still fall thereby into venial sin, which as a contemplative she ought to avoid as much as possible. The eighty-third chapter takes up the problem of worldly concerns thrust upon her unwillingly by those who come to her for advice: 'But now you say', that she cannot avoid hearing vain affairs. On this point, Hilton advises her to give what counsel is necessary, quickly, clearly and charitably, and then to fall silent. Whatever the station of the person consulting her, or whatever his reason, if he continues to attempt to make small talk, he will soon grow bored and leave. She is to reprove no one directly, to say only what will be profitable to her fellow Christians, and to keep silent on all other matters, as much as possible: she will soon find that the press of those who disturb her prayers has diminished. This set of chapters relating the dark image of sin to the senses and imagination comprises a single chapter, the twenty-eighth, in the variant system in H and Ch; As leaves off this system (and, apparently, its other textual agreements with H) at the beginning of the eighty-second chapter.

In the eighty-fourth chapter, Hilton attempts to close the discussion of the dark image of sin: 'By this that I have said, you may see a little of the darkness of this image— not that I have described it to you fully as it is, for I can not'. And again, he is interrupted by an objection: 'But now you say', how does he know that she carries around within her such an image as he describes? He answers first from his own experience, using a verse from the prophet Hosea, that he had found an idol—a mahommet—an image—within himself (Hosea 12:8). Further, he argues in exposition of the text that 'the Lord made for Adam and his wife clothes of animal skins' (Genesis 3:21), that everyone descended from Adam bears such a beastly image, clothing his soul. In the eighty-fifth chapter, Hilton uses the exposition of seven different scriptural texts to describe pride as the head of the image of sin, covetousness as its back and hinder parts, envy as its breast and heart, wrath as its arms, gluttony as its belly, lechery as its private members and sloth as its feet. Hilton concludes his treatment of the dark image of sin in the next chapter, continuing in the expository mode. A text from the Psalms, 'Truly, a man goes about in image (as a phantom); and is but troubled in vain' (Psalm 39:6) and the Pauline text 'As we have born the image of the earthly man, so will we bear the image of the heavenly' (1 Corinthians 15:49) allow him to set up again the contrast between the two images. He then asks what should be done with the image of sin, and replies to his own question with the words of the crowd to Pilate, 'Take and crucify him!' (John 19:15), leading to another Pauline text, 'Those who are of Christ have crucified their flesh with its lusts and improper desires' (Galatians

6:24), and to a final exhortation to 'put off the old man, that is the image of sin of the old Adam, with all his members, for he is rotten in desires of error, and shape yourself and clothe yourself in the new man, which is the image of God by holiness and righteousness and fulness of virtues' (an extended paraphrase of Ephesians 4:22, 24). The manuscripts of the N tradition, it should be noted, divide this chapter in two, making the section on the crucifixion of the image of sin into a separate chapter, so that the total number of chapters in these texts is not ninety-two but ninety-three.

The idea of guarding the heart, which had occurred in the discussion of the extirpation of the seven deadly sins, becomes the theme of the eighty-seventh chapter (eighty-eight in N). Hilton points out in an exposition of two scriptural texts that the heart should be well guarded, for life proceeds from it (Proverbs 4:23); but that if it is not so guarded, bad thoughts and unclean affections arise out of it, which defile a man (Matthew 15:19–20). And since a man consists of his thoughts and his loves, by the setting of these thoughts and loves in God or in some other object is he good or evil. In the next chapter, Hilton exhorts his disciple to begin this work: to behold the wickedness of the image of sin within her, and to lift up her desire to God, either to help her bear the pain of this image, or to destroy it in her. She should withdraw her affection from physical things, to the point that she feels no delight in anything which had delighted her before, finds even herself cumbersome, and feels that all things rise up against her. If she will do so, desiring God simply, then he will ease her by helping her to bear the corruption of her body, and by breaking down little by little the image of sin within her. The eighty-ninth chapter (ninety in N) applies this to the seven deadly sins, but primarily to pride, which sins against meekness, and envy and wrath, which sin against charity. Hilton points out that after she has felt the rising against herself described in the previous chapter, she will be able to discern the movements of sin within her, and to beat them down. In the ninetieth chapter (ninety-one in N), he says that she will be better able to do this when she has set her heart upon spiritual desire for God and to please him, love him, know him, see him, and have him somewhat by grace here, whom she shall have in the bliss of heaven with all her being. If she will do this, she will better combat the movements of sin within her than if she were to give her attention to the sin itself; for Jesus will fight for her, and destroy the sin in her. Finally, he points out in the ninety-first chapter (a differently-divided ninety-two in N) that if she will do so, the image of sin will be destroyed in her by which she is distorted from the image of God, and she will be reformed to his image. The final paragraph of this chapter, which states that whoever wishes to live the contemplative life must come to it by this reforming of the image of God in virtues, is divided off to form a separate chapter in H and Ch; the closely related texts of Trinity College, Cambridge, MS.354 and the 1494 Wynkyn de Worde print of the *Scale* also begin a chapter here, repeating the title of the preceding chapter; neither of the other traditions of chapter numbering mark this division. It should be mentioned also that the final group of Christo-centric additions in H all occur in these final three chapters of exhortation to break down the image of sin. Hilton ends with a statement of the theme of the *Scale*, in exposition of the text, ' "No one comes to the Father except by me" (John 14:6)—that is to say, no one may come to the contemplation of the godhead unless he is first reformed by fulness of meekness and charity to the likeness of Jesus in his manhood'.

In the last chapter of the *Scale*, Hilton says that he has shown the end of the contemplative life, and the means to that end; and advises the reader to follow what he has written as she feels devotion in it. When it is no help to her, she is to put it aside, and turn to prayer and other spiritual occupation until such time as she can feel devotion in the work he describes. Further, if he has said anything poorly, for lack either of English or of wisdom, let it be corrected—but only when necessary. Finally, he cautions that what he has written has been directed toward the contemplative life, and not all of it is appropriate to someone leading an active life: again, an indication that Hilton saw at least the possibility of an audience for this book including others than contemplatives. With this remark, he closes.

It has been the intention of this survey of the argument of *Scale* I to show the organization of its material; to point out the indications that Hilton himself left of its progress and its transitions. He first distinguishes the active and the contemplative lives, then defines and distinguishes three parts of the latter; he describes the end, the foundation and the means, or occupation, of the contemplative life that his disciple has chosen; he distinguishes three parts of the foundation: meekness, sure faith and a whole intent to God; the means are reading (dismissed as inapproprate), meditation and prayer; concerning prayer, he discusses how one should pray, where the intention should be set in prayer, and the modes of prayer, of which he distinguishes three: ordained vocal prayer, vocal prayer without set form and prayer in the heart; although he notes that meditation follows no set form, he describes the meditation on his own sinfulness which often comes to a person newly turned from worldly life, meditation on the humanity of Christ and meditation on one's own soul, with the transitions from one to another; under the latter head, he points out that one is drawn from meditation on the worthiness that the soul had by creation as an image of the Trinity, to meditation on its perversion to a dark image of sin and the extirpation of the tendency to each of the seven deadly sins in the destruction of this image. The idea of reformation in meekness and charity to the likeness of Christ is the single aim throughout. It is also interesting to note that two groups of chapters in *Scale* I: chapters forty-seven through fifty-one, describing the process of seeking in the soul the lost image of Jesus, and chapters eighty-five through eighty-seven, dealing with the destruction of the image of sin and the reformation of the image of Jesus, contain proportionately more scriptural exposition and less analysis than the rest of the book. The fact that this reformation forms the primary theme of *Scale* II suggests the possibility that Hilton was not entirely satisfied with his previous treatment of it. Other themes discussed in *Scale* I are treated in *Scale* II as well, often with somewhat more precision in the description of the role of grace in the contemplative life. J. Clark has further pointed out the possibility that *Scale* II contains revisions of ideas unclearly expressed in *Scale* I which had been criticised by the author of *The Cloud of Unknowing*.[14] The relationship between the two books which these considerations suggest is a question that needs exploration.

We have also seen that Hilton interrupted the argument of *Scale* I at several points to take up peripheral issues. Three of these seem to have been raised by the similarity of his thought or expression to key words in the distinctive teaching of Richard Rolle. Another fifteen appear to have been raised by the first reader, or readers, of the book. We must note, however, that this appearance may be deceiving: although these objections have been attributed here to Hilton's 'disciple', the unknown 'ghostly sister' to whom he addressed this book, the primary purpose has been to demonstrate their function as interruptions. It is simply impossible to say whether any actual person raised these objections, or whether Hilton simply found this a convenient method of treatment of certain questions.

This paper began with the idea that the fourteenth century was a time of experimentation in the forms of major devotional prose, and pointed out the relative positions of Rolle and Hilton in this respect. Perhaps something should be said of the other writings in this tradition as well. We may note that although the structure of *The Cloud of*

Unknowing is not as prominent as that of the *Scale*, much the same kind of analysis could be made of it as we have seen here. The *showings* of Julian of Norwich present a rather different case: the material even of her later reflections is organized according to the original revelations, and normal considerations of conscious authorial choice of form simply do not apply. Nor do such considerations apply to the *Book* of Margery Kempe: for an English writer three centuries before Laurence Sterne, there was only one way to write a biography. Some of the late fourteenth- and early fifteenth-century compilations, however, are interesting from a structural point of view: one finds that the compiler/translators of such works as *The Chastising of God's Children* or *The Seven Points of True Love and Everlasting Wisdom*, in culling the separate appropriate sections of earlier writings and tailoring them to a preconceived argument, produced works organized in a way that the late Professor Vinaver described as modern when he found it in Malory's treatment of his French sources, better than half a century later.[15]

NOTES

1. R. Jordan, *Chaucer and the Shape of Creation*, Harvard, 1967.
2. J. Leyerle, 'The Rose-Wheel Design and Dante's *Paradiso*', *University of Toronto Quarterly*, 46 (1977), 280–308.
3. M. del Mastro, *The Stairway of Perfection by Walter Hilton*, New York, 1979, pp. 15–47.
4. Cf. Jean Leclercq, *L'Amour des lettres et le désir de Dieu*, Paris, 1957, pp. 72, ff.
5. J. Alford, 'Biblical *Imitatio* in the Writings of Richard Rolle', *English Literary History*, 40 (1973), 1–23.
6. J. Russell-Smith, 'Walter Hilton and a Tract in Defense of the Veneration of Images', *Dominican Studies*, 7 (1954), 180–214.
7. N. Orme, *Education in the West of England 1066–1548*, Exeter, 1976, p. 19. Although Orme's statement is applied particularly to school-masters, it is probably capable of generalization to the extent of denying the statement in Gerard Sitwell, *The Scale of Perfection by Walter Hilton*, London, and Wesminster, Maryland, 1953, ix, repeated in B. Wykes Plamtin, 'An Edition of Book I of *The Scale of Perfection* by Walter Hilton', Dissertation, University of Michigan, 1957, 8, and del Mastro, *Stairway*, op. cit., p. 342, that 'he is generally given the title of Magister, which at this time was reserved for doctors of theology'.
8. See J. Russell-Smith, op. cit., pp. 204–5, 209–10; the description of Hilton as 'Parisius in sacra pagina laureato magistro' is to be found in MSS Marseilles, Bibliothèque Municipale 729, written in the Charterhouse of Villeneuve-lès-Avignon in 1498, later—possibly at the suppression of that house in the seventeenth century—given to the Charterhouse of Marseilles (founded 1633); Paris, Bibliothèque Nationale, Fonds Latin 3610, written in the Charterhouse of

Villeneuve-lès-Avignon in 1529; Utrecht, Bibliotheek Rijksuniversitet 5.F.34, written *ca* 1500, with probable Netherlands Carthusian connections, see E. Colledge, *De nobilitate anime* and *De ornatu spiritualium nupciarum*,' *Quaerendo*, 9 (1970), 149–59; and Naples, Biblioteca Nazionale VII.G.31, written *ca* 1525. The provenance of this latter copy is unknown, but it belonged in the eighteenth century to the convent of St Bernadine in Aquilonia, where some Franciscan, apparently moved by the same parochial interest which first produced the Paris connection, found an English Franciscan named 'Walter' in Luke Wadding's *Scriptores Ordinis Minorum*, Rome, 1650, and triumphantly identified the author as W. Brinkeley, scholar not only at Paris, but Oxford as well.

9. S. S. Hussey, 'Walter Hilton: Traditionalist?' in Marion Glasscoe, ed., *The Medieval Mystical Tradition in England*, Exeter, 1980, p. 7.

10. R. (Birts) Dorward, '*The Scale of Perfection* by Walter, Hilton, Canon of the Augustinian Priory of Thurgarton: Book I, Chapters 38–52, Dissertation, Oxford, 1956.

11. See Helen Gardner, 'Walter Hilton and the Authorship of *The Cloud of Unknowing*', *Review of English Studies* 9 (1933), 129–47, and M. Sargent, 'James Grenehalgh as Textual Critic', Dissertation, University of Toronto, 1979, p. 224.

12. J. Clark, 'Intention in Walter Hilton', *Downside Review*, 97 (1979), 204–20.

13. For a discussion of the problem of the authority of this passage, see M. Sargent, 'Walter Hilton's *Scale of Perfection*: the London Manuscript Group Reconsidered', provisionally accepted for *Medium Aevum*, 1984.

14. J. Clark, 'Sources and Theology in *The Cloud of Unknowing*', *Downside Review*, 98 (1980), 83–109.

15. E. Vinaver, *The Works of Sir Thomas Malory* (Oxford, 1947), I, xli–lxxxv; see also *King Arthur and His Knights: Selected Tales by Sir Thomas Malory*, Oxford, 1975, pp. viii–x.

Printed and bound by CPI Group (UK) Ltd, Croydon, CR0 4YY

14/04/2025

14656927-0001